The P

of baseb

The Prehistories of Baseball

SEELOCHAN BEHARRY

McFarland & Company, Inc., Publishers
Jefferson, North Carolina

ISBN (print) 978-0-7864-7797-5
ISBN (ebook) 978-1-4766-1363-5

LIBRARY OF CONGRESS CATALOGUING DATA ARE AVAILABLE

British Library cataloguing data are available

Cover illustration by Eric Sonnendrucker

Printed in the United States of America

*McFarland & Company, Inc., Publishers
Box 611, Jefferson, North Carolina 28640
www.mcfarlandpub.com*

To
Martha, Matthew,
Joshua and Alice

Acknowledgments

Any work of this diverse nature can never be the efforts of the author alone, but is rather a reflection of the accumulated contributions and knowledge of friends, family, colleagues and other authors. They are too many to name individually here, but even small contributions were essential to this book.

I am particularly indebted to some outstanding baseball coaches and friends whose continued encouragement was appreciated, especially Douglas Anderson, Gary Bowden, Mike Kelly, John Masuhara and Ian Ross. I would also like to thank some non-baseball friends who helped or encouraged me: Dr. Janette Bulkan, James Croal, Jennifer Ettinger, Dr. Jairaj Mattai, Sandra Osborne, Pat Ross-Adamson, Dr. Umadatt and Patricia Singh, Eric Sonnendrucker, Christine Upright and Dr. Phillip Whiting.

Dr. Anand Daljeet and Cynthia Hou were continual sources of help during the entire writing of this project. Dr. Daljeet and I have been in regular contact, and he has been an excellent sounding board for various ideas and proposals throughout the last seven years. Both Dr. Daljeet and Hou have given much of their time and made efforts that exceed the obligations of friendship. Their comments were essential during all stages of the project.

The help of the staff at the Vancouver Public Library (VPL) is gratefully acknowledged. They helped me throughout my research with several book searches and numerous interlibrary loans. The regular assistance of Nancy Singbeil, Desiree Baron and Hilary Tait of the Marpole Branch was most helpful.

The friendship of my sister-in-law Ruth and her husband Gordon Eszes was invaluable to me. Gordy is always willing to share his expertise and knowledge of baseball and send old articles of baseball with some from his family's collection. My mother-in-law, Alice Kocel, former civil, women's and human rights advocate, is a source of family pride and inspiration. Her love for baseball and the Detroit Tigers illustrates how this game bridges gaps of time, place, culture and nationality, and she makes us understand how much it means to all of us.

My late mother Basmat Beharry has been and will always be an inspiration to me. Her personal sacrifices to ensure that I received the best education possible were the driving force to excel that helped sustain me on those numerous occasions when life got tough. Her encouragement to me continued until her last day. I am also indebted to my late father, James Beharry, who instilled in me to give my best effort at whatever I attempted to do, to be daring and take chances, and to never bring dishonor to the family name. My late brothers, Bissoondyal Beharry and Clifton Beharry, had always hoped that I would someday pen my thoughts. My late sisters, Daisy and Edith, are likewise always in my thoughts. The love of a family is truly eternal. I would like to thank my brother, Atma Ram Beharry, and sister, Katie Somwaru, sister-in-law, Carmen Beharry, and first cousin, Pearly Harry, for being supportive of my efforts.

I thank my wife, Martha, for putting up with me during the research and writing of this book. Her allowances of my idiosyncrasies coupled with her patience and support during these long years were crucial to the success of this study. The help and encouragement of our sons, Joshua Beharry and Matthew Beharry, were beneficial to the completion of this project. Josh's help leaves me forever grateful and indebted to him; his timely help and editing was pivotal to the narration and coherence of this story.

The cover design was based on an illustration done by Eric Sonnendrucker, a neighborhood friend and local artist. This was refined and polished by McFarland.

Last but not least, I have been blessed with the company of our Cairn terrier, Cinder. It is believed that Cairn terriers were originally bred to guard the cairns or sacred burial places and to watch over or play with the children during their games. Cinder often sat next to me throughout the writing of this book and let me know when it was time to take a break and enjoy the midday sun or go out and enjoy the pleasures of being outside and meeting people.

Table of Contents

Preface

Life is an unpredictable journey. What matters is not where it begins or ends, but what happens in between. Life for me began in British Guiana, which in 1966 became independent Guyana. In pursuit of graduate studies, I ended up in another British Commonwealth country, Canada. In the English-speaking Caribbean, including Guyana (as in all former British colonies), there is an unabashed love for sports, especially cricket, soccer, and track and field. This inherited passion and love of sports is part of our British heritage that has been endowed to and actively encouraged over the centuries in these former colonies. The British understood the power of sports as a way of bridging gaps between peoples. They knew their subject peoples had to have outlets for physical, artistic and cultural expressions. In addition, sports provided avenues for achievement and societal recognition such as a knighthood or commendation by the ruling monarch of Britain and the Commonwealth (now Queen Elizabeth II). British colonies and former colonies share this promoted passion for British-originated and -developed sports.

Caribbean peoples take with them this enthusiasm for sports when they leave the shores of the English-speaking Caribbean for elsewhere. In my own case, I stayed in Canada after graduate and post-doctoral studies. As my two sons grew up, the sport which I got most involved with was baseball. I first coached with Marpole Little League Baseball in Vancouver, British Columbia. The basic techniques and fundamentals of catching, throwing and fielding of cricket and baseball are the same. The similarities and differences between these two games are both interesting and fascinating to those who have a background in both games.

The more I read, I realized, like many others, that I knew very little of the origins of these two games. I attended numerous baseball coaching workshops and conferences, yet the answers to the fundamental questions about baseball's origins remained elusive. During my years of coaching this game to youths, some questions which unfailingly always came to mind were how and where this game began and who first played it? Unfortunately, time travel

1

into the past has yet to be invented, and researching our history is the closest we can come to discovering our roots. It follows that we would want to know what adaptations were made and what aspects were dropped as time moved on. Because of my background and employment as a researcher in science, it occurred to me that the answers for the inherent attraction of so many for this game may lie deep in our past. Baseball likewise evolved and adapted in response to early situations, and finally emerged in its present form. Relics of earlier times are still around with some hidden in the current game. The adventure lies in the exploration of our past and present.

During my years with Vancouver Community Baseball, as part of my coaching responsibilities, I began to write a summary and analysis of each game to send to players and parents. This allowed parents, grandparents and other family members to follow along with the fortunes of our team and provided opportunities for input. Each summary began with a philosophy of life as reflected in baseball. The summary was used to both ask and introduce some of the philosophical underpinnings of what was right before our eyes in each game we played. These writings led me to ask and research the unanswered questions about the early beginnings and development of baseball.

My extensive training and background in scientific research (I am a biochemist/chemist by trade) equipped me with the investigative tools, fortitude and determination to probe deeper into the game's origins and evolution. My broad interests and background in other fields such as philosophy, religion, anthropology, culture, education, etymology, sports and history all contributed to my research efforts. Like other major aspects of human activities, complex questions cannot be answered by the limitations imposed by using a single approach or discipline, but must rather be examined by including a broader range of fields, knowledge and expertise. This wider approach proved essential to our unraveling of the origins of baseball, taking us into unfamiliar places and times. This investigation takes us into our primal and more recent past, which shows the groundings of our military, social, fertility, mythological and religious beliefs and practices that were incorporated into rites and rituals in sacred or communal spaces. These traditions were modified and changed in modern times, but underlying causes for assembly at these places of worship still beckon the faithful as they did yesterday.

Living in the twenty-first century has also given me unprecedented access to historical works through online databases and interlibrary requests not available to others who may have hoped to explain the game before. It is only in recent years that the research going into this book could be accessed by a single person, and I feel lucky to have had this chance to explain the game before me.

My initial writing began in 2000; the research became more focused from 2004 to 2008, but from then it became a full-time project since I realized the complexity and range of the subject matter. The devotion to and passion for this project has occupied me more than my research at graduate schools, post-doctoral studies and employment projects. Many fortuitous events brought books or relevant and timely information to my attention.

There is a potent drive within us to probe the origins of the universe, life, and humankind occupying us from time immemorial as the subject of investigation and often obsession of some of our finest minds. Likewise we seek an understanding of many other things that we enjoy throughout our everyday lives. In particular, we seek to understand those events, routines and games that consume us with a passion and dedication which in some cases approach almost religious fervor and sanctity. This work is a reflection of our inner human drive to search for answers to satisfy our quest for the beginnings of baseball, a game that connects us with our past, each other and the world around us. In so doing we will see our shared humanity and our connection with the "elements," the sun, and our eternal quest for life, survival, fertility and immortality.

My hope is that this work also sparks more enquiries into the true origins of a game which is enjoyed all over the world by millions of people. Let the quest begin. Who knows what surprises await us as we seek to unearth, understand and connect with the past through the game we love?

Introduction

"Imagination is more important than knowledge. For knowledge is limited to all we now know and understand, while imagination embraces the entire world, and all there ever will be to know and understand."

—Albert Einstein (1879–1955)

Baseball is regarded by its faithful as "the greatest game on dirt." The game is not only used as a metaphor for life, love, death and rebirth, but also reflects the analogous daily and seasonal rhythms of our lives. We know a lot about baseball as evidenced by the vast amount of written literature on nearly every aspect of the game. Yet deep down we know there is far more to baseball than what we see, hear, think and feel. Baseball compels us to keep coming to the game again and again as if to reconnect ourselves with our ancestral past and find deeper meanings of the familiar baseball acts, rituals and stages.

Baseball not only arouses our imaginations of past actions, present doings and future possibilities, but brings to mind a certain degree of comfort and soothing familiarity as if we have seen something of this script or have been here before. It brings not only the dramas of earlier struggles for survival, but unconsciously and consciously recalls relics of ancient practices and rituals in places and settings that no longer exist except in our fertile imaginations.

The fundamental skills in this game of throwing, hitting and running are the same ones that facilitated human survival on our rise to the top of the food chain and dominance on the planet. Such innate tendencies and proclivities suggest that an exploration of our past is necessary to discover baseball's roots, through survival skills, beliefs and common evolution of humanity. Like children in search of our parentage, we hope to better understand ourselves, our heritage and our game.

We continue the endemic human tradition of seeking answers to the beginning of things around us. Historian A.L. Basham, in *The Wonder That*

Was India, observes that humankind has always pursued such quests, eloquently expressed by one ancient Indian poet in the wonderful Hymn of Creation of the Rig Veda.[1] In this book, we shall revisit earlier peoples and walk through ancestral cultural practices that, while they echo in many of our sports today, are nowhere more observable than in the game of baseball.

1

Throwing

Throwing remains one of the most basic human skills. Primates' capacity for throwing was enhanced over time by the development of an opposable thumb on each of the two forelimbs, culminating in two creative hands coordinated enough to do the biddings of a sophisticated brain. As our hands developed, they facilitated the making and gripping of tools for diverse purposes, including throwing. These dexterous instruments enabled the appropriate offensive and retaliatory usage of rocks and sticks as long-distance weapons, aiding humankind's survival and dominance over other competing species. It is no coincidence that the most dominant animal on Earth is also the best thrower and that throwing has survived as a major component in several sports. In this chapter, we will look at throwing as one of the innate imperatives of humans and see how it is still eloquently expressed in baseball.

The act of throwing objects at others has never stopped and is still evident in sports, games, hunting and war. The importance of throwing in our evolution and survival is also reflected in numerous expressions in everyday language and cultural activities.[1] Throughout the course of human history public disapproval was often expressed by the throwing of injurious objects at offenders.[2] This practice was and is still often seen when repressed groups and individuals rebel against enforcers of law and state. In certain situations, the goal of protesters is even referred to as "throwing" their oppressors out of office.

Rocks, in the hands of otherwise unarmed protesters, embolden them to face their opponents, even when they possess superior manpower and weaponry. A rock in the palm of one's hand gives an individual, even the disadvantaged, a feeling of empowerment to risk life and limb for his immediate cause.[3] This act of throwing readily attracts and infects bystanders thereby eliciting their participation in this ancient and communal expression of public disapproval.

These throwing tendencies are also evident at many sporting events today. Baseball fans often voice their displeasure of opposing teams and officials by throwing handily available objects onto the playing field. Major League Baseball (MLB) parks and other major sports arenas have stopped offering beverages in glass bottles and aluminum cans, substituting less harmful paper and plastic cups.

This uninhibited response of needing or being compelled to throw is not limited to adults or even the young and rebellious. In fact, this response is noticeable from early infancy onwards; before a child walks his first steps he has already shown tendencies to throw as seen with the throwing and retrieving of objects between a child and his caregiver. This act is particularly noticeable with a child sitting in a high chair. This game of throwing and retrieving is repeated again and again and is one of the child's first physical and social acts.[4] The act of throwing continues throughout toddlerhood as objects are thrown whenever the opportunity arises, out of car windows, and into the water at lakes and beaches. The act can consume and entertain children for long stretches at a time. These early throwing actions reveal the special significance of throwing in our development. Children and adults alike are often caught in this inherent compulsion to throw.

Where did this desire to throw come from? This question takes us further than expected. Inevitably, this search for answers will take us deep into our past beginning with the early rise of humankind, currently and conservatively thought to be about 250,000 to 400,000 years ago.[5]

The development of throwing grew with the rise of humans and similar primates. In Africa, even before our ancestors emerged from the trees, they threw fruits, twigs and branches at offending siblings, extended family members, playmates, sexual rivals, and others. These primates threw whatever was available at others competing for the same territory and food sources (fruits and leaves). Defenders dodged these early thrown objects and retaliated with their own. As primates struggled to survive, throwing became an essential skill in these early competitions and combats. Not surprisingly, this early basic skill of throwing became ingrained within us and continues to seek outlets for expression.

As time progressed, our ancestral primates descended from the safety of their trees to the plains, and early humans became more sophisticated both in their throwing skills and selection of objects to be thrown. They found that when standing in an upright position, with their feet apart and with a step or two in the direction of the target, it was easier to throw accurately. The rise of bipedal gait also helped this throwing process. They ran and threw and threw and ran, slowly developing their throwing expertise over time. They threw various objects such as rocks, sticks, dried mud and animal dung.

These life-experiences led them to choose more spherically shaped objects that fitted well in their hands and were easier to throw more accurately with a higher velocity at targets further away.

In addition, the more intelligent throwers soon learned that the keys to accurate throwing required proper positioning of the opposable thumb and fingers around a rock, the depth of the rock in the palm of the hand, and the correct point of release. Power was enhanced when these hand actions were coupled with stepping or running in the direction of the target with sideways body-positioning just before release of a held object.

Other discoveries in perfecting these throwing strategies and skills were (1) keeping the eyes on the target; (2) using a running start to gain momentum before throwing; (3) moving the arm in a circular or semi-circular motion to increase throwing power; (4) pointing the opposite shoulder and elbow or arm toward the target before throwing; (5) placing the feet at least shoulder-width apart; (6) lining up the forward and back foot with the front shoulder pointing toward the target; and (7) finally rotating the hips, throwing arm and shoulder when releasing the rock. These effective throwing skills were the accumulated wisdom of thousands of generations of throwers. These principles of throwing are still evident in numerous sports where throwing a ball long distances is required.[6]

These rock-throwing attacks were even more effective when rocks were thrown from a point of higher natural elevation, such as from the side of a hill or mountain on opponents or predators below.[7] This was advantageous because rocks thrown from higher ground were now moving downwards in a straighter line rather than in an elevated and curved trajectory. These directly thrown rocks had greater velocity and could cause more harm. In addition, direct throws gave an opponent less time and chance to dodge incoming rocks. Together a great arm and an appropriate sized and shaped rock were a lethal combination in early distance combats. Better throwing was recognized as a strategic advantage in early warfare.

This ability to throw rocks faster, farther, and more accurately meant an increased capability to deal with opponents without direct face-to-face physical or disadvantageous confrontations. This was especially important when the odds of physical size and number of opponents were not in one's favor. Further, there were increased chances of successful attacks by lying in ambush before engaging the enemy. In this approach there was some safe distance between attackers and attacked. More advanced strategies also planned for an exit from these areas of combat. Attackers visualized the possible outcomes of their actions and planned ahead accordingly to minimize their own casualties.

As war strategies progressed, so did the discovery, development and use of spears and shields.[8] The spear evolved as another effective weapon that was dependent on proper throwing techniques. The addition of the spear to the human arsenal of weapons earned the possessors of powerful throwing arms even greater adulation and material benefits. Moreover, excellent throwers became a group's prized warriors and celebrated heroes. Beneficiaries (children, women, the old, and other throwing warriors) of these combats expressed their appreciation of the feats of their finest warriors by honoring their heroes during evening entertainment that included acting out stories of battle scenes, dancing, and singing songs and ballads. The tales became early forms of oral storytelling traditions, and fostered the active portrayals of decisive battle scenes at social meetings held around fires, caves and encampments. These social occasions were used not only to entertain and lionize old warriors, but to inspire others to newer and greater acts of heroism.

As time progressed, their stories were revised and exaggerated and eventually became their own societal myths, wherein heroes became legends and legends became minor and major deities.[9] Youngsters imitated the actions of their power-throwing heroes in daily games, knowing that they too had a chance to be heroes in future stories. The human quest for fame, fortune, and immortality had begun as felt by the need for our names, accomplishments and memories to live on in the minds of others.

This hero worship further fueled a competitive drive within other warriors to excel and reap the benefits awarded to the best throwers. Inevitably, disputes arose as to who was the most effective thrower of a group. Pride always mattered. This desired ranking had its special privileges in the form of status, mates, food, and power. After such argumentative gatherings, a peaceful strategy or solution was needed to settle these disputes. These intra- or inter-tribal conflicts were settled in throwing contests and competitions. Consequently, "judges" had to find a way of quantifying the number of "hits" or "kills" by each competitor to a certain targeted area. This scoring was done by etching marks (lines or pictograms) on dwellings, ground surfaces, or rocks. This aided the birth of the earliest mathematics needed to resolve the throwing effectiveness of these warriors and determine their throwing skills. Soon the limits of this simple accounting system would be tested, as tie breaking rules developed.[10]

At the same time, as disputes arose and survival became more pressing, the need to train future generations in this valuable skill increased. Throwing was taught to the young by the accomplished, injured, disabled or older warriors. It is easy to picture targets being marked on trees to which trainees aimed. Other target possibilities included the use of captured prisoners and simple effigies of enemies. More vulnerable areas of the human body were focused on as the "strike zones." These targets were set up at various distances from the throwing points. Each young thrower learned the limits and strengths of his throwing ability. These warriors learned to throw as a team, launching volleys of rocks to maximize damage.[11] They collected rocks used in combat, regarding them as prized trophies. Battle stories related to these rocks were told repeatedly by tribal elders, historians, storytellers and bards.[12]

Naturally, throwing, as an essential battle skill, was incorporated into games. Our throwing and dodging games—e.g., dodgeball—are likely rooted in such pastimes, in which one person might sharpen his targeting skills while the other practiced dodging. These games kept warriors prepared, honing their defensive and offensive skills.

As these acts of throwing were incorporated into games or sports of children and young adults, it follows that soon the catching of thrown objects was also practiced. It takes little imagination to envision children, friends, and family members throwing non-injurious objects among themselves and participating in a game of "throw and catch."[13] Throwing to children and friends required that the objects not be thrown as hard since the intention was not to injure. Objects were therefore thrown with lower velocity as adults developed deviations in pace when throwing to children. Adults lobbed softer objects to children, providing opportunities for them to use their hands to catch without injury.[14] With older youths or adults, higher-velocity thrown objects were better received by cupped hands, cushioning the object against the chest to absorb its impact. The foundations of throwing and catching in baseball and other similar games were laid very early on in human development.

Throwers practiced frequently and diligently since throwing was a matter of life or death and a way to achieving respected societal status. The game of "throw and catch" became an ancient bonding ritual between parents and children. In modern times, reenactments of this ancient ritual are still acted out in informal games between parent and child—a traditional form of bonding from childhood through youth and often into young adulthood.[15]

In this modern era, the amounts of time and effort spent learning and practicing to throw far outweigh any practical use. Throwing, which was one of the evolutionary necessities, is rarely used in everyday life. Parents are still driven to teach these skills to children, especially in the United States of America—the most technologically advanced nation in the world. Throwing remains one of the oldest and most rapid, but also most elusive, pathways to fame and fortune.[16] Many parents still wish for their children to become one of the greatest throwers of all time.

In modern sports throwing remains one of the most difficult, competitive, and toughest routes to the acquisition of glory, adulation, status and wealth. Any young person who throws unusually fast and reasonably accurately has a better chance of being drafted as a potential power pitcher by a Major League Baseball club. Other types of finesse pitches can be taught to those who already have power arms, but the opposite situation is less likely. International talent scouts scour the world for these unusual human specimens who luckily inherited these power-throwing genes from their ancestors. The wide range of peoples around the modern world in which throwing talent is found demonstrates its once universal value for human development and survival.[17]

These throwing skills are still evident in other sports, including modern-day Olympic Summer Games (javelin, shot-put, and discus throwing events). In addition, several cultures have preserved their own special throwing events. Scots display their physical prowess and skill with caber tossing and the throwing of tree trunks or fence posts.[18] Another early British practice (especially in Wales) continues today with the throwing of a heavy bar usually made of metal.[19] Australian Aboriginals still throw boomerangs. Some North American indigenous peoples have continued playing lacrosse or some form of this game where a ball is thrown and caught in a webbed "bat." The ancient Greeks had some ball-throwing games.[20] It is hard to find a society in which the act of throwing is not incorporated in some form or another in its national games or pastimes (baseball, softball, cricket, rounders, rugby, American, Canadian or Australian football, basketball, lacrosse, and soccer). These games and pastimes satisfy our basic human need of still wanting to be involved in a throwing activity.

Modern warfare has also shown the necessity for throwing. For example, in World War I, World War II and other more recent conflicts, human arms and grenades made lethal weaponry. These arms and "rocks" were and still are effective and destructive combinations in major conflicts. Since good arms are still valued in the modern period of guns and other sophisticated weaponry, it is now easier to imagine and judge the value of good arms in earlier conflicts involving rocks and spears.

The origins and development of throwing from primal to modern times is clear. Throwing has paralleled and propelled the rise of *Homo sapiens* in our bid to become the most dominant animal on the planet. The passion, allure, fascination and respect for throwing that resides within are also clear. Throwing is an ancient act which allows us to connect not only with our parents, siblings and community, but also our distant and early primal ancestors. This reconnection with our past helps to account for the popularity of many simple and sophisticated throwing games that exist today. This act of throwing which was once essential to our survival has been preserved in sports throughout the world. We stood up to throw and threw to survive our battles. In response to these old imperatives, we now throw not because we must, but for our inherent enjoyment and entertainment.

2

Hitting

Parallel to the discovery and development of throwing expertise, hitting skills and techniques likewise emerged in the evolutionary progression of humankind. These two major skills played essential roles in human survival and were expressed in early games and sports. Today, these basic throwing and hitting skills are still preserved and have become the foundations and featured activities of both baseball and cricket. This section will show the development of hitting as also pivotal to human survival. In addition, this discourse shows the emergence of dueling confrontations as hitting and throwing skills and strategies began to be pitted against each other.

As primates evolved, development of the opposable thumb enabled more effective gripping of objects and consequent making and using of tools. Primates soon realized a rock in one's hand was an effective striking weapon. The limitations of hand-held rocks were apparent as a hitter's reach was limited by the length of his arm. Close-quartered combats favored larger opponents with longer arms, bigger hands and greater strength. To overcome this size disadvantage in early confrontations, hand-held sticks became the preferred weapon of choice. A fundamental shift in fighting strategies occurred.

Using their developing hands, our ancestors were not only able to wield sticks more effectively, but also to break off branches and make individualized striking weapons. Consequently, they were relatively better armed to defend themselves against others who threatened their personal safety and interests (food, territory, social or military status and acquisition of mates). With these hitting or striking tools our ancestors became more daring in their attacks, they could not only throw and run, but stand and fight with a better chance of survival.

Once the usefulness of hitting weapons was recognized, it was just a matter of time before our human ancestors improved their effectiveness for close-quarters combats. For example, it was found that sticks about an arm's length were easier to wield, especially with differently sized ends. A narrower end made both gripping and wielding easier, whereas a wider end made hitting contact more likely. Sticks, with wider and heavier ends, delivered deadlier blows and were less likely to break on contact. These weapons were naturally available from knotted or gnarled pieces of wood or forks of branches. Pieces of charred or sun-dried wood also made lighter and stronger weapons. With the development of better tools for scraping and shaving, the handle of a club was made narrower, making it easier to hold and wield. Indentations and coverings were added to the handle to facilitate easier gripping. We can readily envision early hobbies or pastimes which included refining, polishing, and decorating these treasured clubs. Our ancestors capitalized on these discoveries and collected, refined and carried their early clubs. Modern baseball bats still resemble these early weapons, each providing a primal feel and appeal. A big man holding a huge club was and still is an imposing and intimidating force.[1]

Early clubs were skillfully used not only in killing animals to acquire meat for food but also for defense against enemies and predators. These offensive and defensive skills and strategies were practiced in friendly bouts and competitive contests within groups and eventually became in effect a sport or war-game. The art and science of club-wielding (hitting) skills were taught to young warriors of their own group. Children also practiced club-wielding skills, with lighter and less harmful sticks, in their own imitation war-games.

Some ancient stick-fighting techniques that were developed and practiced in the earliest forms of martial arts have survived in several distinct communities.[2] The practice of fighting with sticks also laid the foundations for the earliest forms of wooden-sword fencing. These same skills were helpful in the transition to later fighting with more potent metal swords.[3] The foundations of these combative practices have survived as stick-fighting skills in many cultures, as in Japanese *Kendo* and Indian *Silambam*, forming part of ethnic and cultural identity.

As time progressed, humans were able to use other tools to reduce the circumferences of handles while simultaneously retaining wider barrels toward the hitting ends of their clubs.[4] In addition, they were able to reduce some natural irregularities in shaping their chosen pieces of wood. They spent significant amounts of time trying to make perfect war-clubs to fit their personal needs. Our ancestors learned that their sticks and clubs had both offensive and defensive capabilities when they were made and wielded properly. Engagements with enemies were more likely to be successful than attacks with bare hands or hand-held rocks. In these face-to-face challenges, whoever more skillfully used his club was likelier to survive. Smaller, quicker, and smarter individuals now had a chance against bigger and slower adversaries.

In conflicts fought with clubs, the most skillful, intelligent, agile, and ferocious club-wielders had better chances to emerge as winners. They were the earliest heavy hitters. Such naturally dominant and exceptional hitters gained the respect and admiration of others. The prized skills of the earliest heavy hitters were passed on through their descendants to today's best players.

A club gave its wielder not only a better tool to reach and strike an opponent, but also a better and far safer option to block close-range attacks.[5] From various artistic depictions and surviving war-clubs from different times and places, the ideal length of a war-club was about the length of a user's arm; for example, in ancient Hindu myth, Lord Shiva is depicted with one arm holding a powerful war club. In effect, a club-holder in combat almost doubled his normal reach in attacking and defending maneuvers. Length of a club was only one of the factors to be resolved in making a club to suit an individual's needs. Heavier clubs with the same lengths as lighter clubs were more difficult to wield effectively in combat and had to be pared down. The weight of each club was best near the striking end, that is, the bottom section of the club which will be making contact preferably with the head or upper body of an opponent.[6] Preferred clubs were those which balanced length, weight, circumference and ease of dexterous handling with speed in combat. Modern baseball hitters likewise have personalized needs and desires, and the basic bat-selection criteria are still essentially the same as those for primitive war clubs. Major League Baseball now has standards and limits with regards to weight, circumference and length of bats.

Like throwing, hitting was based on very similar fundamental principles. These included: (1) a proper stance, that is, feet wider than shoulder width apart with the hitting side's foot being slightly behind; (2) flexed knees for easier maneuverability; (3) movement toward the target to gain momentum; (4) initial chest high position of the hands; and (5) faster swinging velocity of the arms toward the target. These hitting skills and strategies were incorporated in the instruction of young warriors in pre-war training camps. Warriors schooled in hitting became a specialized and valued labor pool. These efforts were designed to prepare warriors to defend against potential enemies, and to invade the terrains of others.

In addition, during their close-quarter combats, our ancestors learned that successful club-yielding skills depended on their ability to evade incoming blows from their enemies and to position themselves for counterattacks. They anticipated the actions of their opponents and became more prepared to take suitable counter-measures. Savvy thinking was necessary to plan, anticipate, take evasive actions and become more deceptive in their maneuvers. As time progressed, the levels of athletic, emotional and intellectual sophistication of these combatants were also raised. These inherent qualities were essential for the survival of older, injured, or smaller combatants.

Since fighting was a constant preoccupation necessary for the survival of a community, older and injured warriors, in addition to teaching and sharing their experiences, also contributed to war efforts through the crafting of weapons. Their skills and experiences went into the production of wooden clubs for more able and frontline warriors. In the process, specialized club-makers became respected members of their communities. These weapon-makers employed rites and rituals believed to endow their skillfully hand-crafted and decorated weapons with magical and spiritual forces. For some it was thought that during the preparation process a spirit of a past warrior or animal was infused into the weapon, thereby increasing its fighting powers. A widely known example of such ancient practitioners is the skillful metal-craftsmen of the revered and legendary Samurai sword-makers of Japan. Similarly today, highly skilled Japanese craftsmen seek special trees to make baseball bats for their best hitters in professional Japanese baseball leagues. These specialized bat-makers encapsulate art, skill, ritual and mystique reminiscent of an old and honorable weapon-making profession. To a more limited extent, specialized commercial companies using only select wood make custom-ordered bats for elite major-league hitters.

Since each major battle was a matter of life or death, it was prudent for both clubs and warriors to be blessed by religious authorities such as wizards, witches, shamans, medicine men and women and witch doctors. These hitting warriors carried their favorite clubs with pride.[7] Some, like modern baseball players, did not wish to have their clubs touched by others as they thought this would compromise their club's effectiveness. These club-wielders had their own idiosyncrasies, superstitious beliefs and pre-war rituals, such as a war dance or a particular routine action or diet. These quirks or irrationalities of human behavior are still evident in modern-day baseball hitters. Each baseball hitter has a specific routine before and after entering the batter's box, for example, clapping or spitting on hands or crossing oneself. Old superstitious beliefs and practices are prevalent in baseball and discussed further in Chapter 11.

As weapons developed in parallel with warrior-training, so did rivalries between contestants. Nothing was more absorbing than watching two warriors fight with fists and clubs in a high-stake duel of life-and-death. Such a dramatic spectacle was heightened when the contest for supremacy was between an older experienced warrior and a younger stronger challenger, or when two of the best warriors of a group were vying for supremacy. These scenarios were resolved by combat—winner takes all. In such troubled times, onlookers knew from experience that change was the natural order of things. It is easy to picture a scene wherein a community stood spellbound as the dueling drama unfolded—some could not bear to look, yet they could not walk away. The sound of a club hitting a head and delivering a deathblow hushed or thrilled the onlookers. The vanquished was left behind, while his followers consoled with thoughts that his spirit would join his forefathers in the abode of the brave and heroic. The victor standing over the fallen hero was cheered and honored. Spectators moved on behind their new acclaimed hero.

Supporters of this new hero felt they had collectively contributed to the champion's victory and the loser's demise. These admirers touched their new idol, each hoping that his power would rub off on them, thereby gaining them privileged societal status. They wanted to be associated with the winner of the duel. Over time our human ancestors witnessed many man-to-man dueling battles, knowing instinctively only one would emerge alive and victorious. These brutal battles were repeated again and again in humankind's primitive and recent past. Over thousands of years, humans acquired and inherited a taste and fascination for violence, blood and gore, best illustrated by the gladiatorial contests of ancient Rome.[8]

One continuous thread which runs through generations is the fascination with these classic duels between one man or group and another. Early war strategies between two rivals began with the throwing of rocks or spears, after which clubs were also used. These were common communal duels. Simple man-to-man duels follow the same pattern and began with each opponent being armed with rocks and a club. They first threw rocks at each other before getting into close-quartered combat. Over time a continuous rivalry between the best throwers and hitters developed. They competed to be recognized as the best warrior of one's group. The best thrower was not necessarily the best hitter. Each weapon required skills which favored a particular body type. In situations in which different persons occupied the top spots, rivalries led to disputes and confrontations. These conflicts were settled by duels. These contests were more fascinating since each opponent was armed with a different basic weapon (rock or stick).[9] One throwing rocks as the other charged with his club increased the drama and suspense for those watching.[10] The thrower moved to stay outside the reach of his opponent, while the hitter used his club to deflect incoming rocks as he closed in on his combatant. Both knew that with one solid hit or blow the fight would be over.

These primal reenactments of ancient confrontations occur in the duels between pitchers and batters in baseball. A pitcher tries to hit an invisible yet identifiable strike zone beside the hitter. Throwing directly to hit the batter is far too dangerous.[11] In critical moments, viewers of a baseball game are often hushed or thrilled by that special sound of solid contact between a bat and a ball. A perfect and solid blow by a hitter now produces a home run. Spectators still rise in joyous adulation when their hitting hero is victorious, or slump in silent empathy with their defeated pitching hero. This is a scene one can often return to again and again in baseball. Modern hitters and their supporters enjoy powerful and solid hits in baseball, likely as much as their primal counterparts enjoyed lethal blows in earlier times. A late 1990's Nike baseball commercial and slogan, "Chicks dig the long ball," reveals the inherent primal and sex appeal of heavy hitters.

Hitting, like throwing, has always been a part of primal and human existence. These acts still enthrall viewers showing that, despite modern technological accomplishments and sophistication, we are not far removed from our archaic past. We are still seeking and enjoying the ancient excitement and thrills of these confrontations. This human fascination with duels which prominently pit ancient skills of throwing against hitting is beautifully encapsulated in modern baseball. A thrower and hitter match different skills and body types against each other. Soon thereafter, each member of the dueling pair added others to his cause escalating the confrontation and thereby increasing drama. These conflicts moved from simple man-to-man duels toward team combats and games. The next chapter will take a look at baseball as a team game and how it recreates not only a duel between individual warriors, but also references numerous battle scenes throughout the evolutionary development and history of humankind.

3

Warfare,
Games and Play

War and threats of war have been constant factors in human affairs as ways of settling disputes, ending rivalries, acquiring property, making territorial expansions, expressing aggression, creating distraction, and providing outlets for excitement, risk-taking and adventure. Unfortunately such wanton acts of aggression and seizures of the assets of weaker tribes or states continue despite efforts of the international community. The ancient inner drives for aggressive attacks and defenses, demanded by war and survival, are still with us. Sports and games provide healthier and safer outlets for expressing these inner desires. In the previous two chapters, we traced the developments of both throwing and hitting as well as the re-creation of duels between two basic ancient warrior-types. In this chapter we will continue to explore the allure of baseball as it reconstructs ancient scenes of battle and their associated war skills. In particular, we will trace the earliest roots of human warfare and try to understand why and how baseball alleviates our aggressive tendencies.

As we know, humans and other primates threw rocks, sticks and spears against undesirables of their own groups, or at rivals from other groups.[1] They did this until their victims and opponents were well beyond the reaches of their thrown weapons. Heavy-hitters and their clubs, with or without primitive shields, stood beside their rock-throwers and thereby added further menace to the group's threats to the banished. This use of power arms to throw objects at others contributed to early primate dispersals by literally driving expulsions and subsequent creations of new sub-groups.[2] These chased-out individuals or groups in turn explored new environments and established their own communities. Forced expulsions and migrations also spurred within the rejected an inner thirst for revenge and motivation to strike back at their own kith-and-kin. The rejecters feared the banished would return. Both groups knew it was inevitable they would meet again, and both prepared for attacks by devising defensive measures to secure a more favorable outcome in forthcoming conflicts.

This whole process of voluntary or involuntary formation and dissolution of groups was repeated again and again until some of the dispersed became established tribes and states. The weaker groups, usually being either numerically less or with weaker power-arms and heavy-hitters, were assimilated, eliminated or forced into less desirable environments.[3] Groups with the best survival skills, the ones with earliest baseball-like offensive and defensive skills and the fortuitous, usually occupied the most sought-after places within their environment. It is no coincidence other non-human primates with lesser inherent throwing and hitting abilities and developed skills have only survived in the most remote and least accessible regions on Earth.[4] Presently, these former inaccessible regions are being intruded on or invaded by better-equipped humans. Even without sophisticated weaponry, humans being both more numerous and better throwers and skilled hitters will emerge as the dominant species over other non-human primates and animals.

Humans moving in search of water, food, shelter and adventures crossed paths with others at natural divides, such as narrow rivers, streams, gorges and valleys. In some places relics of these early encounters survived. For example, William Crooke, in *The Popular Religion and Folklore of Northern India* (Vol. II, 1896), writes about rock-throwing fights in India and neighboring Nepal:

> Of these mock fights we have numerous instances in the customs of Northern India. Thus, in Kumaun, in former days at the Bagwah festival the males of several villages used to divide into two bodies and sling stones at each other across a stream.[5] The results were so serious that it was suppressed after the British occupation of the country....
>
> In Nepâl, after the Sithi Jâtra feast, the people divide into two parties and have a match at stone throwing; formerly this used to be a serious matter.[6]

These are but two of the recorded cases of re-enactments of early rock-throwing battles.[7] Similar to the above rock-throwing scenarios, Richard Holt in *Sport and the British* (1989) writes:

> Around 1800 the Govan "rowdy" mob in Glasgow habitually spent part of their New Year's Day "throwing the cudgel for gingerbread cakes" and fighting with "single sticks," in which the combatants often had one hand tied behind their back. Stone fights were popular too. On a small island in the Clyde a boy was killed at the end of the eighteenth century in just such a fight between the weaver lads of the Gorbals and their enemies from the other side of the Clyde. Stone-throwing was not confined to the lower orders.[8]

Rivals or strangers met on an open field or saw each other across a divide.[9] Both groups viewed each other as a threat to their personal and communal interests and survival. These events created uncertainties, and potential battles were usually preceded by exaggerated acts of intimidation and scorn for the other side. They made loud noises by yelling, banging clubs, shouting obscenities and grunting in order to scare real or presumed threats away. These intimidating sounds were accompanied by visible acts that included thumping of chests, butting of heads, and waving of clenched fists. In addition, they made lewd gestures such as displaying their genitalia and buttocks.[10] They also waved weapons such as rocks, sticks, wooden clubs, spears, and shields to show their readiness to fight and prove their war skills and manliness. Such actions excited and energized the combatants for the battles ahead. In some cases these ritualistic displays of bravado and intimidation were enough to cause one side to depart, thereby preventing war. In January 1879, the British, in their sojourn in Africa, encountered such intimidating foreshadowings of war from the Zulus. Maori warriors of New Zealand have also maintained their own intimidating rituals and dances now surfacing as preludes to sporting events like rugby.[11] Some of these ancient pre-battle scenarios are still evident, but as sophisticated pre-game rituals and cheers at sporting events. These are now done to inspire and promote team spirit, camaraderie, and to get the home crowd involved. During baseball games, irate fans still express some of these ancient practices as seen by the taunting of a hated visitor, or in the hurling of verbal insults or objects at offending players.

The intensity of early pre-combat exchanges especially increased when both sides felt secure behind natural or erected barriers and were confident in their own numbers and abilities to win the upcoming confrontation. Each was testing the *fight or flight* response of the other side. When ensuing and ongoing intimidating threats and rants of bravado failed to cause a departure of the other side, someone eventually got too excited and began to throw rocks at the enemy. (This first rock thrown at the start of a battle may be analogous today to the ceremonial throwing of the first pitch at a Major League Baseball game.) A thrower on the other side retaliated in like fashion. The able-bodied of each side joined in and threw rocks at each other across this natural divide. Their best power-arms manned the frontlines of this active rock-throwing battle. Before long someone on one side or the other got hurt and fell. The killing instincts of both sides were aroused as adrenalin levels and emotions rose higher and higher; now there was no turning back and combatants on both sides wanted to inflict greater casualties.

There was jubilation whenever one of their opponents fell after being struck down by an outgoing rock. Such expressive behavior is still evident as modern pitchers likewise celebrate a critical strikeout with clenched fists accompanied by words of jubilation or acknowledgment of divine intervention such as pointing to the heavens and crossing oneself. Sometimes it took several direct hits to bring an opponent down. Injured combatants went voluntarily or were dragged by comrades to a safe place behind a rock or tree or in a trench. Participants seeking temporary refuge or a place to regroup also went to their own protective areas. Much the same was occurring on the other side of the ensuing conflict.

Incoming rocks striking one's head caused serious injuries. In addition, rocks whizzing past an opponent's head were frightening and intimidating. Precision rock throwers manned the frontlines of such battles, saving rocks and energy, as it was essential to make every throw count. A supply of rocks would be more limited inside any enclosure. (Later, rocks were complemented or replaced with spears, javelins and arrows.) Over time, fear of being struck in the head by a rapidly incoming object became part of our human survival instincts.

Hitting is made especially difficult for some after experiencing the ill effects of being previously struck in the head by an incoming fastball. This fear of personal injury is strong even among the best professional hitters. Some Major League Baseball hitters in the 1993 and 1997 All-Star games did not want to face Randy Johnson's high velocity and erratic fastball. Modern baseball hitters take exception whenever a pitcher throws a ball intentionally or unintentionally close to their heads. They become furious and may glare at or even charge the offending pitcher on the mound. (These modern responses are no different from those in old conflicts.) Any pitcher who wants to intimidate hitters must be prepared to throw hard and inside to a hitter.[12]

Victorious outcomes of such conflicts were influenced by the side whose warriors threw heavier rocks with higher velocity and accuracy. The abler rock-throwing warriors achieved more strikes and caused greater injuries and deaths. The superior fire-power of better rock throwers enhanced the survival of their side since they not only inflicted more casualties and intimidation, but chased away their opponents. Good rock-throwing skills decided the outcomes of battles, much as good pitching performances usually determine today's games of baseball.[13]

Incoming rocks provided additional weapons to be used against opponents. The direct stopping or catching of arriving rocks risked injury to one's self. Individuals, like outfielders today, fared better when they had a more developed personal visual tracking system in addition to superior judgment of trajectories of aerial objects. Combatants, like modern catchers, put themselves in harm's way to block incoming rocks, requiring a combination of excellent eye-hand coordination, timing, concentration and patience. A less injurious way to stop an incoming rock was to block or knock it down with a club or shield, and where possible redirect it to an appropriate place or person for re-use.[14] Defenders then threw these rocks back at their opponents. In situations where rocks were in limited supply, it was more efficient to pass the rocks to the better throwers of one's group.

Skilled hitters, like current bunters, also emerged from the pool of warriors who knocked down incoming rocks. Some heavy hitters attempted to hit rocks into the ranks of the other side, but this was difficult to do accurately across a wide divide.[15] Success favored a side with the best coordinated efforts of throwers, catchers, fielders, and hitters as these specialists emerged as respected members of a group. Leaders and rulers emerged from those who best exemplified and coordinated these different battle roles.

During these combats participants also sought refuge behind natural protections such as trees, rocks and hills. As combatants ran from one safe place to another, they were exposed to the dangerous arrival of rocks from opposing rock throwers.

In such battles, speed was essential to get safely from one haven to another. Running from one refuge to another without getting injured or killed by incoming rocks required not only speed, but also courage, daring, timing, and agility. These were the earliest equivalents of modern day stolen bases. Some agile and fast runners also used themselves as targets to draw their enemies' attention. These diversions gave others enough time to move through hazardous zones to regroup or escape. Such runners' unselfish and risky acts for the benefit of the group were among the first deliberate sacrifices by humans for the common good. These commendable, intentional and personal sacrificial actions are part of the evolutionary dictates of each individual. This nobler side was evident and rooted in early humanity. Survivors of the group expressed gratitude by acknowledging these heroic and sacrificial efforts of their runners. These trends are still evident in baseball.

*   *   *

As the physical skills for war developed, thinking and planning of battles emerged as necessary factors to enhance one's chances of success and survival.[16] An intellectual component included having previous knowledge and scouted information of enemies and battle terrains. Strategizing before battles allowed for adaptations and improvisations to changing battle situations. Consequently, in ensuing battles participants used their imaginations, thought like the enemy, anticipated opposing strategies and tactics, took preventative countermeasures, planned retreats, and learned from mistakes and losses. Humans learned that besides physical skills, planning and intelligence, qualities like courage, determination, and risk-taking determined the outcomes of fights. Such actions, thoughts and intangible attributes lead to success at all levels of baseball.

Survival of any particular human group was a constant struggle to find new and better solutions to continuous threats to its existence. Early communities, whether residing on open plains, treed areas, or on sides of hills and mountains, were vulnerable to attacks and ambushes by predators ranging from other humans to wild animals. In response to these vulnerabilities, they built barricades and simple protective perimeters. Wherever possible, they chose higher grounds in areas that offered natural protection with limited possibilities for surprise attacks. Consequently, they were better able to coordinate defensive strategies at one or two key locations.

In one early scenario, the offensive attackers (hitters) stood at the end of a narrow "bridge" outside the stockade and challenged the defenders (throwers) to come out and do battle. When defenders refused to leave the more secured area, an attacker issued a direct challenge for a duel between a leading hitter and thrower. The rock-thrower from his higher vantage point threw rocks at the offensive clubber as he advanced to the entrance of the barricade via the open space between them. The defender's goal was to disable the rock-hitter as soon as he stepped into the line of fire.[17] The defender delivered a barrage of rocks at his target and quickly stepped out of the way of any retaliatory action. As many rock throwers as possible guarded their entrance, avoiding exposure to the weaponry of their enemies. If the offensive challenger was hurt, another attacker took his place, and the dueling continued.[18] The defenders of the main entrance threw rocks at any attacker as he tried to run this gauntlet.

Whenever frontline offensive challengers were incapacitated or killed (struck out), other attackers (on-deck hitters) took their places and the battle continued. The attacking rock hitters would try to reach the entrance to this fortification via makeshift bridges or under shields in their attempts to break down the "gates" of the barricade, using their clubs as battering-rams. The rock throwers' objectives were to disable and stop these attackers. Usually, only a numerically superior force would attempt to attack a well-barricaded position. The leader of an attacking force would determine whether he could afford the casualties to reach his objectives of breaching the defenses. (This situation is analogous to baseball in which hitters one at a time, at home plate, try to batter their way into the "fortification" or diamond, as balls are thrown to him from a mound.)

Once an attacker entered this fortification, other defenders inside dealt with this intruder as defenders of the barricade continued to try and prevent entrance. At the same time, the intruder who broke through tried to create havoc and confusion. He sought possible safety or storage places where valuable provisions or "spoils of war," such as food, drink, clothing and mates were kept. This intruder ran from one safe place to another with his stolen booty until he was struck or captured, joined by fellow attackers, or escaped from the defended territory. The analogous situation of throwing a ball at a runner survived in some precursor games of baseball. In such invasions, successful attackers brutalized the defenders or took them prisoners; victorious defenders likewise showed no mercy to attackers. This situation is not unlike baseball, in which the objectives are to breach the enemy's defenses, create havoc, and let fellow intruders in to join the battle; defenders try to prevent or minimize the impacts of any entry.

The victorious placed the heads and bodies of captured enemies outside the entrances and walls of their fortifications to intimidate other potential invaders. In some cases, they also placed images of ferocious animals and mythical beings to act as talismans and guardians. By such acts they invoked the spirits of these feared and revered animals or supernatural-beings to offer protection and aid for their causes. Analogously, modern stadiums have statues and engravings of "guardian spirits" including depictions of tribal warriors, predatory animals, or mythical beings. These images are placed above and outside the gates of stadiums to help protect and inspire the home team. Modern players are expected to exhibit the fighting qualities and attributes of the mythical creatures and ferocious animals depicted in their stadiums. Busts, statues and pictures of past baseball superstars now adorn modern stadiums serving to encourage and inspire current players to reach the same heights as their warrior predecessors.[19]

Defensive situations were also improved as humans progressed from natural barriers to man-made barricades and primitive forts. In time, societies progressed from building primitive stockades to more secure forts and well-fortified castles. As some human societies grew more sophisticated, elements of newer technologies were incorporated in their defensive strategies to offer better protection from invaders and sudden attacks. Fortifications of wood, mud or stone were universal. Some forts were so well built that remnants or almost entire structures survive despite the passage of centuries.[20]

The corners of these early forts or simple castles later evolved into guard towers or safe places for those on watch duties. Such reinforced safe areas had narrow openings from which occupants were better able to observe possible attackers without being struck by incoming objects such as rocks, spears and arrows. From these higher elevations a wider view of the surrounding landscape to spot the enemy was obtained. The walled distances joining the corners facilitated safe movements of defenders from one refuge to another, providing an excessive number of objects were not raining down on them. In baseball, the intruder on gaining entry into a fortification finds haven in analogous designated safe-areas (bases) from other defenders. In a game, of course, both sides get equal opportunities (innings) to be attackers and defenders.

∗   ∗   ∗

Art and games often imitate and reflect life. Early games mimicked and reflected the realities of living as well as the survival strategies and responses of peoples to their particular circumstances. The game of baseball has patterned itself on these early attack and defense situations. There were three major adjustments in early baseball necessitated by practical considerations. First, the divide or dueling distance between hitter and thrower was moved within the staged area. This meant an invading attacker was now positioned at the entrance or exit (home plate). Second, the main defending rock thrower was moved from the entrance to an area near the center of the defended area. In these ways, participants were also able to use less space within their protective enclosures without getting in the way of others going about their business. Consequently, adults and other passersby were able to move more freely behind a hitter without interrupting a game. Lastly, wherever possible, a person threw from a mound thereby mimicking the higher ramparts of forts and castles from which objects were more effectively thrown at incoming invaders.[21] Games imitated war as much as circumstances allowed.

Intra- and inter-tribal groups held competitive games for prizes or as other ways of settling friendly rivalries and disputes. In their games, throwers would no longer throw directly at the hitters' vulnerable spots but beside them over a marked area, especially where children were involved. In addition, players took turns being either invaders or defenders. These games became their natural training grounds for attacking and defending fortifications. The booty or prize became a point for every trip an attacking player made around the bases. In baseball, the intentions of the offense are to score runs, whereas the defense fights to prevent this.

Throughout human history, there have been constant struggles of combat necessitating the practice of survival skills. In more modern times, for example, in early Europe and elsewhere, numerous forts and castles were built by various groups because of constant territorial disputes and battles for supremacy or survival.[22] Children also had numerous opportunities to develop and play games which closely mimicked the attack and defense of a defined territory. These essential components of early primal battles were reflected and survived in early games. One such early game that survived in old Ireland was described by Alice Bertha Gomme in *The Traditional Games of England, Scotland, and Ireland* (1898):

> A circle of stones is formed according to the number of players, generally five or seven each side. One of the out party stands in the centre of the circle, and lobs at the different stones in rotation; each hit a player gives all his side must change stations, in some places going round to the left and in some places going round to the right. The stones are defended by the hand or a stick, according as a ball or stick is lobbed. All the players are out if the stone is hit, or the ball or stick caught, or one of the players is hit while running. In different counties or places these games are more or less modified. Mr. Kinnahan, who describes this game, adds a very instructive note, which is worth quoting:
> "These games I have seen played over half a century ago, with a lob-stick, but of later years with a ball, long before a cricket Club existed, in Trinity College, Dublin, and when the game was unknown in a great part of Ireland."[23]

In this game of *stones* there was both hitting with a bare hand and hitting with a stick. Generally, a ball can easily be thrown both underhand and overhand, but a stick is best thrown overhand for more accuracy. This ancient game of *stones* shows some of the basic elements (throwing, hitting, and running) preserved in other old British baseball-like games.[24] Gomme mentions the game of *stones* varied in different places. As with most practices this game was adapted to suit its local participants and circumstances. *Stones* was a relic of ancient times just as the throwing of rocks at each other across a divide by two groups of males in ancient India and Nepal were. The survival of this game of *stones* or rock-throwing in old Ireland into the 19th century is not surprising.[25]

The foundations of early baseball, which include throwing, hitting and running, reflect the most basic and essential skills needed for early survival. Like the mentioned game of stones in old Ireland and the rock-throwing festival of 19th century India and Nepal, baseball has a wider historical past than is apparent at first glance. Baseball appeals to primal urges and desires, in a sense allowing us to revisit our collective past, reenact, and relive the dangers and thrills of battles.

4

Baseball Emerges

The ancient roots of baseball lie buried in unknown places once marked by the presence of humans. In Europe, particularly Britain, relics of past practices survived as folk games, but were not recorded until more recently when oral and observed descriptions were written down. It is therefore likely that in Europe (and elsewhere) similar and relevant practices, or relics of them, survived until recently but were not recorded.[1] This chapter examines games played in Britain from the fourteenth to the twentieth century that are relevant to baseball and subsequent development in North America.

In an earlier chapter, we saw that stones and sticks were used in some early throwing and hitting games. As time progressed, rocks and sticks were replaced by less harmful objects. One such game is described in *The Girl's Home Companion: A Book of Pastimes in Work and Play* (1891), edited by Mrs. Valentine.[2] This game was called stool-ball and sounds similar to the game *stones* but with a chair or stool substituted for a stone to mark the bases and only one ball thrown at a striker. The use of a stool instead of a stone also allowed for indoor play during inclement weather. Valentine writes:

> A number of stools are stood in a ring to serve as wickets, with a striker at each—the bat being a fives-bat or such is used in Trap Ball. The bowler stands in the centre and bowls one ball to each striker in turn, going round the ring the same way as the hands of a watch go. If a ball is hit well away, the striker runs towards the next stool to hers, and the other strikers all run as if the game were rounders. The bowler endeavors to hit one of the stools with the ball before the player has finished her run.... Stool Ball on the circular system is a busy game.... It is sometimes called Sun and Planet.
> In the South of England, Stool Ball is an outdoor game.[3]

This account describes an early version of stool-ball, as it mentions a striker at each stool and the clockwise action of the bowler, neither seen in other early descriptions of stool-ball.[4] The person hitting the ball or defending the stool was called a "striker," the same term used with similar meaning in early descriptions of baseball in America. William Baker in *Sports in the Western World* (1988) writes:

> Compared to football, games such as stool-ball and bowls, or bowling, were mild exercises. Utterly simple, they were popular pastimes in the towns and villages of medieval England. Stool-ball was originally a game played by milkmaidens who used the familiar implement, the milking stool, and a ball. One player stood in front of the stool while another threw the ball in an attempt to knock the stool over. At first the "batter" wielded no bat or stick, but rather used the hand. Every time she successfully defended the stool from a pitch, she scored a point. When the pitcher finally knocked over the stool, or caught the hit ball before it touched the ground, she changed places with the batter. Soon the game was played by boys as well as the girls, adults as well as children. It was the basis of the games of rounders and cricket, and from rounders American baseball evolved many centuries later. Although modern baseball is primarily American, urban, and male, its roots are medieval, English, rural, and female.[5]

This is a reasonable explanation for the origins of the stool-ball game and its relationship to ball games such as rounders, cricket and baseball which involve hitting a thrown ball and running. But these games seem to have older roots. Sidney Oldall Addy, in *A Glossary of Words Used in the Neighborhood of Sheffield* (1888), mentions two older games *Munshets* or *Munshits* and *Hittera Ball* that are no longer played, though they were common about fifty years before, in the 1830s.[6]

Valentine's work also mentions the game of rounders being played with five bases as well as a home base: "The ground for the home is marked out by four sticks stuck in the ground, or by four stones, or by a line scratched on the ground, and the five bases are marked at a distance of about fifteen yards apart by a stick or stone."[7]

In this description of rounders, the five bases and home also made a circular pattern. Despite similarities in these early descriptions of stool-ball and rounders, Valentine mentions them as distinct entities. Both games of stool-ball and rounders described above were similar to the older game of *stones*, except a ball was used instead of a stick or stone as the thrown object. The similarities between rounders and stool-ball are also evident, but it is hard to tell where they differ, the biggest apparent difference being that in rounders the base-markers were sticks or stones, whereas in stool-ball they were stools or chairs.[8] Different geographical locations had varying versions of the basic games, as over time each in turn was affected by its own local environment and participants. Joseph Strutt points out in *The Sports and Pastimes of the People of England* (1876) that there were apparently two versions of stool-ball: (1) a simple type in the northern parts of Britain, in which one stool was involved; and (2) a second more sophisticated version in other parts of the country wherein a circle of stools was used.[9] (It is tempting to suggest one version led to cricket and the other early baseball, but both contain elements found in the old games of one old cat, two old cat, and so on.[10])

In Britain, there were several variants of established ball-games which contained elements in common with early baseball. For example, the British played: British base ball, stool-ball, tut-ball, pize-ball, town ball, trap ball, stow ball, rounders, wicket, and cricket. The names for these two-worded games were often written in different forms. Earlier, baseball was written as two words, *base ball*, then as a hyphenated word, *base-ball*, and finally as one word, *baseball*. Similar situations existed for stool-ball, tut-ball and pize-ball.

In addition to Valentine (1891), Francis Willughby (1672), Peter Roberts (1814), Sidney Oldall Addy (1888), Alice Bertha Gomme (1898), F. W. Hackwood (1924) and Alan S.C. Ross (1968) of the seventeenth to the twentieth centuries also use rounders and cricket as frames of reference in their descriptions of any baseball-like game for their respective readerships. F.W. Hackwood in *Staffordshire Customs, Superstitions and Folklore* (1924) writes:

> "Tut-ball" was a similar game [to rounders] in which the bat was dispensed with, and the open hand used to smite the ball—once highly popular with the poorer children of the Black Country whose means precluded the possibility of providing other apparatus than a penny ball. The sport was played as follows: A number of players having selected in much the same fashion as already described, stones or bricks, were placed at intervals in a ring, which in most places were called tuts, from which, indeed, the game was called "Tut-ball." Here, however, the players, instead of throwing the ball into the air with the left hand and striking it with the bat as it descended, placed one of their number in front of the striker to bowl the ball for striking, and when the ball was struck the striker ran around to the various tuts or stations as in the game of rounders.[11]

This is one of the simplest descriptions of a surviving form of early baseball in early twentieth century England. Tut-ball literally meant "stoneball" or "brickball," possibly connecting this game with *stones*. It must be noted that even though Hackwood writes that tut-ball was similar to rounders, he likewise also gives a separate description of each game, thereby viewing each as a separate entity.

Another variant baseball game of late medieval England was pize-ball. Ross in his article "Pize-Ball" (1968) writes: "Pize-ball is a game which in many ways resembles the well-known games, Rounders and Baseball."[12] Notably, rounders and cricket were again used as frames of reference. Addy (1888) defines *tut* as "a stone or other thing set up for a mark or bound" and *tut-ball* as "a game of ball. The same as Pize-Ball."[13] He therefore linked the two games of tut-ball and pize-ball as the same. Addy describes pize-ball:

Sides are picked, as for example, six on one side, six on the other side, and three or four marks or "tuts" are fixed in a field. Six go out to field, as in cricket, and one of these throws the ball to one of those who remain "at home," and one "at home" strikes or *pizes* it with his hand. After *pizing* it he runs to one of the "tuts," but if before he can get to the "tut" he is struck with the ball by one of those in the field, he is said to be burnt, or out. In that case the other side goes out to field.[14]

According to Addy, pize-ball differed from rounders in that hands were used to hit the ball. Ross points out that "pize-ball was evidently much played up to the mid-nineteen twenties; after this date it became rarer."[15] He also mentions in the same work that the game was not confined to Yorkshire, but was known in Derbyshire, Lancashire, High Westwood, Cumberland and New Castle upon Tyne. This game was therefore known in several areas of Britain during time-periods when people were migrating heavily from Britain, and was also still being played by some of those who remained behind. Ross points out that there were two versions of pize-ball, one informal (without sides) and the other formal (with sides), with some formal games requiring an umpire. The presence of an umpire means some unwritten or agreed-upon rules were being enforced. The formal version was often played on Sunday School outings and on Whit Monday.[16]

This tradition of Sunday School baseball likewise migrated and continued with baseball in the Europeanization of North America, including Canada. The foundations of the game were well laid here. Don Morrow in his chapter "Baseball" in *A Concise History of Sport in Canada* writes: "From Manitoba to British Columbia—where baseball was at a feverish pitch with 60 teams in Vancouver's Sunday School baseball league—strictly amateur was very popular in the first twenty years of the century [20th]."[17] (The implications of this and other games being associated with religious holidays will be the subject of later chapters.) Morrow also states: "Four bases, called 'byes' marked the infield area" in early baseball in Canada.[18] In this sense the word "byes" is analogous to the word "tuts." Morrow continues: "Hits and runs were numerous, since the real fun was in getting runners out by 'plugging'— that is the runner, when caught between the bases, could be tagged or hit (plugged) by a ball thrown at him."[19] The word "plugged" had the same meaning as "burnt" in pize-ball.

Ross's work further reveals several interesting pieces of information about pize-ball summarized here. The place where the batter stood to hit the ball from the *pizer* or thrower was called *home* or *homey*. Pize-ball was played on a square (each side about fifteen to twenty yards), and each of the four corners was called a *hob,* numbered 1, 2, 3 and 4 in a counter-clockwise direction. The players waited in the *den* for their turns to bat. The striker on hitting the ball was forced to run and if tagged or struck with the ball before reaching a *hob* was out. One complete circle or run was called a *rounder* or a *round*. Two players were allowed to share a base, a formation called a *sausage*, if they called out "*Sausage*" before the fielders made their call of "*No sausage!*" The *pizer* was allowed to practice deception, in the form of a pick-off move, and could pretend to throw the ball to the hitter but instead throw the ball at a player at a *hob*.[20] In cases where the *pizer* pretended to throw the ball toward the striker, the team waiting to bat shouted, "*No balking!*" Balking or a thrower's pick-off move in trying to deceive the runner at a base was already established. The term *burning* was also used in reference to one of the fielders hitting a runner with the ball. The winner of the game was the one with the highest number of runs or *rounds* after an agreed upon number of innings. This game showed the rudimentary beginnings of several standard baseball practices, such as a runner being safe at a base, attempted pickoffs, balks, and tagging a runner out. (See note 12 for reference to Ross's work.)

The distinctions among the various games discussed so far are primarily: in stool-ball the home plate was a stool; in pize-ball the bases were called *hobs* (as well as *tuts*) and the thrower the *pizer*; in tut-ball the bases were *tuts*, stones or bricks; town ball was the version played in early towns or communal gatherings; round ball described the circular direction of running around the bases to score a point or round; in British baseball the bases were round pillars or blocks of stone; and in rounders the bases were markers such as sticks, or piles of stones as was seen in Staffordshire, England.[21] Of these games, stool-ball was the earliest and most often-mentioned in diverse places.[22] The Viscountess Wolseley mentions in *In a College Garden* (1916): "Games of ball are all much alike, if we go by the descriptions given to them in old books, and it is difficult to make out exactly the difference between 'stowball,' 'stool-ball' and 'bittle-battle.'"[23] Stowball was the hard ball variant of stool-ball. In some early games such as tip-cat, kit-cat and old cat, pieces of wood were used as the ball.[24] The game of one old cat was recommended and described by educator Frank. J. Lowth, for use by country school teachers in rural America in the early twentieth century.[25]

The relationship between stool-ball, tut-ball and rounders is further supported by the work of others. Gomme in *The Traditional Games of England, Scotland, and Ireland* mentions tut-ball being played as a folk game. She states tut-ball is an ancient game and in other places called stool-ball. Gomme also gives a description of rounders; the similarities with baseball are apparent, but the differences harder to distinguish. In addition, Gomme mentions another game called *bittle-battle* as the Sussex game of stool-ball.[26]

It seems that stool-ball, tut-ball and British baseball, though bearing some differences, were essentially versions of the same basic game being played from the seventeenth to the twentieth centuries of what is now Britain.

Of these games, rounders, town ball, round ball, tut-ball, pize-ball, stool-ball and baseball were most similar.[27] Though some of the differences have been mentioned already, the similarities involved running in a circle around four or more markers after hitting a tossed ball. Hitting of the ball was either by hand or with the use of a wooden object, depending on the occasion. In general, one person threw the ball to the batter who hit the ball or defended a stone, tut, base or stool on the ground. If a struck ball was caught in the air, the side or individual was out. A runner was declared out if tagged or struck with the ball before reaching a base or home. In rounders, the team on the field was called the *outs* and the team waiting to bat was called the *ins* (Appendix C). In most of these games there were also some informal rules of fair-play to avoid or resolve disputes such as determining the winners in controversial situations. Likewise, each of these games had variations depending on participants, places, and situations.

Unfortunately, the histories of these formerly well-established British games are rarely acknowledged, so their influences on modern baseball are not well-known and remain underappreciated. Many wonder about the roles of both cricket and rounders in the development of baseball; these issues will be directly addressed later in the chapter. For now we will continue to explore the development of these co-existing games in old Britain.

*　　*　　*

The two games of rounders and cricket were well known to British immigrants from 1600s to 1900s and became frames of reference that led to the common misperception that American baseball was derived from these games. This reference-relationship between British baseball and cricket was an old one. British writer Francis Willughby (1635–1672) in *Francis Willughby's Book of Games: A Seventeenth-Century Treatise on Sports, Games and Pastimes* gives a description of stool-ball and mentions that a stool was the target of the thrown ball, and when the ball was thrown between two stones (*tuts*) the game was called tut-ball.[28] The score being kept by nicks on a stick thereby indicated a competitive game. The version of stool-ball (or tut-ball) described here was simply a throwing game since the stool was not defended. In 2003, modern day editors (David Cram, Jeffrey L. Forgeng and Dorothy Johnston) of Willughby's 1672 unfinished work give a description of stool-ball or tut-ball using the familiar cricket as a frame of reference: "A game called Stool-ball is attested as early as the fifteenth century. It has traditionally been supposed that this game was akin to Cricket, and essentially identical with the Stool-ball played in the eighteenth and nineteenth centuries."[29] In this way these editors are able to describe the game of stool-ball to their readers who understand cricket. If the intended readership had been primarily American, the editors would have likely chosen baseball as the frame of reference.

Stool-ball remained popular in other parts of Britain, especially in some working-class communities. These same low-income districts supplied the pool of migrants and laborers who came to America. David Underdown in *Revel, Riot, and Rebellion: Popular Politics and Culture in England 1603–1660* (1985) writes:

> Football [soccer] was less popular in the cheese country, but bat-and-ball games like stool ball and trap-ball were more widely played. Stool-ball's popularity in North Wiltshire might be ascribed to the fact that its structure expressed, better than football, the more individualistic nature of the wood-pasture community. Stool-ball was a team sport, to be sure, but wood-pasture villages were also communities. In stool-ball, as in cricket, the confrontation between batsman and bowler is an individual one within a team context; there is an analogy here with the place of the individual in the wood-pasture village, which was still, however fragmented, a community. In both the game and the community the individual had a greater sense of his personal role.[30]

Underdown then mentions several places in England where stool-ball was played.[31] Stool-ball clearly was widely played in England in numerous regions and villages in the seventeenth and eighteenth centuries. In addition to the dairy districts, stool-ball was also being played by people in animal-husbandry and clothing-manufacturing districts.[32] The specifically-mentioned places (e.g., in Worcestershire, Lancashire, Bedfordshire and Hertfordshire) were similar to other low-income areas in which people played stool-ball, specifically on Sundays (Note 31).

In agricultural and dairy communities, since workers (men and women) were outside in the fields, it was natural for them to use their stools as bases. Wooden stools were replacing the use of stones or bricks as bases in these non-permanent structures and boundaries of the game were more easily set up. In addition, the game was just as easily dismantled if disapproving officials appeared. The game was now portable and quickly arranged on any cleared piece of land. Children, young people and adults of both sexes likewise played stool-ball. The seventeenth-century British poet Robert Herrick, whose work was collected and published in *The Poetical Works of Robert Herrick* (1893), penned a poem, "Stool-Ball," that grants the game a role in courtship (Appendix C).

Underdown also mentions variants of stool-ball across old Britain. The version played in then Wiltshire involved the use of a hard ball and a wooden staff which resembled a baseball bat. Apparently, this use of a bat to strike a ball depended on the social occasion of the game. Underdown points out the common team-to-team and individual-to-individual confrontational aspects of both cricket and stool ball. Here again the similarities between cricket and baseball are mentioned with respect to confrontations between hitters (strikers or batters) and throwers (bowlers in cricket and pitchers in baseball).

Author and poet John Newbery, in his popular *A Little Pretty Pocket-Book* (1744), describes stool-ball and British baseball as two separate games:

> Stool-Ball.
> The Ball once struck with Art and Care,
> And drove impetuous through the Air,
> Swift round his Course the Gamester flies,
> Or his Stool's taken by Surprise.

> Base-Ball.
> The Ball once struck off,
> Away flies the Boy
> To the next destined Post,
> And then home with Joy.[33]

Newbery's descriptions of the two games are similar in that both used a ball and a bat. His work describes the use of stools for markers in stool-ball and posts in baseball. The marker at the beginning and end of the circuit was already called "home" in baseball. Newbery also poetically describes cricket, trap-ball and other popular and distinct games of his time.[34] This work by Newbery, which specifically mentions baseball, was written long before Abner Doubleday (the supposed founder of baseball in America) was born. Since Newbery specifically mentions the games of "cricket, trap-ball, base-ball and stool-ball," then these games were by 1744 all considered distinct entities at least in some areas of old Britain. There must have been subtle differences between the two games of stool-ball and British baseball, such as the materials used for bases and ground rules. From Newbery's woodcuts and poetical descriptions it is difficult to discern the subtle differences, but the essence of these games is the same.

Peter Roberts, then Rector of Llanrmon and Vicar of Madeley, Wales, in *The Cambrian Popular Antiquities; or An Account of Some Traditions, Customs, and Superstitions of Wales* (1814) writes:

Another species of this game, called stool-ball, resembling cricket, except that no bats are used, and that a stool is a substitute for the wicket, was in my memory, also a favourite game on holydays, but is now, like many other rural games, I believe, seldom, if ever, played. These amusements generally began on Easter-eve, and were resumed after Easter-day....

Easter-day itself is kept as the Sunday generally kept in Wales, that is, with much and becoming respect to the sacredness of the day.... In some places, however, after morning-prayers, vestiges of the Sunday sports and pastimes remain.[35]

The game of stool-ball was also played in Wales. It was played on Sundays and religious holidays, but by this time (early nineteenth century), like other rural sports, it was becoming less common in some areas. The Welsh played an early version of baseball, as the people of England did, but they also continue to play an interesting and re-vitalized version today. The game was not confined to the working classes but to others as well in British High society, For example, in 1748, the family of Frederick, Prince of Wales, and his friends partook in the playing of a baseball-like game.[36]

In addition, distinguished British novelist Arnold Bennett, in *Anna of the Five Towns* (1902), writes about the hardships ordinary people faced in the pottery industry in late nineteenth century in Britain. Bennett mentions the playing of tut-ball at annual school functions, and describes it as "a quaint game that owes its surviving longevity to the fact that it is equally proper for both sexes."[37] This supports the argument that tut-ball was becoming a folk game enjoyed by the working classes. Hackwood likewise states that tut-ball was played by children of the poorer districts.[38] The game of tut-ball, like stool-ball and early baseball, did not require expensive equipment thereby helping to explain its popularity among the children of the working classes.

A familiar argument by some that early American baseball was directly derived from cricket or rounders is now less plausible. As seen above, British baseball, stool-ball and tut-ball were already standing on their own as three versions of the same basic game in Britain and had laid the foundations of what later became known as American baseball. The game of rounders also seemed to have been influenced by these games and in turn contributed to American baseball as well. (This point will be discussed in more detail later.) In addition, since Newbery used stool-ball, baseball and cricket to teach morals to children and young people, then all of these games were likely already being played and established and socially accepted within eighteenth century Britain.[39]

In 2008, the diary of deceased solicitor William Bray of Surrey, England, was discovered. Bray, a young man in his late teens, records that he played baseball with his gentleman and lady friends.[40] Bray writes:

Easter Monday 31 March 1755.

Went to Stoke Ch. This morning. After Dinner Went to Miss Jeale's to play at Base Ball with her, the 3 Miss Whiteheads, Miss Billinghurst, Miss Molly Flutter, Mr. Chandler, Mr. Ford & H. Parsons & Jelly. Drank Tea and stayed till 8.[41]

David Block wrote about this find in the fall 2008 issue of the journal *Base Ball*, and had earlier shown in *Baseball Before We Knew It* (2006) that British baseball was already a distinct game and played mainly by children, especially schoolboys and young girls. According to Block, British baseball was a game with familiar elements of "pitching, batting, and base running—with antiquated characteristics that have long been forgotten."[42] He notes that "baseball" was mentioned in two novels of the eighteenth century, Jane Austen's *Northanger Abbey* and Ralph Vesey's *Battleridge*.[43] Block also makes a strong and credible case that British baseball served as a basis for the development of baseball in America. It must be noted that since most of the early British (and European) immigrants to America were members of the lower or middle classes, they brought with them not only their desires for a better life but also their own games, sports, pastimes and festivities. These immigrants and their children played their versions of baseball (and other games) in America just as they had done in their former homelands. It was a comforting game in their new surroundings and provided entertainment between or among various groups of incoming and recently established settlers.

In early America, baseball, cricket, and rounders were distinct games. The evidence points to stool-ball, tut-ball, British baseball and other early related games as modern baseball's true antecedents.

*   *   *

Why many people have some notion that cricket and rounders were directly involved in baseball's development is understandable.[44] These two games are often used as frames of reference in descriptions of earlier related games. For those not familiar with cricket, after hitting the ball, two runners move back and forth between two sets of wickets (three stumps make a wicket) set up twenty-two yards apart on the cricket pitch in the middle of the playing-field.[45] "Bowling" (pitching) takes place in turn from alternative ends of each wicket after each "over" (six deliveries or six pitches). The batsman is declared out if the wicket is struck by the ball delivered by the bowler, the batted ball is caught in the air by a fielder, or if the runner does not reach the safety line before the thrown ball hits the wicket.[46] Over time, only upper- and middle-class adults could afford the luxury of sports played at a leisurely pace with time out for tea and biscuits. Since cricket was enjoyed by the educated professional and upper classes, it is not surprising that cricketers would have standardized and written rules so that members of the upper strata from different regions of the country could better socialize, without disagreements. The British, in addition to writing standardized rules for cricket (1724, 1744, and 1774) also long had an unwritten code of gentlemanly conduct, indeed before any other known team-game in the Western World.[47] In contrast, the game of rounders was mostly played by those with less leisure time on their hands. The British later adapted the standardized written rules for cricket to rounders in the 1880s. According to Collins, Martin and Vamplew (*Encyclopedia of Traditional British Rural Sports*), "the first English rounders organization was set up in 1889 in Liverpool, a city which has a strong baseball tradition. The Scottish Rounders Association was also set up in the same year."[48,49] This quotation reinforces the argument that early baseball and rounders were distinct games since both were being simultaneously enjoyed in Liverpool. As elsewhere in Britain, baseball had no set of formal written rules, and consequently each community had its own set of informal guidelines. This likely contributed to the large number of names and variations of baseball described earlier in this chapter.

In light of what is known, this game of baseball, or its early variants, does indeed also have elements (as seen above) found in the then more well-known games of rounders and cricket. In cricket, a bowler tries to hit the visible wickets; whereas in baseball, the pitcher tries to hit a defined strike zone. The distances from which they try to do so are approximately the same (sixty six feet for cricket, and sixty and a half feet for baseball).[50] In both rounders and baseball the batter, after hitting the ball, runs in a circle from marker to marker or base to base. Gomme states that in early rounders the hitter tosses the ball in the air with one hand before hitting the ball; whereas, in tut-ball the ball is tossed to the hitter by another player.[51] From Gomme's writings, rounders and stool-ball were similar but still distinct games.

In modern times, anyone who has played rounders can see the similarities with baseball (e.g., four markers and nine players). Likewise, anyone who has played cricket can sense the relationship (man-to-man duels) and observe that the basic skills (throwing, catching, fielding and hitting) are the same. Cricket has eleven players per side while rounders, like baseball, has nine. The similarities between rounders and early baseball make it a natural way of describing baseball to others not familiar with it. Henry Chadwick, who played rounders as a child in England in the 1830s, writes in 1860 that baseball was of English origins and was derived from the game of rounders.[52] Historian and baseball scholar Block points out that Chadwick, the "Father of American Baseball," was born in the town of Exeter, in Devonshire.[53] A Devonshire manuscript of 1771 indicates that tut-ball was played at Exeter particularly at Easter time. Chadwick's mentioning of playing rounders, but not tut-ball, as a child in the 1830s, suggests tut-ball was by then a less popular or common game in Devonshire, as was the case elsewhere in England.

So far no documentation (pre-nineteenth century) specifically mentions "rounders" as a distinct game or a game related to baseball, tut-ball or stool-ball. It is not until the nineteenth century that rounders is mentioned in written works. Even though rounders is not mentioned earlier, in the nineteenth century rounders was being played by boys, girls, and youths of both sexes. It was more common and therefore used as a frame of reference for baseball and related games. It is striking that Hackwood describes tut-ball as being played by the poorer children of Staffordshire and considers tut-ball as a quaint game. This supports the proposition above that while tut-ball was diminished to the point of being unfamiliar to many, rounders was or remained more widespread. Many of the poorer people were also migrating elsewhere and taking their games or folk games with them.[54]

Chadwick, in *The Sports and Pastimes of American Boys,* notes that baseball was "essentially 'Americanized,'" that it arose as a product of "evolution" from "the old English schoolboy game of 'rounders.'"[55] Chadwick had seen and played rounders but was unlikely to have ever seen tut-ball being played in his lifetime, since while still a child he had left England for America.[56] Like others, he used his experiences with rounders as a frame of reference in writing about baseball. Chadwick became the leading authority on the game of baseball in America; in the 1860s and later, Chadwick was the editor of *Beadle's Dime Baseball Player,* the most authoritative and influential publication on baseball. He was therefore an important voice when commenting that baseball was derived from the British game rounders. Despite sharing similarities with rounders, other games were even closer in their approximations to American baseball and existed in Britain and Europe long before British and European immigrants came to settle in the United States and Canada.

The Rev. J.G. Wood in *The Boy's Modern Playmate: A Book of Sports, Games, and Pastimes* (1891) writes: "The simple and almost abandoned game of 'Rounders' has risen to a science under the name of 'Base Ball.'"[57] Wood's thinking is in line with earlier work of Chadwick since Wood himself also uses rounders as the frame of reference with regard to baseball. The acceptance of the later standardized version of baseball led to the decline of previous variants of the game, but knowledge of British rounders was still common as British immigrants were still coming to America.

Both cricket and rounders were used as frames of references for the descriptions of early versions of British baseball in Britain. This pattern also continued in the United States and Canada. Now that the misconceptions of baseball's relationships and connections with cricket and rounders have been explained, it is time to explore baseball's rise to national and international prominence.

* * *

In the 1600s, the people of Boston were playing early forms of baseball with names such as barn ball, town-ball, and the Boston or Massachusetts game. For example, Mayflower Pilgrims played stool-ball on Christmas Day in 1621 at Plymouth. Governor William Bradford deemed this activity inappropriate. Settlers were permitted then to play on other occasions (for example, Thanksgiving) and later elsewhere (away from windows).[58] This shows young colonists were falling back on their enjoyable pastimes from Britain. An account of these beginnings is also given by James Otis in *Mary of Plymouth: A Story of the Pilgrim Settlement* (1910), in which he describes newly arrived immigrants enjoying the games and festivities of their former homelands.[59] Children and adults alike played variant forms of baseball in the numerous safe forts or communities founded across North America. These early arrivals played their own versions of inherited games and interacted with others who played variants in their new communities. Accordingly, we find various versions of baseball which existed earlier in America before standardization. Modern American baseball was derived from British (and European) originated games of town-ball, round ball, goal ball, stool-ball, pize-ball, tut-ball, and British baseball.[60]

The game was again mimicking life and serving some of the same roles for newcomers to North America as it did for their ancestors. Whether or not immigrants realized it, their game of baseball most befitted their times and present circumstances. British and European immigrants who came to the New World, particularly North America, fell back on their past fort-building and defensive strategies.[61] The fortification and defensive strategies, incorporated into baseball, served British and Europeans well in their bids to wrest control of the land and its resources from well-established indigenous peoples of North America. In these forts, British and European defenders no longer used rocks, arrows, and spears, but more sophisticated weaponry of devastating guns and bullets. (Arriving immigrants also unintentionally and intentionally waged biological warfare whereby multiple diseases decimated native populations.) New waves of arrivals brought superior technologies, better and more coordinated war strategies, and an almost limitless numbers of personnel from the exiting masses of Europe.[62]

As various immigrant communities became settled and grew, the need for sports and games to keep youths occupied in constructive activities, particularly after school, became necessary. Boston-based Robin Carver says he is indebted to the earlier English edition of the *Boy's Own Book* for some of the material for his book. Carver in *The Book of Sports* (1834) states that his work is written specifically for American boys:

> My young friends have often come to me, after they have been dismissed from school, and begged me to think of some new sport for their amusement. Now, though somewhat of an old man, I have not forgotten the games and pastimes of my boyhood, while those of later years have quite faded away.[63]

Carver also notes:

> The use of the ball was well known to the children many hundred years ago.... The games with the bat and ball are numerous, but somewhat similar....
> Base, or Goal Ball.
> This game is known under a variety of names. It is sometimes called "round ball," but I believe that "base," or "goal ball" are the names generally adopted in this country.[64]

Moreover, Carver's work supports the argument that baseball and other similar ball-games brought over from Britain were being played in America. Carver writes that the game was called "round ball" and "base ball" in Boston where he was located.[65] It is easy to picture various versions of baseball existing to meet the needs of tough immigrants, as any too gentrified game would lack appeal to their senses of pride and manhood.

British baseball, besides being a rustic game, required less time to play than cricket, which moved at a leisurely pace with stoppages during the game for tea and biscuits. During break periods players visited with their dates and friends. Not only is the time-frame for a game of cricket longer, the game can also end in a draw. Ordinary laborers and skilled workers did not have much leisure time, and a non-decision may not sit well with some. British cricketers had a code of sportsmanship that would not sit well with the average baseball attendee.

Equally important, Americans saw the social and financial potentials presented by the growing and widespread popularity of various versions of baseball and recognized the need for standardization. The British had already developed a standardization of rules for cricket in 1727, 1744 and 1752.[66] British football was another popular working-class game played mainly by tough men that similarly had to be standardized because of its money-making potential and intense rivalries that often resulted in fights and severe injuries. The British had legal copyright and therefore a say in any adoption of their cricket and football rules.[67] Americans did not want to be seen as adopting a British game with its cultural trappings.[68] Baseball and its precursor games had no such legal or political implications or restrictions for Americans who sought to capitalize on its ever growing popularity or exploit its financial potential.

In the early nineteenth century, various North American communities (for example, Boston and New York) had their own versions of unwritten rules, and before critical games, ground rules were outlined to avoid later disputes or fights. A game was usually played in accordance with local house rules set by the home team. Traditions demanded the captains (later coaches or managers) of opposing teams meet with umpires before each competitive game to spell out local ground rules and possibly exchange "line-up" cards. In earlier times, leaders of two rival groups would meet to determine the terms of battle. This ancient tradition is still evident before each baseball game.

The New York Knickerbockers are generally credited for codifying, in 1845, a set of twenty rules that were drawn in part from variants of baseball being played at the time. (Too often, they—and Alexander Cartwright in particular—are also given credit for inventing rules—such as three strikes or nine innings—that either came earlier or later.)[69] Their compilation and publication of the rules not only helped spread the New York Game but made baseball safer. For example, Rule 13 eliminated the old practice of *soaking* or *plugging*—that is, throwing the ball directly at the runner. This 1845 standardization of the rules put the game on a path to faster development and acceptance across the nation, despite examples of what may now appear as strange practices (e.g., hitters calling for their pitches and pitchers not allowed to throw overhand) as seen in Wood's work (1891).[70]

As the New York Game ascended, advocates of the Massachusetts rules saw their numbers shrink and elements of the game they loved drop away. The Massachusetts Game, for instance, featured overhand pitching, whereas the New York prohibited it. Also, in the Massachusetts game, a catch was only valid if a ball was caught in the air, whereas in the New York game, a catch was also valid after one bounce. New York's game quickly killed the Massachusetts variant (also called "long ball"), where *soaking* continued into the late 1850s. The Massachusetts game was viewed as manlier and was more popular among soldiers during the American Civil War (1861–1865). Thorn also describes and comments on New England's version of baseball, and concludes:

> The Massachusetts game of baseball was in many ways the superior version, for both players and spectators....
> There is no overestimating Americans' love and fear of organization, then as now. It is certain that variants of the Massachusetts game were older than variants of the New York game. No matter, the Knickerbockers brought in *system* before the New Englanders did.[71]

Eventually, some aspects of the Massachusetts game became the accepted norms, such as the rules for pitching and catching a ball before it bounces. Only in 1864 was the ruling made that a catch was only counted as an out if the ball was caught in the air, not on the bounce. There is still no rule about whether or not a pitcher should pitch overhand or underhand.[72] Thorn also documents the incredible story of how the "unmanly" version of the game triumphed.[73]

Once a set of formal rules was in place in the relatively large metropolis of New York, other clubs, towns, cities, states, and countries eventually fell in line. By the 1860s, the battle between the two dominant regional strains of baseball had been decided, and the game was on a path toward the version we have today.

* * *

From the seventeenth through the eighteenth and nineteenth centuries, steady streams of British and other European immigrants came to North America. Many of these peoples, primarily the socially and economically disadvantaged, left their respective homelands in search of a better life. As most of these immigrants were from wide cross sections from the working classes of their respective societies, they were familiar with one or possibly more of baseball's early variants as folk or country games. It is natural to expect individual variations of their games as people came from numerous backgrounds of the Old World. This and all the other pieces of evidence provided throughout this chapter merely add to the mountain of evidence that already stands against the arguments of those who believe baseball is distinctly and purely an American invention, altogether denying its British and Continental roots.

The best-known and most thoroughly debunked false narrative holds in 1839, Abner Doubleday, an American, invented baseball in Cooperstown, New York.[74] Vernon Bartlett in *The Past of Pastimes* (1968) writes: "In 1908, an impressive but somewhat biased 'committee of research' had reached the conclusion that the rules, and even the name, owed their existence to General Doubleday."[75] In contrast to the Doubleday myth, Dr. James Naismith who invented basketball in 1891 had thirteen written rules for his proposed game. His new game was based on a game he had played as a child in Canada. In the case against Doubleday's invention of baseball, such a historic document with the written rules of his invention of baseball has never surfaced in the debate on American origins, nor has any mention ever been made of what earlier games this invention by Doubleday was based upon. David Voigt in *American Baseball: From Gentleman's Sport to the Commissioner System*, Vol. 1, states that despite people knowing better the idea thrived.[76] Additionally, why would the New York Knickerbocker Base Ball Club be writing rules in 1845 for a game that was supposedly already invented in 1839 by the legendary "founder" of American baseball? As seen above, the New York Club and others compiled their rules from those already used in variant versions of baseball being played in America

*   *   *

As the game was being played across America, it found suitable conditions to grow and thrive in early British and European colonization periods. Many who fled Britain knew that rigid class and societal structures were burdensome impediments to social and economic advancements. On leaving Britain, they also wanted to put these negatives behind them. These immigrants did not want a continuation of the same class domination for their children that they and their parents experienced in the lands they left behind. Americans needed a game that would reflect their independence from British and European aristocratic domination and control.[77] The stage was set for accepting the already popular resurgence of grass-roots baseball.[78]

As immigrants moved in wagons and trains from the Eastern seaboard, the game spread further inland until it reached the West Coast and Southern regions of North America.

British settlers and their children also took the game to Canada, where early baseball variants were likewise introduced.[79] British Loyalists who fled America during or after the American War of Independence (1775–1783) took their games north to present-day Ontario, Quebec, Nova Scotia, New Brunswick, Prince Edward Island and parts of Western Canada. Americans who came north during the Fraser River Gold Rush of the late 1850s brought their versions of the game to present-day British Columbia, Alberta, North West Territories, and the Yukon. This movement of peoples helped to reinforce and spread early baseball traditions. The introduction of the Canadian Pacific Railway (ca. 1881–1885) helped to further spread the game across the North American continent from east to west. These east-west and north-south commercial routes and migrations helped to account for the rapid spread and acceptance of the game across North America.

Baseball, besides being more familiar to working-class migrants, also helped to bridge class and societal divisions in North America, since in both America and Canada the game facilitated the integration of immigrants from various regions of old Britain and Continental Europe. Usually, in these emerging colonies of America, there was no longer any necessity to maintain the previous rigid ethnic, cultural and class divisions of old Britain and Continental Europe, since these immigrants essentially shared common cultural and religious (Christian) heritages. (Notably, others from mainly non–Christian cultures such as China and India were kept out and away from these new lands.) Their immediate and common enemies were foremost the visibly different indigenous peoples, i.e., the "Indians" or "Redskins." Of course, there were inter-European power and ethnic rivalries in North America. For example, in 1755, the British subsequently fought and displaced the French Acadian settlers from Annapolis Valley, Nova Scotia. As the English-speaking immigrants "ranked higher" in status than non–English speaking peoples, British language, culture, judicial systems, entertainment, and games eventually dominated North America.

It is uncertain whether British (or European settlers) introduced British or early baseball to the tropical lands of the then mighty British Empire, though they did establish rounders, cricket and British football.[80] For example, rounders was still being played by schoolgirls in the colony of British Guiana (now Guyana, South America) in the late 1960s.[81] Rounders seemed to be the game with the closest similarities to baseball to be exported from Britain to the British West Indies and other places of the British Commonwealth. In the end, only cricket and British football thrived in these places, whereas other related games did not. Cricket was mainly played by middle and upper classes of British society, and they continued doing so when they migrated to the colonies.[82] British personnel in non–North American colonies were mainly from the middle, upper or professional classes (cleric, medical, judicial) of society.[83] Such personnel had more leisure time on their hands and cricket provided a medium for business networking and social mobility.[84] The game of cricket became the dominant sport in many of these non–North American countries. The local populace of these countries got into the act of playing cricket, as it afforded an opportunity for social interactions with their British or European Colonial rulers. Educational programs in the British West Indies, including then British Guiana, had to cater to the needs of British children. The curricula of elite British schools, including both academic and non-academic pursuits, were implemented in primary and secondary schools. Sports and games taught were similar to those in then British school systems; for example, boys mainly played cricket and British football while girls played rounders in the British West Indies.

The emigrants from Britain, including those who played early forms of baseball and related games, went mainly to North America, where better economic and social advancement opportunities existed than in the other British colonies. Workers did initially go to some of these other colonial places but not in overwhelming numbers since governments and industries required mainly management, administrative and professional personnel from Britain. It was more economical to use local or other imported populations (including slaves or indentured servants) for unskilled labor. In addition, people in working-class areas in Britain where baseball was played did not seem to migrate as much to other colonies such as Australia, New Zealand, Zimbabwe (formerly Rhodesia) and South Africa. Instead, the majority of people went to North America, where the prospects and chances of owning land were better. In addition, the climate was more similar to that of Europe.[85] Immigrants to non–North American countries or colonies identified with the powerful ruling British elites who played cricket. They now had more leisure time on their hands, and it was in their interest to join the British upper-class establishment. (It must be noted that there were several well-established cricket clubs in the British colonies of both early America and Canada, though most of these have long since disappeared.)

It is reasonable to assume some immigrants also took their early game of baseball to other British enclaves of the British Empire.[86] Since these other colonial places were too far from the influences of America (at this time a former ex-British colony and a rebel state), the game was denied its standardization and development. The immigrants of other British colonies were apparently unlike Americans in that they were content with their privileged socio-economic, political and loyalist status and did not rebel against British rule, nor did they develop any set of independent rules to radically distinguish their own games from British-inherited ones. The non–North American colonies remained loyal to Britain for the time being. In several of these places, people are still content to be under the British flag; Canada, New Zealand, and Australia have yet to assert their full political independence from Britain.

Americans, on the other hand, forcefully expressed their mistreatment by the British Government in the American War of Independence, also called the American Revolutionary War (1775–1783).[87] Still resentful of the British, and with their sense of national pride threatened, Americans readily promoted and believed the more acceptable idea that baseball was invented in America. This denial of British origins can be seen as consistent with the fact that the words of the 1776 American Declaration of Independence were likewise based on the earlier 1689 English Bill of Rights.[88] It is highly improbable for any game to be both suddenly invented and rapidly accepted across vast and numerous places by peoples of different ethnic, cultural, and social backgrounds; even with modern technology this would be difficult.

Americans responded to the need for uniformity of rules in a game they would call their own in much the same way they had earlier responded to their political needs and interests. Baseball has since become part of American Independence Day traditional celebrations.

The New York Knickerbocker Base Ball Club's formalized rules of September 1845 eventually became the standard in and outside the United States.

Some of the terms used in early baseball showed their British origins or influences; for example, the conditions under which games should not be played and restarted were almost identical to those written earlier for cricket.[89] It is a credit to nineteenth-century Americans that they took some of the best components of the various inherited versions of baseball and standardized, refined, and wove together one superb master-game. In effect, Americans were able to adapt what they received from their working-class British and European roots to produce their own national game and reflect American character. This American character was a continuation of the grit and determination shown by peoples of various cultural backgrounds who were forced initially to endure harsh struggles in their bids for survival in the New World. Baseball allowed them to express their individuality within a team concept.

American baseball influenced the development of the Canadian game owing to the impacts of strong family and cultural relationships, movement of peoples, and marketing strategies of American sporting business concerns.[90] Early forms of baseball were similarly played in Canada before the introduction and acceptance of American standardization. Don Morrow in *A Concise History of Sport in Canada* (1989) writes:

> Baseball was very much a working-man's sport and caught on quickly.... The overwhelming representation of the working-class at both in the playing and organizational levels also characterized other clubs in nearby communities ... across the country, and (at least among the players) puts a stamp on baseball today. It had the salutary effect of exempting baseball, relatively speaking, from the class manipulation prevalent in other sports....
>
> It must not be assumed or implied that middle-class and professional men did not relish participating in, and watching, informal baseball games.... It is interesting that rarely, if ever, did men from dissimilar occupational backgrounds intermingle to compete with each other.[91]

Canada, like other parts of the United States, saw this new trend coming, joined in and enjoyed baseball, as press coverage of American leagues increased, as it dominated the sporting news in the early part of the last century in America.[92]

Other neighboring countries of the United States, including Cuba and Mexico, also benefited from America's baseball influence. Eventually, more countries in the western hemisphere, including the Dominican Republic, Nicaragua, Panama, Puerto Rico and Venezuela also embraced the American-favored game.[93] This spread of baseball outside the United States accompanied the rise and dominance of American economic power and culture.

Many have already documented the development and history of baseball in America as well as players, various issues, and impacts of baseball in the life and history of Americans. What has remained indisputable is the superb marketing strategies and consequent popularity of baseball in the United States. The game has influenced Americans and helped them through major wars, terrorist attacks, and other severe national hardships.[94] It must be added that some variants of baseball entertained and sustained Americans even before they became an independent nation in 1776. Later, in the American Civil War (1861–1865), both Union and Confederate soldiers played baseball in their respective camps. The American passion for baseball was and still is infectious, usually finding receptive ground wherever people are exposed to this entertaining and challenging game.[95]

Spalding in *America's National Game, 1839–1915* writes:

> Base ball is the American Game *par excellence,* because its playing demands Brain and Brawn, and American manhood supplies these ingredients in quantity sufficient to spread over the entire continent.
> No man or boy can win distinction on the ball field who is not, as man or boy an athlete, possessing all the qualifications which an intelligent, effective playing of the game demands. Having these, he has within him the elements of pronounced success in other walks of life … [including] men of eminence in all the professions and in every avenue of commercial and industrial activity, who have graduated from the ball field to enter upon honorable careers as American citizens of all the highest type, each with a sane mind and sound body.[96]

The idealism and potential benefits of baseball expressed by Spalding in 1911 hold true today.[97] It is an unfortunate reflection of the times that the term "American" did not include Native, African, Chinese, Japanese, Mexican and other Latino Americans until Jackie Robinson broke the color barrier in 1947. George Vecsey in *Baseball: A History of America's Favorite Game* (2006) accurately and skillfully describes the long journey to acceptance and the implementation of the principle of equality to all, irrespective of ethnicity, language, religion and culture through baseball.

Baseball has emerged as the best team-game for teaching quick physical and mental responses to rapidly changing situations. This makes baseball different from other sports or games. Teachers, parents, and others familiar with the game know that a boy or girl who goes outside and plays baseball with his or her friends has to make more rapid decisions in response to changing circumstances than a child who stays inside and plays chess. It also involves watching and waiting for an opportunity to contribute.

As mentioned in earlier chapters, baseball is the ultimate warrior game. Spalding puts it best: "Cricket is a gentle pastime. Base Ball is War!"[98] It is rather difficult to develop a better "war game" than baseball without violence being involved. Baseball not only tests physical and mental skills and prowess, but also reveals strengths, flaws and weaknesses in a player's character. It is not surprising that the Japanese, with their rich martial-arts and Samurai-warrior traditions, work-ethic and discipline, have readily embraced baseball.[99] Japan is a source of several accomplished star players for Major League Baseball. Taiwan and South Korea have likewise made significant contributions to the MLB, and baseball is now expanding into mainland China.[100] If present trends continue, soon this highly-populated country will also be producing potential MLB players.[101] Some American baseball players and coaches currently find employment in Japan. The newly created World Baseball Classic reveals the international flavor of the game.

In each country and culture where baseball has been adopted there is an inherent insertion or blending of national identity. The American game generally places a premium on power, both power-pitching and power-hitting by well-built athletes. Everything is done to enhance the power-aspects of the game and players.[102] Latin American players bring their own unique style, enthusiasm, and flavor to the game. Japanese players display finesse, and attention to small details and subtleties.[103] Canadians are said to bring an aggressive "hockey mentality" to the game. Current trends show a return to favoring speed and athleticism.

Each player today is judged on his own merits and what he can contribute to the success of his team. These days, extraneous factors such as ethnicity, nationality and religion matter very little, if any, in the selection of players. Inherent qualities such as the degree of baseball skills, work ethic, and potential within an individual player are what matters most. Each player now has the opportunity to express not only his inherited skills of throwing, hitting, and running but also the added efforts of his practice and refinement. During a baseball game, the participants' pasts are unfolded for all to see— whether they be players or spectators, all are inexorably linked and connected. The game of baseball reflects human struggle for survival, and the struggles of humanity are reflected in baseball.

As we have seen, the basic game of baseball and its variants were played under names such as stool-ball, tut-ball, pize-ball and British baseball in old Britain and Continental Europe before they came to North America. Though rounders and cricket were often the frames of reference used to describe baseball to others, early baseball itself existed a long time before. The British and Continental European immigrants, particularly those of the working class, who came to America and Canada, brought games that provided solace, enjoyment and thrills in their new settings. This rich heritage was rekindled by the right conditions and time. The standardized game found fertile conditions on American soil and has since thrived and swept the continent of the New World and beyond. It is rather curious that other major non–British European colonial powers such as Spain and Portugal did not have baseball or that baseball never became a national game in their dominions as it did the former British and some other European dominions of North America. This suggests that the game was played predominantly by the British and certain European groups. The following chapters will travel further backward in time to find baseball's truest origins and the basis for its wide appeal.

5

European Roots and North American Expressions

What is striking about baseball is its broad appeal to people of different social, cultural or national backgrounds. This is evident by the numerous players and fans who have participated in, excelled at, and enjoyed this game through its various progressions in America and Canada. This holds true not only for Americans of British descent (being, for example, of pre–Celtic or Celtic, Roman, Anglo-Saxon, Norman, Welsh, Irish and Scottish heritages or a melding of these), but also for others of European origins (French, Germanic, Dutch, Italian, Russian, Polish, Nordic or Scandinavian), or African roots. It turns out that besides the old British, many others of old Continental Europe were playing some earlier forms of similar ball games.

The birthplace of formalized modern baseball in America (as written rules) was New York, from where the early game spread. Melvin L. Adelman in *A Sporting Time: New York and the Rise of Modern Athletics, 1820–1870* (1986) gives some idea of this early city:

> The city of New York has almost always been in the midst of change. After the departure of British troops in 1783 a variety of demographic, political, economic, and social forces undermined the character of colonial New York....
>
> The population explosion following independence most immediately transformed New York. Between 1790 and 1820 the city's population almost quadrupled, from 33,131 to 123,706; by 1810 New York had replaced Philadelphia as the most populous American city. While the normal birthrate obviously contributed to this growth, New York's ability to attract and keep newcomers was really the key to its swelling ranks. People arrived there from a variety of places but especially from New England. These New Englanders, inclined toward a more conservative life-style, had a profound impact on the city's economic, religious, and social life. Despite the cultural differences between them and the native Knickerbockers, New York in the period 1783–1812 "was more truly an American city,

in the sense that the ethnic background of its population reflected its national composition, than in any other period of its history."

While the majority of newcomers were American citizens, New York continued to attract sufficient numbers of European citizens to sustain its reputation as a polyglot community. The lion's share of foreigners came from the British Isles, especially Ireland; German and French immigrants also constituted a major addition to the existing settlements of Danes, Swedes, Italians, Portuguese, and Spaniards.[1]

Adelman gives some insight as to the cultural diversity and ease of social interactions of the peoples of New York and America at the early stages of British and Continental European colonization. The swift rise in popularity of baseball, in peoples of such wide cultural and national backgrounds, raises the question whether some aspects of it were inherently familiar and re-exposure aroused the dormant passions for their folk games. We shall now look at the possible pre–American baseball roots of some of these various nationalities who embraced the game in North America.

As discussed in Chapter 4, several versions of baseball (such as British baseball, tut-ball, pize-ball and stool-ball) were being played earlier in Britain, from the seventeenth to the early twentieth century. In addition to these games, other similar ball games also existed in and around the same time in Britain. Block in *Baseball Before We Knew It* (2006) notes that Wales was a likely hotbed for early baseball. Centuries earlier, John Taylor, the "British Water Poet," in *A Short Relation of a Long Journey Made Round or Ovall by Encompassing The Principalities of Wales from London* (1562) writes with regard to the ordinary Welsh people's lack of strict observation of the Sabbath on Sundays, the Lord 's Day:

> There is no such zeal in many places and parishes in Wales; for they have neither service, prayer, sermon, or preacher, nor any church door opened at all so that the people do exercise and edify in the church yard, at the lawful and laudable games of trap, cat, stool-ball, racket etc., on Sundays.[2]

These isolated Welsh communities were not yet fully Christianized (or under strict Christian influence); hence these communal gatherings on Sundays were occupied with ancestral games and pastimes in the absence of available churches and clergymen. The games of trap and cat have elements or skills (hitting, catching, running, throwing) that were also found in versions of stool-ball. The choice of game (e.g., trap, cat or stool-ball) being played depended on the occasion and number of participants available. Taylor mentions that though these games were lawful and commendable, they should not be played on Sunday during times expected to be devoted to religious services. In some areas of Britain, Sunday was a day to also enjoy traditional sports and pastimes after religious services, but activities such as bear-baiting, cock-fighting, wrestling, and so on were unlawful. Strict Sabbatarians frowned on games and pastimes on Sundays and wanted these days to be used only for religious observances.[3] Early Pilgrims to America were in search of a place where they could practice strict observance of the Sabbath, the seventh day, in response to the Fourth Commandment of the Ten Commandments given by God to Moses. The same playing areas in the churchyards were used for these games and pastimes until these practices were stopped.[4]

Supporters of Welsh baseball have claimed the American game came from their version.[5] National championships of this variant Welsh game have been played between England (North West) and Wales (South) since 1908.[6] In the Welsh game, the inner field is shaped like a diamond with four points serving as bases. Each base is marked by a pole planted in the ground which the runner touches upon reaching or passing it. The batter's box, called the *center peg*, is 15 feet (4.6 meters) in front of home plate which, is 100 feet (30.5 meters) from second base. The bowler delivers the ball underarm from a rectangle 10 feet (3.1 meters) long and 2½ feet (0.76 meters) wide that is 50 feet (15.2 meters) from the batting point. Catching gloves and other protective gear are not used. All eleven members of a team bat before the inning is completed, similar to cricket. Welsh baseball has deep roots within Wales and England. Rob Light in Tony Collins, John Martin and Wray Vamplew's edition of *Encyclopedia of Traditional British Rural Sports* (2005) mentions that the game of cricket may have been derived from an old folk game or pastimes which used a bat or stick.[7]

Block writes of Welsh baseball in old Britain:

> A likely legacy of this hot-bed of stool-ball is the remarkable game of Welsh baseball. In the early twentieth century, organized teams playing a form of baseball reminiscent of nineteenth-century Massachusetts round-ball took root in Wales and parts of western England. For several decades this game enjoyed great popularity, and given its popularity, and given its great proximity in form and geography to earlier English variants of baseball, it is almost certainly a modern reemergence of these older pastimes....
>
> No other game contributed more to baseball's early formation than stool-ball. The game was a popular fixture on the English scene for centuries, and in its multiple bases version featured a familiar combination of ball play and circular base running.[8]

The deep roots of early stool-ball in Wales were likewise documented by others after directly observing and living with the Welsh people. Peter Roberts in *The Cambrian Popular Antiquities; or, An Account of the Traditions, Customs, and Superstitions of Wales* (1814), also writes that stool-ball was being played in Wales:

Another species of this game, stool-ball, resembling cricket, except that no bats are used, and that a stool was substituted for the wicket, was, in my memory, also a favorite game on holydays, but is now, like many other rural games, I believe, seldom, if ever, played. These amusements generally began on Easter-eve and were resumed after Easter-day....

 In some places, however, after morning prayers, vestiges of Sunday sports and pastimes remain.[9]

This supports the earlier observations of John Taylor in his 1562 work connecting stool-ball with Sunday activities. From the mid-sixteenth to the nineteenth century, stool-ball was being actively played.

Oliver Goldsmith articulates the losses occurring throughout Britain as people were moving from the countryside to the cities or elsewhere overseas in "The Deserted Village" (1770):

> Sweet Auburn! loveliest village of the plain,
> …
> Seats of my youth, when every sport could please,
> …
> The decent church that topt the neighbouring hill,
> …
> How often have I blest the coming day,
> When toil remitting lent its turn to play,
> And all the village train, from labour free,
> Led up their sports beneath the spreading tree;
> While many a pastime circled in the shade,
> The young contending as the old survey'd;
> And many a gambol frolick'd o'er the ground,
> And sleights of art and feats of strength went round;
> And still, as each repeated pleasure tir'd,
> Succeeding sports the mirthful band inspir'd;
> …
> Thy sports are fled, and all thy charms withdrawn[10];

Goldsmith mourns the rapid losses of traditional scenes and events that were occurring in older village communities.

If the loss of traditions, including games and sports, occurred in the eighteenth century as mentioned above, then by the nineteenth century the decline would have progressed even further.[11]

Gomme, whose work was quoted in Chapter 4 with reference to tut-ball, stool-ball and rounders, writes that stobball, another alias for early baseball, was likewise known in Ireland, Scotland and England. Block has raised some questions about whether or not stobball was the same game as stow-ball or stool-ball or both. The game of stobball was popular in areas such as North Wiltshire and North Gloucestershire, located in the Southwest corner of England, near Devonshire, and Swansea of Wales just across the Bristol Channel.[12] These areas of Britain, called Britannia in pre–Roman times, were once heavily populated by early British peoples and their descendants.[13]

* * *

Descriptions of similar games (tut-ball, stool-ball, stobball, pize-ball, British baseball, or simply bat-and-ball) can also be found in several parts of Europe beyond Britain. (Appendix F for cultural backgrounds of Germanic and Scandinavian peoples.) Erwin Mehl, in his two articles "Baseball in the Stone Age" and "Notes to Baseball in the Stone Age," mentions that early popular batting games were played by Germanic, Scandinavian and Slavic peoples.[14] Block extends the findings on some variants recorded in Germany (*das deutsche Ballspiel*, or the German ball game) and France (*le grande théque, la balle empoisonée, la balle au camp,* or bat and ball, poisoned ball, and field ball, respectively). France, including the Huguenots, and Germany were also major sources of immigrants to early America.

Block further points out that J.C.F. Gutsmuths (1796), an eighteenth-century German expert in the field of education and recreation, compared British baseball and the German folk game or pastime, *das deutsche Ballspiel*. Gutsmuths unable to find suitable instructions to teach popular games and sports, wrote his book *Spiele zur Uebung und Erholung...Games for Exercise and Recreation...*(1796).[15] Gutsmuths was the first modern educator to acknowledge the suitability of baseball (English and German versions combined) as a means of training both mind and body.[16] Gutsmuths, besides pointing out many elements (e.g., pitching, base running, and outs) that were in common with the British game, also mentions in the German version the counterclockwise direction of running after hitting the ball.

Despite the passage of centuries, early forms of baseball were known and handed down from generation to generation in both Britain and Germany. Gutsmuths was able to see the two versions of baseball (British and German) as similar or with common roots, and that a combination of various aspects of both British and Germanic versions would make a better and more challenging game for youths. Block elaborates:

> Gutsmuths described a second method of retiring base runners...called "burning," and came into play when a fielder observed that an opposition runner had overrun or neglected to touch a base. The fielder could then place the runner out by obtaining the ball and throwing it at the base, while at the same time calling out the word "burned." This innovation of directing the ball to the base, rather than at the runner, was an early prelude to the modern baseball method of forcing or tagging a runner at a base, a practice that was not to be introduced for another fifty years [in America].[17]

The term "burning" was also used in pize-ball when a player was put out after being touched or struck with a ball before safely reaching a base.

Writers (for example, Steven A. Reiss, Steven Hardy, Melvin Adelman and Warren Goldstein) of early American baseball history do not mention the presence of early forms of baseball in the newly developing Germanic communities in America. Because of the detailed histories of other games or sports (e.g., gymnastics and boxing) coming over from Europe, we may infer that baseball or similar games were likely not a major factor in these early arriving Germanic communities. Steven A. Reiss in *City Games: The Evolution of American Urban Society and the Rise of Sports* (1989) writes:

> While English and Scottish immigrants adjusted relatively easily to life in American cities, German newcomers had to make greater cultural transition. They were generally well prepared for economic success in the United States because they had education, skills, and some capital. Most Germans settled in cities; in the 1850s they comprised one-third of the population of Louisville and large segments of cities like Chicago, Milwaukee and New York.[18]

The Germans were heavily involved in their gymnastic societies, *turnvereins,* which also included traditional exercises and stunts. Reiss mentions in Germanic neighborhoods their cultural heritage included theater and choral societies.

Adelman expresses similar views as Reiss concerning early Germans' participation in sports. Adelman likewise gave details of early German participation in *turnvereins.* German outdoor activities (including folk games) were also not detailed in these works (Reiss and Adelman), and similarly there is no mention of early baseball-like activities in these urban Germanic communities, despite Gutsmuths 1796 work. Furthermore, Adelman writes:

> Germans also did not share the sports heritage of the native-born population, unlike the English, Scots, or even the Irish. Finally, and perhaps most importantly, the language barrier encountered by most German immigrants served to insulate and isolate them from the general population, thus fostering greater group dependency.[19]

This suggests that the work of Gutsmuths to actively promote his combined version of baseball did not take hold with the majority of the Germanic people (mainly from the working class) who were arriving in early America. The time frame for the establishment of Gutsmuths's ideas among the educated youths was likely too short. Erwin Mehl in "Baseball in the Stone Age" states:

> Unfortunately, dark days of reaction (1820–1840) followed the dawn of German gymnastics. When gymnastics fled from green meadows to gardens and halls, open-air games disappeared. They reappeared only at the end of the nineteenth century in the revival of gymnastics and games.[20]

Early German immigrants in America were achieving the goals of community, social support and physical fitness in their gymnasiums where they participated in fencing, gymnastics, wrestling, and so forth. As seen with Gutsmuths positive response to British baseball, German immigrants would likewise respond positively to this game when exposed or re-exposed to this old familiarity of their past. With this game in their Germanic cultural background and folk-games (such as *das deutsche Ballspiel* or *Schlagball*), they responded when the social, cultural and language barriers allowed interaction with other citizens in America. (Notably, many Germanic peoples or of Germanic heritage, e.g., Angles, Saxons, and Goths went to early Britain after the departure of the Romans.)

*   *   *

Mehl in his article "Baseball in the Stone Age," states that the early German batting game (described earlier by Gutsmuths as the "German ball game") influenced neighboring societies such as the Finns and the Laplanders. In the old Finnish folk game, king's ball, fielders also tried to "burn," i.e., hit a runner with the ball as he tried to reach the safety of a base. When a struck ball was caught in the air, the runner was said to be "wounded." Safe areas existed within the circles around the bases. The "Kings" were in charge of selecting the two opposing teams.[21] Analogously, in early American baseball, the two captains selected the teams and agreed on the choice of umpires and rules.[22] David Levinson and Karen Christensen in *Encyclopedia of World Sport 1: From Ancient Times to the Present* state that around the 1920s the traditional Finnish folk game king's ball was being modernized and improved by Professor Lauri "Tahko" Pihkala (1888–1981) of Finland.[23]

King's ball has the first written description of marked circles around the bases being used to define "safe" areas, where runners could not be tagged out.[24] These circular or semi-circular areas are seen on modern baseball diamonds, but are only decorative with no necessary function. The Levinson and Christiansen description of the traditional Finnish game seems to be a re-creation and adaptation of old war scenarios in a competitive game (Notes 21 and 23). Finns were not a dominant enough majority in early America to influence the development and adoption of their version of the game.

In the seventeenth century, Finland (like parts of modern Europe such as Estonia, Germany, Lithuania, Latvia, Poland, Norway and Russia) was under the control of Sweden. In 1638 New Sweden (with Swedish and Finnish immigrants) was established in the New World at Fort Christina (now Wilmington, Delaware). New Sweden came under Dutch rule in the 1650s and eventually under British rule in the 1680s. Larger numbers of Swedes and

Finns began arriving in America in the nineteenth and twentieth centuries (1867–1914), leaving deteriorating economic conditions in Sweden. These communities were eventually absorbed by the more established British communities.

Other regions of Europe also had their own versions of a similar peasant or folk games, including *lapta* in Russia. Briefly, in *lapta* a hitter uses a stick to strike a ball as far away as he can and then runs to a marked point and tries to get back to the starting point before being struck by the incoming thrown ball. It is described as a folk-game between two opposing teams that requires attributes such as speed, strong hitting and swift thinking.[25] Such folk-games and traditions were passed down for generations among rural peasants in isolated communities. European peasants generally continued with their traditional and non-threatening ways and forms of entertainment, until new traditions took hold.

Russians have also claimed that the American game was derived from their games, as brought over by Russian immigrants. This claim is doubtful as Russian immigration to America, and in particular to the East Coast, was neither widespread nor relatively large in numbers until late in the nineteenth century, compared to other European immigrants.[26] Further, Russian settlement patterns were such that they had insufficient population density to play and spread *lapta* to the rest of America in such a short time frame. In addition, Russian immigration was negligible in eastern Canada, where early immigrants from Britain played similar early versions of baseball as those played by others on the Eastern seaboard of America. German Russians were immigrating to America, but it is difficult to discern what version of their folk game, if any, they played. The Russian folk game seems to be an old independent version which survived in isolation for centuries, and there is no evidence currently available to suggest its influence on neighboring European countries. The existence of *lapta* helps to explain why the Russian immigrants who came to America were likewise readily drawn to baseball because of its cultural and pastime familiarity. In addition, it shows the wide folk roots of baseball across many cultures.

* * *

In the seventeenth century, Dutch arrivals established New Netherland (*Nieuw-Nederland*) on the Eastern seaboard of America. This former Dutch state (Republic of Seven United Netherlands, 1614–1667) included areas of the mid–Atlantic states of Delaware, Connecticut, New Jersey and New York with smaller outposts in Pennsylvania and Rhode Island. The population in this early new Dutch state consisted mainly of Native Americans, Europeans and Africans. The Africans were brought in as slave laborers. In the 1600s, Dutch settlers were documented as playing a variety of ball games in New Amsterdam, and elsewhere in New Netherlands. Esther Singleton in *Dutch New York* (1909) writes:

> In the Seventeenth Century, the majority of people were fond of games that required violent exercise, such as disc-throwing and all varieties of ball games. Nobles, burghers, and peasants shared this taste. Games of "short ball," "long ball," balls driven through gates or wickets, balls thrown against a stake, balls struck by the gloved hand or ungloved hand, racket, stick, club, mallet, subject to various rules and known under various names, such as tennis, golf, paile-maile, bowls, skittles, ninepins, hockey, etc., were favorite pastimes with the New Netherlanders.[27]

The games of "short ball" and "long ball" are not described. It seems that long ball was similar to stool-ball in other early British American communities. The situation becomes intriguing when William Rankin, a baseball writer of the *New York Clipper*, on December 17, 1904, states that baseball was invented by the Dutch.[28] From the above quotation, it is apparent that the early Dutch settlers were heavily involved in a variety of ball games (including stick ball) for recreation and entertainment. (Washington Irving in *Knickerbocker's History of New York from the Beginnings of the World to the End of the Dutch Dynasty* (1824) gives a satirical view of Dutch youngsters, but no mention is made of them being involved in baseball.[29])

The Dutch city of New Amsterdam, incorporated in 1653, became the British city of New York in 1665. Alan Ross mentions in his article "Pize-Ball" that numerous Dutch workers were brought to England in the early seventeenth century (around 1626 to 1629) to work on the drainage of the "Level of Hatfield Chase," a place not far from Doncaster, Yorkshire, England.[30] Whether the Dutch immigrants brought their own version of stool-ball or a version of the game they learnt in Britain is unclear. Unfortunately, no record is found of stool-ball or similar games (long ball, short ball, or stick ball) being played or survived in other former Dutch colonies around the world. As noted before, some early Pilgrims who arrived via Holland were playing stool-ball in their new environment.[31]

The Dutch, as did other ethnic or subordinate non–British groups in America, had to eventually conform to the values of the dominant British culture. Writing in particular about the Dutch in New York, Robert C. Ritchie in *The Duke's Province: A Study of New York Politics and Society, 1664–1691* (1977) notes:

> New York was unique among North American colonies. After conquering New Netherland, the English found themselves in control of Dutch colonists whose

loyalties and culture differed from their own. As the number of English colonists grew and the interrelationships within and between communities became more complex, the Dutch came under pressure to Anglicize. They were the first European group confronted with this problem, and their experiences prefigured those of many later immigrant groups to America.[32]

If the Dutch colonists, who were once friends of the British Pilgrims, were forced to assimilate, then the same pattern could be expected with other nationalities (for example, Swedish, Finnish and French) in these now predominantly British occupied and controlled lands.[33] This meant that other groups (particularly those from the working classes) who arrived then or later would likewise have to adapt or participate in the British versions of early baseball or take up the standardized New York versions. The seeds were sown for more ready adaption of the dominant British sports and games.

The other dominant cultural group among the early European newcomers to North America was the French who settled mainly in New France (Canada, Acadia, Hudson Bay, Newfoundland or Pleasance, and Louisiana). David Block documents the possible baseball related or ancestral games (*théque, la balle au baton, la balle empoisonée, la balle au camp, au grand théque*) that were played by the French. He concludes that these games were rudimentary forms of baseball of an earlier time and were more related to rounders. Therefore, the French had some form of early baseball or related games in their history. The question is whether or not the early French settlers brought their versions of baseball-related games to America and did these games thrive in their communities.

In his chapter "Baseball," Morrow writes that, "unlike the team sports of lacrosse, football, and hockey, which originated and developed in Montreal, the Canadian origins of baseball were in Southwestern Ontario."[34] William Bennett Munro in *Crusaders of New France: A Chronicle of the Fleur-De-Lis in the Wilderness* (1921) mentions the various activities of the early French, but no mention is made of any early baseball-like game such as *théque, la balle empoisonée, la balle au camp*, or *au grand théque*.[35] It is surprising that these very early settlers of New France in their spare time were not playing any ball games.[36] People from Normandy (that is, of Scandinavian origins, Northmen) settled in Old France and Munro notes that some traditions that came from France were Norman-influenced. These Scandinavian peoples also had some versions of early baseball. But games, such as *théque* and *langbal,* were not mentioned as being played in their early communities in New France or elsewhere in the New World. Block finds in an 1899 issue of *Le Soleil* (a French Language daily newspaper in Quebec City, Quebec, Canada) that a game called "Grand théque" was played. This game was similar to rounders in that there were ten players per side and the playing area was pentagon-shaped with wooden base or sand bags used to mark the position of the bases. In addition, the pitcher and batter were both from the same team with the former throwing the ball so that it was easily hit. Therefore, some version of an early French game did come over to the New World.[37]

Old Colonial France could be viewed as consisting mainly of a few basic cultures and regions, such as: (1) Normandy, peopled mainly by Normans and people of Scandinavian origins by permission of the French King; (2) Brittany (*Armorica*), peopled mainly by those of Celtic roots; and (3) Old France, peopled mainly by the Gauls (before being conquered by the Romans) and Germanic tribes such as Franks, Burgundians and Visigoths. The people from Brittany were closer culturally to the Welsh people who enjoyed stool-ball as part of their early British cultural heritage. Several Bretons (from Brittany, France) distinguished themselves in service to America in its War of Independence; therefore there was old common ground between the Bretons and the Britons (Britain). (Appendix A has further details about the common cultural backgrounds of insular British and their related Continental Europeans.)

As we have seen, of the various other non–British European groups, such as the Dutch, German, Russian, Scandinavian, and French, who came to North America none was dominant enough (numerically, socially, culturally and politically) to determine the national pastime of a then-emerging British North America. With the current available information, the possibilities are slim that other non–British European nationalities could have significantly affected the sporting culture with regards to early baseball in the New World. Therefore, only one of the major European groups, that is, the British could have strongly influenced the emergence of baseball in North America. This dominant group, with its subsets of diverse populations from Great Britain, had the potential to affect America. Within the population under then British control and influences were many nationalities, e.g., the English, Scottish, Welsh and Irish peoples (each in turn was comprised of peoples from various heterogeneous ethnic and diverse cultural backgrounds) who came to North America and brought over their pastimes and games, including those related to early forms of baseball.[38]

The conclusion is that early forms of baseball were brought to America, initiated, played and promoted mainly by those of British descent. The fact that baseball found ready acceptance across diverse cultural divides in America meant that in some cases (as seen above) there was already a cultural familiarity with some version akin to the game played here. To have such broad appeal the game of baseball taps into the common ancestral past and human heritage of all peoples.

6

Religion, Culture and Sports

The previous chapter shows that other European nations, such as Germany and France, had versions of an early or precursor baseball-like game bearing similarities to those seen or documented in areas of Britain such as Wales and England. At the same time, the British exerted the most influences on early American culture. In this chapter, we seek to understand the roots of early baseball and why the game thrived in Britain.

The British people's rich cultural heritage shows a remarkable diversity arising from the contributions of different historical groups from Europe, who added to those of local or indigenous populations. Those who came and conquered Britain (e.g., tribal peoples of Celtic origins, Romans, Angles, Saxons, and Danes) left, were in turn conquered by others (Normans), or assimilated with the passage of time. Folk games survived where and when they conformed or adapted to their present situations, within the possibilities and limitations set by new rulers or the political, religious and social environment. The chances of survival of folk games and their associated rituals depended on the depth of their roots and the roles they played in the lives of their communities. Folk games were also most likely to survive in situations when and where conqueror and conquered or old residents and newcomers shared or once shared common myths and religious practices (with Germanic and Scandinavian generally viewed together as Teutonic). The survival of folk games and associated rituals reflect a people's history. (Appendices A and F give further general information on the early British, Teutonic and other European peoples.)

* * *

Let us now focus mainly on the peoples of Britain to shed light on the earlier origins and propagation of the game of baseball. In the early Europeanization of America, the dominant culture, language, institutions, sports and games (including early baseball) were inherited from the British. Britain was not only the former colonial ruler of America, but also supplied most of its early immigrants.[1]

The Romans who influenced Britain (in particular England and Wales) during their periods of arrival and rule (43 to 410 CE) have no record of playing any early baseball or any similar precursor game.[2] (The Romans gave these lands the name *Britannia* because they defined the various tribal groups as one people.) The Christian era under the Romans, beginning about 200 CE to the Roman departure 410 CE, was not noted for promoting "heathen" games. Many of the British (now pagan meaning pre–Christian or non–Christian) practices such as festivals, holy days, traditions, rituals, and games were adapted to fit into early Christian-sanctioned ideology, doctrines and culture. Centuries later during the Christian eras (both Roman Catholic and Protestant) as Christianity became more firmly entrenched (especially under overzealous Roman Church officials and Puritans), religious authorities were even less tolerant of folk games and their accompanied rituals.[3] Any game associated with old pagan customs, idolatry, sexuality, courtship and "ungodliness" was actively discouraged or sanitized. Reformists and Puritans were most opposed to games on Sundays or Sabbath, particularly since these recreational events were often also associated with undesirable behaviors such as drinking, fighting and gambling.[4]

The foundations of these folk games lay past the Christian era in Britain as evidenced by the apparent non–Christian philosophical and religious nature of these games. Rationally, the peoples who must be examined are those who occupied early Britain before the Romans came. Accordingly, all British peoples (Britons, later identifiable as English, Welsh, Irish and Scottish of the Iron Age, about 700 BCE to 100 CE) must be considered, as well as the earlier inhabitants (Bronze Age, about 2500 to 700 BCE) of these lands.

Besides the British peoples of pre–Roman England and Wales, other neighboring and related peoples of particular interest here include the Irish and Highland Scots of Britain, and the continental Bretons. These peoples are all thought to be of Indo-European origins of the Goedelic branch (Irish Gaelic, Scottish Gaelic, and Manx) and the Brythonic Branch (Welsh, Breton, Cornish and Gaelic).[5] Various British kings and kingdoms were found all over Britain before the Romans arrived in about 43 CE.[6] In fact, there were at least 17 different British kingdoms spread over Britain. In these old subsets of British societies, their priests (including Druids) formed the powerful religious and professional classes. It must be noted that Druidism is not the name for the religion practiced by these British and related peoples. James MacKillop in *Myths and Legends of the Celts* tells us: "The Druids were a religious order among the Celtic peoples of Ancient Britain, where perhaps the order originated."[7] (Appendix A gives further relevant background information on the British peoples.) The distinct warrior classes of various British clans and kingdoms were held in high esteem with regard to their fighting skills and bravery. Despite these warrior qualities and military advantages, the British were a disunited people with numerous inter-tribal and inter-kingdom conflicts. This failure to unite even for a common cause against the invading Romans led to their downfall. The Romans gradually gained control of Britain (England and Wales), and remained in power until about 410 CE.[8] The decimations and subjugations of British warrior and military traditions (specifically England) during Roman rule left them militarily weakened and defenseless after the withdrawal of the Romans. Indeed, many of their warriors were killed, conscripted into the Roman army, or condemned to serve in mines. The leadership, such as the nobility and priesthood, was reduced.

On departure of the Romans, the British peoples were vulnerable and at the mercy of other invaders including many Germanic tribes (Saxons, Angles, Jutes and Frisians), Danes and Normans who raided and ruled Britain. Notably, the Germanic tribes (Saxons and Angles) who dominated the British peoples were also Indo-European people with similar beliefs and practices that were prevalent before the introduction of Christianity. Germanic tribes had some form of early baseball-like games in their folk games as seen in the previous chapter. The Danes and others who came and stayed had similar beliefs and practices. The Normans ("Norsemen" or "Vikings") and others from Normandy (included Danes, Norwegians, Hiberno-Norse, Frankish, Orkney Vikings and Anglo-Danes) under Viking control and led by Duke William II of Normandy (later William the Conqueror) with French and Flemish help, defeated King Harold II of England at the Battle of Hastings in 1066 CE. The Normans replaced the Anglo-Saxon nobility as the ruling class of England. With time the Normans' traditions and language merged with that of the conquered peoples of England. Similar courses of Norman conquests and merging or intermixing occurred with the neighboring British domains of Wales, Ireland and Scotland. The traditions of the Germanic, Teutonic and Scandinavian peoples and others merged with that of the resident British peoples, particularly those of England and Wales.

Block notes the contributions of the incoming groups in relation to early or precursor forms of baseball, such as Longball, that were known to several European groups such as the Goths, Vandals and Franks.[9] Block acknowledges the contributions of the Angles and Saxons, who came and settled in Britain (then predominantly peopled by those of varied Celtic backgrounds) and became assimilated into the British diversity.

The Christians who arrived during the Roman period found that the local British religious traditions, culture, sports, societal values and so on were very strong.

Despite various overlords and their accompanied subjugations, and often harshness and intolerance of Christianity, several aspects of early British culture survived. Traditional British games were modified to accommodate the times and circumstances of their subjugations, with variations of ancestral versions being retained or changing in isolated locations.

We know that people were playing games such as stool-ball on church properties on Sundays (Chapter 7, Note 15 provides details). Some of these same churchyards, graveyards and playing fields were also former sites of early British ancestral sun god worship with their accompanied rituals. The Romans built temples dedicated to their own gods on former destroyed British religious sites, and in turn, the Christians built or rededicated temples to Christ on the Roman sites.[10] These sites were places where various early tribal peoples once met listening to the poetry (triads), songs and music of their enchanting bards.[11] Matrimonial unions were blessed by British (likely Druidic) priests at these sites. Here votive offerings, vows and pledges of fidelity were also made. Early British peoples learned of earth, air, fire and water, from which "elements" they themselves and all life were made. It was here the people were also taught about entering and exiting the Otherworld, the realm of the afterlife.[12] Other religious services, such as celebrations of births and honoring of the dead, were performed in these sacred grounds, all in the presence of both sexes. Some British peoples obeyed an ancient command as Isabel Elder in *Celt, Druid and Culdee* states, "Hu Gadarn had established, among other regulations, that a *Gorsedd* or Assembly of Druids and Bards must be held on an open, uncovered grass space, in a conspicuous place, in full view and hearing of all the people."[13] Before or after each *Gorsedd* or mandated assembly, *guiftal* or game exercises were held. These game exercises included activities that honored their ancestor and Sun God, Hu, or other deities.

These sacred grounds (some of which later became Christian churchyards and graveyards) provided places for games and rituals allowing male-female interactions, uniting gods and goddesses, and enabling symbolic mating of bulls (sun) and cows (earth), as stressed in their folklore and mythology (discussed in later chapters). Training and taking of oaths to uphold honor and duty to family, clan and kingdom were solemnized here. Warriors were further bonded and schooled as they listened to exploits of war from British heroes of yesteryear. In British pagan times, religion was expressed in games and both were deeply intertwined. Likewise, games served as a vehicle for military training, and warring attributes (for example, courage and risk-taking) were in turn also expressed in games. Together, war, religion, and games formed the interrelated structural and philosophical foundations of British culture. (In modern societies which were later influenced by British peoples, these formerly intertwined aspects of life have now evolved as separated and distinct entities, but to these peoples they were one.)[14]

British games influenced their societies, and each society was in turn affected by the basic foundations of their own early customs. Games were a way of preparing the young in the skills and strategies of combat; maintaining a combat ready force of fighters; entertaining the populace and creating diversions or recreational outlets for the young; providing opportunities for social interactions of the sexes; communicating with the gods; facilitating fertility rituals to ensure successful propagations of their own kind, animals and crops; celebrating victories, religious occasions and special occasions as mandated by their core beliefs, customs and traditions; honoring heroes of the past; and passing on and reinforcing core values, beliefs, and traditions to future generations.

Since the influences of the early British are also evident in several aspects of the game, subsequent chapters will reveal the influence of their religion and peoples as well as the contributions of others in the process to explore and understand baseball's earliest foundations and roots. These traditions blended well into those of other incoming groups from Europe producing a more dynamic and ever-changing British society.

7

Grounded in Religion

Baseball has its beginnings in religious practices or rituals, once thought essential for survival. The intellectual Jacques Barzun observed that to understand America, one must understand baseball. Therefore to truly understand baseball, or America, one needs to look at the religious roots of the people who brought their games to North America during colonization. Early colonists from the Old World were mainly from Britain and the rest of Europe. The first recorded game played by the religious British Pilgrims (or European colonists) in North America was a version of stool-ball.

Americans are a religious people, and many of their forebears who came here did so because of their desires to pursue religious freedom without fear of penalties and persecutions or interference by the state or crown (Chapter 5, Note 38). Even though the core religious beliefs of these arrivals were Christian, various immigrant groups sought to express their religious values with their own prescribed rituals and worship. Religious beliefs and expressions were essential to the societal development of America, and many facets of society bear religious imprints (for example, "God Bless America," "In God We Trust," and "One Nation Under God"). Deanne Westbrook in *Ground Rules: Baseball and Myths* (1996) writes:

> Whatever our declarations to the contrary, the shades of the sacred have not been dispersed by science or displaced by facts. Harold Bloom says of Americans in particular that "we are a religiously mad culture, furiously searching for the spirit, but each of us is subject and object of one quest, which must be for the original self, a spark or breath in us that we are convinced goes back to before the Creation.[1]

There is hardly any doubt about the religious nature of those who came during and after the formative years of both America and baseball (Pre- and Post- New York Knickerbocker Rules, 1845). This also holds true for the people who later came after the basic American values and foundations (Post-Revolutionary and Civil Wars) were laid and developed. (Religious beliefs of candidates for high political offices are still among the primary factors considered by the electorate of the United States.)

Despite profound modern advancements and achievements in fields of human knowledge such as philosophy, science and technology, we are still irresistibly drawn to events and happenings whose roots lie buried in our distant past. We feel the invisible pull of primal urges, needing and wanting to assemble with others, sometimes under higher guardian beings. Meetings at special places and occasions were held by our forebears and their forebears and their forebears' forebears *ad infinitum* reaching into the mists and shadows of our past, as revealed today in our common myths, beliefs and practices. Not only were our genes transmitted over thousands of years, but also myths, cultures, practices, religions, traditions, games and sports. All aspects of human activities were and are intricately intertwined. For example, our myths also tell of our religious beliefs and are often reflected in our games and vice versa.[2] In particular we will explore how the game of baseball was connected and associated with religious or former "pagan" practices of the more recent ancestral past of the multi-ethnic and culturally diverse British peoples, thereby solidifying strong underlying general pre–Celtic, Celtic, Germanic, Scandinavian foundations and other European contributions. In addition, we will examine the contributions of others who came into contact with the diverse British people.

As with other old cultures, certain games, in addition to being played in numerous regions in early Britain and elsewhere, were associated with religious and festive occasions and observances on Holy Days (holidays).[3] These games also provided ample opportunities for the social interaction of both men and women. Such necessary and desirable opportunities for mixing of the sexes on religious and festive occasions uncover one of baseball's early functions.

*   *   *

Games for Social Interactions

In 1755 William Bray writes that he and friends of both sexes play baseball on Easter Day after Church services (referenced in Chapter 4). The survival of this game at Easter time, that provided opportunities for such social interactions, was particularly noticeable in older Celtic and Germanic communities in Britain.[4] It is established that Easter has its origins as a spring fertility ritual in the pagan (non–Christian) world of many cultures. In 2003, Cram, Forgeng and Johnston, the editors of Francis Willughby's unfinished work, note that "Contemporary references suggest that stool-ball was considered a rustic pastime, and one of the fewer sports in which women freely took part. It seems to have been especially associated with Easter."[5]

Robert Herrick (1591–1674) in his poem "Stool-Ball" records similar observations:

> 1. At Stool-ball, Lucia, let us play,
>   For Sugar-cakes and Wine;
> Or for a Tansie let us pay,
>   The losse or thine, or mine.
> 2. If thou, my Deere, a winner be
>   At trundling of the Ball,
> The wager thou shalt have, and me,
>   And my misfortunes all.
> 3. But if (my Sweetest) I shall get,
>   Then I desire but this;
> That likewise I may pay the Bet,
>   And have for all a kisse.[6]

The speaker plays this game for a kiss, which he gets win or lose. Stool-ball was used for promoting social interactions and courtships.

The association of the game with religious affairs was not merely confined to Easter; Gomme writes that in Britain it was believed those who did not participate in stool-ball on Ash Wednesday would fall ill during the harvest. Gomme notes that both Christian clergy and laity participated in the traditional game of stool-ball to avoid misfortune.[7] The association of these old games with Lent and Easter was not introduced by Christianity, but was part of pre-existing ritual observances deemed necessary by the pre–Christian peoples for good health and welfare. Christian religious leaders and their communities kept up and tolerated to a degree long established traditions that may otherwise hurt their chances of survival, especially when misfortune was preventable by simple observance of a seemingly harmless and enjoyable game.[8] Local-born priests were more apt to understand the old traditions. Over the years, involvement in this game declined, so much that in the nineteenth century it rapidly became a faded ritual with even more accelerated loss of its deeper meanings and significance in Christianized communities.

Others support the idea that in some parts of rural Wales, stool-ball was becoming a folk game or pastime, enjoyed mainly on holidays (Easter) but stripped of any religious meaning. For example, Rector and Vicar Peter Roberts in *The Cambrian Popular Antiquities; or, An Account of the Traditions, Customs, and Superstitions of Wales* (1815) writes that in his boyhood days stool-ball was played on Holidays, Easter and after Sunday morning's prayers, but was fast becoming only a rural game.[9]

Poet John Taylor in *A Short Relation of a Long Journey Made Round or Ovall by Encompassing the Principalities of Wales from London* (1562) mentions that in some areas of Wales, people were playing stool-ball on Sundays in the churchyards, as if this was customary and also without fear of any penalty for breaking the Sabbath. These activities were therefore in existence long before the later arrival of strict Christianity in these rural communities where both males and females played stool-ball in the churchyards and graveyards. Evidently people retained or were reverting to old traditions which they knew and enjoyed to occupy their leisure times. In many places the Christian burial places or graveyards were on church properties since these were considered consecrated grounds. Church properties often had open communal spaces where children, youths and adults met and played. In many societies, church or temple properties were often the sites for communal gatherings and festivities, since life was centered on religious beliefs and calendars.

Robert W. Henderson, in *Ball, Bat and Bishop: The Origin of Ball Games* (1947), sums up his observations on stool-ball:

> The four characteristics of the old game of stool-ball are very evident: first, the constant association of the game with the Church, and the churchyard as a place where it was usually played; second, the association with the Easter season; third, it was played by young men and maidens, and fourth, the use of flavored cakes, usually tansy, as prizes.[10]

Such observations led Henderson to also suggest that stool-ball or baseball (in the 17th and 18th centuries) was likely a Christianized adaptation of an early pagan spring fertility ritual:

> And the element of romance—it was definitely a period of merrymaking of particular concern to young men and maidens, a time of courting *par excellence*. There can be no doubt that this characteristic of the Easter stool-ball festivities has a direct association with the ancient pagan rites, with connotation of human fertility and child-bearing....
>
>   That stool-ball was merely a local adaption of the ancient pagan rites there can be no doubt, and many writers have suspected it.[11]

Henderson's view of ball games being associated with religious practices at Easter is not isolated, and he also points out that the curious relationship was addressed as early as 1725 by an English clergyman, Henry Bourne.[12] Adelman in *A Sporting Time* supports Henderson's view that ball games were linked to fertility rituals:

> Unlike other sports which sprang from day-to-day activities, ball games originated in religious and magical functions and were closely associated with fertility rites. The Church adapted these ritualistic ball games and used them for Christian purposes, with some modification in their meaning. In Europe

various ball games became part of the Easter observance and other springtime customs.[13]

In these ball games, sexual courtship rituals and religious practices were intertwined and preserved as sexually maturing or matured persons, youths or young adults and adults were involved.[14] These more recent views are in line with the observation of Roberts' who shows that the playing of these bat-and-ball games was not limited to children since the community was involved. This means that the game was learned during childhood and continued through youth and adulthood.

In Christian Britain, the playing of ball games on Sunday and in church-yards was later frowned upon by powerful church authorities, who thought that the solemnity of religious observances was disrupted and violated.[15] The fact that the church threatened to punish and fine offenders verifies the participation of sexually-matured youths and adults in these games.[16] This means that stool-ball and other early baseball activities were also considered as corrupting, undesirable and pagan activities by the church.[17] Church authorities knew about the non–Christian nature, context and connotations of these games and often found them in conflict with their own beliefs and practices.[18] If such pagan acts could not be adapted to events of the Christian calendar, they were frowned on, discouraged and prohibited. In the late 18th and early 19th centuries, industrialization in Britain was just beginning, and people were moving from rural into urban areas to work in factories and offices. In cities, migrants used convenient and available churchyards and communal spaces as places to play. These religious and sacred sites were a natural draw for people longing for familiar communal games, pastimes and the camaraderie of friends left behind. This movement of peoples from rural areas also served as a way of reintroducing rural games into urban centers where such practices dwindled or were long curbed by ruling or religious authorities. In urban settings, a team-game attracted a wider variety of participants, and thereby facilitated its subsequent spread and reintroduction in other places.

Disapproval by Christian Church officials gives further proof toward these games older pre–Christian origins. These precursor and foundational games (stool-ball) fit the traditions of the early pre–Christian British peoples and also show the impact of other European (Teutonic and Scandinavian) peoples who later came to Britain. In order to further explain these findings and grasp a deeper understanding of the foundations of baseball, this investigation will now turn to briefly view the relevant beliefs and practices of pre- and post–Roman peoples of Britain.

* * *

Public Meeting Places for Games and Sacrificial Rituals

Peoples and nations existed in Britain long before the Romans and others, such as Germans, Scandinavians and Normans, came and added their own significant contributions and impacts (See Appendices A and F).[19] Games or athletic exercises were previously practiced by, for example, the Irish at their public meetings.[20] Physical prowess in activities, such as games and war, was well regarded and integrated into informal and formal educational and societal programs. Elder in *Celt, Druid and Culdee* gives an indication of those practices:

> The educational system adopted by the Druids is traced to about 1800 BC when Hu Gadarn Hysicion (Isaacson), or Hu the Mighty, led the first colony of Cymri into Britain from Defrobane, where Constantinople now stands....
>
> Dr. Henry, in his *"History of England"* has observed that collegiate monastic institutions existed among the Druids....
>
> Their recipe for good health was cheerfulness, temperance, and exercise. Certainly, the power of physical endurance displayed by the early Britons was a strong testimony to the salutary laws of hygiene enforced and the general mode of life encouraged by the Druids.[21]

These British and neighboring communities therefore had a system in place which actively promoted and integrated physical activities into their cultures and lifestyles.[22] It should be noted that the priesthood, the Druids, were said to be actively involved. Other groups, Teutonic and Scandinavian, who came after the Romans were similarly committed to physical fitness via games and sports as seen in their traditions and culture, including religion and war.

The ruling Christian Church later became very puritanical and repressive of festivals, sports and entertainment which were viewed as not being devoted to the glorification of the Christian god or Holy Trinity. Other related practices which may now seem relatively innocuous were frowned upon and condemned because of their histories, associations and connotations. For example, the strange but harmless Easter (the Solar New Year) activity of *heaving* or *lifting* was deemed undesirable. In this regard, T. Sharper Knowlson in *Origins of Popular Superstitions and Customs* (1972) writes:

> For instance there was the custom of *heaving* and *lifting* at Easter, a custom which took a long time to kill, and one where it was possible to trace stages of development from seeming improprieties to respectability. In the Northern counties, as will be seen, there was a roughness which is absent, in the same custom in London and the south.[23]

In *Observations on Popular Antiquities* (1841), John Brand quotes a 1784 writer for the "Gentleman's Magazine" (February 1784) stating the practice of *lifting* at Easter time in which a spread-eagled man or woman was lifted in the air by at least four women or men, respectively.[24] Knowlson writes that this Easter tradition of *lifting* or *heaving* was part of the sports and game festivities accompanying the occasion: "But *lifting* was only one of the sports of old Easter-tide. There were games on land and water, and much eating and drinking, indeed it was a season *not* kept holy but devoted entirely to merriment."[25] It is remarkable that such practices survived as late as the 18th century despite centuries of Christian suppression. These activities are indicative of early fertility rituals and sacrificial offerings to the British sun- and earth-gods or goddesses responsible for reproductive successes and regenerations as celebrated at Easter time.[26] Such processions and actions were deeply embedded in rural folks who were less inclined to give up time-honored traditional practices, as fertility rituals were deemed necessary for the success of crops, livestock and survival. Knowlson notes that these rather strange practices of "the lower class of people" were becoming less rustic, and consequently there were rapid losses of their original forms, intents and meanings.[27] The *heaving* or *lifting* practices, as early versions of stool-ball or baseball, were especially associated with Easter or springtime and included social interactions of couples with eating, drinking and merriment.[28] The participants of *heaving* and *lifting* were involved in a procession through the community. In general, processions were usually aimed at the mobilization of their religious communities, and like dances and games also functioned as prayers dedicated to particular deities.[29,30] Communal processions on festive and religious occasions invariably led to sites where the occasions were capped with games and entertainment.[31] Despite legal and church prohibitions, these practices and early ball games rose again and filled the need for games, sports, and entertainment.

It should be noted that this desire to meet in special places is deep-rooted. This old practice of *heaving* or *lifting* in connection with Easter also illustrates the necessity for the real or symbolic sacrifice of a high-ranking male such as priest or king for the good of the community. This is an ancient Indian practice that continued and apparently survived in remnants as Indo-European fertility rites.[32] This noble concept of willingly sacrificing oneself for the communal good in a sacred ceremony witnessed by the community was a long entrenched tradition in many old cultures. Such ancient concepts of self-sacrifice were endorsed in the earliest of times as exemplified by Indian, British and other European peoples in their philosophical teachings, attitudes, practices and cultural and religious perspectives. It should therefore be expected that their games in their special places also reflect their traditions and values.

* * *

Fires at Ritual Sites

We are all connected by fires, not only do they enable our survival but they also played a key role for ancient humans in religious and communal ceremonies and celebrations.[33] Fires still command our attention, and continue to be a significant part of some major religious ceremonies, for example, Christian and Hindu. Instead of simple wooden fires, bonfires and wicker-fires of yesterday, fireworks are now often used to mark special holidays and occasions such as New Year's and Independence Day. Modern men, women and children still assemble to watch and enjoy fireworks lighting up the skies. On such occasions, youths and adults, like their counterparts of bygone ages eat, drink and make merry. These occasions likewise promote social inter-actions. Bonfires and their associated traditions were important rituals which continued despite the years of established Christianity. Brand writes about fires called *bonefires or Nedfri,* that is, bonfires, and that they caused people to act foolishly and must be stopped.[34] The *Nedfri* was also called "Need Fires" and "Will Fires." These bonfires originally included the burning of bodies with bones, hence the early literal term *bonefires.* The Christian authorities found these bonfire activities not suitable for their Christian pop-ulace. Knowlson notes that the introduction and acceptance of Christianity were responsible for the termination of these older practices.

The earlier bonfires or burnings were part of the rituals that accompa-nied joyous celebrations. The descendants of the former practitioners of these *Nedfri* or *bonefires* continued in their ancestral footsteps with sanitized bonfire traditions. The participation of both the early laity and some Christian clergy showed how deep-rooted "those sacrilegious Fires" were, and the Church authorities clearly knew the meanings and implications of such "pagan" activities (Note 34).[35] The punishment for participation in pagan practices such as bonfires and accompanied dancing was not only excom-munication, but also the possibility of death. Even the local British clergymen were not exempt from the proposed harsh penalties imposed for participating in these then undesirable and prohibited practices. In spite of these prohibi-tions and purges, fragments of old customs survived as Addy in *A Glossary of Word* observes in old Celtic and Germanic communities of Britain.[36] William Borlase in *Antiquities of Cornwall* (1754) writes his observations on festival bonfires in places such as Cornwall.[37]

The fire-associated rituals, like the rituals of *heaving* or *lifting,* involved participation of both sexes dancing around bonfires, going from one neigh-boring community to another. These rituals involved perambulations around fires presided over by their Druidic priesthood. Relics of dancing around fires were not confined to rural or peasant classes but also church and law officials.[38] The church therefore associated these fire and dancing sacrilegious practices with relics of the pagan past and a continuation of worshipping the devil.[39] Consequently, these perambulations were similarly condemned and violators punished.

Addy also writes about the dancing and perambulations around fires.[40] The dedicated sites where bonfires were lit and people assembled for their essential fire and dancing ceremonies emerged as communal "squares" or "open-air temples." In addition, early churchmen (some former Druids) were involved in these old non–Christian ceremonies, a relic of the religious duties of the former pagan priesthood. The sites used for such involvement of open-air fires, people and priesthood were used again and again as dedicated spaces set aside by the community, as often evidenced by place-names (e.g., *Bell Hagg* and *Burnt Stones*).[41] In support of this idea of dedicated sites for these fires, Knowlson remarks that at such sites and ceremonies, children and young people played and the whole local community turned out.[42] Since these were rural agricultural communities they would likely play communal games such as stool-ball. Fire ceremonies associated with superstitions or religious worships were not limited to one people or nation, but were universal and provide a common connection among many peoples. Today we still gather at ballparks to watch fireworks after ballgames on special occasions.

As Christianity moved in and time progressed, these fire ceremonies faded away, but human need for assembling still remains. It is remarkable that anything entertaining or fun such as games, racing, dancing or other social events survived under such austere and intolerant religious conditions. The Reformation of the Church (1517 CE) eventually led to the rise of the Puritans to power (ca. 1649 CE), and zealous Puritanism was a repressive and intolerant force intent on sweeping aside all remaining superstitions and idolatrous practices, beliefs and customs.[43] Under the Puritans, traces and hints of pagan practices were ruthlessly magnified, vilified, condemned and their eradication promoted. In 1646 CE, Sir Thomas Randolph responds in a poem to the greater harshness of the actions and the consequent social climate created by the Puritans.[44] Christian Church authorities condemned any game or practice perceived to be associated with old idolatrous practices such as the worshipping of Baal.[45] The British world, as the poet Randolph further laments, had been turned into a "no-fun" place.[46] This prohibition of games, dances, sports and entertainment on Sundays meant many people of the working classes were not allowed to participate in their own traditional pastimes and recreational activities. These had evolved over the centuries and there were now no proper substitutes to meet social and recreational needs.

The number of feast days and Holy days for social festivities were also considerably reduced. The consequences of both prohibitions and reductions of times available for recreational activities naturally led not only to the loss of some traditional games, sports and festive events, but also an unhappy and unhealthy populace.

*   *   *

German philosopher Hans-Joachim Schoeps in *The Religions of Mankind: Their Origin and Development* (1961) writes about a wide variety of religious and historical situations that were reenacted in drama, mock battles and games.[47] Schoeps gives an example where ball games reenact the path of the sun:

> The ritual [Aztecs] included ball games played at certain times outside the temples; apparently these were scenes from an ancient religious drama representing the course of the sun and intended to influence the same. In some parts of Mexico these religious ball games have continued down to the present day.[48]

Accordingly, there is known precedent in which ball games were associated with religious ceremonies. Since the sun was viewed as the major deity of old Britain and Europe and elsewhere, a celebration of Easter, the Solar New Year, would reasonably be expected to incorporate ball games in religious and communal practices.

It is generally recognized that sacred and other important acts, rituals and ceremonies of great consequence to early communities were and still are usually done in special or consecrated places and with an evolving priesthood. One that involves larger fires would be done outdoors. These occasions and ceremonies filled a great human need of wanting to assemble at a special place for the benefit of ourselves and our communities to reaffirm kinship with others. Philosopher J. Krishnamurti writes: "Events, technology, and all those things are happening in the world, are producing great changes outwardly. Yet inwardly most of us remain more or less as we have been for centuries."[49]

The New Testament's exhortation to assemble ourselves as believers, shows this basic human necessity of connecting with each other and reaffirming our identity as a group to survive.[50] People met and still meet to re-establish our sense of belonging to a group or place, in special ceremonies with accompanied rituals. Americans are generally regarded as a society that respects individuality, but individuality stills needs identification with a group and its rituals to continue thriving. Baseball, with echoes of its religious past, quietly fills and enmeshes the assembled, soothing ancient needs and inner commands.[51]

It seems that modern baseball evolved to fulfill these inner needs and reconnect us with our past. We are responding to an ancient drive and survival strategy of meeting together as a village or religious community. This aspect of the foundations of special places being required for such meetings and accompanied ritual practices will be addressed in the next chapter.

8

Shaped by Functional, Sacred and Communal Places

The early people of pre–Roman Britain, like others of Europe and else-where, chose not to keep written records of their rituals and ceremonies, fearing this privileged information would fall into the hands of enemies and outsiders.[1] The Germanic and Scandinavian peoples who later came to Britain held similar beliefs.[2] With this in mind, the search for confirmation and meaning of baseball's deepest origins now turns to the architectural sites of early Britain and the later-arriving Germanic and Scandinavian peoples. Early British peoples, like others, held important religious events and rituals in appropriately selected and designed places which reflected their traditional respect for fields, trees, springs, waterfalls, groves, hills and other landscape features. Such sites will be examined for possible baseball-like field designs, constructions, adaptations and symbolism. These sites and their functions melded together to form the foundations of what would later evolve as an international game. In addition, similarities of ancient peoples who embraced common widespread beliefs (for example, Celtic, Northern European, Hindu and Buddhist) will be pointed out. (Appendix E gives further details about Indian backgrounds to these beliefs.)

The early Indo-European peoples, in their northwestward migration across Europe, were prodigious stockade and fort builders. These well-built structures and fortresses were designed and developed to safeguard against the constant threats and realities of warfare in their everyday lives.[3] Numerous old Gaelic words for death, killing, war and warfare have survived the cen-turies as recorded by William Shaw in *A Galic [Gaelic] and English Dictionary* (1780).[4] This noted predilection toward fort building is discussed by Anne Ross in *Everyday Life of the Pagan Celts* (1970). According to Ross, the evi-dence suggests the Celts had a professional class of fort builders. Such archi-tectural tendencies spilled over into the building of other structures for commercial, entertainment, educational, social and religious functions. These functions were often interrelated, and old religious sites served multiple purposes. Games were an integral part of religious rites and military training. The sites used for such interrelated activities followed a construction plan similar to that of forts and stockades, on a relatively smaller scale. These same basic building plans of a square or circle were used for games and religious activities. Insular British and Continental European peoples knew circles are easily formed both outside and inside a square.[5] When needed, these same or similar sites could easily be adapted to teach offensive and defensive war strategies.

This investigation will now focus on the basic characteristic plan of early structures before and during subsequent Roman and Christian control in Britain, which provided venues for early games like stool-ball. They reveal a deeper meaning to the terms "baseball fields," "baseball squares," or "baseball diamonds," mirroring the layout of their predecessors' ancient and religious sites.

Numerous early cultures held groves of trees as places of early worship, for example, the Old Testament mentions the groves of Ahab (I Kings 18:33) and Manasseh (II Kings 21:3 and 7).[6] One of the British Grail legends mentioned a temple surrounded by a thick grove on a hill, only accessible to the divinely selected. Many groves are featured in British myths and folklore. Alexander Porteus in *The Folklore of Myths and Legends* (1928) describes the basic design of early sacred groves and places:

> In our country [Britain] and in Northern Europe, the worship of the Druids was carried on for many centuries. It was an article in their creed that it was unlawful to build temples to the gods, or worship them within walls or under roofs. Consequently all their places of worship were in the open air, and it was generally on high ground whence they could view the heavenly bodies to which much of their adoration was directed…. These sacred groves were watered by some consecrated fountains, and were surrounded by a ditch or mound to prevent the intrusion of strangers. No one was permitted to enter these sacred groves except through a passage left for the purpose. These passages are guarded by Druids of an inferior standing to prevent intrusion into the sacred mysteries. Some of the groves were circular, others oblong, and they were large or small. In the centre of the grove was a circular area enclosed with one or two rows of large stones set perpendicular to the earth, which constituted the temple, within which the altar stood on which sacrifices were offered.[7]

Such sacred groves were the earliest natural temples in Britain and Continental Europe. The above description suggests the origins of the structures which would later be found or reverted to in modern baseball. This particular description of a typical British or Northern European grove evokes images of a modern baseball field with an infield (area), bases (altars) and a guarded pathway (bared earth lane used by the priesthood) from the infield's exit (home plate) to the foul area/stands (grove). Porteus elaborates on the many and widespread transitions from sacred groves to temples.[8] Fergus Flemings, Sharukh Hussain, C. Scott Littleton and Linda A. Milcor in *Heroes of the Dawn: Celtic Myth* (1996) record: "[Julius] Caesar had reported that the druids originated in the British Isles where Gaulish novice druids were sent for training."[9] Likewise, James G. Frazer in *The Golden Bough: A Study in Magic and Religion* (1958) points out that in old Europe and elsewhere, others held groves as sacred places or temples.[10] Therefore, many sacred places or groves in Britain and Europe followed similar plans.

The numerous sacred old groves in Britain and Europe, as elsewhere, did not survive the ravages of invaders, time, population pressures and industrialization. But analogous ground plans between the sacred groves as "open-air" temples and other old British, Germanic and Scandinavian structures show striking similarities in design.

Ancient peoples, in their movements across the northwestern landscape, built four-sided rectangular earthworks which in Germany were known as *viereckschanzen*, a term meaning "rectilinear enclosures." Sometimes other written sources refer to these similar shaped structures as "squares" or "rectangles." The basic plan of each rectilinear structure is similar to that of a fort. Anne Ross writes in *Everyday Life of the Pagan Celts* (1970), "In the main they [rectilinear enclosures] seem to date to the first century BCE, and culturally to go back to the square Iron Age burial enclosures and forward to the Gallo-Roman temples, built usually of stone and square or circular on plan."[11]

These earthworks were found in many locations throughout Europe including France, Bavaria, and Britain. One in Britain was dated back to 1400 BCE. According to Ross, these approximately squared areas were varied, from about 100 to 200 yards (91.4 to 182.8 meters) in length or width.[12] The perimeter of the field area within each was demarcated by an earthen or stone embankment which in turn was surrounded by a ditch, with or without water.[13] In modern times, some early baseball parks with similar earthen embankments or "hills" likely formed the basis of the expression "hitting one over the hill" or "out of the yard."

Ross also elaborates on possible activities within these rectilinear enclosures:

> We know from Irish sources that Celtic ritual gatherings were accompanied by lavish feasting and drinking, and that games and races and marketing of wares played an integral part in the solemn religious festivals…. The evidence, then, serves to indicate that, far from worshipping their Gods in groves and other

features of the countryside alone, the Celts did in fact have a variety of built structures of some sort, in which their rites were performed.... There is also a body of evidence for wooden temples, constructed within these banked, earthen enclosures. The Celtic word for "sanctuary" was *nemeton*; there is no reason to suppose that the term did not include these earthworks, as well as referring to the clearings in a grove which also served as sacred places.[14]

Ross therefore underlines the importance of these banked earthen enclosures as not only centers of local marketing (i.e., market squares) and other social activities, but also links them with religious festivities. Such sites were therefore an integral part of any community, similar to how modern temples, churches, cathedrals and baseball parks contribute to the lives of people today.[15] Medieval and modern cathedrals of Britain and Europe were built to mimic the effects of sacred groves. As mentioned in Chapter 7, the restrictive Christian Church would later ban these pagan festivities in Britain and Continental Europe. The loss of these activities created a void, and sanitized versions of games, without religious trappings, emerged to fill basic recreational needs. One such acceptable game, stool-ball, was played within the framework of these old abandoned religious sites. Stool-ball filled the social, emotional and cultural needs of the people, and connected them, however faintly, with their ancestral roots.

The traditional old British game-day atmosphere Ross evokes in her above mentioned citation is mirrored in an old poem "Stool-ball, or the Easter Diversion," in the British magazine *The London Magazine, or Gentleman's Monthly Intelligencer* (1733). The anonymous poet's description of an early baseball-like scene gives some indications of the field location chosen for a game as well as the audience and participants in Swansea, Wales:

> And in the market's guarded square
> ...
> They chuse that open area most,
> Where stand the stocks and pillory post;
> Where justice shows a worn-out face,
> And sinners seldom meet disgrace:
> While servile bands, of mean renown,
> Enjoy the out-parts of the town.[16]

The game was therefore being played in an open area such as the market square, a public place where the stocks and pillory post (instruments of punishment) were present, and where others assembled for various purposes to form a multi-functional communal site.[17] In addition, Ross mentions evidence of wooden temples built within these earthworks. These structures were likely used as sacred places, or *nemeton*, but just as the more renowned sacred groves of Anglesia or ancient Mona's Isle, Wales, Britain, they were destroyed by the

Romans.[18] The Romans destroyed these sites because of their association with the influential British priesthood. They knew the importance of these sites to all aspects of life of these people. In addition, the Romans seized similar sites for their own religious, administrative and personal uses, while abandoning others altogether.[19]

Ross's work also includes three relevant photographs. Two depict pieces of pottery from the Romano-British periods in which a naked figure is seen holding a ball or other spherical object (perhaps a human head) in one hand, and a curved stick in the other. The third photograph shows a plaque of a ritual crown or diadem on which another naked figure is seen holding a ball in one hand and a similar curved stick in the other. This latter image shows an approximate square framed by four balls, one in each corner.[20] These early scenes suggest some connection between a ball-game and religious rituals involving sacrificial offerings or the trophy collection of heads and square or diamond-like designs.[21]

These *viereckschanzen* are a likely place from whence early baseball precursor games emerged. This multifunctional use of religious spaces continued in later times in Britain. For example, theatrical plays were performed in the Churches of Britain right through the Reformation of the seventeenth century. The nave of the renowned St. Paul's Cathedral, London, was initially used as a public market square in the early eighteenth century. This tradition of the multifunctional stage (including weddings and funerals) of religious places in Britain and Continental Europe was a part of its pre- and non–Christian heritage. It is important to remember that although we may have separate places for rituals, sports, markets and other activities, to the people of old Britain and Continental Europe these activities were often overlapping and interrelated.

The exact configuration of these playing fields is difficult to determine from descriptions of early baseball. A section of the previously cited poem, "Stool-ball, or the Easter Diversion," gives a feel for the playing field:

> And stretching to a wide extent,
> To seize the ball before it grounds,
> Or take it when it first rebounds.
> The youths their stations have a-far,
> Enjoin'd to guard the distant rear,
> With nimbler limb, and manly strength,
> To strike the mark from utmost length,
> To watch the ball that farthest speeds,
> And tow'rs above the ladies heads.[22]

Since this description indicates young women were closer to the hitting action while young men, with stronger-throwing arms, occupied spaces in the playing fields further away, this implies that some versions of stool-ball already showed tendencies for the separation of infields and outfields (or infielders and outfielders). Later on, the same poem also mentions women were catching fly balls with their aprons (perhaps the first gloves or mitts).

* * *

Infield and Outfield

In the modern game, the use of the terms infield and outfield describes the arrangement of a smaller squared field or diamond within a larger field.

As a variety of early games were held within places, such as *viereckchanzen*, the possibility for an infield and outfield arrangement existed (Chapter 3). Whether or not these two terms were actually used in early baseball or when they became incorporated is unknown, but these terms do show old agricultural origins or associations. For example, in Britain, Samuel Hibbert in *A Description of the Shetlands Islands Comprising an Account of their Scenery, Antiquities, and Superstitions* (1822) writes with regard to the concepts of infield and outfield:

> It is usual to give a land a distinction that was no doubt introduced into the country by the Scottish settlers; that is, into *Infield* and *Outfield*. In Scotland, the land lying near the homestead was kept for successive years in tillage, and under the name of *Infield*, received all the manure, mixed with earth, which the farm afforded.... In Perthshire, for instance, any portion of land which lay in a valley at a distance from the house, and was sufficiently free from stones, was under the name of *Outfield*.[23]

It is easy to see the analogy between old agricultural designs of farmsteads with their houses or homes, infield and outfield areas, and the modern game's diamond with its home plate, infield and outfield, respectively.

On the basis of what is generally known about religious rituals we would expect to find a smaller defined area within the center, or in another specific location within the larger field, where the major rituals took place.[24] A central location of the main staging or inner area (as in cricket) would have maximized equal viewing by surrounding audiences.[25] On the other hand, the one corner location of the main staging area (as in baseball) allows the creation of mystique and indicates a more hierarchal type of priesthood or society, since some are closer and others farther away from the main action or rites.[26]

Porteus writes that sacred groves were guarded and situated to prevent easy access by the uninitiated. Many religions prefer a special section where the high priesthood performs their duties. In addition to this latter type of arrangement facilitating the needs of a hierarchical society, it also permits more multi-functional stages of a cleared space, since other communal activities could be permissible without intrusions into the sacred domains of the infield area.

Modern baseball fans are better aligned (when sitting close to the infield area) to observe the subtle movements of the ball and experience the tensions of man-to-man dueling confrontations.[27] This is in contrast to the situation in cricket, where a more uniform (equidistant) view of the field is offered to all.[28] It is also possible both arrangements were in use at one time or another in different places or times. Curiously, Chadwick's 1884 work shows a hard, bare and smooth ground forming a pathway from the center of the infield (pitcher's mound) through the home plate area and leading off the field.[29] Several pictures or photographs of old ball parks show this pathway from mound through home plate to off-field.[30] A similar design is still seen at the baseball diamond in the stadium of the Detroit Tigers (Comerica Park). In former times such an area was created for personnel (priests and bards, dignitaries and other religious attendants) to enter and exit the main staging area of rituals and ceremonies. This is much the same as the carpeted paths to altars in churches, cathedrals and temples. No such pathway from the wicket to off-field has been recorded in old cricket fields.[31,32,33]

*   *   *

Sacred Places of Worship

Ross, cited earlier with regards to early British and continental European sacred places, *nemeton*, indicates that wooden temples were constructed within these earthen enclosures and that *viereckshanzen* were comparable to sacred groves. Porteus similarly describes the basic design of early sacred groves and places marked with stones. Elder also provides further support for the use of stones to mark early British sacred places:

> The word "temple," in its primitive meaning, is simply a place cut off, enclosed, dedicated, to sacred use, whether a circle of stones, a field or a building. In the old British language a temple or sanctuary was called a "caer," a sacred fenced enclosure. The stone circles or caers of Britain were, therefore, essentially temples and held so sacred by the people that reverent behavior in their vicinity was universal.[34]

The fact that encircled areas were clearly marked with stones indicates these were dedicated for regular religious or important purposes with accompanied rites. In these places, the British priest-philosophers and magician-sages were the mediators between the early British and their gods and goddesses.[35] Here the priests worked, imposing their mystique and promoting their own societal philosophies and traditional values.[36] In early times, the corners of each inner sacred area or temple were marked with stones, bricks or wooden poles, some of these practices survived in places as seen in the earlier versions of baseball. Newbery's 1744 work, the earliest known written reference with the specific term "Base Ball," shows a picture of the game being played in Britain with what appears to be slabs of stone or wooden posts as bases. This use of markers is also consistent with what was mentioned in Chapter 7, where stones and wooden poles were similarly used in Welsh baseball and other predecessor games.[37]

This traditional way of defining sacred places with markers was well known in Britain and Europe. Similar places to *viereckshanzen* and groves were found in other areas of Europe, as seen for example in the old dedicated sacred places of Germanic, Scandinavian and French peoples. These latter groups also held stones, called runes to be of religious and cultural significance.[38] Ralph Blum in *The Book of Rune: A Handbook for the Use of an Ancient Oracle: The Viking Runes* (1982) writes: "Numerous *hällristningar* [rock carvings, petroglyphs], as well as the runic standing stones, can still be seen in the British Isles, in Germany, and throughout Scandinavia."[39] The runes were symbolic markings, or glyphs, used to convey thought. Blum says: "Those first glyphs, were called *runes,* from the Gothic *runa,* meaning 'a thing, a mystery.'"[40] Therefore, it is not surprising that stones would mark sacred places of worship.

Markers of Sacred Spaces

The question now arises with regard to the number of stones or posts, i.e., bases that define this inner area and help to give baseball its unique diamond shape. It is difficult to know how many markers were used in these early rituals, or if one standard amount was preferred. The actual number was likely dependent on location, time and event. As was seen in Chapter 5, the quantity of bases in early versions of baseball-like games varied from two to six.

The use of a square and four bases in early baseball fields in America was well documented. Carver states that in baseball: "Four stones or stakes are placed from twelve to twenty yards asunder," and thereby form an approximate square.[41] In addition, Wood states: "Each corner of the square shall be marked by a flat iron plate or stone, six inches square, fixed in the ground even with the surface."[42] It is interesting to note the use of four bases in connection with the sites of former sacred places. Numbers played a significant role in the beliefs and mythologies of certain societies. The number four is also prominent in old British and European mythology, as in other great spiritual traditions and practices of many other recorded cultures.[43] Accordingly, a case can be made for the use of four bases, mirroring the rectangular designs of the *viereckschanzen* and other sacred places reflecting the religious and philosophical importance of the number four in, for example, early British and continental European life.[44] Exactly, how early baseball settled on four bases is unclear, but the choice in design is closer to plans for original religious sites.

The term "home" is used for the final stone or post by Newbery in his 1744 description of baseball.[45] Both Carver and Wood, mention that in early American baseball games, home plate was likewise made of a stone, often marble. The modern home plate in baseball is now represented by a pentagonal-shaped plate, a combination of a rectangle and an isosceles triangle sharing one common side.[46] Addy in his 1888 work writes that "the plan of a house, &c. was formerly called the plate," which suggests that the pentagonal shaped home plate may literally have been a pictogram to indicate a "home" or "house."[47]

* * *

Origins of Terms in Early Baseball

With markers including stones and posts in mind, terms such as "burning," "soaking" and "wounding," used in early baseball games when a runner was put out before reaching the safety of a base can now be better explained. As we know, in early British and continental European folklore the oak tree was venerated as the most sacred of all trees.[48,49] Elder indicates that "the oak was held by the Druids to symbolize the Almighty Father, self-existent and eternal."[50] In old British beliefs, mighty oak trees were symbolic of the "Trees of Life, Light and Knowledge." Elder further describes the sacredness of the oak tree:

> In the earlier days the Druids used the oak for the same purpose. They sought a tree having two principal arms springing laterally from the upright stem, roughly in the form of a cross. Upon the right branch they cut the name Jesu; upon the middle or upright stem Taranis; upon the left branch Belenis; over this they cut the name of God—Thau. The Hebrew prophets, it will be noted, referred to the expected Messiah as "The Branch."[51]

Taken in this light, the right branch (that is, first base) may be said to symbolically represent *Jesu*, the middle branch *Taranis* (second base), and the left branch *Belenis* (third base).[52] As will be seen later, spellings and pronunciations of these gods' names varied with time and location. Under the influence of Christianity, by 530 CE these triunes or trinity of gods merged together to form a monotheistic entity.[53] Even though the temples and gods changed in British and continental Europe, older religious influences are still seen in buildings and art forms on present day structures. In this regard, Anne Ross's chapter *The Celtic Consciousness* contains a photograph (plate 8) that shows a three-headed figure, three arched windows, and a row of the four circles joined to a central circle in a mandala-like structure. Its legend states: "The Three-Headed Grotesque, Bayeux Cathedral, Calvador, France; the cathedral was constructed over a temple dedicated to the Celtic God Belenos."[54] This cathedral was built in the eleventh century with its sculptures, stained-glass windows and architecture still reflecting old religious influences despite 500 years of Roman and Christian rule. John Davies in *The Celts* (2000) provides intriguing insights:

> Writing a century after Caesar, Lucan gave particular prominence to the names of three gods: Teutates, Taranis and Esus.... Lucan states that those sacrificed to Teutates were drowned, those to Taranis were burnt and those to Esus were hanged.[55]

Another scholar, Ward Rutherford, in *Celtic Mythology: The Nature and Influence of Celtic Myth from Druidism to Arthurian Legend* (1990) also notes the similarities of Celtic sacrifices: "There is little doubt that Druidic sacrifices included the triple death mentioned by Lucan. Usually this involved hanging or strangulation, followed by burning or stabbing and immersion in water."[56] The Rev. C. Arthur Lane, in *Illustrated Notes on English Church History* (1896), writes about similar practices adding to the observations of Elder, Davies, and Rutherford.[57,58]

In connecting these latter statements and previous works, it can be imagined that sacrificial offerings were made to each of these three gods at various altars. The altars, stones or wooden posts that once marked areas of religious significance have survived as bases. Sacrificial offerings were made at various altars: (1) hanging or strangulation (death by lack of air, first base) at one altar releasing the spirit; (2) burning (death by fire, second base) at another altar sending the ashes back to earth; and (3) drowning or soaking (death by water, third base) at the third altar putting the person in contact with the underworld or Otherworld.[59]

The survival and use of these terms ("burning," "wounding," "plugging" and "soaking") used in early ball games are relics of earlier times describing the methodology of sacrificial offerings.[60] These descriptions once accurately, but now colorfully portray what happens to a player when put out. Today, the triple play or "triple death" as it may once have signified is rare.

Within these four bases (pillars, posts or altars) the foundations of early British and continental European societies and consequently modern baseball were laid. After sacrificial offerings ended during Christianity's rule, changes emerged, such as the former altars (bases) or their immediate areas, becoming places of safety and refuge. Early players likely sought protection from the attacks of pursuers by hiding behind or holding on to the former stones or altars. Chapter 7 discussed with reference to the Finnish game that not only the bases, but areas around them were designated as "safe zones." In one early form of baseball (pize-ball), more than one player could be safe at a base, providing they were linked to each other hand in hand, and where the term "sausage" was used. A game that catered to social interactions of young men and women needed to include safe areas, where the chased can avoid being caught by the chaser.

* * *

Mounds

In many cultures, sacred places for rituals and religious activities are generally focused in the center of or near designated sacred and special areas. These chosen places, for example, groves, hills, wells, springs, rivers and fields add to the aura, mystique, and solemnity of the prescribed rites and ceremonies, increasing the depth and impact of religious experiences on participants and worshippers.

This need to gather at mounds runs deep in our common human evolution. This central area was where sacrificial offerings were made and high priests performed their public duties. These acts were best presented on higher ground for better visibility. In addition, the reenactments of battles between two heroic figures and honored deities (for example, friend versus foe, good versus evil and heaven versus earth) with the appropriate rituals were best presented on elevated ground.

Another basic human need is to ensure the continuation of oneself or a loved and honored one in his or her transition and continuation to the afterlife. This need likewise required the setting aside of areas in special places. Mounds were created to house the deceased and were filled with anything the departed souls were thought to require in their continuation in the afterlife. This building of mounds seems to have been a universal human phenomenon as seen in both the cultures of the old and new worlds.[61] Religious, ceremonial, social and recreational activities were interrelated, and the traditions, myths and legends, including old duels, were likewise reenacted.

Since the game came to America via Britain and continental Europe, we look to these places and cultures for the presence and impact of mounds on earlier times. In fact, mounds were an integral part of many cultures of European peoples, for example, British, Germanic or Scandinavian (Appendices E and F). This propensity for building barrows (earth mounds) and cairns (stone heaps) in early Britain is documented in the works of Cyril Fox, E.O. Gordon, R. Hippisley Cox and Barry Mardsen.[62,63,64,65] The Mound People of Denmark, about 1000 BCE, is documented by Danish archaeologist P.V. Glob.[66]

The mounds that occurred across Britain and Europe, as seen in Wales, London and Denmark, were built on a similar plan and match that given of the sacred spaces by Porteus in *The Folklore of Myths and Legends*.[67] The mounds of Britain and Denmark were likewise defined by free-standing stone circles, or in the latter also by posts interweaved with twigs. Gordon states: "The footprints of the first settlers have been traced by the remains of their religious monuments."[68] Ross states that in addition to wells, springs, groves and trees, the burial mounds and *viereckschanzen* were hallowed sites for religious rituals and were similar in Britain and Denmark.[69] Jan Filip in his chapter, "Early History and Evolution of the Celts" in *The Celtic Consciousness*, writes about the widespread use of *viereckschanzen* in Europe.[70] Hilda Roderick Ellis Davidson in *Myths and Symbols in Pagan Europe: Early Scandinavian and Celtic Religions,* reminds us that if suitable places for use as sacred places did not exist naturally, then humans would create them.[71]

Anne Ross in *Everyday Life of the Pagan Celts* describes the presence of ritual shafts in, for example, the British and European, *viereckschanzen*:

> Some *viereckschanzen* contains pits or offering-shafts, like the remarkable examples at Holzhausen, in Bavaria. Here two earthworks, set close together, were found to have timber palisades underneath; the enclosures contained deep shafts in which traces of offerings were found, including flesh and blood, presumably sacrificial. In one of these enclosures traces of a timber-built temple were found. Many deep shafts, mostly circular in section, have been found in Britain.[72]

In addition, estimations from the diagrams in Ross's work reveal that a ritual shaft was about 15 feet (4.8 meters) in width at the top and extended downward about 30 feet (9.1 meters).[73] These shafts, lined with wicker or wood, were used for the underground storage of food, shelter of priestly insignia and other religious objects, and placement of religious offerings and propitiations. The entrances to these shafts were the domain of the priesthood and likely occupied a central or defined area at ground level. It is possible this defined area was at the center of the circle or square where the rituals were performed since this was the domain of the respected priesthood.[74]

Elder provides further thoughts on the presence of underground constructions at some early British sites including chambered barrows and cairns with built-in fireplaces and exits for smoke.[75] Early British and continental European gods were often depicted with two faces, one looking into the underworld and another looking backwards into the world of the living. Areas above these shafts would have been clearly marked to signify the entry and exit point between worlds (living and Otherworld). Chadwick (1884) refers to a rectangle, 4 feet by 6 feet, near the mid-point of the infield square.[76] Wood (1891) describes a similar rectangle: "The Pitcher's position shall be within a space of ground four feet wide by six feet long, the front or four feet line."[77] In addition, Welsh baseball continues to make use of a similar, yet larger rectangle 10 feet long and 2½ feet wide from which the pitcher throws.[78] The use of these rectangular shapes is analogous to the central location of the pitching mound where previously older practices occurred in former consecrated grounds. Anne Ross in *Pagan Celtic Britain* writes:

> Primitive or Polytheistic religions are concerned with death as with life, and the duality of the Chthonic/fertility deities is illustrative of this preoccupation with the two extremes of human experience. Death is regarded as a stage in the progression of life. This concept makes it natural for grave mounds and other burial sites to serve as a focal point for ritual and for the religious games in which the Celts indulged.... The burial mound, like the well, and the sea, was regarded in Celtic belief as one of the entrances to the otherworld of which the Celts were so conscious.[79]

Many such mounds, after being abandoned, weathered and sank over time. Yet as Jacob Grimm in *Teutonic Mythology* (1844) points out: "people trod their old paths to the accustomed site," for communal gatherings, sport and games.[80] This deep need to gather is still powerful and draws us to analogous sacred places with a central focus of activity. Today our main point of focus is likewise the pitcher on the mound who controls the fate of the game, as a Druidic priest of yesteryear controlled his rituals.

Field Designs and Mandalas

Geometric patterns (circles, squares, triangles and lines) are often incorporated in the design of sacred places and in rituals, holding special meanings and significance as seen in Buddhist, Hindu, Navajo and other old practices.[81] Similarly, early British and continental European priests incorporated squares, circles, lines and numbers in their artistic designs of sacred places and as practical teaching aids.[82] Such geometric designs were in effect mandalas. Cassandra Lorius, author of an introductory work in *Mandalas and Meditations*, explains:

> A Mandala is a pattern of power that represents the whole circle of existence … mandala is a primal circular pattern that has existed in nature since the beginning of time…. Anthropologists have discovered that representations of mandalas have long been used in many cultures as vehicles for shamanic journeys…. Mandalas can be used as a path to power, describing an inner journey to the center.[83]

In essence, a mandala is a shape or pattern that helps one to connect and remember religious beliefs through visual designs. In places where these old sacred sites later re-emerged as rudimentary "baseball fields," one may expect to find relics of earlier mandala-like designs and expressions. Markers which once defined many early British and continental European rituals and sacred areas, now define the main playing area of a baseball "diamond." Lines or paths can be found linking the bases, and the pattern of running the bases adds a further circular dimension.

Early British and European attachment to square and circular designs is also expressed in the most renowned stories of Western literature and philosophy including the *Grail Castle* and the *Holy Grail*.[84] In addition, old British and European-inspired mandalas are seen in the beautiful stained-glass rose windows of the famous Chartres and Notre Dame cathedrals in France.

Worshippers, who accepted the sun as their major god or one of the many gods, began morning prayers and rituals facing the east and the rising sun. The daily journey of the sun from the eastern direction is constant and became the reference point for facing and bowing to the sun to show respect.[85] Outdoor and indoor places of sacred worship were often chosen and built to align with the path of the rising and setting sun. Ross in *Pagan Celtic Britain* notes, "Here again a Romano-Temple has been superimposed upon a pre-existing native site…. The temple was oriented north-east and south-west."[86] This means early British and continental European sacred places that were razed, seized or abandoned were so aligned before the Romans arrived. The abandoned sites, which later became game and communal sites, kept the old alignment. Modern baseball diamonds are now generally set with a northeast and southwest orientation to avoid the setting sun getting into the eyes of the hitter, catcher, and home plate umpire. Svensson makes some interesting remarks that a diamond symbol on ancient runes is associated with fertility.[87] (Further details with regards to similar symbols and their meanings used by the ancient Indians are given in Appendix E.)

As with the mandalas of Buddhism and Hinduism, early British and European designs used concentric circles, squares or rectangles (often three) in their artistic expressions.[88] Baseball fields lend themselves to, and each diamond provides outlets for, these artistic patterns and repetitions. Many modern baseball groundskeepers also intuitively express similar artistry in the patterning of cut grass within these larger and outfield designs.[89]

Modern baseball fields with their British and European heritage show a high level of sophistication reflecting and paralleling the designs of ancient philosophical Buddhist and Hindu mandalas.

In summary, we have seen that early British and European *viereck-shanzen*, groves, trees, stupas and mounds were sites for sacred rituals presided over by religious authorities, with a central figure or focal point. Some of these sites, defined with stones or wooden markers, also served as analogous "fire altars," where incantations and sacrificial offerings for the well-being of individuals and the community were made. The sacrificial processes involved fire ("burning"), water ("soaking") and hanging or strangulation ("wounding" or "plugging"). Rituals also involved participants moving around in a circular fashion as many still do at sacred places. Together these aspects of the game echo its past, connecting us with early peoples and each other.

9

Special Features of the Diamond and Game

Several of the distinctive features of the modern baseball diamond (and its relatives like softball) are not seen in any other game. These features evolved not only from deep British and European mythical, religious and historical roots, but were influenced by the cultural and social traditions of several societies, places and times. This game was grounded in human roots thereby explaining its international appeal across cultural, language and religious divides.

Gathering at the Mounds

One of the most definitive and striking features of the modern baseball diamond is the central pitcher's area or "mound." In this area stands one of the key combatants, the pitcher, who faces and initiates the attack on his opponent, the batter. Confrontations between two individuals and groups have deep roots in our primal heritage. Cleared or elevated areas, or mounds, were chosen for such contests or fights. Regular usage of such combat places give birth to the battle fields with their flattened places or mounds, seen as circles, rings and rectangles.[1] As time evolved the combats (or mock-battles and re-enactments) became sports and games. Holt in his Chapter "Old Ways of Playing" in *Sport and the British*, gives us a flavor of the survived rationales for sports as they provided opportunities for meeting, forming local community bonds, inter-communal rivalries, and facilitating recreational and social needs.[2]

Propitiating local deities or regional gods and goddesses with sacrificial gifts or votive offerings to ensure health, survival, good fortune, and victories in battles and games was a major personal and communal need.

This ancient and seemingly embedded attraction and tendency to gather at mounds for religious, snake or sun worship, and other purposes is still with us. Ramsay MacMullen in *Christianity & Paganism in the Fourth to Eight Centuries* (1997) gives additional explanation as to why mounds survived and why this traditional respect and affinity for such places provided a common bond between the old paganism and the new Christianity:

> The faithful of both religions sought out the same cemeteries, there to mourn, though cheerfully and even boisterously to mourn, the recently deceased, and then periodically to return to recall them in the company both their friends of any faith at all, in a social gathering—since these were the facts of their ordinary life, there can be nothing surprising in the ambiguity, call it, of our evidence. Or it may equally be said: for hundreds of years, the pagan cult of the dead was a common part of Christianity.
>
> For, in the fourth and later centuries, the evidence continues in the same character. Finds in cemeteries and other excavations repeat in detail all of that picture of graveside banqueting.[3]

MacMullen concludes that this attraction to graveyards, churchyards and mounds has a long and wide history:

> These scenes have been offered as convincing indications of a changeless religious usage. It seems safe to assert not only this much but, further, the virtual universality of the Christian grave cult in the Mediterranean world at the commencement of my period of study and for a period thereafter—in some regions, only over the length of a few generations but, in others, for a very much longer time, even to our own age.[4]

For the most part in our history, we have lived with these mounds. People went to the mounds to pay respect to their ancestors and on special occasions they prayed, sang, danced, played, feasted, socialized, renewed family or clan and tribal connections.[5] In this way they also re-established their religious ties and cultural foundations with others. Jacob Grimm in *Teutonic Mythology* (1844) states that old traditions and festivals adapt or continue, because they are so interwoven into the fabric of life.[6] The people of old Britain and continental Europe likewise assembled at burial places which were places of sanctuaries and ritual practices.[7] Ross in *Pagan Celtic Britain* writes:

> Death is regarded as a stage in the progression of life. This concept makes it natural for grave mounds and burial sites to serve as a focal point for ritual and for religious games in which the Celts indulged.... The burial mound, like the well, and the sea, was regarded in Celtic belief as one of the entrances to the otherworld of which the Celts were so conscious.... The so-called *sid* mounds which are a regular feature of the early Irish world, probably originated in beliefs associated with burial mounds.... It is therefore clear that the burial mound was yet another place for cult practice.[8]

Such a gathering at the mounds was an ancient practice in several cultures and was practiced more recently (before, during and after the introduction of Christianity) by the ancestors of the early British and continental European peoples whose descendants later came to the New World.[9] The mound and its significance have never left us, and its inherent attraction as a site for communal gathering is still effective and connects us with our past. We are responding to the "call of the mounds."

*   *   *

Circumambulation in Our Universal Roots

In addition to the natural pull of the central mound in the theater of action, another striking related feature of the baseball field and game is the circular and counterclockwise motion of the runners around the bases. Peter Morris in *A Game of Inches* (2006) writes, "In many of the forerunners of baseball, the bases were run clockwise. The reasons for the change are not known, but it is interesting to speculate on the consequences. Imagine how different baseball would be."[10]

Many religious rituals include circular motions about a central place during worship. Such practices began a long time ago in stone-, tree-, serpent- and sun-worshipping ceremonies. Edward Burnett Tylor in *Religion in Primitive Culture* (1873) writes:

> It is especially interesting to survey the stock-and-stone worship.... [T]here belonged the stone pillars of Baal and the wooden ashera-posts, but how far these objects were of the character of altars, symbols, or fetishes, is a riddle....
>
> There are accounts of formal Christian prohibitions of stone-worship in France and England reaching on into the early Middle Ages, which show this barbaric cult as then distinctly lingering in popular religion. Coupling this fact with the accounts of the groups of standing-stones set up to represent deities in South India, a corresponding explanation has been suggested in Europe. Are the menhirs, cromlechs, &c., idols, and circles and lines of idols, worshipped by remotely ancient dwellers in the land as representatives or embodiments of their gods?[11]

Such old worshipping practices go deep in our historical roots ranging from India to France and England. Tylor further points out that the old practices lingered on, despite the advancing strides of civilization.[12] Jane Ellen Harrison in *Ancient Art and Ritual* points out that sacred tree-worshipping (occurred along with, after or even before stone-worshipping) was done in many places and that primal man saw it as a necessity.[13] Grant Allen in *The Evolution of the Idea of God*, writes about similar observations, makes similar interpretations and notes how universal such practices were.[14] Going around the tree or stone was a way of making active supplication to the revered deity as the more recent "rain dance" or "war dance."

These constant footsteps over time marked a path that the faithful followed. Once the tree died, faithful believers still trod the familiar paths to these old stumps since they also believed that the soul/spirit of the tree still resided there. These old and revered stumps in turn gave rise to the earliest stupas, as recorded in ancient India. Even today, as in the past two millennia of Christianity, when a person is declared to be a saint the person's tomb is revered and his/her body parts become treasured relics in sacred shrines. The boundaries (paths and corners) were set to mark the path of the faithful and to separate the sacred from the ordinary as seen in the ancient Indian and Buddhist temples.[15] (Appendix E has further details.)

Trees were revered in many cultures, and such reverence and deification were almost universal to the extent that many believed they were children of particular trees.[16] An explanation of the widespread phenomenon is offered by Sir James Frazer in *The Golden Bough: A Study in Magic and Religion* (1922):

> To the savage the world in general is animate, and the trees and plants are no exception to the rule. He thinks they have souls like his own, and he treats them accordingly....
>   Sometimes it is the souls of the dead which are believed to animate the trees.... In these cases the spirit is viewed as incorporated in the tree; it animates the tree and must die with it.... Thus the tree is regarded, sometimes as the body, sometimes as merely the house of the tree spirit.[17]

These old beliefs and religions died slowly and evolved in new forms as time progressed. Frazer mentions not only the ancient premises for the worshiping of trees, but also the marriage between two trees in both India and Germany.[18] A wedding ceremony is a more joyous and festive occasion; therefore people gathered at these tree sites for both religious and celebratory rituals. The rationale for the worship and reverence of trees was to ensure fertility of crops and cattle and to procure healthy offspring. In addition, there were ritual purification and reenactments where youths were involved in ceremonies with sacrificial offerings and feasts.

In ancient India, in addition to stone and tree worship, serpent worship was common, as indicated by several early writers, including Grant Allen, William Crooke (*An Introduction to the Popular Religion and Folklore of Northern India*), John Bathurst Deane (*The Worship of the Serpent Traced Throughout the World*), Jacob Bryant (*A New System of Analysis of Antient*

[Ancient] *Mythology*) James Fergusson (*Tree and Serpent Worship*), and E. Washburn Hopkins (*Origin and Evolution of Religion*).[19] These practices were not confined to ancient India, but universal as noted by these authors. From stone-, tree-, and serpent , early people moved to sun-worshipping practices; and these co-existed, merged or were abandoned over time. These universal practices have left their impact without our knowing. (Appendix E has the details.)

* * *

Circumambulation in Our British and Continental European Roots

We shall now look to Britain and continental Europe with regard to these ancient practices of circular movements and later influences on the peoples' culture, including the foundations of baseball. Relics of tree worship survived in Britain and Europe. For example, the Maytree or Maypole was regarded as having magical powers, helping the fertility of women and cattle. Maytree bushes were set up in barns and stables at the stalls of cattle and horses.[20] The celebration of Maypole festivities, including dancing and singing around a central tree, was observed throughout Britain and Europe, but with individual variations of the basic theme and form.[21] Maypole celebrations in Britain were condemned by the Puritans as a heathen or pagan activity associated with immorality, until they were restored by the Stuarts.[22]

Trees were sacred to early British peoples, and like other European peoples, venerated the oak tree.[23] Ross writes that some regarded themselves as children of their particular revered trees, and these trees were similarly focal points for local assemblies.[24] For example, the term *bile* meant "sacred tree," *dar, derw, duir* or *drus,* "oak," and *nemeton,* "sacred grove." Other names incorporate a combination of words—for example, *Drunemeton,* "the Oak Sanctuary." Tree- and serpent-worship were often linked together or related as shown in their art.[25] Ross examines the existing evidence for the cult god depicted on the famous Danish Gundestrup cauldron in early Britain. This cult god, known as Cernunnos, is a horned creature, "Lord of the Animals," who sits in a crossed leg position with a serpent in his right hand. Ross finds that there are variations in the themes of this deity, who may be associated, among other things, with the underworld, fertility, protection of herds and flocks, treasure and the military.[26] This god on the mound, carried a square shield and a spherical stone, the picture is therefore one of a Cernunnos type of god in warrior-mode, standing on a mound ready to hurl spears or stones. Early games of throwing from a mound could have been an imitation of this god in presumed action.

Ross in her summation of "The Horned God of Britain" in *Pagan Celtic Britain*, concludes that there is evidence for a horned god in early Britain as in continental Europe.[27] There are numerous instances where serpents, snakes and dragons are mentioned in early British and continental European myths and legends, and seen on various iconographic structures.[28] Often, serpents are associated with mounds and water—wells, springs, lakes and rivers. Ross writes:

> On the whole, the evidence suggests that serpents, ram-headed, crested, aquatic, were of very considerable importance in the mythologies of both the European and the insular Celts, and that in Ireland, the comparable paucity of traditions concerning reptiles is explicable in terms of the attitude of the Church and its desire to suppress, as far as possible, all traces of the cult of the horned god and his serpent companion.
>
> The dragon is of greater importance in Welsh than in Irish tradition.[29]

The practice of serpent worship was stronger in Wales, a former hotbed of early baseball. The serpents that St. Patrick banished from Ireland are thought to be those of the cult of the serpent worshippers. Such thoughts were recorded earlier by Deane (1883).[30] He also notes the connection between tree- and serpent-worship in several cultures and comments on the similar nature of the religious or superstitious beliefs of the priesthood of the early British and continental Europeans. He contends that his British ancestors moved from serpent to serpent-solar to solar worship.[31] Deane notes that these early British and European practices were related and deeply embedded in Britain. The title of the high Druidic priest included being called an architect, a prophet and a serpent. Earlier, Jacob Bryant in *A New System of Analysis of Antient [Ancient] Mythology* (1807) notes the universality of the symbols such as serpent, bull or sun being used with regards to the same deity.[32] He traces the serpent in various depictions (e.g., single headed, two headed, winged and without an orb or sun). It is apparent that as one set of incoming religious beliefs and practices changed into or merged with a pre-existing one, the symbols and rituals likely remained the same, but with newer interpretations.[33]

Early British people like others tried to make their places of worship and rituals emulate their deity and its actions.[34] The early British colonists brought their Maypole activities to North America, but these were seen as pagan and therefore condemned by the Puritans, as is noted by, William J. Baker in *Sports in the Western World*.[35] It is notable that in this particular recorded Maypole celebration in New England, the tree was erected on a higher ground called Merry Mount. It shows that traditions die slowly, even when the early significance and meanings are long lost, the revelry, dancing and fun remain.

In addition to stone-, tree-, serpent- or sun-worshipping rituals and actions, the art and sculptures of old Britain (and its neighbors) show numerous spirals or circles which are viewed as representing the sun. Spirals (circular forms) and swastikas (crossed forms) had then or earlier symbolized the serpent or relics of serpent-worship. The familiar zigzag line used to represent lightning likewise represented a serpent before it became associated with the sun god or goddess. These symbols and their origins are discussed by John Deane and Jacob Bryant.[36] More recently (2007), this topic of serpent worship was also addressed by Philip Gardner in *Secret Societies*.[37] The ceremonies of old serpent/dragon-worship practices would likewise have involved imitations of the circular or spiral patterns of serpentine movement about a mound.[38] Such old practices were evidently brought from elsewhere since snakes in far Northern Europe including old Britain, Ireland in particular, were relatively rare. This was pointed out by Balaji Mundkur in *The Cult of the Serpent: An Interdisciplinary Survey of Its Manifestations and Origins*:

> The importance of the serpent in far northern European mythologies, however, is quite out of proportion to the actual rarity of serpents and infrequency of their attacks.... Pre-Christian ophidian traditions that survive in modern rural Swedish and other northern European domestic customs are well documented.
> The fauna of Ireland totally lacks serpents, yet the latter are depicted, alongside solar symbols, in the passage-graves of the fourth millennium BCE and antedate by at least two and a half millennia the very extensive repertory of fantastic serpents of pre–Christian Irish (and Welsh) mythology and iconography. These much later traditions stem from migrations from central Europe of a people, the Celts, who venerated serpents and gave them a prominent place in their bestiary. The most important attributes of their major god Cernunos were the stag and a ram headed serpent. Despite this, Irish, Welsh, and continental Celtic myths are replete with gory tales of heroes burning or slaying dreadful water-dwelling serpents. The symbolism of modern British folklore on serpents (or dragons) hardly reflects Christian attitudes toward heathenism, Satan, and moral evil.[39]

Serpents played key roles in early British and European societies. The fear factor was likely the driving force behind these ophidian myths and cults. It should be noted that in places where these reptiles were dangerous and feared, that a priestly class with specialist knowledge arose to handle and perform the appropriate propitiatory rites in the sacred ceremonies to these feared creatures. In addition, the priestly class, predecessors to the later Druids, would be the ones at or near the core of the religious sites directing the circumambulations. Ernest Block, in *Atheism in Christianity*, states that the snake cult, associated with the Tree of Knowledge, was not totally wiped out by Christianity showing that old beliefs and traditions die slowly.[40]

As people moved away from serpent-worship to more powerful gods, it would be expected that the newer gods have control of the feared serpent. It is therefore not surprising to see depictions in which the deity Cerunnos holds the serpent in his hand to show that he has control; or, that the Sun god has serpents pulling his chariot across the sky; or, that Jesus Christ has power over the serpents and grants such power to his believers.[41]

As the sun became the object or deity of veneration, the old religions adapted and incorporated the new incoming deity into their old cultural and social order, rites and rituals. The sun also moved in a circular pattern in the sky. Circular movements mimic the action of this sun deity, who rises in the morning, reaches overhead at midday and sets in the evening, and repeats this process daily. (See Appendix E with regards to salutations to the sun deity in India.) For example, Hu Gadarn, who was regarded as the legendary founder and hero of the Welsh people of early Britain, was deified as the sun god, Esus. Worshipping rituals included circulatory movements in mimicry of the sun's movements across the sky, and lit fires in selected or consecrated places represented the sun. For example, James Frazer in his chapter "The Fire Festivals of Europe" writes:

> In most parts of Europe the peasants have been accustomed from time immemorial to kindle bonfires on certain days of the year, and to dance round them or to leap over them. Customs of this kind can be traced back on historical evidence to the Middle ages, and their analogy to similar customs observed in antiquity goes with strong internal evidence to prove that their origin must be sought in a period long before Christianity.[42]

In the Highlands of Central Scotland, the fires lit on the First of May (called Beltane Fires) bore traces of human sacrifice as seen in the neighborhood of Collander in Pertshire in the eighteenth century.[43] The early British peoples were steeped in these practices and every sizeable community had its religious places where the people likewise danced around fires in their acts of worship and festivities. Fraser mentions one example where participants sat on a turf around the wood to be lit, and that the number of persons required to turn a square wooden frame around the axle tree was three, or multiples of three, these being nine and twenty seven.[44]

It is therefore not surprising that a game that maintains these embedded and ancient traditions of circular movements would survive in some form and be a natural draw for their descendants. This was observed when they moved to other unfamiliar lands overseas, where the comfort that traditions provide was most needed. The game's circular movements, founded on ancient religious practices of humanity, touch something deep and familiar in its participants and spectators.[45]

Religious Foundations of the Battles of the Ins and Outs

Games such as stones and stool-ball featured a person standing in a central position and throwing stones or balls to others (Chapter 2). In early British and continental European cultures, religious rituals involved perambulations about a mound, with its shaft, presided over by the appropriate personnel. Religious officials had to be in an advantageous position, and were best positioned in the center or near central location to direct rituals. In concert with British and European myths, on the circular hallowed-center resided the old deity *Cernunnos*, the "Horned One," "Lord of the Animals" and Forests, and Ruler of the Otherworld.[46] Since shafts also represented a symbolic or real portals between this world of the living and the Otherworld, then the person in the central position likewise controlled movement to both domains (the *in* and *out*, *up* and *down*) to this natural living world and the Otherworld. One side of early baseball-associated games was called the *ins* and the other the *outs*. The *ins* represented those from the Otherworld or from inside the shaft or mound, and the *outs* those outside, in the world of the living. The contests or battles were between the *ins* (hitters) trying to invade the turf of the *outs* (fielders); whereas, the *outs* tried to send the *ins* back to their world. These old terms and games together suggest that their roots lie in antiquity and were reenactments of contests between the two worlds, living and Otherworld.[47] (Appendices E and F provide more background information.)

The use of these obsolete terms *in* and *out* in the games of cricket, tutball, stool-ball and rounders, suggest a common origin or association of these games (Note 47). Portals that allowed movement, entry or exit, from one world to the other were regarded as real, in both early British European and ancient Indian beliefs.[48] Early British, European and Indian philosophies were similar in that neither world was feared since gods, peoples and Otherworld beings could transition from one to another, on certain calendar occasions. (More details in Chapter 9 and Appendices A, E and F.) Such beliefs made them fearless and willing to face death despite overwhelming odds. British myths mention there were great battles with contestants such as the incoming Tuatha de Danaan and the indigenous Fomors.[49] Likewise, Germanic and Scandinavian myths describe *Ragnorok*, the final battle between the Aesir and the Vanir gods (Appendix F).

Old Love of Man-to-Man Combat and Fair Play

Where early British and continental Europeans gathered to celebrate or commemorate an event, one can expect to find their inherent "warlike nature" coming to the forefront. For example, Ross, in *Everyday Life of the Pagan Celts*, gives us some snapshots of the strong love of single combat by the early British. In these societies, war was the norm and it was considered necessary and commendable that the young be engaged in single combat activities.[50] The young responded and aspired to be warrior-heroes.[51] Ross writes:

> War and the technique of warfare clearly had a high priority in the everyday life of the Celtic peoples everywhere. As a result we may expect strong emphasis on weapons, battle tactics and elaborate codes of honour. This predilection for battle and single combat is reflected not only in all the evidence for their daily life, but is very much emphasized in their religious tradition and cult legends. The tribal god is first and foremost a superb warrior. The semi-divine hero may stand in for the god in single combat; the god could come in and aid the semi-divine hero in similar situation.[52]

Such celebratory meetings and occasions provide avenues and opportunities for competitive games. It is easy to picture games involving throwing and hitting occurring when family or clan members gathered on these mounds, burial places, or *viereckschanzen*. When warriors met, their games would not only become more challenging with man-to-man and team-to-team combats, but more codified.[53] Ross states:

> Another important feature of Celtic warfare was the custom of fighting in single combat. There were strict Irish rules about this, and one of these was known as *fír fer,* lit: "fair play," whereby a man offering single combat should only be opposed by a single opponent.[54]

Stories of personal combat between heroes or deities are found in their myths.[55] The types of popular games expected to evolve with peoples, such as the early British, are therefore those that allow individual as well as group confrontations and rivalries. Early stool-ball games were associated with the Welsh and others of Britain and continental Europe. This inheritance, respect and importance of "fair play" in games were commented on by Chadwick, who used baseball to illustrate what this term meant.[56]

In addition, when friends and families met to commemorate the lives of warriors at burial places, they would reenact the triumphant battles of the warriors or the last battles in which the fallen heroically fought, and honorably fell. The spirits of the commemorated deceased were invited to the occasions with food, drink, music and entertainment offered. One scenario, where two teams were formed include: one team representing the deceased or residents of the Otherworld called the *ins* or *insiders* emerging from the burial mound; and the other team representing the living or this world, the *outs* or *outsiders*. Only a fiercely competitive game with a code of fair play was a fitting tribute to past heroes. Others also had games to honor past heroes and events.[57] Spalding partly captures the warrior spirit in which a baseball player's total dedication would be a fitting tribute to any hero of any time.[58]

Despite attachments and tribal loyalties of various British and related peoples, there was still respect for fair play in accordance with the unwritten rules and code under which their battles were fiercely fought. The old warrior's code of honor frowned upon cheaters or violators of their ancient rules of war and games. Today, baseball fans likewise do not condone cheaters and violators of ethical codes and principles of fair play and competition.

Return of the Throwing Combatant in the Man-to-Man Duel

In the drawings or sketches of early baseball (after the formalization of the games in America), the approximately central throwing position was defined by rectangular and later circular areas with no mounds visible.[59] It is hard to identify what varieties of the early forms of the basic game with regards to the various types of throwing existed and what died out, particularly after the New York standardization. People in search of socializing and building relationships in communal gatherings were likely to throw underhand to children and potential sexual or marriage partners. In more competitive situations harder/faster underhand or overhand throwing was likely used to meet the demands of tough participants (who wanted to prove or showcase their prowess). As seen earlier, participants had already figured that it was easier to throw from a mound or from higher ground where they often assembled and played. Each competitor in this duel tried to have the advantage. In warrior cultures (such as that of the early British, Germanic and Scandinavian), people had long figured out that throwing from higher ground would be more advantageous. The fundamental principle of "fair play" was part of their cultural heritage, and this established tradition was later encouraged as part of manliness wherever they went and in the games they played.[60]

In early baseball in America, this personal man-to-man dueling was not initially followed after standardization, as Morris points out in *A Game of Inches*:

> It appears that the intention of the Knickerbockers was for the pitchers to be the least important players on the field, their role being simply to lob fat pitches to the batter. As their name implied, they were required to "pitch" the ball in the manner of a horseshoer. Instead pitchers almost immediately began to hew out a larger role in the game, and rule makers tried in vain to reclaim the lost ground and to restore baseball to a game of hitting and fielding.[61]

In *Revel, Riot, and Rebellion: Popular Politics and Culture in England 1603–1660*, Underdown notes that ordinary people preferred the individual confrontations within the team context as in stool-ball and cricket. The people's natural inclination for personal combat within a team context was lacking and they responded as there was now hardly any competitive fairness in this duel between pitcher and hitter.[62,63] Consequently, their cultural and traditional respect for "fair play" and need for competitiveness in dueling competitions became the driving force in the search for balance in the modern man-to-man confrontations, pitcher versus hitter, in baseball. Morris outlines some of the poignant points in the history of the mound story in the American game.[64] In America, once faster overhand pitching and the role of pitchers became accepted in competitive games, modern pitchers sought to gain the advantage from the allocated distance and location of the pitcher's box. Throwing underhand would not have lived up to the "manliness" ideals set for American baseball by Spalding. In cricket, no player except the catcher uses gloves to field the ball, and can boast of being manlier. Each modern pitcher seems to have his preferences with regards to the shape and downward slope of the mound. In general, throwing the ball from a raised mound, releasing it from above the hitter's eye-level and a sharper downward angle (altogether resulting in increased velocity) are conditions that favor the pitcher and simultaneously disfavor the hitter.[65]

The distance between the combatants in the duel is another critical factor. A closer distance means less loss in velocity by the ball from the time of release from the pitcher's hand to the time it reaches the plate, and this in turn means less time for the hitter to react to a ball coming in relatively faster. The distance between the pitcher and hitter affects the time a hitter has to react.[66] Each individual differs in his reaction time to an incoming object. It took a while for the height and diameter of the mound and its distance from home plate to become standardized, and its preparation along the way became an art form.[67] The spirit and fascination of old duels between two powerful combatants returned and still lives.

An Old Running Game Influences Base Distance

Running was a competitive survival skill and sport in many cultures, places and times in the history of humankind. Determining the winner of men and women's racing competitions required that fixed lengths be used. The exact measured distance between any two markers of early inner areas or squares was also varied, and likely depended on local circumstances as seen with the variations in size and location of sites (sacred groves and rectilinear areas, *viereckschanzen.*) (Analogously, in modern baseball fields, the distances between home plate and outfield fences still vary and are often adjusted to suit local needs and preferences.) The 90-foot length from home plate to first base was instituted as the standard in American baseball in 1856.[68] Recently, Morris writes on this subject of length of 90 feet being selected.[69] A few other modern baseball commentators have claimed that it took a genius to decide on the 90-foot distance between bases. This distance lends itself to numerous close calls at first base, adding to the excitement and uncertainty of a game. This choice of dimensions was most likely influenced by another once popular old British game in which running without being caught was the key component. Hackwood (1924) mentions a game called "Prison Base" or "Prisoner's Bars" thought to be an old warrior's game.[70] This game involved the running of players 20 to 30 yards to a stake or stone before returning home, similar to today's game of capture the flag.[71] Earlier, Strutt (1838) states:

> There is a rustic game called Base or Bars, and sometimes written Bays, and in some places Prisoners' Bars; and as the success of this pastime depends upon the ability of the candidates and their skill in running…. It was much practiced in former times, and some vestiges of the game are still remaining in many parts of the kingdom.
>
> The performance of this pastime requires two parties of equal number, each of them having a base or home, as it is usually called, to themselves, at the distance of about twenty or thirty yards….
>
> About 1770, I saw a grand match at base played in the fields behind Montague House, now the British Museum, by twelve gentlemen of Cheshire against twelve of Derbyshire, for a considerable sum of money, which afforded much entertainment to the spectators. In Essex they play this game with the addition of two prisons, which are stakes driven into the ground, parallel with the home boundaries, and about thirty yards from them.[72]

Strutt mentions that this game was popular with youths as well as adults, especially in Cheshire and other adjoining counties in Britain (1770s). It had to be a very competitive running game, with some rules, since money was involved. Hackwood gives insight as to the former widespread popularity of the game as early as fourteenth-century Britain:

> Prisoners' Bars was highly popular with adult youths of Staffordshire, as it appears to have also been in other parts of the country. As early as the reign of Edward III, it was played with such zest that a proclamation was issued prohibiting it to be played in the avenues of the Palace of Westminster during the sessions of Parliament.[73]

As indicated before, Staffordshire was a former British area that retained some old traditions. This area was once likely occupied by members of the Cornovii tribe (ca. CE 50) during pre–Roman Times. Hackwood adds, "In olden times, when customs were more primitive, we can imagine grown men playing this game to while away the long summer evenings on the village greens of Staffordshire."[74] Several others including Spenser (*Faery Queen*, Book V) and Shakespeare (*Cymbeline*, Act 5, Scene 3) have referred to the widespread popularity of this game, particularly at Easter and Whitsuntide.[75] This game was therefore not only confined to Staffordshire, but was played in several other places across Britain. It is likely this game emerged from the same places and times as stool-ball and tut-ball, since it is often mentioned alongside descriptions of early British and European games. As immigrants from the Old World came to America, they also brought practical knowledge of all their pastimes and games, especially those deeply entrenched. Prisoner's base was played by early British immigrants in America. Robert Carver, writing of children's games in America, also describes the game of prisoner's base and mentions "This game may be played by five or nine on each side, and there is no objection to more or fewer players."[76] Chadwick describes prisoner's base as "one of the best of the running class of games.... Players are chosen from the swiftest runners of the crowd."[77] This once-common and thrilling British game is no longer played in Britain or in America. Block argues against the idea that it exerted "any influence on baseball's evolution," but one cannot help but notice that the distance between bases in prisoner's base—the "twenty or thirty yards" described by Strutt—is roughly the same as the standard set by baseball, whose runners would later attempt to avoid a tag, as they had in this earlier game.

*   *   *

Early British and European (Celtic, Germanic, Scandinavian and others) practices and beliefs find direct expression in baseball and other pastimes.

The drives motivating our ancestors to ritual and belief are still with us, whether they are satisfied by recognizably religious activities or by those apparently secular. Baseball satisfied this need in the American culture when it took root. David Voigt points to the demands and new-found freedoms of an increasingly industrialized United States:

> That baseball should have undergone so swift a transformation from rudimentary child's-play origins to a stage of formal organization with the feature of gentlemen's baseball clubs, and even farther, to the point where it was becoming an organized spectator sport for mass consumption, is perhaps best explained in terms of leisure revolution. It was as if the Americans needed new rituals to unify and sustain themselves in the new world of city and factory. As a sports spectacular, baseball met both challenges by providing fans with a tension-relieving spectacle of two hours' duration, played by skilled new heroes.[78]

10

Early Language, Folklore and Myths

The previous chapters point to the early British and continental European peoples, whose descendants, in particular, laid the foundations for the modern game of baseball in North America. Since known early British and continental European physical structures, practices and beliefs help to explain various aspects of the game, this search continues by looking at other aspects of British and related peoples whose languages, folklore and myths impacted the game of baseball. The findings in this chapter will help to provide a more comprehensive understanding of the conditions and histories from which baseball emerged.

One of the best ways to control the early British and neighboring peoples was to eliminate and replace their spoken and written languages.[1] Consequently, conquered peoples of Britain and continental Europe were forced to abandon their traditions, languages, and cultures, in particular those aspects perceived as a threat to the supremacy of Imperial Rome.[2] Later under the hammer of the Roman Catholic Church, old British cultures, symbols, languages and actions fell under closer scrutiny, especially when and where these were perceived as abhorrent, heathen and idolatrous. Centuries later, the Protestant Christian Church, successor of the Roman Catholic Church, was even less tolerant of surviving pagan words, practices and cultures. Over time, the net result of domination and persecution by foreign rulers and religious overlords was the abandonment of early British words of the various subdued communities with the concomitant rise to greater prominence of the tongues and cultures of their masters.

Modern baseball requires great imagination to prepare for the myriad of possibilities in every game situation. Even older and experienced coaches, players and fans are often faced with the new and unpredictable. This sense of wonder which baseball continuously provides is one of its inherent attractions. Baseball's capacity for potential growth, increasing complexity and enthralling unpredictability, are such that many devotees believe baseball was intentionally designed and adapted by imaginative and fertile minds.[3] Many terms used in early popular games, rituals and so on have found their way into common language.[4] Much of the abandoned early British words which survived the various purges have also been lost. Fortunately, over two centuries ago, Reverend William Shaw and numerous others saw the need to preserve the surviving old Gaelic and Irish words which were fast disappearing. They worked together toward the production of *A Galic* [Gaelic] *and English Dictionary* (1780).[5] This account was keeping with early British traditions of passing words and their meanings to succeeding generations. The true meanings, connotations and contexts of these survived words may still be difficult to understand; and most of the relevant words needed for this particular quest may be lost altogether. With these difficulties and limitations in mind we shall proceed knowing the rewards are worth the efforts of reconstructing this game's oldest past and foundations.

Languages of Old Places and Times

Shaw's preserved and predominantly old Gaelic words together with known folklores, tales and myths provide valuable insights into the lives of early British peoples. Moreover, their words, folklores and myths will give some answers with regards to the underlying foundations of baseball. This game reflects early British and continental European religion, culture, and philosophy. The same major rituals and beliefs were also common to a broader sphere than European peoples. Both intra- and inter-tribal interactions among various early British and continental European kingdoms were promoted by inter-tribal priests, particularly the legendary Druids.

Some of the surviving early British words and beliefs will now be examined. Unlike England and Wales, Ireland was never conquered by the Romans and only part of Scotland was under Roman rule; therefore there is a greater likelihood of old intra- and inter-tribal words, practices and cultures surviving longer in these non-militarily conquered areas. In modern times, there is still evidence of distinct cultural identities of the Irish, Scottish, and others in more isolated parts of Britain and neighboring places. In Shaw's work are found some Gaelic words which referenced these old cultural identities, for example, *goideal,* "the Gaelic tongue"; *goidhhleag,* "the Irish, Gaelic, or old Celtic tongue"; *goideal, gaoidhal,* "an Irishman, or Scotch Highlander"; and *goidhealach,* "Irish, Highland." (Throughout this chapter, old words from Shaw's compilation will be italicized, followed by their meanings.) Old Britain itself was home to several related tribes or kingdoms. The peoples of these adjacent places such as England, Wales, Ireland, Scotland, Brittany and Isle of Mann were all related, that is, in effect they were a *gaoil*, "family or kindred," or a *fine*, "a tribe, family, kindred, tribe and nation."[6]

In Shaw's work are found several words which suggest that the early language for a game as a possible tribute to a sun god existed. From this dictionary are taken a set of related old words and meanings: *raidhe, raithe*, "an umpire, an arbiter"; *raidhteachas*, "a contest, trial of skill"; *rath*, "a fortress, an artificial mound"; *ratha*, "running"; and *rathdan*, "bowling." Since the word *rath* meant an artificial mound, and *rathdan* bowling, these old Gaelic words together suggests a person was bowling, that is, throwing from a higher elevation.[7] This is much the same as today where related words often imply related meanings, e.g., bat, batter, batsmen. James Bonwick in *Irish Druids and Old Irish Religions* writes, "The round mounds, or Raths, enclosing the round dwelling, related to early sun-worship."[8] Numerous mounds occupied the British landscape. There could have been contests or trials of skills occurring in the presence of an umpire or arbiter in a possible sun-worshipping ritual.

Another set of old words include *faoghaid*, "a game, and men that start the game"; *fioghait*, "a four-square figure"; and *fiughidh*, "hero."[9] Together these words could indicate a person became a hero in this square when he plays this game in the presence of officials. These old words therefore suggest the place, game, and participants were closely intertwined.[10]

Shaw also mentions an area with an open temple being named:

> *Magh-adhraidh.* A plain or field of adoration, where an open temple, consisting of a circle of tall straight stone pillars, with a very large flat stone called a Crom-leac, serving for altar, was constructed by the Druids for religious worship. These Druidic temples, whereof many are still existing in Ireland and Scotland.[11]

Shaw notes that such places can be given a specific name, citing *Beal atha magh-adhoir* as an example and breaking the name down in this way: *Beal*, "the God Belus"; *atha*, "blast of wind"; *magh*, "field"; *adhram*, "to adore, worship"; and *adhradh, adhras*, "adoration." It was not only places which bore testimony to this particular sun god (*Beal, Belus*), but other activities and events also commemorated and honored the god's name. Some of these traditional practices have survived the centuries long enough to be remembered by participants of Shaw's eighteenth century compilation.

In Shaw's work, the importance attached to the sun god is also documented in words and practices of old Scotland and Ireland. He mentions the celebration of the fire festival, *Bealteine*, on the first of May (or May Day) in honor of *Teine Bell*, the fire of the god *Belus*.[12] These were apparent reenactments of an acknowledgement of the gift of fire from the god *Belus*. From this sacred fire other fires of the communities were rekindled once a year on May Day. The sacred fires were also believed to offer protection from diseases and misfortune. The peoples of old Scotland and Ireland, like others of Britain and continental Europe under the leadership of their priesthood, were ritually purifying themselves and protecting their animals as was previously done in ancient practices with sacred outdoor fire altars. (A similar tradition of ritual purification by fire is still maintained by Hindus.) Ward Rutherford in *Celtic Lore* writes of the deeply-embedded practice of honoring the sun in these older times:

> Fire festivals are invariably linked with the ultimate givers of life, the sun gods. This and the name *Beltaine* supports the belief that it was dedicated to *Belinus*, whose solar character is beyond doubt. We know that in Ireland, St. Patrick was condemning sun worship in the fifth century and vestiges were to be found until very recent times. In the Shetlands it was customary on May Day to look-skyward and greet the sun with the words, "Good morning and show your eye"....
> The solar connection is endorsed by the practice of circling holy wells, normally visited on this day, sunwise. However, in the Hebrides, a graveyard rather than a well was circuited and a dance ... took place.[13]

These early peoples were fully aware that the sun (or sun god) was the sustainer of life and the ultimate energy source of all living things on "Mother Earth." Like other cultures, they too were steeped in the honor and deification of the powerful sun god who was often referred to with many names, *Belus, Belenis, Beli, Beal,* and *Belteine*.[14] This acknowledgement and tribute to the glory of the sun god found expressions in religious worship, rituals and games. In such early societies, since religion, games and social practices were interrelated, some communal expressions survived as relics in activities, such as games, despite being sanitized to remove their pagan aspects and influences.

Early British and continental European peoples had different names, *Belenis, Taranis,* and *Esus,* for the sun god at different stages of its journey across the sky. Shaw's dictionary reveals several old Gaelic words and expressions existed to differentiate this daily journey of the sun.[15] Other old Gaelic words for the sun included *Tiotan, Tiothin, Telhin, Titin, Grian* and *Grioth,* thereby emphasizing the widespread recognition of the sun god amongst the various clans.[16]

* * *

Earlier, large stones or piles of stones in a circle were used to represent the sun (or its daily journey) to form altars on which offerings were made to the sun god. Bonwick mentions both residual behaviors and places of sun worship:

> When Martin was in the Hebrides, he came across observances reminding him of solar worship. "In the Island of Rona," said he, "off Ness, one of the natives needs express his high esteem of my person, by making a turn round about me sun-ways, and at the same time blessing me, and wishing me all happiness."... The Reverend MacQueen mentions that every village in Skye had a rude stone, called *Grugach,* or fair-haired, which represented the sun; and he declared that milk libations were poured into *Grugach* stones.[17]

As discussed in Chapter 4, Hackwood observes that poorer children in isolated sectors of the community of Staffordshire used stones or *tuts* as markers in their tut-ball games. These stone markers or *tuts* were likely relics of former communal worshipping. One of the early alternative names of baseball Carver mentions in *The Book of Sports* is "Goal Ball." This is similar to the old Gaelic word *gaoil,* "family, kindred, love." Another similar old Gaelic word is *goal,* "love, liking, fondness." This name of "Goal Ball," synonymous with one early term "Base Ball," now suggests family members, relatives and kindred were involved and possibly playing against other families and clans, especially at their family and festive occasions.

Shaw writes old Gaelic words *base,* "red, round," and *ball,* "a spot, mark, a place; a ball, globe; a weapon, member, a cable."[18] Together *base* and *ball* suggest a rounded place or marked spot, where a red and spherical ball was used.[19,20] Another interpretation is that the game was played in a circular or rounded place like a ball or globe representing the sun or moon. Carver also mentions another earlier name for baseball was "round ball." The word Gaelic *base* literally means "round," as well as indicating the possible nature of the activity therein, such as running in a circular manner. As seen above, the old Gaelic word *ball* had several meanings that easily suggest a rudimentary baseball-like game being played in a circular area marked by a cable or path. The use of the color red (blood) is consistent with the idea that in earlier times sacrifices were also performed at the bases. The old Gaelic word *ball* was also used to mean both a weapon and a person who used that weapon; these meanings were in keeping with early developmental stages of the game.

Other old Gaelic words such as *caoin, suirach,* "a base" show some relationship. The word *caoin* is similar to the words *cuainn,* "a corner," and *cruinn,* "a round area." The word *suirach,* "a base," suggests an obvious connection with the sun or sun-worship and a base. Old Welsh words *sail* and *sylfaen,* "a base," also indicate their derivations from words for the sun. These old words suggest an association with a place or round area and its connection with the sun.

Additionally, old Gaelic *bas*, "death," has some possible implications. The name *Beul* or *Beal* refers to the same sun god.[21] Interestingly, when *bas* and *Beul* are put together, they sound like baseball. This *Bas Beul* as "Death by or for *Beul*" would be a more accurate description of the original purposes accompanied by sacrificial rituals in early baseball like games.

The second given meaning of *bas*, *bos*, "the palm of the hand," suggests this area or activity, *Bas Beul*, was in "the palm of the hand of *Beul*." In this sense the sun god, held human destiny and all Earth like a ball in "the palm of his hand."[22] This interpretation means that "baseball" is simply a game or ritual: "In the Hands of God *Beul*."

Alternatively, the second meaning of *bas* or *bos*—i.e., "the palm of the hand"—may simply indicate that in one version of the game, the palm of the hand was used to hit the ball. Using the palm of the hand represented a simpler version of the game as seen in descriptions of tut-ball, whereas in the more sophisticated versions a hitting instrument (club, staff, bat, or weapon) was used.[23] Piecing together the origins of baseball is challenging, but what stands out is the religious connections.

* * *

Belenis or *Beli* was the rising sun god and healer. On an outspreaded branch of the revered oak tree, *Belenis* would be symbolically represented by third base side.[24] The morning sun was believed to have healing and curative properties. The sun rises in the east to *tuis*, *tus*, or "begin," its *tur*, "daily," journey across the *speur*, "sky." Secondly, *Taranis* the *Thunderer* was the mysterious sky god, sometimes called the god of the wheel analogously located on the middle branch of an oak, representing the midday sun, i.e., second base.[25] Thunder accompanied with lightning created burning trees which were sources of life-giving fire.[26] Thirdly, *Esus*, "Lord," was the high god who *fuin*, or "ended," his journey in the western sky and went down into the western sea. *Esus* would be represented with a location on the right branch of an oak, or first base.[27] The gods were thought to live in or play near the top of tall trees which represented the houses of gods and deities. The tree's crown represented the daily path of the sun in its journey across the sky.

* * *

Shaw also mentions *solus*, "a round ball thrown in the air in honor of the sun," and *solas*, "comfort, consolation, vast pleasure; applied to the intellect."[28]

Solas or *solus*, likely referred to a religious ceremony honoring the sun or sun god, the ball rising would have represented the morning sun, at its peak height midday or noon, and sinking the setting sun.[29] Any tribute to the sun god with its religious significance would be done as perfect as humanly possible, both in appearance (red or white ball in appearance as different colors of the sun through the day) and in its path travelled (hemispherical or rainbow like).[30]

The second meaning of the old Gaelic word, *solas*, suggests this past tribute to the sun god's activity was full of "vast pleasure," and indicates more than mere enjoyment of sunrises and sunsets were involved. Old Gaelic words *sol*, *sul*, "sun," shows derivative words associated with solar-related activities.[31] Examples are *solafach*, "full of pleasure"; *suiridh*, "courtship and wooing"; and *solafaim*, "to comfort and console." A tribute to the sun god was also not only a comforting and consoling activity, but pleasure and associated sexuality were aspects in early games, such as tut-ball, baseball, and stool-ball. This connects them with early sun-worshipping and games.

The solar rites were ways of seeking the blessings of the sun god on personal relationships, and to find comfort from earthly problems. In addition, this ball-game activity is described as *solas*, "applied to the intellect," perhaps implying that their ball game was emotionally, physically and spiritually enjoyable as well as being "intellectually stimulating."[32]

* * *

Whether facing north or south, our perception of the sun is east to west in a clockwise direction. In earlier games, players ran in both clockwise and counter-clockwise directions. As it got closer to modern times (pre–American migration), running in an anti-clockwise direction prevailed. In the Christian-dominated era, clockwise directional movement was likely reminiscent of pagan-worshipping acts or a continuation of ritual tributes to a pagan sun god, *Beul* or *Belus*.[33] The importance of this direction of movement is supported by John Brand in *Popular Antiquities*:

> When a Highlander goes to bathe, or to drink waters out of a consecrated fountain, he must always approach by going round the place *from East to West on the South side* in imitation of the apparent diurnal motion of the sun. This is called in Gaelic going round the right or the lucky way.[34]

Early British peoples had customs in which the dead in funeral services were first carried sun-wise to burial sites, a boat setting sail must first go sun-wise, after a marriage ceremony the couple must turn sun-wise, and in any desired prosperous venture the first movement is sun-wise.[35] This first movement of peoples from east to west, in a clockwise direction, was well-entrenched in these early societies. As a way of honoring the sun, it is therefore not surprising that this pattern of movement was also deeply rooted in their games.

It is likely that as the game was sanitized and Christianized to remove obvious relics and traces of pagan sun god worshipping, the sun-wise direction of running in rituals and games was avoided or reversed.

Shaw (1780) notes *solus* or *solas*, the old game and its religious significances were no longer in vogue by 1780. The ball game was already fully sanitized or cleansed of its older religious connotations.

The old Gaelic word *sul*, "the sun and the eye," indicates a connection between the two meanings.[36] Societies of the early British peoples with their Druidic priesthood standing among the oak trees of a sacred grove looked at their places of worship and saw what appeared to them as an eye.[37] Areas with sunken shafts through which light entered the domains of the Otherworld were analogous to light entering an eye.[38] An eye represented the sun keeping watch over earth.[39] Here the symbolic depiction of an eye representing the sun, about the center of a sacred area, tracked the movement of the above deified sun.[40] Eyes like the sun awake, smile, captivate, glare, and sleep. The eye was also an ideal symbol to represent the desire that society's eyes look toward the sun god. A dot in a circle was a symbol of the sun as well as an eye, and sometimes an eye itself was another symbol for the sun. In today's game, we say "keep your eyes on the ball," but early sun worshippers were more likely asked to "keep your eyes on the sun."

Ward Rutherford (*Celtic Lore*) writes that in Shetlands, Scotland, an old May Day practice was to look and greet the sun with the words, "Good morning and show your eye."[41] The eye of a sacred circle or square greeted the sun. It was noted earlier that circles around the bases were designated as "safe areas" in some places. These circles originally may have also represented smaller "eyes," tracking and representing the sun god at sunrise, midday and sunset, respectively.[42] The game, as a tribute to the sun, was and still is, best enjoyed in sunlight and played outside in the house the sun built.[43] Indeed, enclosures in the Highlands were called *Grianan*, or the House of the Sun.

Such old words survived not only in a few remote places in early Britain, but also in other areas. A publication, *The Anti-Jacobin Review and Protestant Advocate*, volume X (1801), edited by John Richards Green and John Gifford, states:

> Thus *Heul, Syl* is the sun in Cornish. *Haul, Heyle, Heyluen* in Welsh are the sun, as *Sul* is the Sunday. *Soil-bheim* in Irish is a flash or bolt of light; a thunder-bolt. *Solas, Solus* is light, *Sul* the sun, *Dia Suil* the Sunday, *Suil* the eye, *Sulbeim* is a bewitching by the eye; *Sul* in the Armorick is Sunday, *Sul Pafk* is Easter Sunday, *Suliou* are Sundays, *Ur-Suluez* is a Sunday's journey. *Heule,* Welsh to bask in the sun or to shine as the sun or to shine in general.[44]

The old words for sun and an eye were similar in peoples of older communities of early Britain (Scotland, Cornwall and Wales) and neighboring Brittany.[45] The "Armorick" mentioned above referred to the former country of Brittany or Armorica, now the southwest part of France. The quotation also shows that Sunday, the first day of the week, was named in honor of the sun. Shaw mentions that there were regional variations in the pronunciations and consequently the spellings of words overlap, but with similar meanings. In communities that were closely related and adjacent to each other, these variations in words are accounted for by natural boundaries and limits to traveling. Often ordinary people were confined to live and work in their parishes; for example, the Reverend Addy (1891) defines his parish of Sheffield, England as reaching the counties of York and Derby.[46] He mentions that with no natural barriers the dialects within a five- or six-mile radius were not significantly different, but beyond ten-miles, the dialects began to change.[47]

The impact of the sun on the lives of early British and continental Europe pervaded religious, social and game rituals.[48]

* * *

The worshipping of the sun and its influence on adoring societies extended beyond early Britain and continental Europe where the sun god was similarly identifiable and named. Charles Squire in *Celtic Myth and Legend* writes:

> The summer solstice was also a great Celtic feast. It was held at the beginning of August in honour of the god called *Lugus* by the Gauls, *Leug* by the Gaels, and *Lleu* by the Britons—the pan-Celtic Apollo, and probably, when the cult of the war-god had fallen from its early prominence, the chief figure of the common Pantheon....
> The same great Gods were, no doubt, adored by all the Celts not only in Britain and Ireland, but of all Continental Gaul as well. Sometimes they can be traced right across the ancient Celtic world.[49]

Lugus or *Lugh* was a triune god consisting of *Esus*, *Toutatis*, and *Taranis*. *Lugus* also meant light in the common language of early British and related peoples. Peter Beresford Ellis in *The Druids* offers more details about the widespread impacts of *Lugh*.[50] *Lugus* was equated with the Roman god Mercury or the Greek god Hermes. The god *Lugus* had a wide following in the ancient European world. For example, in Ireland, *Lugus* was viewed as skilled in the arts; and in other places, he was also responsible for trade, commerce, and travel. Many early British and Continental European tribes were warlike peoples and honored their god of war in games and war preparations.[51]

In Shaw's work, related terms are defined as *leus*, "a light, a ray or beam or blink of light," and *leug*, "a diamond, a precious stone, a jewel."[52] Note that the diamond shape can also be viewed as representing an eye and would be an appropriate representation of a sun deity. Stones and rocks would have been used to define areas, called a "diamond," where the god *Leug* was worshipped. In addition, early British people believed that diamonds had curative properties against diseases; their Druidic priests also used them as ornaments to display the authority of their office.

This "diamond" was a powerful symbolic shape. George Frederick Kunz in *The Mystical Lore of Precious Stones* (1915) writes: "The diamond was often associated with and was sometimes believed to owe its origin to the thunderbolt."[53] This meant it was thought the sun god, the "Thunderer," was responsible for the formation of diamonds. Like fires, diamonds were thought to be gifts from the sun god. Diamonds were also thought to have reproductive powers, to be either male or female and nurtured by the dew of heaven.[54]

The "diamond-shaped" appearance of a sacred square, viewed from an entry point behind the sacred square would have been a perfect place for the early British and continental Europeans to pay homage to the tri-cephalic god, *Leug*.

*   *   *

Any place of former pagan worship, associated with fertility rituals, was a necessity to secure health and continuation of people, animals and crops. This need for union and balance between male gods (usually for war, sky and tribe) and female goddesses (fertility, earth, and locality) was strong. Lewis Spence in *The Mysteries of Great Britain* comments on the writings and teachings of Myfyr Morganwg (the late nineteenth century Arch-Druid in Wales— "The Druids of Pontypridd") and Owen Morgan ("Morien") with regards to the value of these sources for early British peoples' folklore.[55] With their limitations in mind, folklore can be useful in revealing our hidden past and providing some insights into understanding our present thoughts and actions. Spence summarizes and comments on the writings of Owen Morgan with regard to Triads of the sun and the Earth as three males and three females, respectively.[56] Spence writes:

> The whole earth was known as *Buarth Beirdd*, or the *Bovine Bardic Enclosure*. That is, the earth's fertility was symbolized by a white cow and the generating sun by a white bull. The Avanc or Beaver is said to have been drawn ashore by Hu Gadarn, and typified the sun disappearing every evening in the western seas. There were three cows and three bulls employed as symbols by the Druids in their sacred cattle-pen or circle.[57]

The *buar*, "oxen," was the standard of Hu Gadarn, the legendary founder of Wales, who was later regarded as the sun god.[58] The fertility of "Mother Earth," represented by a white cow, needed the energy of the sun, represented by a white bull. In these rituals, Druidic priests used three cows and three bulls to represent different stages of the sun, and enhance the chances of reproductive successes for the benefit of the community.[59,60] This type of ritual ceremony also seems to be a blending of two major philosophies, the incoming and often dominant Indo-European male sun god and female Earth Mother Goddess, with that of the mainly female older Earth Mother Goddess of pre–Celtic peoples of early Britain. The Mother Goddess concept was almost universal and her incorporation in this sacred pen or circle is natural. Peter Gelling and Hilda Ellis Davidson in *The Chariot of the Sun* add that humans often played a vital part in such ceremonies acting in the roles of the gods and goddesses.[61] Evidence of similar situations were found as occurring in Mohenjo-Daro in ancient India.[62,63]

The creation myths of many cultures include divine beings often visiting human beings (and animals) and mating with them to produce semi-divine or superhuman beings to aid humankind. In the case of these rituals, there is the continuous enactment of ritual creation myths by priests, kings and heroes with priestesses, queens and virgins. In established communities, such ritual re-enactments occurred in special and dedicated places (e.g., *Bovine Bardic Enclosure*, "cattle-pen or circle"). These rituals overlapped with those of the sun's daily journey involving circular paths and movements.

*   *   *

Gods of the Sun and Underworld

In addition to *Lugh* and *Belinus*, another major patron god of old Britain and Continental Europe was Dagda, the "Good God" and "Lord of Life and Death." Dagda was also known as the *Eochaidh Ollathair*, or "Great Father," and *Ruath Rofthesa*, or "Mighty One of Great Knowledge." He was regarded as Lord of the Underworld and Knowledge, a great magician and artisan, controller of weather, crops and fertility, and a musician who played a sacred oak harp, which brought joys, sorrows and dreams. This deity was most renowned for two attributes, his magnificent war club and his cauldron. Dagda the great warrior, regarded as "The Good Striker," wielded his war club and with one swing destroyed his foes, as many as nine men. The other end of the same club on touching the fallen, healed the injured or revived the dead. When dragged, Dagda's club left a deep track behind on the earth. His cornucopia-like cauldron was a source of food. Dagda was also Lord of a *sid*, or "mound." Dagda's attributes and skills made him the favored god of the old Druidic priesthood of early Britain and elsewhere.[64] Since Dagda was both a "Good Striker" and "Lord of a Mound," then we can expect a fitting tribute on a mound to this triune god as well.

These two popular deities, Dagda and *Lugh*, had many worshippers in early Britain and continental Europe. The worship of either one of them would in all likelihood have been incorporated in their sacred rituals in places such as groves and temples, as seen earlier for the triune sun god, *Esus, Taranis* and *Teutates*. The most likely place for Dagda and *Lugh* to be represented in a sacred square would a place marking the beginning and end (home plate— cornucopia, and great striker), or on the mound itself (entrance and exit to the underworld) at the central point of focus befitting major deities. As the gods *Esus, Taranis* and *Teutates, Lugh* and Dagda shifted or merged with another, their powers, attributes and domains become enmeshed.

* * *

Early British and continental European peoples believed in the significance of the numbers three, its multiples, and four. These numerical features were deeply entrenched in their societies including their religious structures, beliefs and practices.[65] In addition the triune sun god, *St. Brigit* was once a triune goddess of fire and water.[66] The same goddess with similar names and functions was *Brigandu* in Brittany, *Brigantia* in England, *Brigid* in Ireland, and *Bride* in Scotland. One *St. Brigit* was associated with culture and poetry, one with healing, midwifery and sacred wells, and one with fire, smith-work and other crafts. The vocabulary in Shaw's dictionary shows several words for the number three such as, *triur, teoir* and *teora*.[67] It can be expected that this old cultural and societal absorption with numbers was incorporated in games, sports, and recreational activities.[68] Use of three-fold views of god has precedent with ancient Indians and others.[69,70]

Anne Ross and Don Robins in *The Life and Death of a Druid Prince: The Story of Lindow Man, an Archaeological Sensation* make a convincing case that the Lindow man, a likely British prince, suffered a triple death (a blow, strangulation, and drowning) as an offering to the triune gods or goddesses for help to defeat the invading Romans.

Even though the sacrificial and religious aspects of these rituals changed and became folk games, three acts were still required to produce a symbolic kill. The sacrificial traditions associated with games mimicked their former religious practices. David Block notes that the "three strikes required for an out" rule dates back as far as can be traced even in the earliest related games, such as "kit-cat" and trap-ball.[71] In 1887, the number of strikes for an out was changed to four, but promptly changed back to three for the 1888 season.

Three outs would be the expected intuitive choice to end an inning in early ball-games and was likely brought over to early communities in America. The New York Knickerbockers Club adopted this rule from various versions of related baseball games being played at the time. Earlier exact origins are unclear, but the rule was quickly accepted with lack of opposition. The proponents of Boston's or Massachusetts' game, who were opposed to other New York-imposed rules, did not reject this New York-implemented rule, or it was already known to them.[72]

It is now easier to understand the significance of three bases representing gods and goddesses in triplicate forms and rituals ending after three sacrificial offerings, corresponding to three outs per inning, one half-cycle of events. After three outs per inning, the roles of gods and goddesses switched, as in ancient Indian sacrificial ceremonies (early British *heaving* or *lifting* traditions, and Appendix E).

As discussed above, the sun and worshipping of the sun god were regarded as essential to early British peoples' survival, and relics of these worshipping rituals have survived in baseball. Several early British and continental European symbols for the sun, sun-worshipping ceremonies and places can still be expressed in baseball: the dot in the center of a circle, represented by a central area with or without a mound in the infield; the solar cross or solar wheel, represented by the four bases in the infield circle when opposite bases are joined diagonally; and the curved swastika, derived from the solar cross, the solar wheel of the sun god's chariot in motion, represented by the circular movements around the bases.[73] The solar cross is equivalent to two pieces of wood which when rubbed together produced fire, like the sun god. The swastika, an ancient Indian symbol, also represented two pieces of wood with each having handles at the ends; these more easily handled sticks produced fire when rubbed.

Circular movement is often expressed pictorially as a spiral, and in triplicate form three such circles are joined in one continuous path from the smallest innermost circle through the middle to the largest outermost circle. The distinctive triple spiral (*triskele* or *triskelion*) is regarded as both an early British and pre–British symbol. There are various suggestions as to what the triple spiral means, the most common being that it represented the sun and its rotation around a central point.[74] For example, one *triskelion* symbol for the sun (seen on the flag of the Isle of Man, an island in the geographical center of the British Isles) depicts three legs running in a clockwise direction.[75] There are versions of these spirals which once conveyed different meanings of the sun and its motions to the early British and continental European peoples. Loosely wound anti-clockwise spirals were thought to have represented the summer sun, whereas tightly wound clock-wise spirals, the winter sun. This indicates the importance of directional movements to these early peoples, and the likelihood of such mimicry being expressed in their rituals. In addition, the spirals may suggest that their physical representations in sacred sites created varied distances between altars in summer and winter.[76] This may well be an explanation for the varying distances of 60 to 90 feet between bases seen in some early British games. In their philosophical views, these movements and orbits of the sun correspond to an expanding and contracting universe, in line with other more ancient Indian beliefs.[77]

* * *

As mentioned above, some of the early British and continental gods were represented as being three-headed, but multi-headed statues with nine and eighteen heads were also found. The use of nine, like the number three, would likewise also be represented in their ancestral cultures including games. There are nine players per baseball team and nine innings per game, choices likely also based on old myths and traditions. Nine is a sacred number, often marking the beginning and end of all things in the myths of various world cultures.[78]

The number nine is also well documented in early British and European renewal and regeneration myths. Consider, for example, that (1) after nine years, a Scandinavian king's rule may be terminated if the omens for continued prosperity were unfavorable[79]; (2) nine men using nine different types of wood and rubbing two pieces of oak lit the new year's renewal fires of the Beltane "Fires of Beli" festival in England and Wales[80]; (3) the breath of nine maidens continuously heat the cauldron of the Lord of the Otherworld that was the desire of King Arthur's quest; (4) nine virgins perpetually attended the fire of Brigit or Bride, a powerful goddess once invoked widely over the early pagan British world. Brigit in Christian times was venerated as Saint Brigit of Kildare.[81]

In addition to the number nine being mentioned in myths of renewals, there are other events where the number nine plays a role. According to another British legend, the most sacred spring, shaded by nine hazel trees contained the wisdom of the world, where the salmon of knowledge lived. These salmon gained their knowledge by feeding on fallen hazel nuts and whoever ate the salmon became blessed with their knowledge.[82] Dagda, the "Good God" of the old British and others, carried a war club that could kill nine men with a single blow.[83] Kai or Sir Kay of Welsh mythology, a senior warrior in King Arthur's court, was regarded as having magical powers; he could go without sleep for nine days and nine nights, and also stay under water without breathing for nine days and nine nights. There are several old Gaelic words for nine and ninth.[84] According to Hinduism, the body has nine apertures or gates, two at each of the ears, eyes, and nostrils, and one at the mouth, sexual organ and anus.

The essence of modern baseball, a nine-inning game, mirrors its early British and European origins. Knowlson (*Origins of Popular Superstitions*) cites the work of Sir John Sinclair's *Statistical Account of Scotland* (1794) describing the customs performed on the first of May. The rites included a ritual shared meal which included a cake with nine square knobs, with each knob representing an animal or entity responsible for the wellbeing of crops and livestock. These offerings are flung, while facing backwards, into a central fire while invocations are made to appease a particular entity or guardian animal.[85] Analogously, each inning in baseball is a symbolic sacrificial-offering of three members of the opposing team to the gods. The same work mentions that one person was ritually sacrificed by jumping through the flames and this victim was considered physically dead and not to be mentioned as alive for a year.

In British peoples' myths, *Morgan the Fate* was at one time honored as the nine-fold goddess whose domain was the *Fortunate Isles*, a place reserved for dead heroes. Shahrukh Husain writes in *The Goddess*:

> *Morgan the Fate* (Celtic, *mor*, sea) was only reduced to the status of a wicked sorceress when the Arthurian cycles were transcribed by medieval Christian clerics. Nimue, the "Lady of the Lake," is sometimes thought to be a personification of Morgan; she was the arbiter of Arthur's success as a monarch, and his savior in death.[86]

Early British folklore and myths provide strong reasons for the selection of the number nine as the number of battles or innings which should be fought between the *ins* and *outs*.[87] The goddess, *Morgan the Fate*, waited to welcome heroes after death, and the courageous and valiant efforts of warriors were therefore rewarded. This predisposition to the number nine was also in Scandinavian beliefs. For example, the god Odin hung on a tree for nine days, and the warrior band of the Valkyries (Odin's handmaidens or "choosers of the slain") operated in groups of nine on the battle field.[88] Ancient Indian practices likewise placed emphasis on the number nine.[89] (Further details are found in Appendix E.)

There is little doubt about the religious, social and mythical significance of the number nine in early British, continental European and Indian cultures.

A complete modern day Major League Baseball game requires twenty-seven outs, unless ending before the bottom of the ninth. The goal of any pitcher is to pitch a perfect game of twenty-seven straight outs without anyone reaching first base safely. This is the magical feat or the "Holy Grail" of any aspiring or professional baseball pitcher.

The number of players per team similarly has roots in insular British and continental European cultures. Johnson and Elsbeth in *The Grail Castle* write:

> Finn MacCool was the leader of a warrior band called the Fiana or Finians. He and his men protected Ireland against invaders and perils. The physical training necessary to become a member of the Finians was arduous. A candidate had to be buried up to his knees in a pit and armed only with a shield and a wand of magic hazel, to ward off nine warriors who attacked him with spears. He had to run through the forest, pursued by other Finians; not only must he avoid being caught, he must not break a single branch of the forest. In addition to these physical requirements, there were ethical ones: A Finian had to renounce his clan or family and dedicate his energies to the brotherhood, he had to be a bard as well as a fighter, he could not refuse hospitality to anyone, never turn his back in battle, and never be cruel or insulting to women.[90]

The analogy of a Finian being tethered and fighting nine others is similar to what one now sees in modern baseball, where a hitter has to face nine opponents in each confrontation while initially confined to a batter's box, and then run through a gauntlet to get home safely. It seems that codes and standards of an esteemed and respected warrior were set a long time ago in myths.[91] Finn MacCool, the prototype of an exceptional warrior, serves as a model for any aspiring great baseball player. Training to become a Finian was a long and arduous process similar to what is usually required to become a great baseball player in Major League Baseball. Moreover, those wanting to join the Druidic priesthood of early Britain had to undergo even more arduous training. Elder writes that each theological student underwent an arduous training for nine years, which involved examinations, after every three years.[92] Training of early British military, civil and religious leaders was therefore rigorous.[93] This long and rigorous training is analogous to that of drafted players today who progress through thorough screenings from Single A to Double A to Triple A. Many players are eliminated during this arduous selection process.[94] The situation in MLB, i.e., the transitions from rookie (three years) to young player (six years) to veteran (nine years) is also analogous to the long and difficult journey undertaken by an apprentice to become a professional priest of old. Baseball is the only game where young players undertake such a long period of training before being ready for professional leagues.[95]

The preserved old languages and myths of early Britain and continental Europe show sophisticated old words linking fertility, religious and social rituals which later re-surfaced to produce a sanitized game still encompassing core beliefs. These peoples have ingeniously designed intellectually pleasurable and stimulating places where they met as sun god worshippers. Though the true meanings of early rituals may forever elude us, their vestiges live on in a game we have come to view as our own.[96]

We, like our ancestors, are responding to inner social imperatives to assemble and participate in comforting rituals, but we assemble for our own and societal well-being and enjoyment of our heroes.

11

Superstitions and Traditions

The evolution of and adaptations made by humans in our survival and cultural development are reflected in the early foundations of baseball. Over time, early peoples and their descendants incorporated war maneuvers, religious structures, philosophical beliefs, fertility rituals, and entertainment into their games. Early British and continental European peoples were deeply religious as seen in their legends, myths and structures.[1] These religious natures were part of their survival strategies, adaptations and practices to appease feared or loved gods, and local deities thought to reside in special places, plants or animals.[2] Old beliefs were eliminated, lay dormant, and melded with new and approved practices.[3,4]

Despite being a sophisticated, philosophical and intellectual game, there are many embedded superstitions prevalent in baseball.[5] In addition, a closer look at game participants including players, coaches, spectators and media personnel reveal there are numerous entrenched beliefs in taboos, rituals, omens, signs, luck and lucky charms. These observations seem particularly odd, when viewed in the light of modern advanced science and technology.[6] The superstitious nature of both baseball and its participants lies in the very foundations and structures of the game.

Early British and continental peoples believed unseen forces, deities, spirits, luck or fate played a major hand in determining outcomes of communal events (war and games), as well as individual destinies.[7] People sought to deal with the uncertainties of life by observing taboos and restrictions, performing appropriate religious rituals, heeding and interpreting forewarning omens, making sacrificial or votive offerings, and taking preventative actions such as wearing protective talismans and jewelry.[8] These necessary actions were taken on the advice of the professional, military, cultural and religious hierarchies of their civil societies and priesthoods, including the legendary and respected Druids. These precautions were executed to ensure and enhance the survival and happiness of individuals, families, clans, and tribes. Such ancestral responses are still expressed today, even though they seem irrational and quaint. Superstitions provide a time-machine for travelling back into the past to glimpse how early peoples coped with forces beyond their control.

As science and technology advanced providing rationalizations for previously misunderstood natural phenomena, the number and extent of superstitions or formerly cherished religious and societal beliefs and fears decreased.[9] Consequently, the tenacious hold of superstitions lessened both with time and succeeding generations. Alternatively, some old superstitions were replaced with newer beliefs and doctrines. For example, under Roman control, Roman gods replaced early British gods in religious services. Chicken entrails, used in ceremonies to learn the will of the gods or divining the future, replaced the use of human entrails and heads. Later under the teachings of Christianity, the ultimate sacrifice of Jesus Christ, on the cross, negated the need for any further sacrificial offerings for human transgressions.

Knowlson writes on the roles of superstitions in societal evolution and points out that superstitions were based on ignorance allied with fear.[10] Early British and related peoples likewise believed spirits or local deities (benign or malicious) lived within everything, and that necessary and appropriate actions must be taken to placate or avoid offending these supernatural entities.[11] Knowlson mentions the superstitious nature of even well-educated and trained minds of their own times and that the passing on of old beliefs, often unedited and unquestioned, to succeeding generations occurred in all societies. Sometimes, members of modern societies still think it is prudent not to take unnecessary chances by avoiding superstitions, just in case, as seen today with the practice of "knocking on wood" with our knuckles to avoid evil or misfortune.[12]

Raymond Lamont Brown writes:

> Every religion has tended to accumulate superstitions, until the word has now, ambiguously, come to include peripheral beliefs. Caius Cornelius Tacitus (55–*circa* 120), for instance, said that Christianity was a pernicious superstition, while Constantine (*circa* 272–337), Emperor of Rome, called paganism superstition. Christians would regard aboriginal totem worship as superstition, while those aboriginals might equally well look upon the veneration of Christian saints' relics as superstitions.[13]

Therefore, whether or not a set of chosen or inherited beliefs is viewed as religion or superstition, they had major impacts on their believers and cultural, societal and technological development.[14] Brown continues:

Nevertheless, the study of superstitions is of great importance ... for they reflect thought patterns of very ancient times; beliefs once tenaciously held which are now either forgotten, changed completely, or but remnant shadows in the mind.

Carefully assessed, superstitions throw light on the history of our ethnic groups and help to understand the thought processes of our ancestors in relation to our own.[15]

Surviving or adapted superstitions exerted strong influences on rituals and practices which emerged in early folk games and predecessors to baseball.[16] The superstitious routines and rituals of baseball have their origins in early British and continental European peoples' beliefs and practices.

* * *

In addition, the leadership of these early British and continental European peoples were reluctant to have their religious secrets exposed via written records. The religious natures of these peoples may have died very slowly, but it seems they have also been recorded and stored in their descendants' memories for safekeeping and withdrawal at appropriate occasions and times. The early British and European peoples may yet prove that the best way of recording a people's past is via oral history and their own trusted people. F. Marian McNeill in *Scotland: A Description of Scotland and Scottish Life* gives a general idea of old religious beliefs and practices that have passed into history as superstitions or enchanting and fascinating folklore, as in the Beltane festival, May Day, Halloween and bonfires.[17,18] McNeill points out that these formerly religious rituals, including the Beltane festival, have continued and retained their hold upon the early British people despite the acceptance of Christianity and the passage of centuries of time.[19]

In early Eastern religions and related practices, it was and still is in some cases, customary to pray at sunrise and sunset. These devotees pay due reverence to their supreme deity, who originally was the sun god. One such symbol is seen when the arms are raised with palms facing the sun, the thumbs and two index fingers of the opened hands touch. The net effect is that of an approximately four-sided diamond-shaped ($\Diamond$) figure. Through this diamond-shaped figure the worshipper viewed the sun and sky. In some Eastern martial arts forms such as Japanese Kyokushin Karate, one advanced kata, *Kanku Dai*, begins with this traditional sky-gazing symbol, *Kanku*.[20] As Eastern monasteries and centers of learning paid tribute to the sun or sun god in their religious practices and martial-arts teachings, early British and continental European peoples similarly honored their sun god. This may have provided a partial justification for a shift of the central area to one corner of the field so a diamond shape was more approximately obtained when viewed from behind the place that marked the beginning and end of a journey, i.e., home plate. This was likely another way of denoting to all that this place was intended to honor the sun god.

* * *

Early British and European peoples viewed the whole scene from behind the sacred area (home plate), and saw what appeared as a diamond, a powerful symbol with positive attributes. The imaginative priesthood must have thought that a diamond was produced by the sun god and it thrived when nourished with sacred dew, also produced by the sun god.[21] The importance of a diamond was further justified in that it was thought to have special talismanic properties. George Frederick Kunz records that a diamond was thought to have such powerful talismanic properties that even gods and monarchs (considered as gods' representatives on earth) were unable to counteract its protective powers.[22] In olden times, the *Droch Shúil* or "Evil Eye" was much feared since it was thought some persons of evil intent with mere malicious looks could bestow harm and misfortune upon others.[23] But the destructive powers of the Evil Eye were neutralized by the greater protective powers of a diamond.[24] Individuals took matters in their own hands by wearing diamonds as a precautionary method of protection against the Evil Eye. Earlier, Indian princes and princesses wore diamonds in the middle of their foreheads as a charm against evil. People of Northern India also wore lampblack to ward off the Evil Eye and for protection against eye infections.[25]

In early British societies, beliefs in the powers of the Evil Eye were strong, and had a long ancestry. In response to the need to provide some relief and antidotes to ever present evil forces, such as the Evil Eye, Brown writes:

> Since the Bronze Age the profusion of semi-precious stones to be found in Scotland led to a regular commercial intercourse between Scotland and Ireland, the latter a country rich in superstitions from very early times. To combat the dreaded Evil Eye, Scotland exported stones dipped in sacred peat water and fashioned amulets in great numbers wherever veins of quartz were found among the hills.[26]

Scottish craftsmen, whose work was deemed essential to health and fortune, were highly regarded and given special social status in their societies.[27] Individuals of these societies took to the wearing of these stones or gems as charms for protection against evil.[28]

It was not only individuals who needed protection against evil bewitching powers, but the entire local population. The early British and European priesthood offered this protection to individuals as well as their local and tribal communities. The priests designed the shapes of religious places as protective devices for the entire group. Each sacred enclosure, a square, oval, or diamond, was in effect an outdoor talisman which guarded the local neighborhood against evil.[29] Intra- and inter-tribal rivalries also involved priests or "wise-men" of one community casting spells on rival communities for real or perceived wrongs.[30] Early temple grounds which were later used in folk games were originally guardians of local communities from evil and other bewitching powers. Most communities had at least one such religious site that also offered its protection.

Each sacred enclosure's inner space or "diamond" also doubled as an eye or a representation of an eye, which kept watch on the sun across the sky. In this way the sun god was viewed and appeased with offerings, rituals and ceremonies.

Early craftsmen responded to the needs of individuals, while the priesthood responded to both the needs of the individuals and the entire local community with outdoor adaptations of their sacred spaces as a charm against harm and misfortune.

Shades of duels are often found with these beliefs. In Irish mythology, *Balor*, a Formorian, was the personification of the Evil Eye. After exposure to fumes of a magic potion, *Balor*'s eyes became poisonous to onlookers. Four of his men held his eyelid open on a battle field, and no one was able to resist the paralyzing power of his gaze. *Lug* or *Lugh*, the sun god, destroyed *Balor*'s eye with a thrown stone.[31]

* * *

Sometimes, the grass of modern baseball diamonds is cut in a pattern which shows numerous small "diamonds" facing the sky, or into small squares resembling Scottish tartan patterns. In the past, more "diamonds" would have meant more protection against evil onlookers.

Though in and out of fashion, as recently as the 1990s and early 2000s, baseball players were more commonly bedecked with jewelry. To this day many players wear chains, crosses, rings or other items for good luck and fortune. Such pre-emptive and protective actions passed down from previous generations provide players with a reminder of and link with their ancestors.[32] Kunz further shows the powers attributed to diamonds:

> It was thought to bring victory to the wearer, by endowing him with superior strength, fortitude, and courage. Marbodus tells us it was a magic stone of great power and served to drive away nocturnal spectres; for this purpose it should be set in gold and worn on the left arm. For St. Hildegard the sovereign virtue of the diamond was recognized by the devil, who was a great enemy of this stone because it resisted its power by day and by night.[33]

With night it becomes more imperative that protection be available since evil forces of darkness are then most apt to be waiting for unsuspecting victims. Earlier, in the absence of sunlight and the sun god, it was thought that Lords and Princes of Darkness or evil forces were more active and powerful; and the most feared Prince of Darkness, equivalent to the Devil in Christianity, ruled at night. Even today when venturing out at night or to unknown places, players and us alike reach for protective items to wear and reaffirm our courage. Many professional players also wear gold necklaces with plain or diamond-studded crosses. The cross, often also displaying a crucified figure, a crucifix, later became a Christian symbol worn as a charm against the evil forces of Satan. The cross was an earlier pre–Christian symbol dating back to the early British sun god *Taranis*.[34] When players make the sign of the cross before taking the pitcher's mound or batter's box, they unknowingly invoke ancient symbols of protection. It now seems appropriate that after successful efforts some professional baseball players unknowingly look up to thank the sun god whose adoration has left a legacy for their livelihood and lifestyle.[35]

Pearl necklaces are also worn by some modern players. Kunz writes about the appropriateness of the combination of diamonds and pearls:

> The diamond is to the pearl as the sun is to the moon, and we might call one the "king gem" and the other the "queen gem." The diamond, like a knight of old,—brilliant and resistant, is the emblem of fearlessness and invincibility; the pearl, like a lady of old,—pure and fair to look upon, is the emblem of modesty and purity. Therefore, it does not seem unfitting that the diamond should be presented as token to the pearl, and that pearls should go with diamonds.[36]

The protective power of a diamond or any stone is further enhanced if it is "holed" like a donut, called a "Holed-Stone." Steve Roud in *The Penguin Guide to the Superstitions of Britain and Ireland* writes:

> By far the most widespread superstition about a mineral concerned stones with a natural hole in them, which were prized as lucky and protective. They could be hung up to protect a building against witchcraft, or carried on the person to ward off an EVIL EYE.[37]

A baseball diamond with the pitcher's mound about the center may appear like a sacred "Holed-Stone." The pitcher's mound becomes the symbolic hole in the center of the analogous diamond-shaped stone. Sometimes, there is a path linking the mound and home plate area reminiscent of a holed-stone suspended on a chain as also seen in old pictures or depictions of early diamonds.[38] The Druidic priesthood symbolically had a diamond-shaped gem preferably with a hole thereby doubling its effectiveness as a charm. The sacred area or diamond had all the requirements not only for protection against the Evil Eye, but combined with a "Holed-Stone" had added effectiveness as a powerful community amulet. This superstitious nature of early British and others was evidently incorporated into the game and these old protective responses are still evident.

Ross in *The Folklore of the Scottish Highlands* captures the essence of the charms and incantations against the Evil Eye.[39]

It is common to see baseball players wearing necklaces or chains containing "heavy" metals such as copper, silver, gold, titanium and platinum (from the d-block families of chemical elements or transition metals of the modern chemistry periodic table). Some claim these elements, and chemical compounds and alloys made with them, have special health-promoting and curative properties. The efficacies of these health claims are yet to be substantiated by modern science. The wearing of these metallic chains provides a rationalization for continuation of the wearing of old protective amulets and charms. To enhance these putative protective effects, some players wear two or three of these necklaces bearing their team colors.[40] Some modern players still wear protective amulets and good luck charms which are discreetly tucked out of sight.[41] We generally see it as "why take chances, at least it does no harm."

* * *

A peculiar but common sight within most MLB dugouts is players, coaches, and managers spitting. Normally, spitting in public places is considered unsanitary in many cultures, especially in the light of modern knowledge of how infectious diseases and illnesses, colds and influenza, are spread.[42]

The origins of this custom are buried deep in antiquity in many cultures including that of the early British and related peoples. Brand writes:

> According to Pliny, [spitting] was superstitiously observed in averting witchcraft, and in giving a shrewder blow to the enemy. Hence seems to be derived the customs pugilists have of spitting on their hands before they begin their barbarous diversion, unless it was originally done for luck's sake...
>
> The boys in the North of England have a custom amongst themselves of spitting their faith (or as they call it in their northern dialect, "their Saul," *i.e.*, Soul) when required to make asseverations in matters which they think of consequence.
>
> Colliers and others about Newcastle-upon-Tyne in their combination for the purpose of raising their wages are said to spit upon a stone together, by way of cementing their confederacy. Hence the popular saying, when persons are of the same party, or agree in sentiments, that "they spit on the same stone."[43]

Rabbi Dr. R. Brasch, in *How Did It Begin? Customs & Superstitions and Their Romantic Origins*, further clarifies the spitting superstitions and substantiates Brand and Knowlson's works.[44] In addition, according to Steve Roud, spitting practices were common and widespread in Britain. In evidence, Roud cites Harland and Wilkinson's *Lancashire* (1882):

> Spitting was formerly an integral part of boys' traditional code of behaviour, when swearing an oath or preparing to fight.... In Lancashire boys spit over their fingers in order to screw up their courage to fighting point, or to give them luck in battle.[45]

Analogously baseball players, like workers of yesteryear, spit on the dirt, strengthening their ties of brotherhood. Hitting is an exceptionally difficult skill, one of the most difficult in sports, and hitters spitting on their hands is also a reversion to old ways of making a difficult task easier.[46]

The superstitious British and related peoples were constantly engaged in war and games. In these physical confrontations they understandably wanted to do everything possible to gain the advantage over opponents and neutralize the effects of adverse spells and evil entities. Spitting was one of the ways of shifting the odds in their favor. Knowlson, Brasch and Roud support the idea that fighters spat on their hands not only to ward off evil, but also to increase their luck and the efficacy of their blows.

Another notable reason for spitting was the belief that if anyone found himself in the presence of the Evil Eye, he should spit three times on the ground.[47] Players may also spit over their left shoulders toward whatever real or imagined evil lurks there, as the Devil was previously thought to reside on the left-side or shoulder. Players also spit on the ground, like warriors to ward off evil on the battle grounds. Some players are in the habit of constantly spitting on the field or dugout, ignoring any sanitary implications.[48]

Modern players frequently spit on their hands or batting gloves not only to increase their grip when batting, but also in the hopes of enhancing their batting prowess. David Ortiz, one of the greatest modern power hitters, immediately comes to mind. In one Major League Baseball's television commercial, he is shown teaching young players how to hit with confidence, and humorously begins with spitting on the palm of his hands and then rubbing his hands together.[49] The spitting that occurs in modern baseball had its origins in superstitions and old religious beliefs.

Often when it is a modern hitter's turn to bat, his actions may include one or all of these now-considered superstitious acts (making the sign of the cross on his body to invoke the blessings of his god, spitting on the ground to ward off evil or make an offering to a deity, and spitting on his hands to increase his own batting prowess).[50] Other curious rituals may follow. He may pick up some dirt, where others have frequently spat, and rub it on his hands or throw it over his shoulder. Knowlson writes that salt was used with sacrificial or propitiatory offerings by both the Greeks and the Romans to appease the gods and that a pinch of salt held between the fingers was thrown over the left shoulder to avoid bad luck.[51]

*   *   *

Many hitters take three swings before stepping into the batter's box. Some batters also tap home plate three times before each at bat. This tapping practice was done in earlier times to wake up or chase away evil forces or residents. This old practice of knocking three times was also done to ask permission for entry into the abode of an unknown resident. This habit is much the same as the clinking of drinking glasses in a toast to good health, as those sounds were made with the intentions of scaring away evil spirits. In some places, before crossing a body of dark or muddy water such as a trench, canal or swamp, the surface of the water is struck hard three times to chase away any evil force which may be lurking underneath. In addition, this would warn dangerous creatures such as snakes and other reptiles to move away. The idea is that since one is trespassing into the domains of others, visible or invisible, evil or good, one must be polite enough to give sufficient warning to any unseen residents, so they may move away and let one enter and pass safely. The habit of tapping home plate gives notice to whom or what lays ahead. Home plate is analogously the entry point of a sacred site or house and it marks the beginning and end of a symbolic journey.

The superstition of not stepping on the foul-lines to avoid misfortune, though common in baseball, is either of more recent vintage or unknown origin. Anyone who has coached or done field-preparation for children or youth baseball knows once the lines are laid down with lime, chalk or paint, players are asked not to step on them. This is requested so the lines do not get smudged or erased before the game starts. No record or indication is found of this avoidance of stepping on lines or cracks as being of early British origin, though in Britain, where chalk was and remains abundant, it may have been used to define religious or game areas.[52] Michael Edwardes in *Everyday Life in Early India* writes, "but most [houses] were of one storey with a floor covered with an outer mixture of lime, earth, and cow-dung."[53] This indicates that the use of lime was likely known and used by others of Indo-European origins such as the early British and European peoples. In addition, early British and European peoples would have respected their defined mandala-like boundaries. Stepping on these lines which separated sacred from ordinary was likely taboo as in Hindu and Buddhist societies.

*   *   *

One tradition long associated with baseball is chewing tobacco and gum. In America tobacco companies vigorously promoted their products using elite baseball players as their spokespersons, and sponsoring baseball teams and tournaments. Later, chewing gum with enclosed cards was introduced, that both children and adults bought. These baseball cards of bygone heroes are now prized possessions, often with high monetary value. Baseball players and coaches are still seen actively chewing gum and even tobacco. There is evidence that the early British chewed an equivalent substitute at sacred sites.[54]

The habit of chewing on a finger or thumb is also reminiscent of superstitions in vogue before and after the introduction of Christianity. This was later replaced by church-approved gesture of a person "crossing" themselves.[55] Superstitions die slowly even when superseded by newer knowledge. As it was dangerous or impractical for someone to chew on his thumb or cross himself and simultaneously work in a highly industrialized society, an alternative substitute was provided. A stick or wad of gum or tobacco, a proxy thumb, fitted well with the old needs, making chewing both possible and enjoyable while simultaneously working. In early British and European cultures, which deified trees, the chewing of leaves of sacred plants was viewed as of special significance. They, like other old cultures, saw chewing of leaves as a "Holy Communion Service" in which the faithful participated.

Modern players, like their old British counterparts of yesteryear, are responding to natural and perceived supernatural forces just outside of their control with the same basic responses. In the game, the margins between success and failure, hero and loser are often negligible. The results are often not a true reflection of the efforts and sacrifices which losers or winners give. Many times it seems that luck, fate, destiny or chance are involved. Naturally, a player tries not to offend those who control these forces beyond his. Superstitions (old or new) will always be a part of baseball.

* * *

Major League Baseball stadiums seek to create a special aura so both non-players and players feel privileged to walk or work in these hallowed grounds. For example, in the old Yankee Stadium, baseball lore and myths of the greatest Yankee players permeated the atmosphere as baseball history seemed to ooze from the old walls.[56] In the new "cathedral," Yankee Stadium, one finds bronze busts and statues of the greatest Yankee heroes creating a carefully-crafted ambience. It is as if these baseball gods are critically watching and weighing members of visiting teams to see how these modern mortals measure up to their own godlike and iconic status. Younger players of visiting teams are often awed, intimidated and sometimes so unnerved that their performances suffer. The shock to subtle intimidation of the Yankees mystique produces trepidation in others and reduces their successes. Yankees players, on the other hand, are inspired to excel. Before each game, some Yankees players visit these shrines and touch the busts of their favorite players for good luck, similar to the use of the charms and talismans of yesteryear.

Warriors of early British and continental European peoples were known for collecting the severed heads of respected opponents, and hanging them around their fortifications. This was a way of intimidating others, boasting about military accomplishments, and inspiring their followers and descendants to greater achievements. Ross (*The Pagan Celts*) writes that the symbol of the severed human head was common, and besides being a trophy was regarded as having mystical powers. Stones carved into the shape of heads have survived to this day, but others have long since decayed.[57]

It is not surprising the hallowed shrines of baseball reflect the practices of past warrior societies. In America, where immigrants of British and continental European ancestry fought indigenous Indian tribes or nations, adversaries like the Indians (Cleveland) and Braves (Boston, Milwaukee, and then Atlanta) were also used to represent teams. Both teams still feature a head of an Indian warrior depicted on their respective logos, though controversy around the use of such symbols has increased in recent years.

No observer of the "Red Sox Nation" at Boston's Fenway Park doubts baseball is a "religion." The fervor and devotion of a "Red Sox congregation" supporting their team in unison is legendary. In Boston, the "cathedral," Fenway Park, is full for every "religious service." This "religious fervor" reflects the deep connection of fans and their game. Earlier in its history, Fenway Park had an embankment in left field where spectators sat, as their early British and related ancestors previously did in their own enclosures.[58] Bostonians have inherited and passed down a natural affection for their cultural heritage which includes a love of learning, competition and sports. The various societal classes and socioeconomic strata of Massachusetts were and still are united by a common love for ball games. Their passion for baseball unites them as the "Red Sox Nation." The rival New York Yankees are often referred to as "The Evil Empire."[59]

*   *   *

Before and during wars, bards and priests (their roles were sometimes interchangeable) sang about the noble deeds of their ancestors to inspire them to fight with bravery and honor. This power to inspire their fighters was acknowledged by the invading Romans, who singled out bards and priests for slaughter. Inspiring renditions of anthems before baseball games are a relic of times past when the warriors were roused before battles. These patriotic songs were used to unite the related tribes before, during, and after battles or games. The brilliance of bards and priests was evident in the powerful "magic" of their lyrics and voices whose soul-stirring songs inspired their warriors.

After the September 11, 2001, terrorist attacks at the World Trade Center on American soil, Irish tenor Dr. Ronan Tynan gives us a glimpse of the Irish bards at early battle scenes. Dr. Tynan's singing performances during the seventh inning stretch, in the games between the Yankees and the Red Sox, like the bards of yesteryear, captivated his listeners. His beautiful rendition of "God Bless America" is an inspiring and soul-stirring clarion call to arms. Listeners are bonded with each other and connected with the past.[60] Similarly, warriors heard the clarion call of early "Armorica," the ancient name for Brittany, invoked before a fight with Roman invaders. They felt that their ancestral warriors and heroes were present, and now it was their turn to stand up and be counted. Early British and continental European peoples understood the magical power of words to inspire and to motivate. Some tribes likewise responded to the sound of bagpipes, marching fearlessly onwards to life or death including that of the famed Gordon Highlanders, for whom the Yankees were earlier named.

* * *

Not all of the old traditions were associated with earlier religious practices or warding off evil. Early British and continental European sites were also places of celebrations which are mirrored today. In modern times, occasionally, young men continue the tradition of publicly proposing to their beloved in baseball settings.[61] This sacred square or "diamond" was not only a place to find and promote relationships, but was also associated with health and protective rituals.[62]

Many of baseball's superstitions are founded on, and are a continuation of old beliefs and practices. These acts and behaviors have deep origins and foundations with philosophical and religious underpinnings.

Early British and other peoples' contributions spread far beyond former domains with the rise and global reach of colonization. British and other Europeans carried with them their Christian practices still reflecting earlier beliefs and customs. Many of these special events were eventually incorporated into the Christian calendar, including Christmas, Easter, St. Valentine's Day, Halloween, May Day and Groundhog Day. If the British and European peoples wanted to preserve their beliefs and practices, they could not have chosen a better vehicle than a game which encapsulates so much of their ideas and values.

12

Baseball and the Sun

Before the sixteenth century, the Earth was thought to be the center of the universe, with the sun literally rising over and setting below us. It was considered obvious that the sun was orbiting the earth and this was regarded as a universal truth. This view was held by many from the earliest of times, and has influenced our lives in all areas. Even when the first scientific evidence was gathered, it took centuries before we accepted the "heretical' view that the Earth orbits the sun and not the other way around (first proposed by Copernicus in the fifteenth century and advocated by Galileo in the seventeenth).[1] The sun, long deified by humans, has powerful influences on us, as the Earth and its life are controlled by the gravitational attraction and energy-fields of the sun. Advances in knowledge have reinforced the concept of the powerful impacts the sun has on all life. This insight would have made the sun even worthier of veneration in the games of ancient peoples, including the priesthood of early British, continental European and other peoples. Modern players, fans and others involved in baseball may be surprised to know how much the sun affects this game, which originated long ago as a tribute to the sun. Everything in our world obeys the law of gravity, but a myriad of unseen forces controlled by the sun also influence the path of a baseball in every game on every diamond.

The Earth orbits the sun in a process which takes one solar year, 365.26 days, traveling through space at 30 000 meters per second or 67,000 miles per hour. The average distance between Earth and sun is approximately 150,000,000 km or 93,000,000 miles.[2] As Earth orbits the sun in an approximately elliptical path, it also spins about its own central axis, a process which takes 24 hours or one solar day to complete. This spinning process creates day and night. Throughout history, societies such as the early British and continental European peoples used these light and darkness patterns to set their calendars.

The Earth spins in a counter-clockwise direction about its own axis, meaning that the atmosphere and oceans of Earth are also forced to move or spin.[3] Every atom or molecule of our atmosphere and oceans are in motion.[4] This rotational movement accounts for the winds, clouds, weather patterns and ocean currents. Even a ball released in the air will minutely move to the right in the Northern hemisphere and to the left in the Southern because of this spin.[5] The Earth's rotation creates the illusion that it is the sun which is moving across the horizon. This optical illusion underlied early religious beliefs that the sun controlled Earth's destiny.

The Earth not only spins on its axis as it orbits around the sun, but also tilts toward or away from it causing the sun to appear higher on the horizon during summer. This spinning and tilting of the Earth in its orbital path around the sun is responsible for the four seasons: winter, spring, summer and fall.[6] Life adapts to these cyclic seasonal rhythms.[7]

Games and entertainment are likewise affected by the passing of the seasons. All sources of energy (wood, coal, oil, natural gas, fuel, wind and tidal), except those derived from nuclear, geothermal and hydro-electric sources, are solar in origin or solar-dependent.[8] Despite centuries of technological and scientific advancements, weather has remained predictably unpredictable. In trying to understand and predict the weather, scientists with sophisticated satellite and computer technologies have replaced the priests and magicians of early insular Britain and continental Europe. Modern science attempts to forecast the weather, replacing old religious incantations, spells, rituals, offerings and sacrifices previously used for the same purposes. Despite current modernizations, humankind is still in the dark with serious consequences for our failures to predict and avoid the consequences of extreme weather conditions. Mother Earth is still at the mercy of the sun and whatever natural forces influence her.[9]

The game of baseball is affected by these complex interactions of the sun and Earth. It is poignant that baseball, originally dedicated to the sun, is more strongly affected by it than other outdoor ballgames. It still often seems as if some unseen forces have powerful hands or decisive says in the affairs of this game. The sun's influences on global weather conditions in turn affect our local community which in turn affect the game. Our ancestors imagined a mandala-like design with representations of the seasons and "elements" (earth, air, water and fire) as the four end-points or spokes of a spinning wheel, which carry the chariot of the sun god.[10] The interactions of these "elements" control the game.

Early British and other peoples were very concerned about the weather and used their observations of the skies, clouds and winds to make crude weather predictions. Their agricultural successes were dependent on weather conditions and some of their lyrical expressions survive in folk-wisdom.[11]

The weather and its effects remain a determining factor in the outcome of war and sports. The technology of controlling weather to wreak havoc on an enemy still remains an elusive weapon of war. The early British and others knew that the sun controlled the weather and to ensure its welfare employed symbolic fertility rituals between sun and Earth, including votive and sacrificial offerings. In effect early British and continental European peoples sought to appease their sun god. In times of war, they invoked it with incantations and rituals, hoping to harness the power of the sun in their favor.[12]

The early British and continental European peoples also paid tributes to the sun or sun god in their games.[13] The seasons affected the appropriate times for such tributes as locations of these desired rituals were outdoors. Such activities were held throughout the year, but were practical more often in spring, summer and early fall avoiding dramatic changes in weather patterns. During winter, because of adverse weather conditions and reduced availability of daylight, fewer games were played outdoors. People still need play, and in 1621, early Pilgrims in America played stool-ball during winter on Christmas day. It must be noted that stool-ball was recorded as both an outdoor as well as an indoor game. The Reverend Wood writes, "In the North of England, a variant of the Old English game of Stool Ball is played indoors in wet weather.... In the South of England Stool Ball is an outdoor game."[14] This deeply entrenched game was enjoyed outside and in adverse weather shifted indoors, where appropriate game adaptations were made. The popularity of stool-ball was exceptional and it continued to be mentioned as indoor games in the eighteenth and nineteenth centuries.

In summer, longer daylight hours and better weather conditions are more conducive to being outdoors. Hackwood mentions children played rounders and tut-ball during the summer in Staffordshire (Appendix C). Ross also writes that ancient pagan activities were influenced by the changes of the seasons.[15]

The playing of stool-ball was thought to be essential for good health before harvest. Like other early religious practices performed in public places at appropriate times, this playing of stool-ball was influenced by seasonal patterns. Modern baseball in North America generally still follows the dictates and rhythms of the four seasons.[16]

The amount and duration of sunlight and its warmth influence when and where games are played. In early and sometimes in modern unlit parks, games are called off or postponed on account of darkness. Today most Major League Baseball games are held in the evenings in well-lit parks or stadiums.[17] The advent of electrical lighting made it possible for more working class people to attend evening games. (In North America, spring training and pre-season for Major League Baseball take place in Florida and Arizona.)

Players have difficulty seeing balls when running against the direction of the sun, and when hitting, catching, and fielding with the sun shining directly in their eyes. In such situations, baseballs are said to be lost in the brightness of the sun.[18] On sunnier days the air receives more of the sun's energy and becomes warmer and more energetic.[19] These energized constituent molecules of the air move about more rapidly and in effect assist a baseball, going in the same direction, to travel further and faster. When the temperature rises, warmer or hotter air becomes less dense and offers lower resistance to a baseball moving through it. A decrease in barometric pressure results in the air becoming less dense at higher elevations allowing a baseball to travel further.[20] This effect is most pronounced at high elevations like that of the Colorado Rockies' baseball stadium. On both cooler days and those with higher barometric pressure the opposite holds true as both a baseball's velocity and distance travelled are reduced. In early spring or early fall (with relatively colder conditions) a baseball falls earlier than it would in summer. This small effect can often be the difference between whether a baseball just leaves the park, or stays in with a chance of being caught. Such situations illuminate why baseball is called "a game of inches."

The sun's energy also heats up the earth (or turf) which in turn passes this energy into the layer of air directly above.[21] This now energized layer of hotter air rises and is replaced by heavier and cooler layer of air previously above.[22] This cyclic process continues and small air currents are produced. As temperatures rise and create more active air currents, the movements of a ball become less predictable. Sometimes a spinning ball seems to have "a mind of its own" as its trajectory is affected by local air currents. All these minute effects lead to the unpredictability of where a ball will finally land, be it in front of or behind a fielder, in fair or foul territory, or inside of or over the fence. Together all these factors affect key plays in a game and often determine the outcome.

In evenings when the sun sets and the air cools, the remaining heat from the warm ground becomes the strongest source of energy for heating the air. This layer of air near the warm earth gains energy and becomes warmer and rises. Layers of air nearer the earth are warmer and less dense than those higher above it. For example, a sinking fastball pitch delivered over-arm will sink a little more quickly as it approaches home plate. Conversely, a pitch thrown with an under-arm delivery will rise slightly less as it approaches the plate, as these fastballs move upwards through cooler layers of air as they approach home. Life is made more difficult for the hitter who tries to judge the flight path of a ball to his bat. Line-drives hit in colder evenings do not travel as quickly as those hit closer to the warmer ground. Here again the physical parameters that the sun controls can be of great significance.

When the air is humid and contains more water vapor, it becomes less dense and movement of a ball through the air is easier.[23] This can determine whether a hit ball makes it over the outfield fence or a home run, or falls just short enough to be caught. When the air is too damp or supersaturated with water particles, aggregates of water molecules become attached to the leather ball, and its waxed red cotton/polyester threads, making it slightly heavier. Any slightly dampened ball, because of the added weight of water, will be slowed down to a small extent.

When the ground is very dry, a ball bounces more than it would on a wetter surface. Dry ground acts like a trampoline and balls often ricochet in unexpected directions, referred to as "bad bounces" or "bad hops." On very wet ground or dampness, a ball is either slowed as water acts as an adhesive, or "shoots" in unpredictable directions as water acts as a lubricant. The longer and more often a ball is in contact with wet ground the heavier it becomes. Likewise players are slowed down in such conditions as running speed is reduced and the risk of slipping or injury increases. Players adjust accordingly to the amount of moisture on the field.

On windy days, the molecules which constitute air, move more rapidly and determine directions and velocities of any ball travelling through it. Likewise a ball going in the same direction as the wind travels farther and faster. A ball going against the wind encounters more resistance to its movement and therefore falls earlier.[24] Wind can be a major determining factor in the game.

Outfielders grab blades of grass and drop them to see how and where they fall, a simple test to check the direction of the wind. Outfielders can also get a general idea of what direction the winds are blowing by looking at flags flying within the stadium. Outfielders take these into account, adjusting their fielding positions to the specific area the current batter is expected to hit the ball. An outfielder's position may be the difference in whether or not a catch can be made or throw delivered in time.

The same conditions (temperature, wind and humidity) which affect the path of a ball after it leaves a bat similarly affect a ball after it leaves the pitcher's hand. These smaller environmental effects together help determine whether the pitched ball is just in or out of the strike zone.[25] The consequence of this may be the difference between a strike or ball producing an out, or a base on balls, respectively. The velocity of a fastball is helped by favorable conditions which facilitate less resistance to the direction of movement of the ball. The effects of atmospheric conditions are felt on a "curve" ball where denser air conditions are expected to help the "curve" land in the strike zone. Knuckleball pitchers are the most concerned about local weather conditions. Windy conditions make the already unpredictable path of a knuckleball even more erratic and hitters have great difficulty tracking the ball to hit it squarely.

A strong crosswind, between the pitcher and batter, affects both the velocity and path of a ball. A crosswind can affect the final destination of a breaking ball, such as a slider, enough to determine a hitter's or an umpire's response.

The path of a ball also depends on the spin generated by the pitcher's release off the tips of his fingers. How and where a ball is held before release determines if the pitcher gets the desired minimum or maximum number of collisions between the stitches along the seams of a ball and surrounding molecules of the air. With a four-seam fastball, the number of effective collisions between stitches and air are maximized; the ball stays in a straighter line longer and is called a "rising" fastball. In the case of a two-seam fastball, the number of collisions between stitches and air are reduced; consequently, the ball drops more and is called a "sinking" fastball. There are three different types of spin: (1) topspin, a ball spins in the same direction that the ball is moving; (2) backspin, a ball spins in the opposite direction that the ball is moving; and (3) sidespin, a ball spins sideways to the direction that the ball is moving. A regular four-seam fastball is thrown with backspin. A "cut" fastball has backspin and some sidespin. The "curveball" has more topspin; whereas the "slider" has more sidespin. Spin can be measured in the number of revolutions per minute, a 100 mph fastball spins at 1900 revolutions per minute (rpm).

The ball, upon reaching and colliding with a bat, leaves the bat still spinning. The spin (rpm) a ball leaves a bat with is dependent on the point of contact with the bat. The contact places range from being hit "squarely," to the top or bottom of the ball. In addition to the force applied to the incoming ball, the spin on the batted-ball determines both its direction and movement. This is dramatically evident when a ball leaves a bat with backspin in an almost vertical direction; the ball goes up toward the backstop and then moves back towards the infield. Catchers are trained to expect this movement. Similar unpredictable movements are often seen with infield pop-ups.

Weather conditions not only affect the movement of balls in the air and on the ground, but they also affect players. Cold temperatures affect the hands of players as heat is lost from the exposed hands to the colder surrounding air. As the hands become colder, the body metabolizes energy resources to maintain a constant body temperature; and, as more warm blood is pumped to the hands more heat is lost. Players often rub their hands together, swing their arms or jog on the spot to generate warmth from within. The body's natural priority is to first protect the internal organs and brain, and blood supplies are preferentially routed to these organs instead of the hands and feet.

Cold fingers make it is difficult to properly grip a ball and throw it accurately to a desired target in a hurry. Pitchers are the most affected by coldness, and often try to warm their throwing hands by blowing on them when off the mound. In general, pitchers are not allowed to bring their hands to their mouths while standing on the mound because of concerns about adding spit to the ball. Under cold, wet and windy conditions, umpires may allow pitchers of both teams to blow on their hands while standing on the mound. A pitcher must properly grip a ball before release. Movement and accuracy are also dependent on arm-slot and point-of-release. (Chapter 2 has more details on throwing.) Each pitch (four- or two-seam fastball, change-up, sinker, splitter, slider, curveball and knuckleball) is gripped and released differently to get the desired interactions between the stitches of the ball and the air it passes through. This is a crucial factor in pitching since a pitcher needs to control both the desired location and velocity of delivery. It is difficult to control the precise location of a ball into the strike zone even under ideal playing conditions; and the effects of colder temperatures only make this task more difficult.[26] On very cold days, a pitcher may lose his advantage in this game of accurate throwing.

Each stadium has its own site-specific environment with miniature characteristic weather patterns. The physical location of a stadium gives an idea of what general environment can be expected. Two examples are the baseball stadium in Denver, Colorado, which is high above sea level, and the stadium in San Francisco, California, in the San Francisco Bay area, at sea level. Barometric pressure decreases as height above sea-level increases, and a ball travels further at higher elevation. The Rockies' stadium favors home-run production by power hitters, while pitchers are more likely to give up home-runs here. To compensate for any field becoming "a pitcher's graveyard," the outfield is moved farther away from the infield allowing balls to stay within the walls and be caught.[27] Conversely, in the San Francisco Giants' stadium home run production is more difficult, as a batted ball is more likely to be "knocked down" earlier by the air. Pitchers may fare better here for the same reason.

The home team knows how a ball travels at its park in daytime and nighttime, and on warm, cold, windy or wet days. Visiting teams often watch

what the home team does to learn the peculiarities of local weather environment, or when possible get advance scouting reports on a particular park.

The thousands of fans in a stadium also affect these local micro-weather
environments. Fans breathe in cooler air with nitrogen and oxygen, and
breathe out warmer and more energized air and carbon dioxide.[28] The carbon
dioxide content of the stadium increases with thousands of fans breathing in
these confined or semi-confined areas.[29] If the air is not moving or there is
poor circulation, the build-up of carbon dioxide slightly increases the density
of the air within the confines of the stadium. This slightly heavier air offers
more resistance to the movement of a ball. Simultaneously, water vapor is
also breathed out and dampens the atmosphere; the moistened air is now
less dense. Since water and carbon dioxide molecules are given out in equal
quantities, the net effect is heavier air, since each carbon dioxide molecule
(CO_2, Relative Molecular Weight, RMW, of 44) with a water molecule (H_2O,
RMW, 18) is about two times heavier than an oxygen molecule (O_2, RMW,
32). The oxygen content of the exhaled air is reduced slightly, being replaced
by heavier carbon dioxide molecules (Notes 23 and 28). This denser or heavier
air reduces the velocity of a ball travelling through it even more.

With thousands of spectators sitting in the stands and breathing out
warmer air the ambient temperature of the park also increases. The more
active the fans, the more heat they generate and consequently the park gets
warmer. It is therefore not only for psychological reasons that a visiting team
tries to keep the fans quiet and out of the game. A loud and boisterous crowd
generates more energy, heat and sound, than a quiet one. Shouting energizes
the air particles, allowing more collisions. A ball carries more when the stands
are full of cheering fans than when the stands are empty. If the fans are
divided, the side of the stadium where the energetic fans are packed is warmer
and the effects of this warmer area in the stadium are skewed. This affects
both teams equally, but its effect on any individual pitch or hit which takes
advantage at just the right moment can be a game-determining factor.
Warmer air favors power pitchers since both velocity and movement of the
ball are enhanced. Since warmer air rises, the air currents will move upwards
and higher. This situation also benefits power hitters, as a well-hit ball can
ride these warmer air currents over the fence.

Baseball is called "a game of inches" and is influenced by minute factors
which have major consequences in determining a game's outcome. These
close plays can make the jobs of umpires more difficult. Such minute differences require judgments often beyond human visual limitations, and only
slow-motion camera replays can show the right call. Sometimes replays from
various camera angles are necessary to ascertain the correct call such as a

very close play on whether a runner is safe or out, a ball is fair or foul, or a pitch is called a strike or not. In most cases umpires make the correct calls.

The factors which influence these close plays are also determined by atmospheric conditions (air, temperature and water vapor) which in turn are determined by the sun. From an ancient perspective, the sun still attends this game which welcomes it to a performance in its honor. The sun dutifully watches over the game of baseball and participates through an infinite number of small effects. In so doing the sun is not a mere spectator, but rather an active participant in every game. From an early British and continental European perspective, a baseball diamond is the sun's playground and players its playmates. The sun god and its energy meets humans and matter. Which side will gain more from the sun's influences at critical moments is difficult to predict. The modern era of baseball, aided by both the refinements of the ball and the game itself, allow for maximum interactions with the sun and the factors (temperature, pressure, energy, etc.) which it controls. The umpire's raised open hand showing palm and fingers, also an ancient Indian symbol of the sun and rays, still stops the play or game. Baseball is played under the watchful eye of sun, once dedicated to the sun, and still played with its active participation.

13

Not Mere Observers but Participants

Fan participation and devotion can make baseball analogous to a religious service. Players, as living divinities, and coaches, as priests and high priests, know their fans must be actively involved as individual devotees and a larger congregation. The baseball faithful play a vital role in the ceremonies and rituals that sustain and perpetuate this game.

Active involvement in worship services is facilitated as "baseball cathedrals" are designed to seat onlookers as close as possible to the center stage of events.[1] The best seats are those directly behind home plate or just to the sides of the first- and third-base lines. The faithful who occupy these seats are rewarded with increased chances of participation as well as being publicly seen and acknowledged by covering media. Over the years, more and more seating has been packed into these areas. Wider foul territories along first- and third-base lines have been steadily shrinking, and fans have moved closer to the field of play and action. From these closest-seating positions, fortunate viewers can better see the details of the game, e.g., strike or ball, fair or foul, and safe or out. In addition, this closeness to the game's action makes the fans feel more involved in the game. They can better see and sense not only the subtleties and nuances of baseball, but read the body language (fear, tension, confidence, relief, regret, and frustration or anxiety) of each player, coach and official. This is the closest fans can get to living out their own dreams of being in the big leagues.

Likewise, wherever possible, the outfield has been shrinking to bring faithful attendees closer. Most stadiums do not have a bad seat anywhere in their entire "Houses of Worship." All can see, are involved, and interconnected with heightened emotions and enthusiasm.[2]

Involvement of an observer extends further beyond the stadium in modern baseball. Now each action is recorded by both cameras and microphones from various vantage points: above, below, behind, sides and front. Close-up live pictures of remarkable or questionable plays and surrounding decisions are replayed over and over again.[3] In addition, the rightness, wrongness, beauty, near impossibility, and historic moment of the particular replayed action are analyzed by radio and television broadcasters and expert or color commentators. Simultaneously, these replays are also viewed, debated, and judged by fans. Fans are captivated and bonded by these replays, as even strangers momentarily find strong enough common ground to relax social inhibitions and engage and converse with each other. Beautiful and exceptional moments need to be shared with family and fellow fans. This bonding of shared humanity and interests is rediscovered and reinforced in the friendly and safe environment of each "baseball cathedral." This is a place where each can find oneself connected to a larger baseball community, where children are particularly encouraged and welcomed.[4] "Give the kid the ball" is often heard in the stands. We feel this human kinship and a sense of belonging to a larger whole in baseball settings. It is easy to feel comfortable with so much to actively engage one's attention, and at the same time everyone has opportunities to connect with others.[5]

These religious services now reach into every home, shopping mall, place of entertainment or work via radio, television and Internet. No fan feels isolated. A single person at home or elsewhere looking at the game feels connected with the devotees in attendance. Both sets of worshippers, in the "cathedral" or elsewhere, are united by this common baseball service. Tomorrow, they will find further common ground as a game is discussed at work, school or home. All are united by witnessing and sharing common thrills, misfortunes and highlights, experiencing the exhilarating win or painful loss of a game.

Baseball fulfills many roles including that of a mock battle, a substitute for the excitement of war, the euphoria of religion, an avenue for entertainment, and a therapeutic diversion from life's everyday stress.[6] Owners and business managers want spectators to be actively involved in all the details of these live theatrical dramas, including all the various sub-plots of players.[7] In this way attendees have heightened emotional investments in the outcomes of each play and decision. The attention of spectators is directed so they become riveted to the particular scene before them. The game fulfills the needs of each fan, whether viewing the game as a battle, siege, medieval tournament, old-fashioned duel or as an opportunity for social or "religious" gathering. Human imagination knows no limit and the game accommodates the desired freedoms to imagine infinite possibilities and situations. In addition, a fan's mind can easily take him back in time from modern through medieval to primal scenarios. Our minds can also fast-forward us into upcoming battles at future games. The beauty of baseball is that there is no limit to the times, places and persons it can connect us with.[8]

Fans cheer at favorable outcomes, and boo when they wish to voice their displeasures. Both responses unite spectators in one community. When causes for disapproval occur, fans unite in these perceived assaults on their collective persona.

Expectations, exhortations, hype, atmosphere, rivalries, and excitements together result in greater emotional involvement of the crowd. Greater emotional participation makes baseball more exciting for the entire community: onlookers, coaches and players. The total energy of this mass of believers or "mass energy" is directed toward the field of play and its participants. This energy of the home crowd acts like a powerful tidal wave directed to force decisions or outcomes of games in their favor. Music played over speaker systems, often accompanied with mascots or cheerleaders, keeps the tempo high promoting enthusiasm and support.[9]

Each spectator feeds off the energy generated by this "mass effect" of the crowd, and *vice versa*. A home crowd behaves as one breathing and living entity with its own distinctive personality, like the fans of New York's Yankee Stadium, Boston's Fenway Park, and Chicago's Wrigley Field. In such places, an observer sees expressions, hears prayers, and feels the energy, intensity, love and hostility emanating from the local faithful in their stands. Such raw primal emotions and energies can have an enormous effect on umpires, home and visiting team players, managers and staffs. The crowd is now alive, alert, hungry, thirsty, aggressive and ready to consume opponents who stand in its path to victory.

Fans near home plate put each decision of the game's home plate umpire under close scrutiny. The umpire feels the relentless pressure of fans and may succumb to this influence, thereby letting "close calls" go more readily in the home team's favor. It is human nature for anyone, including umpires, to be swayed by such emotionally charged moments. Umpires have to consciously force themselves to be as deliberate and impartial as they can in their decisions. The crowd senses its hypnotic or devouring power, and preys on any vulnerable umpire who can be cajoled, bullied and swayed. The crowd often becomes incensed when they think their superstar or hero is being cheated or unjustly treated. In extreme cases, some fans throw whatever is at hand onto the field to show their displeasure. Irate fans may unite as one enraged entity, and unleash primal instincts, discarding socially acceptable constraints. In times past, these individuals would have been the first to jump into battle, without any fear of losing life or limb. Such enraged individuals were at the forefront of charges fighting for their family, clan, and tribe to the aid of beleaguered brethren in battle. Baseball reveals what we are by showing the instinctive responses of our ancestors through our actions.

Base umpires are in similar situations as the home plate umpire, and learn how to weather verbal abuses and storms of rage. When the decision is clear-cut there is usually little argument from fans, but with a close or judgment call, all umpires can expect vigorous questioning.[10] Naturally, there is an instinctive rebellion against authority when umpires do not give fans what they want. This can create potentially troubling situations, but to avoid chaos and conflicts fans have to accept the verdicts of umpires. Fans know that if their behavior gets out of hand their team may even be punished and victory awarded to their opponents.

Judgment calls frequently occur when a batter runs from home to first, or when a pitcher attempts to pick off a runner. There are many similar potential conflicts such as calls for safe or out, missed tags, and runners being inside or outside the baselines. Some base umpires (like home plate umpires) enjoy making an emphatic and dramatic "punch-out" or "ring up" gesture. When done in a decision favoring the home team, umpires endear themselves to the crowd, at least until the next controversial decision. Alternatively, by an emphatic "punch out," umpires let fans know they will not tolerate any questioning of their calls.[11] Now with video replays being introduced in some scenarios, calls are being reversed and umpires are not threatened by such challenges or reversals.

The "mass effect" of the home crowd also influences actions, thoughts, and strategies of both managers and coaches. Legendary baseball manager Casey Stengel once went to the mound to remove a pitcher, pointed to the stands and said, "Up there, people are beginning to talk." Sometimes, the head coach or manager emerges from his dugout to protest real or perceived wrongs inflicted on his players or team. This can occur when his pitcher is not getting strikes called; or, when his hitter is having strikes called against him even when balls are clearly outside the strike zone.[12] Even though coaches know they are not legally allowed to question judgment calls, they still question the eyesight, viewing angle and concentration of an umpire. The home crowd often expects someone to go out and speak on their behalf.[13]

Fans may spur on a coach or manager to question the integrity of an umpire or the wisdom of his decision, and sometimes this protest may be accompanied by a breach of accepted protocol. Unprofessional and inappropriate conduct of the complaining coach may result in him being tossed from the game. Penalized coaches usually hope their ejections inspire their players to pick up their games.[14] Fans think by actively complaining a coach is doing his job, and is displaying a passion for his team. Coaches and managers want to be publicly seen by the crowd as doing their best for the team. From time to time a coach may go out on the field to argue with an umpire even though he knows he has no valid case. Public approval of a coach's performance is essential, or fans begin to talk and call his job into question.[15] Coaches try to do as much as possible to avert the potential wrath of irate fans and media. The home crowd therefore also affects managing style and the decisions of its manager or coach, altering the strategies, pace and rhythm of a game.

There are often very close plays at home plate concerning whether a runner is safe or out. Questions in disputes include: Did the ball arrive before the runner touched home plate? Was the tag with the ball or ball in glove applied before the runner touched home plate? and Did the catcher have the ball in his hand or glove when the tag was made? The answers to these questions usually depend on which side one is supporting. The home crowd in this "game of inches" will rarely give an inch on questionable calls. Fans form a united tribe and stand up to cheer or do its "war chants" in support of their team. Atlanta Braves' fans are known best for their intimidating chants and tomahawk-chopping arm movements. Such actions add pressure to players, as it arouses buried instincts, fight or flight responses, where one naturally wants to run away from such a massive horde of boisterous individuals.[16] Today, we still have trouble distinguishing between a real possibility of injury or death and the taunts and jeers of a seemingly hostile crowd. It takes experience to distinguish past dangerous situations from present realities. This is why rookies are usually most affected by these external factors, while veterans handle pressure with greater poise.

Infielders and outfielders often pursue balls close to the seats on first- and third-base sides. Though these seats are considered to be in foul territory, if a fielder can reach into or over and catch a ball before it lands or touches someone then the batter is out. If the fielder is from the home team, fans seated in that area usually move aside to allow the fielder a better chance of catching the ball. Fans also try to cushion any fall of their own player.

If a fan of the home team interferes, willingly or inadvertently, and makes a catch himself, or if his actions prevent the home team's fielder from making a catch, other fans do not hesitate to voice their displeasure. The loyalty of the particular fan, as well as his intelligence and sanity are taunted. In extreme cases, an offending fan may be at risk of physical harm from less-forgiving and irate fans.[17]

On the other hand, when a fielder from the visiting team tries to catch a ball, home fans make an effort to catch the ball in their area of foul territory. The visiting fielder knows he is entering hostile enemy territory at his own peril.

Fans are involved throughout a game and their responses may influence its outcome. Knowing we are a part of the game makes baseball more enjoyable. War was never a spectator sport; and fans want to be involved and play a role in battle. War and war games provide agitation and excitement for active physical, mental and emotional involvements in the affairs of a community. Asking members of this community to sit still and be mere onlookers is asking the impossible. Fans seek involvement and participation in their own common destiny. Successful baseball organizations like the Boston Red Sox and New York Yankees satisfy these basic communal needs, and tickets to their games are often sold out. By this and other purchases of merchandise fans further contribute to the war chest, allowing their team to hire better players.

The visiting team wants to take these supportive home fans out of any game. In addition, visitors may be subjected to the crowd's inherent hostility and open intimidation, such as relentless heckling, jeering and taunting.[18] Consequently, each home team strives to get its own crowd involved as it is a big part of its arsenal. Visitors know that no team likes to lose in front of its fans. Encouragement by the crowd often bolsters the home team to heroic efforts, especially when the home team is down, lagging behind, or when the game is on the line. The home side does its best to respond to these clarion calls.[19] Players are pushed to give unbelievable efforts to stave off defeat. They understand this common bond between themselves and their fans. The morale of players can also be supported by fans and players voice their appreciation of fans struggling with them through tough times.

Occasionally, this intensity of overenthusiastic fans can adversely affect the performance of some players who have difficulties handling pressure, closer scrutiny and high expectations. Younger players often struggle at parks in their former hometowns in the presence of families and friends. Successful players learn quickly how to harness the energy of the crowd and know that failure could result in them being traded or released.[20]

The strength of this "mass effect" of the home crowd is dependent on a number of factors: the number of enthusiastic fans in the stadium, the degree to which the game is hyped, the extent to which the crowd is pumped-up, the strength of the rivalry between the home and the visiting team, the history between the two teams and players, the importance of the particular game, the relationship between the fans and the players, and the weather conditions.

The effects of spectators are felt at all levels of baseball, from professional to amateur to children. During baseball games, some parents respond even more viscerally to perceived threats to their child. Some parents are determined to stand up for their own children and team, and cannot distinguish between real dangers and game situations.

The mantra of the crowd can be summed up by a well-known quotation attributed to the legendary American football coach, Vince Lombardi: "Winning is not everything; it is the only thing!"

Our responses at baseball games say a lot about ourselves and how our ancestors responded to situations in our deep past. Baseball great Yogi Berra puts it well: "You can observe a lot by watching." By taking a step back from the game and watching its fans, baseball reflects our personal and societal values. The crowd affects whatever it is focused on; and baseball serves as a great outlet to express our collective energy. Baseball is truly a game in which the masses both watch and participate.[21]

14

Baseball Within
Our Culture and
Its Relevance Today

A people's culture tells the world who and what they are.[1] Baseball is an integral part of many peoples' cultural expressions which reveal their past, occupy and entertain their present, and indicate their future.[2] Baseball is an enjoyable part of popular culture which players and fans are happy to be involved in and proud to publicly show their love and affection for.

In addition to the sights and sounds of the game, there are other unexpected and hidden aspects which over time were consciously or unconsciously captured in baseball. These other facets of baseball reflect deep biological, natural, historical, religious and philosophical underpinnings. They have also helped to give this game its widespread international appeal, transcending societal barriers of religion, language and ethnicity. Baseball is currently being played and enjoyed in more than a hundred countries across the world, yet each country's style of play reveals national traits and social values. A society adopts the game, and in turn the game adopts the society.

There is a natural rhythm in all tangible and intangible things. In the cosmos, for example, there is the expansion and contraction of the universe, and the births and deaths of galaxies, stars, and planets. On Earth, there have been historic rises and falls of empires, kingdoms, dynasties, and societies. During our lives there are readily observable phenomena of rhythmic periods of light and darkness—day and night, sunrise and sunset, and the rising and falling of tides. Likewise, the natural order of living things involves birth and death which are both beginnings and endings. Life in some philosophical perspectives is viewed as a constant battle between two opposite forces such as good and evil, light and darkness, and life and death. This view can be analogously expressed in scientific evolutionary terms or Darwinism, that life is a continuous struggle for survival, determined by the process of natural selection.[3] Yet, survival and success do not always favor the industrious, meritorious, and honorable individuals and societies. Often small unforeseen, inexplicable and untimely acts determine the direction of battles, struggles, paths and lives.[4]

Baseball captures these rhythmic cycles (e.g., beginning and ending, rising and falling, and symbolic living and dying) and struggles as philosophical battles played out in the cosmos and daily life.[5] These aspects help to explain the allure and popularity of baseball throughout the world. This is strikingly true in the East (Japan, China, South Korea, Hong Kong, and Taiwan) where the philosophies of Buddhism, Shintoism, Confucianism, or Taoism prevail. In addition, baseball finds favor in other Western and Western-oriented countries (Australia, Aruba, Belgium, Cuba, Dominican Republic, Holland, Italy, Nicaragua, Panama, Philippines, Puerto Rico, South Africa and Venezuela) where Christianity was or still is the dominant religion and core philosophy. The game has also found fertile ground in Israel, where Judaism is the accepted state religion. Baseball is also played in some Middle-Eastern Islamic countries, where American workers were and continue to be employed in the oil industry.

*   *   *

Duels and Widespread Appeal

The popularity of baseball across so many diverse cultures and societies is formed on the basis of the duels between pitchers and hitters. These primal man-to-man and life-determining confrontations were common to all societies at one time or another in their past. As recently as the seventeenth and to the nineteenth centuries, Western European man-to-man duels and combats were established methods of settling disputes between gentlemen.[6] Such practices and customs were brought to America and exhibited through deadly gunfights. Duels were seen in the early days of British and European colonization in streets and bars of small towns and cities across the frontiers especially of the *wild wild west*. Gunfights were ways of settling arguments or grievances, asserting dominance, removing opposition, and exerting legal or illegal control. As Western societies became more "civilized," such reasons for injurious or lethal confrontations were deemed no longer acceptable and legal. Yet people still longed for the thrills of old-fashioned duels. Baseball provided an outlet for these much-desired man-to-man duels. Women and children were also allowed to attend these sporting duels as no bloody violence was involved.[7] There was also money to be made in these substitute personal duels or team-combats, contributing to the rapid professional development of the game.[8]

In baseball, as in life, one faces his duties and responsibilities. At one time or another everyone is faced by the inevitable confrontation between winning and losing or life and death. In baseball these battles are between a batter and pitcher; only one can win, the other must lose, there is no middle ground.

In the primary duel in baseball, the batter, on lower ground, sees the mound and knows the odds are against him, fully aware that from this higher place comes "death." The pitcher, like a god, on higher ground, controls the action. The batter knows that despite the lower probability of success he has to respond to the will and actions of the pitcher. Not all gods are all-powerful and even gods, or the greatest of ballplayers, fail and have their intentions thwarted. Viewers look at the contestants in this duel on unequal heights (heaven versus earth, or god versus mortal) facing each other. These symbolic life-and-death struggles are played out, again and again, over the course of every game.

The hitter, standing in one of the two batter's boxes beside home plate, knows this journey starts and ends here. He must first touch all four bases before his valiant efforts in this duel are rewarded.[9] The underlying philosophy here is that human life begins with nothing and after a brief period of time returns to the earth. The point of entry and exit, or beginning and end of all life is one and the same. This is the same principle taught for centuries in most martial arts traditions such as in formal katas of karate instructions. Life begins with nothing and ends in the same place with nothing, except for goodness or evil wrought in the brief period on stage. Consequently, one of the fundamental principles of moral instructions espoused in Eastern philosophies, such as Hinduism and Buddhism, is to value the opportunities to serve the common good. This is based on the concept that we are each a divine spark from the same ultimate energy and life source.

In line with their esteemed Samurai warrior traditions, Japanese baseball players, coaches, and spectators show respect not only for the visible aspects of baseball (e.g., rules, umpires, players and opponents), but also for the game's intrinsic objectives, values and traditions. Japanese philosophical and religious beliefs and social values have enabled them to recognize the duel between pitcher and batter or two teams as an old-fashioned confrontation between two opposing forces. This attitude is reflected by Major League Baseball superstars such as Ichiro Suzuki and Hideki Matsui, who approach this game with humility and reverence. These successful players know the "gods of baseball" are watching and traditions demand respectful behavior to the game, players, opponents and officials.[10]

In addition, each confrontation or play in baseball (pitcher and batter, ball and catcher, grounder and infielder, or pop-ups and outfielder) influences subsequent events which determine the outcome of a game. Each inning must be viewed as a battle with smaller battles (e.g., pitcher-fielder and hitter-runner) for every out.[11] Each game is therefore a small war and the entire season is analogous to one long military campaign. Spalding writes in *America's National Game, 1839–1915*:

> Base ball, I repeat, is War! And the playing of the games is a battle....
> But it is a bloodless battle; and when the struggle ends, the foes of the minute past are friends of the minute present, victims congratulating victors, conquerors pointing out the brilliant individual plays of the conquered.[12]

The tough characteristics described by Spalding were a continuation of previous practices of the sturdy British and European immigrants who came to America.[13]

Baseball illustrates the interconnectedness of a player's actions both on himself and others of his team. No other game better confirms the fundamental concept of our interdependence with others, or as John Donne (1572–1631) states: "No man is an island."[14] This is also a team-sport in which each player soon learns his personal actions affect the welfare of his team, and the team's actions in turn affect the welfare of every participant. During key situations, a player's sense of social responsibility toward his group is sharpened and bonds with teammates are strengthened.

Religious and Moral Teachings

Across North America, early British and European settlers established churches for indoor religious worship and moral teachings, schools for educational and vocational training, and baseball diamonds for outdoor recreation and practical instruction.[15] During spring and summer one attended church or Sunday school on Sunday morning and played baseball in the afternoon.[16] Some Sunday school teams were organized and played against other neighboring Sunday school teams. Children and youths learned ethical, moral and religious principles in church, and practiced social skills of respect and camaraderie on the baseball diamond. The theoretical foundations and values of society were in effect taught in one setting while tested and applied in another.

Spalding provides further insight into the values that best reflect the American spirit and its ideals:

> I claim that Base Ball owes its prestige as our National Game to the fact that as no other form of sport it is the exponent of American Courage, Confidence, Combativeness; American Dash, Discipline, Determination; American Energy, Eagerness, Enthusiasm; American Pluck, Persistency, Performance; American Spirit, Sagacity, Success; American Vim, Vigor, Virility....
>
> The genius of our institutions is democratic; Base Ball is a democratic game. The spirit of our national life is combative; Base Ball is a combative game. We are a cosmopolitan people, knowing no arbitrary class distinctions, acknowledging none.[17]

Spalding underlines the differences between the British and American class systems. It was often stated that the British used the "3 Cs" (Christianity, Civil Service, and Cricket) to build and maintain the British Empire. In Britain, football (or soccer) was popular with the working classes, and cricket with the middle- and upper-classes.[18] The British Empire used football to help train and entertain infantry soldiers (drawn mainly from lower socio-economic classes), and cricket for their religious, military and civil officers (middle and upper classes). In general, baseball was more widely played by lower socio-economic classes of British and European heritage. Americans have used their own football game, American football, to keep their soldiers in shape, and baseball to keep young men and soldiers physically and mentally sharp. These games provided a mixing of the various socio-economic strata in America. Baseball was used to enforce common American ideals and value systems in young men and women. America strived to define itself and its national character as a distinct entity as expressed in its national game of baseball.

Such lofty national principles and core values (as articulated by Spalding) of any society must be actively inculcated into its young people.[19] Dedicated outdoor places propagated and reinforced these desired attributes in children, youths, adults, and older citizens.[20] Americans learned to live, love, and die for their cherished national values taught in baseball. Parents, teachers and community baseball coaches all influence and contribute to the development of commonly-accepted core values in young Americans.

Triads (short poetic expressions of folkloric and ancestral wisdoms in groups of three) of early British and continental European peoples best explain how these games were supposed to be played and what was expected from each participant. One such triad states there are "Three duties of every man: worship God; be just to all men; die for your country."[21] Such ideals are reflected in the American Pledge of Allegiance.[22] In addition, the triad: "The three highest causes of the true human are: truth, honor, and duty," is also expressed in the very old and widespread *Semper Fidelis,* "Always Faithful," now a primary principle of the United States Marines.

Many ancient peoples expected every citizen and soldier to act honorably on the battlefield and willingly lay down his life for his comrades and country. These ancient inherited codes and ideals of conduct are still expected and cherished by the American people.[23] The game reflects old inherited and ancestral ideals, principles and attitudes; and likewise, Americans use modern baseball to teach their core societal values.[24] America through baseball prepares its children and youth with the desired mental skills and spiritual attitudes of ancient warriors.[25] In fact, it is known that Little League Baseball [LLB] operates under a special charter granted by the Congress of the United States Government.[26] No other youth championship games receive such wide national media coverage as the LLB World Series in America. At the professional level, winners of the annual Major League World Series visit the White House to meet the sitting president of the United States of America.[27]

*   *   *

Games were designed and developed to teach essential skills for society to survive and progress. Necessary survival skills were taught and practiced in ways to minimize potential injuries to participants while maximizing benefits to both individuals and their societies. The distinction between games and religions were vague in that games besides testing of one's prowess against other competitors also served several functions such as paying tributes to the gods and providing opportunities for social interactions.[28] In addition, games obey the dictates of our inherited genetic information. Our genes can be viewed as the modern equivalent of past unknown spirits within us and demand to be passed on. We and our housing bodies have always sought ways to survive and pass on our genes to the next generation.[29] The chances of our genetic drives for successful perpetuation of ourselves were made more likely by the battle-skills acquired in early games.[30] The various physical combat-skills taught in ancient war games have passed into the realm of today's recreational entertainment and can be seen and displayed in baseball.[31]

Games provide avenues for expressing survival responses of our distant past, and satisfy both ancient and modern imperatives to be idolized and immortalized.[32] Games also provide opportunities for public triumphs and the creation of glorious memories of "epic battles." This need for continued expressions of inner drives remains. Everyone strives to pursue their own quest to achieve ephemeral immortality or their brief moment in the sun.[33,34]

Everyone knows their time to shine is fleeting. Baseball players, coaches and the public recognize the time available for a player to achieve "hero" status is short. The chances of playing for one's favorite Major League Baseball team are small, and the opportunities to be a local hero are few.[35] Yet from early childhood, each youth hopes that one day the uniform he is wearing becomes the Major League Baseball uniform of his favorite team. He begins a quest for his own "Holy Grail," and parents buy into youthful dreams.[36] As time advances for many, reality steps in, the competition becomes too great, the costs financially and socially too high, disabling injuries occur, other interests develop, attractive distractions beckon, and the fires within dim and extinguish. Each who departs, willingly or unwillingly, from this quest does not regret dreaming or trying. The great memories and friendships formed through baseball still remain. More attainable dreams develop and the baseball experiences of youth prepare them for the pursuit of more reachable goals.

The few who still dream continue on their paths, being motivated from within and sustained by the encouragement of others.[37] Each hopeful knows luck, fate or his chosen god must also intercede to avoid injuries and present timely opportunities.[38]

Besides honoring the sun god, teaching war skills and promoting physical and mental fitness, baseball games were designed and adapted to teach the young several essential and intangible life skills. Each player is like a rough gem to be polished on the green baseball diamonds so that he too will eventually radiate under the watchful eye of the sun.[39] Every youth baseball coach hopes to find a rare "diamond in the rough" who becomes the next superstar. Modern coaches, like their ancient counterparts, know that refining talent is an intricate, delicate, and slow process, more of an art than an exact science. Youths are polished through their developmental and formative years by a line of local coaches, each contributing to the work in progress.[40] Each baseball diamond (in effect an outdoor temple as well as workshop) leaves its own characteristic imprint on its players.[41] The processes that produce human diamonds to qualify to perform in the temple of the sun are long and slow. These polished stars, like mini-suns, add sparks, flame, light and energy to our lives.

*	*	*

Learning to Sacrifice for the Team

Each fielder is expected to risk injury in pursuit of a ball in order to get an out, even if it means crashing into walls or diving into stands. Each hitter is expected to produce for his team and be willing to take a hit from a speeding fastball for the good of his team. The game comes first. Respect is lost when any player shows cowardice, hesitation or lack of hustle.[42] This willingness to risk and sacrifice one's body for the benefit of the group was ingrained and endemic in the battle-ready and warring tribes of early Britain and continental Europe.[43] Paying the ultimate price for the benefit of others is an ancient practice preserved in many folk tales and legends.[44] This noble trait was not only recognized during war, but also in rituals to appease the gods for victories and other bounties. Such sacrificial practices continued in peaceful times as seen in religious rituals and games. This embedded practice of willingly sacrificing one's life for the benefit of everyone was and is expected from soldiers and others engaged in the military. The most famed regiment in the British Army is still the Gordon Highlanders, who sacrificed their lives to maintain their ground, reputation, trust and honor of their brotherhood.[45] Since the regiment was formed in 1881, many Gordon Highlanders have died to maintain their fighting traditions and reputations in war after war.

The old religions of British and continental European peoples were replaced by Christianity, a religion that also emphasized this concept of sacrifice for others. According to Christian beliefs, humans were born with sin and continue in sin. A price needed to be paid before humanity could be forgiven and cleansed, since without the shedding of blood there can be no remission of sins. After this price was dutifully and willingly paid by Jesus Christ on the cross at Calvary, outside the city walls of Jerusalem, no other sacrifice of blood or life, human or animal is required. Christians who symbolically "sacrifice" themselves to Christ and his teachings do not have to fear death, as they are assured a place in heaven with their Lord and Savior, Jesus Christ. Similarly, in the days of the old religions of the British and others, sacrifices of one-self did not go unsung and were also acknowledged when one entered into the domains of the Otherworld.[46,47] This concept of sacrifice for others became even more ennobling and obligatory as a holy and sacred duty in early British and continental Europeans beliefs and stories. A noted example in the beliefs of the early Germanic and Scandinavian peoples is that of "Odin, chief of the gods, who must sacrifice his right eye in order to drink from the fountain of wisdom."[48] Pain, suffering and death are the sacrifices dutifully endured for the betterment of the community. The gods, old and new, set the examples of what is expected.

Today, players are often commended when they play through pain and injury.[49] This concept of sacrificing oneself for the team, alias the "team concept," is crucial to success in baseball as seen in the following examples. A defensive player is expected to sacrifice his body in order to stop or catch a ball. He must not be afraid to run into unforgiving barriers and risk breaking limbs or being knocked unconscious, even if resulting in serious head injuries.[50] The catcher is expected to stand his ground and hold onto the ball despite being bowled over by charging runners. An offensive player is expected to sacrifice his body in order to get on base, take out a defensive fielder in order to prevent a double play, take out a catcher in order to reach home safely, and prevent the catcher from making another play to get an out.[51] Players also make running headlong dives into bases, even if it means risking serious injuries.

Some plays are called by the manager or coach requiring offensive players to execute a sacrifice bunt or suicide squeeze in order to move a runner into scoring position or to bring a runner home. The sacrifice fly (when there are less than two outs) is made to bring a runner home from third base.[52] These sacrificial plays are requested in close games or when there are limited opportunities to score runs. Each offensive player in such sacrificial situations willingly becomes an automatic out, although he lowers his offensive statistics like his batting average and on-base percentage. His teammates congratulate him for his triumphant sacrifice on return to the dugout.

Leaders who call for sacrifices during a game are also called upon to sacrifice themselves when necessary. At the professional level, if the team fails, its coach or manager may take the fall for his team and be fired or resign. Sometimes this occurs even when he cannot be justly blamed for the poor performance and injuries of his team. Leadership is the first to be sacrificed.[53]

As discussed, the foundations of baseball included sacrificial offerings to the sun god for betterment of the community. Baseball teaches that dreams supported by devotion, discipline, and work are the paths to greatness. The sacrifices, unselfishness, and willingness to risk life and limb required over and over again are but part of the pact with "baseball's gods." This attitude is well expressed in an old hymn, "Our Prayer," by an anonymous writer:

> Not for ever in green pastures
> Do we ask our way to be;
> But the steep and rugged pathway
> May we tread rejoicingly.[54]

The motives and attributes which drive so many in pursuit of their dreams and quests are evident in baseball. Many can identify with the struggles of players to excel. In baseball, the ancient imperatives to rise to recognition, accomplish great deeds and fall are reenacted again and again, just as the heroes of yesteryear were immortalized in old sagas.

* * *

Relevance to Modern Societies

Baseball with its rich evolutionary origins and diverse places of development has far more to teach us than is apparent at first glance. Early British and continental European peoples, their descendants and other benefactors of this inheritance recognized and developed the rich potentials of the game. The predecessors of the game (in whole or part) were used as teaching tools for many basic religious and philosophical concepts, as well as military and survival strategies. Fundamental concepts needed to be effectively taught if the necessary societal norms and values were to continue successfully from generation to generation. Philosophical and religious concepts were more easily taught to younger people via a game played by almost anyone, irrespective of body type. Spalding understood that baseball was a vehicle to forge a distinctive American national identity.[55]

In particular, societies noted for their warriors (like early British, Germanic and Scandinavian tribal groups) or military traditions recognized that not all persons were suited to serve in the military or priesthood (neither was this desirable for any progressive and complex evolving society). Most importantly, it was acknowledged that all members of society benefited from the physical, intellectual and philosophical rigors of such training opportunities. The desirable fundamental skills the game effectively taught so well were designed to create heroic warriors and citizens willing to die in the service of their own group. Often it was not the dying that was difficult, but continued existence under adverse conditions. Living was most torturous when there were disastrous private and public failures, especially when humiliating events occurred over and over again despite one's best and dedicated efforts. (One example of such dire circumstances followed the conquest and rule of various tribes of early Britain by the Romans.) Often under unfavorable conditions, no fame, glory, adulation or hope seemed possible. Dying was the easiest choice or the desperate path to be taken. It was living which took not only daily heroic courage, but moment-by-moment resilience. Yet live many did, not always for personal reasons but often for family, friends and society. This was indeed the story of many everyday unsung heroes in conquered early Britannia.[56] This state of affairs was not only common to conquered early Britannic tribal and continental European peoples, but to all human societies past and present which faced adversaries.

How does one teach people to endure the unendurable, live with humiliation and degradation of personal failures, and yet maintain one's sanity, self-respect, and dignity? Or, how does one teach the young to avoid tempting self-destructive pathways in life and embark on healthy, productive lives?

Early societies cleverly used games with their cultural, societal, and religious foundations to help teach these most important concepts to children and youths.[57]

The game provides ample opportunities not only to fail oneself, but also to fail one's team and supporters. This latter event is much harder to deal with. The game gives a player plenty of time and opportunity to dwell on his failures.[58] Fortunately, it also provides avenues to learn how to recover from defeats and failures. There is always another chance, inning or game, and another tomorrow, or season. Dealing with failure is the most difficult skill for anyone to learn and master. Successes bring accolades, admiration and friends, while failures bring misery, isolation and loneliness. To rise above the fallouts of failures one must have exceptional determination, character and work ethic. Failing is hard enough and yet when a person is battered and injured getting up is even harder and more challenging.[59] Early British and continental European peoples taught their warriors not to wallow in self-pity when knocked down, but to get up and fight until they were no longer able, so as to die with honor. When the battle was over they could clean up and attend to their wounds. It was not about personal victories, but giving everything on the battlefield.

In some early societies there were divisions and specializations of labor or class systems. The base of this pyramid consisted of numerous ordinary people on whose shoulders, the priest, warriors and ruling elite stood. Non-warriors who formed the base were likewise expected to do everything humanly possible to complete their tasks and responsibilities. They were taught their daily struggles made them better and provided opportunities to advance their status in the next life through rebirth or in the Otherworld. Consequently, each knew that the rewards for faithfully executing his duties would bring merit and a chance to rise above immediate and difficult circumstances. Each person was given hope for advancement and a chance for a better tomorrow here, or in the hereafter.

In addition to giving us dreams and teaching us about dedication and duty to our community, baseball teaches us about dealing with adversities. Baseball is a game of failure. When someone in the Major Leagues bats a 0.300 average (that is, failing 70 percent of the time), he is doing very well. The last person who successfully batted with a 0.400 average for an entire season was the late hitting genius, Ted Williams. John Olerud, while a member of the Toronto Blue Jays, flirted with this elusive 0.400 batting percentage for a few months of the early 1993 season. On the other hand, when a starting Major League Baseball pitcher wins more than half of his games and therefore has a winning percentage greater than 0.500 (i.e., failing about 50 percent of the time), he is said to be doing well. (Other factors such as total innings pitched and durability of a pitcher also factor in evaluating pitching perform-ance.) Baseball players soon learn failure is a fact of life. When a player fails with the bat, he cannot dwell on this failure when he takes to the field. The offensive player must focus on the new task at hand, or else he is likely to fail in his defensive role. Similarly, a defensive player who makes a costly error cannot afford to dwell on his failure, since this will adversely affect his per-formance as a hitter or base-runner.

Personal failures in this game are inevitable and naturally hard for any-one to take, but the failure to learn from mistakes and losses makes bad sit-uations worse.[60] In this game, successful and intelligent players use failures as a motivational tool to work and improve their craftsmanship. Wise players accept the past and move on, they know what is written with the ball, bat, and glove cannot be changed. Each game provides a fresh start and new opportunities to fail and succeed.

Playing this game successfully requires players to have a solid foundation in the basic skills of their position, the intelligence to anticipate the strategies of opponents, the intuitive response to rapidly changing situations, and a love and passion for the game.[61] In other sports like ice hockey, players may express their frustrations through physical hits and fights; in American (and Canadian) football, players may legitimately body-slam their opponents. Yet in baseball, players need to keep their emotions in check. Losing control or lacking emotional intelligence takes a player off his game. Being too emo-tionally charged often results in errors, fielders overthrow, hitters swing too hard, pitchers throw wildly, runners over-run bases, and players make poor decisions. High adrenalin rushes hinder performances and cause undesirable consequences in a game of precision. A player has to be calm and this only comes with experience and maturity.

Although there are many players on each team, baseball can be a lonely sport. In situations when the game is on the line, the pitcher is most alone. Likewise the hitter is alone when he stands at the plate with the weight of his team on his shoulders. A fielder is alone when he fails to make a costly routine play. The manager is alone when he switches players and the situation gets worse. An umpire is alone when he blows an obvious call. Throughout this game there are innumerable moments of loneliness. Each has to learn to deal with failure and to forgive himself. Successful baseball players have learned to handle failures, loneliness, and the roller-coaster of emotions that a game may provide. This is what baseball teaches.

A major difference between many players and spectators is that players expect failures and have learned to live with them. Baseball highlights and records our failures and errors. Many of the greatest players, notably pitching aces Roy Halladay and Chris Carpenter were sent down several times to lower levels of baseball, but rose above these failures and despite pain and adversities reached stardom. Any game which teaches us to accept failure and rise above personal misfortunes is valuable throughout life. Deep inside, fans yearn to see their favorite players climb and beat the odds.

Priests and peoples of early societies lived by the sun god's example: every day the sun gets up from its travails of the night's darkness, travels unfailingly across the sky, and then falls into the abyss of the oceans where it battles to rise again. It does its duties whether or not it is blocked out by dark, angry clouds or storms, and eventually comes shining through. Like the sun god, our own lives are an endless cycle of "births" and "rebirths," failures and victories, sadness and joys, rising and falling, shining and fading and beginning and ending. No other game skillfully illustrates and teaches these concepts as well as baseball.

*   *   *

Respect for the Game

During a baseball game an imaginative observer can picture the "gods of baseball," or the ghosts of past baseball heroes, looking down on the day's action.[62] These invisible attendees are not usually content to be mere observers, but often seem to decide who will be humiliated or exalted during a game, and the "gods of baseball" intercede. This seeming intercession is the unspoken explanation for unlikely bounces or plays, especially when there are unbelievable breaks or miscues which favor one individual or team.[63]

The game is regularly decided by mere fractions of an inch barely visible to the naked eye, as the ball veers slightly one way or another in its path from pitcher to batter to fielder. When the breaks go in one team's favor, it is said that the "gods of baseball" must be on their side. Sometimes it seems that nothing goes right for the disfavored team. The recognition that a player's best performance does not guarantee success undercuts the popular belief that each person holds his fate in his own hands. Often, the proud are humbled, the perfect show flaws, and the mighty inexplicably fail and fall publicly.

The game, like life, has to be played with an appropriate mindset. The best advisable approach is to enter into the rhythms and flows of the game. To be successful, a player must work to develop rhythmic movement in his play so that he participates naturally with grace, fluidity, beauty, and harmony.

Players must enjoy these moments despite possible negative outcomes, since pain, like pleasure, is temporary. Outstanding performers are often richly rewarded by the adulation of attendees. In our past, the overlap of war, survival, religion, games and entertainment were hard to disentangle.

The late Lou Gehrig amply demonstrated, with class and grace, the philosophical concepts of this game through his moving farewell speech, when and where he showed how to deal with our own human vulnerability.[64] Lou Gehrig considered himself lucky to have been blessed with talents and opportunities to play baseball, something he dearly loved. Baseball remembers and honors the past.

Conclusion

Different games evolved with us as we struggled for existence throughout the ages. Various skills and strategies useful in our survival, including war, were valued and practiced.

Over time, skills and strategies useful for survival in peace and war were modified and incorporated into games. Some skills and strategies were discarded altogether, but others had a special hold and significance.[1] Games whether they survived or not carry relics of our histories, languages, religions and myths, and therefore reflect diverse yet common pathways walked by our ancestors.[2]

The earliest forms of games were adaptations of strategies and skills for defending one's home. Ancient arts of war, including acts of throwing (distance warfare), hitting (close-quarters combat), and running (attack and retreat) were woven into early informal and formal games.

As primal humans evolved and became more sophisticated in their outlooks on life, they began to acknowledge the existence of unseen mysterious forces which had powerful influences on their welfares and destinies. Humans respected special places, trees, animals and deceased ancestors out of love, fear, and an acknowledgment of the powers they believed these entities had. At sacred sites and areas of assembly, priests led the populace through circular movements around sanctified objects in imitation of their deities to pay obeisance.

As these early peoples became more imaginative, their philosophical and religious beliefs became more complex. They believed in the continuation of life after death and ingeniously created paths to get to the thereafter.[3] The quest for immortality began along with beliefs and practices to achieve a place of honor with one's distinguished ancestors and gods, and to escape death. Several early cultures had stages for accomplishing such achievements including religious and social rites and rituals in sacred groves.

Early peoples recognized the importance of the sun, knowing that without it life would be doomed.[4] They were comforted by the daily rising sun over the horizon that dominated the sky, and were troubled with its daily setting to the west. Curious and imaginative minds wondered where the sun went at night and where it came from to start the day? They asked why it was chased away by darkness yet was always able to return.[5] Early humans sought to study and understand the sun and its movement.[6] They were awed and troubled by its visible presence and absence, and assigned powerful and mysterious forces to it. The sun was respected and feared. In many cases the sun became the central focus of myths, legends, rituals, and songs. The deified sun became a powerful ally against darkness, and its light and warmth as well as its protection were necessary for survival.

In a changing world of seasons, weather and enemies, the sun was the cornerstone of early religious beliefs and practices. The sun god was known by different names in many diverse places. This ancient universal veneration and deification of the sun provided a shared heritage and common beliefs among humankind, as shared by early British and continental European and ancient Indian peoples (Appendix E).

Adulation and deification of the sun were not enough. The sun was viewed as a living entity and like every being it needed food and drink. Humans offered their lives, or the lives of others, as worthwhile tributes and sacrifices. They sought ways to harness the power of the sun for their benefit, prosperity and collective survival.[7]

Early peoples adapted and developed games which honored the sun god, known as *Beul, Belus,* or *Taranis* in early Britain and continental Europe. Children and youths learned the importance of the sun from older generations who in turn had learned from their ancestors. The sun controlled the length of days and weather. Linkages with past ancestral worship continued with successive generations. Rites were named in honor of the sun, like *solas* or *solus,* and the sun's movements were mimicked in these. In such rites, sacrificial rituals, votive offerings, and beliefs and practices honoring the sun were duly made and became embedded in their religions. Early efforts in natural settings like green fields were among our earliest efforts to harness the energy of the sun to benefit society. These green fields or "baseball diamonds" of early priests or magicians, like today's solar panels, were analogously designed to harness the energy of the sun.[8]

These ancient religious rituals overlapped with training for war and early games. They continued their development under early peoples for centuries and millennia. As the peoples of early Britain and continental Europe, with their leading priesthood, fell under control of the Roman State and later the Christian Church, their customs and practices fell out of favor. These practices were considered politically dangerous, pagan, out-of-touch, irrelevant, or no longer socially acceptable by ruling powers.[9]

Early British and related European sacred groves were destroyed and abandoned, over which Roman temples and later Christian churches were built. Games associated with former pagan sun-worshipping practices were considered dangerous or outdated superstitions, and were forcibly abandoned and later forgotten. Surviving members of early British high societies, under the threat of violence and death for their "idolatrous" ways, embraced Roman and later Christian practices. Since the depleted leadership of early British tribal societies accepted and could not actively promote the public continuation of their hereditary practices, the significance of these sun rituals and games submerged. These sun-worshipping rituals had been interwoven into all aspects of their lives and were themselves based on older religious practices such as tree- or snake-worship, which likewise included circular movements around sacred places (trees, burial places, and other defined sites). Despite natural barriers and distances, the supernatural entities being worshiped or honored, and the rites, rituals and religious practices of humanity were common throughout various communities and times. This essential commonality helps to explain our universal affinity for the comforting and familiar ways of the past, despite modern differences.

After the early Christian Church made vigorous attempts to stamp out pagan practices, the later puritanical zealots of the Reformation worked toward total completion of this task.[10] Early religious rituals survived only as fragments in folk and ball games, stripped of religious meaning, significance and connotation. The fun, entertainment and socializing aspects of these practices were retained to some extent in the games which survived. Stool-ball, an early predecessor or form of baseball, was associated with social mixing and religious holidays.[11] Such aspects (especially the courting by young people) during and at these games were frowned upon by the church and ruling civilian authorities.

Despite all this opposition by officials, ball games and their variants survived the millennia of human development. In the fifteenth to nineteenth centuries, these innocuous games were known and recorded as stool-ball, tut-ball, baseball, and many other names. The early British and continental European peoples (including children and young people) were able to connect with each other and enjoy what remained of their ancestral rites, rituals, pastimes and games.[12]

These various folk games were brought to the New World, where their eventual acceptance and standardization led to the rapid spread and development of the game we know as baseball. Standardization brought the different varieties under one ruling hand. This centralization brought together both strengths and weaknesses (some more desired components were later re-introduced), and the net effect was stability, acceptance and the long term success of baseball.

An examination of baseball throughout our history shows relics of religious rites and folk games, which owe their origins to tributes to the sun or sun god. The game's deep appeal lies in its quiet and deep past. Various war strategies, philosophical principles, religious beliefs, superstitions and traditions embedded in the game reveal its true depth, nature and history. This game, like the sun, has undergone a twilight period and a time of seeming disappearance, only to return.

Today, baseball is not only America's national pastime, but has also found fertile ground around the world.[13] Baseball is played and enjoyed by many, breaking through cultural, language and social barriers.

At each baseball game, we get a chance to witness something new and spectacular. These events transcend boundaries and create shared memories across the baseball world. In this way, baseball brings us all together and we are bonded despite, class, ethnicity, nationality, culture, time and place.[14]

Children and youth worldwide benefit from the opportunity to participate in baseball as it teaches and prepares them for many aspects of life. Today, the sun traverses the sky, from east to west, overlooking a game which once served to honor it. Baseball brings joy and reveals the common roots and heritage of humanity.

Appendix A

A Brief Background of the Early Insular British and Related Peoples

The achievements of any particular group are rarely fully their own, but rather reflect the assimilation and influences of others past. The peoples of early and later Britain are no exception to this rule.

Though the diverse tribal peoples of early Britain forged distinctive groups, they were themselves impacted by others, before and after, sojourning to their present homes. Because of the rich diversity of these groups, continuous interactions and intermingling enriched their communities. These people of Indo-European origins interacted with numerous other tribal groups, of similar or dissimilar natures as they moved across the western world until they reached ancient insular Britain and neighboring areas of Scotland, Ireland, Wales, etc. Some of these related peoples settled in Brittany located in the southwest part of France. On arrival with this vast cultural baggage they merged with the pre-existing peoples of these places. Unfortunately, there is no solid record of the cultural practices of the ancient peoples who pre-existed here in Britain and Europe, before the arrival of the waves of various tribal peoples.

Davies in *The Celts* writes, "There was thus a melding of the old traditions with the far higher moral teaching of Christianity. It is that melding which causes the spirituality of the Celtic Church to be so captivating in its appeal."[1] The respected Druids carried out the priestly functions in these early British societies. The priesthoods (old and new) of the various tribal and inter-tribal groups were also the preservers of ancient traditions, laws, science, scholarly activities and healing practices. These priests and bards were recruited from the aristocracy of each tribal society, since they were part of the leadership class. The priests and the upper echelons of tribal warriors formed the upper classes of early British and related societies. The religious and sacred places of these various groups were carefully attended to by priests, scholars and their apprentices.

Julius Caesar visited Britain in 54 and 55 BCE, and Emperor Claudius began his subjugation of Britain in 43 CE. Roman conquerors and emperors (Caesar, Tiberius, Claudius, and Nero) made it their business to liquidate the powerful and influential priestly class of the Druids, since they were considered politically dangerous to Roman State supremacy. In this way, the ruling Romans ensured there would be no rebellions. Priests who survived and escaped took their religious beliefs and traditions underground. Roman temples were constructed over many of the sites which were then considered "pagan" sanctuaries and holy places. Roman structures built over these pagan sites were in turn later converted to or replaced by Christian temples and shrines.

Following the rise of Christianity and accompanying zealots, many tribal peoples and their priests refused to reject their own entrenched pagan beliefs and were unwilling to embrace Christianity. Later, this refusal led to ruthless persecution by Christian Church officials. Pagan priests and priestesses who refused to convert to Christianity were made objects of derision. Wherever and whenever it was not politically expedient to incorporate or tolerate local religious beliefs, practices and icons into Christianity, there were vigorous attempts by the Christian hierarchy to suppress or totally erase these influences. In the processes, many people were falsely accused of being witches and wizards or magicians and sorcerers, and some were burnt at the stake. This persecution of the priesthood was accompanied by relentless destructions of sacred places, sites, statues, sculptures, buildings and shrines. Survivors took their faith underground and hoped to re-surface again after the current storms of repressions subsided.

Later, the ruling London-based House of the Tudors (Henry Tudor or Henry VII, born 1457, reigned from 1480 to 1509 CE) was most virulently against old tribal traditions. The Tudors made centralist policies and laws which were designed to destroy local tribal languages and culture. Yet this drive for a distinct religious and cultural identity was never extinguished, since committed British pilgrims would seek a place to be themselves. Unlike the religious Protestant Pilgrims who left Britain to practice their religion without persecutions in the New World, some of these descendants of the formerly suppressed peoples found similar persecutions followed them to the New World, often by their own peoples. Old abhorrent practices of burning those accused and found guilty of witchcraft at the stake continued in early British and European colonies in North America. Witchcraft was equated with heathen practices, paganism or worse—the worshiping of the

Devil. Early settlements on the Eastern seaboard of North America held infamous trials and burnings of women and girls in the towns of Salem and Boston, Massachusetts.

These repressed groups hoped their religious beliefs and practices would not have to go underground in the New World. Some were among the strongest early advocates for freedom of religious worship in America. Ellis in *Celtic Dawn* states:

> Over 300 Bretons distinguished themselves as Officers in the American Revolutionary Army, including the Marquis Lafayette and the Marquis Armand Tuffin de la Rouerie, known to the Americans as "Colonel Armand," who was appointed a Brigadier General by Washington at Yorktown.[2]

The various related tribal peoples (mainly from Brittany, Cornwall of Southwest England, England, Ireland, Isle of Man, Scotland and Wales) and their children knew of the persecutions or changes their people had suffered at the hands of others and the Christian Church. Tribal oral traditions facilitated these transmissions of historical wrongs from older generations to succeeding ones. These related peoples and their descendants were therefore inclined to be aligned with the Revolutionaries in America.

The tribal related peoples and their descendants influenced life of America, including its sports, most likely without this being an intentional effort or agenda. Rutherford in *Celtic Lore, the History of the Druids and Their Timeless Traditions* writes:

> As Toynbee [historian and philosopher] says conquered peoples have frequently maintained their cultural identity by the intense cultivation of their religion, as the Jews after the Diaspora. Never, since the Roman occupation, have the Celtic peoples known a time when their culture was not threatened in one way or another, yet that they maintained a cultural identity can scarcely be doubted and we know Druidism continued even if in a radically diluted and corrupted form....
>
> In point of fact, from the fourth century, Druids are again being spoken of as if they had never left the scene.[3]

In addition, as indicated by Davies, "It is that melding which causes the spirituality of the Celtic Church to be so captivating in appeal."[4] Some early British peoples harmonized and adapted beliefs and practices of Christianity to their own. These dilutions and surviving fragments of early British beliefs and practices were handed down to succeeding generations through the centuries to us.

Appendix B

Socio-Economic Conditions Affect Games

Various supporting documentations show the game of stool-ball was played by the working classes in the sixteenth and seventeenth centuries. When the Puritans rose to power (1640s to 1660s) there was little or no time for sports in Britain.

Historian John Rhys, in *The Welsh People* (1906), writes of the extremely harsh conditions endured by the average Welsh farmer and farm worker:

> A word must now be said as to the opportunities for recreation and the means of improvement within the reach of the agricultural population. Few country places have any ground set apart for recreation and athletic exercises and even where ground has been reserved for that purpose under the Acts of Parliament authorising the enclosure of common land, the Commission usually found that it was little used, or not at all. The growth of interest as that of cricket and of football belongs chiefly to the younger part of the population of the towns and mining centres, though football is by no means a new game in this Principality. It used to be a very popular pastime prior to the Nonconformist revival, but as the principal day for it used to be Sunday it was put down with stern severity by all the Nonconformists, who held decided Sabbatarian views. In Catholic times there were numerous saints' day and festivals on which the game might be played, but as these holidays have nearly all ceased to be observed and Sunday is out of the question, football mostly ceased in the country districts.[1]

Rhys also expresses the view that people were too tired from their hard physical labor to be involved in athletic exercises at the end of the day. In winter, evenings often passed as women knitted and men carved wooden spoons while someone read aloud. When they were tired they went to bed. This pattern was similarly seen in early farmsteads in America.

Further evidence of harsh times during the Reformation is supplied by Hackwood who describes the enjoyment of May Day festivities (bonfires, music) and activities (dancing, rustic sports) and courtship rituals.[2] The early

Christian churches, in a few localities, have records which showed expenditure for these festivities.[3] Financial and the church's administrative support for these activities were stopped. The above works shows sports and other entertaining activities were dropped during the era of the Puritans, and some hardly survived in spring times, even in diluted forms.

Sir Walter Besant writes, in *London in the Time of the Stuarts* (1903), about the variety of sports and their demise, and he includes a bit of verse:

A list of sports in 1600 is quoted in Furnivall's notes to [Philip] Stubbes (I No. 6, p. 316).

> Man, I challenge thee to throw the sledge,
> To jumpe or leape ouer a ditch or hedge,
> To wrestle, play at stooleball, or to runne,
> To pitch the barre, or to shoote off a gunne,
> To play at loggets, nine holes, or ten pinnes,
> To trie it out at foot-ball by the shinnes;
> At Ticktacke, Irish, Noddie, Maw, and Ruffle;
> At hot-cockles, leape frogge, or blindman-buffe;
> To drinke halfe pots, or deale at the whole canne
> To play at base, or pen-and-ynk-horne sir Ihan;
> To daunce the Morris, play at Barly-breake;
> At all exploytes a man can thinke or speake;
> At shoue-groute, venter-poynt, or crosse and pile;
> At beshrow him that's last at yonder style.

The prohibition of games on Sunday by the Puritans led to the abolition of working class's amusements altogether, and was therefore accountable for the much of the hideous brutality which possessed that class during the latter part of the eighteenth century. They were not to wrestle, shoot, play at bowls, ring bells, hold masques, wakes, play games of any kind, dance, or exercise any other pastime on Sunday. Now, as Sunday was the only day when the working people could play games or be involved in recreational activities, this prohibition destroyed knowledge of these games, the delights in them, the desires for them, and the skills in them. After eighteen years of Puritan rule a new kind of working man grew up, one who knew no games and could practise none; a duller creature, heavy witted, slow of sight, and clumsy of hand; one who would yield to the temptation of drink without resistance; one who was capable of sinking lower and lower still. This is one of the many adverse effects bestowed upon London by the Puritans.[4]

Besant also catalogues the various choices of winter amusements available to the upper classes which were in stark contrast to what were available to the lower classes of London, as mentioned by Rhys for the Welsh. Besant then cites another list of sports from John Chamberlayn's *Present State of England* (1707) which were being played in eighteenth century England:

The King hath abroad his Forests, Chases, and Parks, full of variety of Game; for Hunting Red and fallow Deer, Foxes, Otters, Hawking, His Paddock-Courses, Horse-Races, etc., and at home, Tennis, Pelmel, Billiard, Comedies, Opera, Mascarades, Balls, Ballets, etc.

The Nobility and Gentry have their Parks, Warrens, Decoys, Paddock-Courses, Horse-Races, Coursing, Fishing, Fowling, Hawking, Setting-Dogs, Tumblers, Lurchers, Duck-Hunting, Cock-Fighting, Guns for Birding, Low-Bells, Bat-Fowling, Angling, Nets, Tennis, Bowling, Billiards, Tables, Chess, Draughts, Cards, Dice, Catches, Questions, Purposes, Stage-Plays, Masks, Balls, Dancing, Singing, all sorts of Musical Instruments, etc.

The Citizen and peasants have Hand-Ball, Foot-Ball, Skittles, or Nine-Pins, Shovel-Board, Stow-Ball, Golfe, Troll Madams, Cudgels, Bear-Baiting, Shuttle-cocks, Bowling, Quoits, Leaping, Wrestling, Pitching the Bar, and ringing of the Bells, a recreation used in no other country of the World.

Amongst these, Cock-Fighting seems to all Foreigners too childish and unsuitable for the Gentry, and for the Common People Bull-Baiting and Bear-Baiting seem too cruel; and for the Citizens, Foot-Ball, and Throwing at Cocks, very uncivil, rude, and barbarous within the City.[5]

It should be noted that stow-ball, another name for stool-ball (or tut-ball), was being played by citizens and the working classes. Here even football (soccer) was only played by the commoners and was regarded as an undesirable game within the city. This information illustrates not only the playing of stool-ball by peasants, but also the absence of its use by the higher classes of society. This can help to explain why ball games were not so widely known or written about.

Appendix C

Further Documented Descriptions of Rounders, Tut-Ball and Stool-Ball

Hackwood gives a detailed description of the game of rounders. He mentions circular running around heaps of stones and the contests between the "ins" and "outs."[1] In addition, Hackwood's work shows some common points with modern baseball, these being: the runner had to touch each heap of stones, i.e., a base, as he ran around them, until safely home; the ball had to be caught before it touched the ground to count as an out; a bat was used to hit the ball; and speed was an essential component of the game.

Hackwood also describes the game of tut-ball and mentions the circular running as in the game of rounders, where players circled the tuts or markers. He noted the chants during the game and that it was played until darkness fell, and resumed the next day.[2] Games were also being played in the morning, and in one of their chants "Ready for morrow morning" children looked toward playing again. This shows baseball-like games were being played by children with great enjoyment, not much different from that of today.

In addition, the distinguished British novelist, Arnold Bennett, published *Anna of the Five Towns* in 1902 (edited with an introduction by Margaret Harris, 1995). In this work, Bennett portrays the harsh economic conditions and life in the late eighteenth century in the Staffordshire's potteries. His portrayal of tut-ball is consistent with the description by Hackwood, except in Hackwood's version, a bat was used to strike the ball; whereas, in Bennett's a hand was used. Bennett writes with regards to tut-ball:

> Then the more conscientious teachers set themselves seriously to the task of amusing the smaller children, and the smaller children consented to be amused according to the recipes appointed by long customs of school treats. Many round games, which invariably comprised singing or kissing, being thus annually resuscitated by elderly people from deeps of memory, were preserved for posterity

which otherwise would never have known them. Among these was Bobby Bingo.... Also, he usually joined in the tut-ball, a quaint game which owes its surprising longevity to the fact that it is equally proper for both sexes. Within half an hour the treat was in full career: football, cricket, rounders, tick, leap-frog, prison-bars, and round-games, transformed the field into a vast arena of complicated struggles and emulations.[3]

As seen from the above, games like tut-ball and prison bars were played at school functions with the elderly passing on their folk games. This was one way of maintaining some of the old traditional games.

Gomme writes:

"Tut-ball," as played at a young ladies' school at Sheffinal fifty years ago. The players stood together in their "den," behind a marked line on the ground, all except one, who was "out," and who stood at a distance and threw the ball to them. One of the players in the den then hit the ball with the palm of the hand, and immediately, ran to one of three brick-bats, called "tuts," which were set up at equal distances on the ground, in such positions that a player running past all would describe a complete circle by the time she returned to the den. The player who was "out" tried to catch the ball, and to hit the runner with it while passing from one "tut" to another. If she succeeded in doing so, she took her place in the den, and the other went "out" in her stead. This game is very nearly identical with "rounders."

A game at ball, now only played by boys, but half a century ago by adults on Ash Wednesday, believing that unless they do so they would fall sick in harvest time. This is a very ancient game, and was elsewhere called "Stool-Ball," indulged in by the clergy as well as the laity to avert misfortune.[4]

This also suggests a religious undertone or an affiliation of a ritual for good health as an old established tradition. Gomme also mentions that Addy, *A Glossary of Words ...*, states that the games of pize-ball and stool-ball are the same (Note 4).

Another writer, Delloyd J. Guth in his compilation of literature on *Late-Medieval England, 1377–1485*, states: "Pize-ball: Popular games similar to stool-ball and tut-ball, or to modern rounders and baseball."[5] This supports the other claims that games similar to baseball were long known in medieval England before they were established in America.

In the work of Robert Herrick, *The Poetical Works of Robert Herrick* (1893), the following is found:

691. Stool-Ball.

1. At stool-ball, *Lucia,* let us play.
   For sugar-cakes and wine:
   Or for a tansie let us pay,
       The losse or thine, or mine.

2. If thou, my deere, a winner be
    At trundling of the ball,
The wager thou shalt have, and me,
    And my misfortunes all.
3. But if, my sweetest, I shall get,
    Then I desire but this;
That likewise I may pay the bet,
    And have for all a kisse.[6]

Herrick's poem, originally published in 1648 in *Hesperides or The Works Both Humane and Divine* captures the socializing aspects of the old game. Both sexes and betting were involved.

Underdown adds in *Revel, Riot, and Rebellion: Popular Politics and Culture in England 1603–1660* that there were two variants of stool-ball.[7] In addition he points out the areas of Britain where the game was played and associated with the culture of different regions and occupations.[8] This early form of the game was widely played in England in numerous communities and villages in the sixteenth, seventeenth, and eighteenth centuries (CE), and was played in animal-husbandry and clothing manufacturing districts.

Gomme in her two volumes of work (1894–1898), writes about rounders and stool-ball.[9] She mentions that rounders was played by boys and that one side was called the *ins* (batting) and the other the *outs* (fielding). Her account of rounders shows that three swinging strikes produce an out, and that the hitter can run on the third strike. The hitter on running can be struck with the ball (referred to as "tagged," "soaked" or "burned" in other places). The base can be crowned, that is, tagged before the runner gets there. A caught fly-ball ends the inning for the entire hitting team. A player who makes it safely around the bases is said to score a rounder. From the above detailed description of rounders, the game has obvious similarities with baseball and therefore many who were familiar with rounders thought baseball came from it. She concludes that an elaborate form of this game has become the national game of the United States of America.

Gomme describes a game of stool-ball being played by the upper strata of society and country folks during the reign of Queen Elizabeth I and gives an example of the game being played and witnessed by the Earl of Leicester and his attendants and local country people.[10] Gomme also mentions that this game was established in North Wiltshire, North Gloucestershire and in some areas of Somerset and Bath. Stobball, noted by Gomme, may well be another variant of early baseball, since the author could not determine whether the game was being played in many other places in England. This game was being played on a turf and rock surface which helped the ball quicken on the rebound.[11] However, Francis Willughby's work suggests the two games stool-ball and stobball were different. The distinction between these two games is unclear. Others had mentioned stool-ball was played in North Wiltshire.

Willughby (1635–1672), a seventeenth-century naturalist, died at the age of 36 before his work on games was published. Editors Cram, Forgeng and Johnston in their 2003 edition of the Willughby's book clarify the two terms in the "Glossary of Games" section:

Stool-ball, Tut-ball
A game called Stool-ball is attested as early as the fifteenth century. It has traditionally been supposed that this game was akin to cricket, and essentially identical with the Stool-ball played in the eighteenth and nineteenth centuries. Willughby's Stoolball is simply a ball-throwing game, and there is no defence of the stool. This does not exclude the possibility that there existed a seventeenth-century version of the game within half a century of the writing of the treatise.
Tuts or Tut-ball is attested in the OED between 1519 and the late nineteenth century. Willughby clearly distinguishes between Stool-ball and Stowball, two games sometimes confused by modern authors....
Contemporary references suggest that Stoolball was considered a rustic pastime, and one of the fewer sports in which women freely took part. It seems to have been especially associated with Easter.[12]

This is the editors' transcription from Willughby's old seventeenth century manuscript with regards to stool-ball:

The plaiers beeing aequally divided according to their skill, they lay a stoole downe on one side, so as the seate or board of the stoole is perpendicular to the ground. All the players of one side stand at the stoole and one of them begins & posts the ball towards the other side, who stand as farre of from the stoole, as they thinke hee can post. If any of them can catch the ball hee must post it back againe towards the stoole. If any of that side catch it they post it back againe, & so backwards & forwards as long as they keepe it up....
Instead of a stoole they sometimes use a great stone.[13]

According to the editors' "Glossary of Technical and Obsolete Terms," the word "post" was a verb meaning "to toss a ball up with one hand and hit it with the other." The documentation from Willughby's writing shows the game was played in seventeenth century England. He describes a simpler version of the game than those later mentioned by others, though it also shows that variants of the game were widespread in England.

Otis in *Mary of Plymouth* (1910) writes about the first set of reformist settlers who came on the *Mayflower* from Plymouth, England:

How to Play Stool-ball
I know not if my friend Hannah has seen the game of stool-ball as it is played in our village of Plymouth because those among us who take part in it use no

sticks nor bats, but strike the ball only with their hands. Of course, we have no real stools here as yet, because of the labor necessary to make them, when a block of wood serves equally well on which to sit; but the lads who play the game take a short piece of puncheon board, and boring three holes in it, put therein sticks to serve as legs.

These they place upon the ground behind them, and he who throws the ball strives to hit the stool rather than the player, who is allowed only to use his hands in warding it off. Whatsoever stool has been hit must himself take the ball, throwing it and continuing at such service until he succeeds in striking another's stool....

Then he [Governor Bradford], with those who were ready to obey the rules, went to their work. On coming back at noon, he found those who did not believe it simply to labor on Christmas Day, at play on the street, some throwing bars and others at stool-ball. Without delay the Governor seized the balls and the bars, carrying them into the fort, at the same time declaring that it was against his conscience for some to play while others worked. This, as may suppose, brought the merrymaking to an end.

For my part, I enjoyed the Christmas festivities as we held them at Scrooby and cannot understand why, simply because certain heathen people turned the day into a time for play and rejoicing, we should not make merry after the custom of those in England.[14]

The author gives a good feel for this game and entertainment brought from England, as settlers resorted to familiar games of their home countries.

Appendix D

The Game of Prisoner's Bars or Prison Base

Hackwood's 1924 publication, *Staffordshire Customs, Superstitions and Folklore* (republished in 1974) is not readily available in many libraries, but Hackwood's Chapter XL—"Children Games: Pastimes and Amusements" is a delightful read since it gives relevant background to British peoples in the early twentieth century. Hackwood gives a detailed description of the game of Prisoners' Bars or Prison Base in his work as he did for rounders and tut-ball.[1]

This game, sometimes known as Prison Base or Prisoners' Bars, is of great antiquity and shows the measured distance of 30 yards (or 90 feet) was already being used in a boys' or young adults' game. This game and its measured distances were widely known, since it was played all across the country and in front of Parliament. The same measured distance, 90 feet, would likely also be used in their baseball, stool-ball, or tut-ball games.

Willughby (1635–1672) gives a detailed description of "Prison Barres" as played in the seventeenth century.[2] The editors Cram, Forgeng and Johnston of Willughby's work write in their "Glossary of Games" that Prison Bars has been around at least in the end of the sixteenth and early seventeenth century.[3] Willughby describes the prevalence "Running of Races" where running competitions were taken seriously since bets were involved. Runners may be naked or with shirts only and with or without weights (lead) added.[4] To compare racers from one event to another, the measured distances run had to be standardized. Such measured lengths had to be well known and were brought to America and used in their sprinting events at folk events.

Appendix E

Roots of the Indo-European Peoples in Ancient India

"Whence this creation arose, whether it created itself or whether it did not? He who looks down upon it from the highest space, he surely knows. Or maybe he knows not."
—*Rig-Veda X. 129.7*–Fuerstein, Kak and Frawley

Many early British and continental European traditions and beliefs found expressions in games. These ideals and accompanied practices can be found in the earlier roots of Indo-European peoples (e.g., British and Germanic). Early traditions run deep into the mists of time in unknown places. Fortunately, the old traditions of ancient India (ca. 2000 BCE) survived to be recorded. We shall therefore look to find the foundations of the traditions and beliefs that have found expression and are hinted at in baseball. India is a place where traditions die slowly.

Several early Western scholars of Indian philosophy, language, culture and religion have noticed similarities between Indian and European practices in the peoples of Indo-European roots. Observers and scholars from Britain were among the first to mention these similarities.[1] These early observations in conjunction with later and modern studies led to the conclusion that the early British and related Europeans were an Indo-European people who journeyed northwestward after passage through or from ancient India.[2] In that long journey, these future British and European peoples assimilated other ideas and modified their own deeply-held and long-established beliefs and practices. Peoples of ancient India likewise absorbed new waves and impacts of powerful conquerors, but managed to continue entrenched and rhythmic patterns of ancient traditions. It is striking how much these survived British and European peoples' beliefs and practices have in common with their ancient Indian roots. Indo-European groups, for example, those who later became identified as Britons (of early Britain) and Bretons (Southwest

France) left ancient India while others remained, yet common heritage influenced both sets of people, as well as the world.

It is noticeable that despite distance and time there are several similar and analogous beliefs and practices of early British and continental European and Indian peoples, that are particularly relevant to the underlying religious and philosophical foundations of baseball.

For migrating ancient peoples, religion, philosophy, and sports were intimately intertwined. The structural foundations and underlying philosophies of this game were etched deep in the early roots of these tribal peoples. Similar or earlier versions of past British and continental European beliefs and practices have survived in modern geographical India. Ancient cultural and religious traditions found all over India provide windows into the British and related European peoples' past. They also provide rationalizations for our inherent attraction and love of the game.

The foundations of baseball were based on ancient sun-worshipping beliefs and practices. The time frame for the beginning of sun-worship in ancient India is lost in antiquity. Swami A.C. Prabhupada Bhaktiventa in *Bhagavad-Gita As It Is* indicates the high regard with which the sun was held: "The splendour of the sun, which dissipates the darkness of this whole world, comes from Me. And the splendour of the moon and the splendour of fire are also from Me."[3] Ancient Indian kings were named either *Suryavanshi* or *Chandravanshi,* i.e., descendants of sun god or moon goddess, respectively. Alexander Cunningham in *The Ancient Geography of India* (1891) writes:

> Here, *Samba*, the son of Krishna, established himself in the grove of *Mitra-Vana* and by assiduous devotion to *Mitra*, or the "Sun," was cured of his leprosy. He then erected a golden statue of *Mitra*, in a temple named *Adyasthana*, or the "First Shrine," and the worship of the Sun thus began by *Samba,* has continued to the present day....
> We know, however, from other sources, that the Sun-worship at Multan must be very ancient....
> For these reasons I infer that *mula* is only an epithet of the Sun, as God of rays, and that *Mula-Sthanapura,* means simply the "city of the Temple of the Sun." *Bhaga* and *Hansa* are well-known names of the Sun.[4]

This sun-worship, continued with the movement of peoples northwestward from ancient India.

The sun in earlier times was considered feminine and its gender was later changed to masculine form. Relics of older ways survived or co-existed with newer practices. Jean Markale in *The Great Goddess* writes:

> Ancient Semitic and Indo-European languages give the masculine gender to the moon and the feminine gender to the sun, as is still the case in modern Ger-

man and in three Celtic languages that continue to be spoken, Breton, Welsh, and Gaelic. There is something troubling here, made even more so by the well-known legend of Tristan and Isolde, which as it is, fully restores the earlier conditions animated by a feminine solar divinity....

Among the Celts, it is a mysterious, radiant sun-woman whose characteristics we find again in the Irish heroine, Grainne, whose name comes from the Gaelic *grian,* "sun," is the prototype for Isolde the Blonde.[5]

In ancient India worshipping the sun was common.[6] *Indra* was the sun god and a sun goddess was also known. In modern India this ancient practice of sun-worship is still celebrated. In the state of Bihar, people celebrate *Chhath Puja.*[7] For one night and day, people gather at the banks of the sacred Ganges River and offer thanks to the sun for riches bestowed on earth and for personal blessings granted. There is also the festival of the sun god, called *Makar Sankranti.* Authors S.P. Sharma and Seema Gupta in *Fairs & Festivals of India* write with respect to this festival of the sun god:

> Prostrations to you, O Sun God! Only You are the eye for the whole world. You are cause of the origin, existence and destruction of the whole world.
>
> We can see only in light. In darkness, we are as good as blind. The Sun is the source of light during daytime. During nights, we get sunlight through reflection from the Moon. Therefore, the sun was worshipped by the peoples of Vedic communities, not once but three times a day.[8]

These ancient practices mirror earlier statements that the three bases (first, second and third) of a baseball field evolved from a time in early history when three such altars represented and commemorated three stages of the sun's daily journey across the sky.[9] In addition, the sun is addressed as an all-seeing eye, in line with the idea that a baseball diamond depicts an eye which represents the sun; and this eye keeps a protective watch over the community. The powerful nature of the sun was well expressed and acknowledged by the diverse peoples of ancient India. The *Rig Veda*, one of the four oldest religious texts of the world's oldest surviving religion, Hinduism, has hymns and prayers which are still used in greeting the morning sun. Nancy Wilson Ross in *Three Ways of Asian Wisdom* notes:

> Let us meditate upon the adorable
> Glory of the Divine Life-Giver
> And may He direct our thoughts.[10]

This worship and deification of the sun spread into other aspects of ancient Indian life, and the sun became the center of their religious and spiritual lives and universe. Feuerstein, Kak, and Frawley in *In Search of the Cradle of Civilization: New Light on Ancient India* write:

The ultimate purpose of Vedic meditation is, as one hymn of the *Rig-Veda* (VI.17.3) puts it, to "manifest the Sun." The sun has since ancient times been a symbol of higher consciousness, or enlightenment, the Self (the *atman* of Vedanta). In the *Vedas*, to realize this inner sun is to become the Light of Lights, the Godhead beyond all deities, the supreme Reality. Once the sun is understood as the essential Self, all the secrets of the Vedic Yoga begin to unfold, not as some primitive Shamanism but as Vedantic philosophy couched in mantric symbols.[11]

In ancient India the sun was regarded as the most perfect of all creations. One of the purposes of sun-worshipping was to become like the sun and thereby manifest all its divine attributes. Consequently, participants were more willingly involved in sun-worshipping rites, rituals and games which allowed them to radiate divine qualities similar to those of their sun god.[12] Baseball, with its rich religious and philosophical foundations, provides opportunities to achieve this elusive, radiant and divine status to any pursuant of such goals toward perfection.

William Sumner, in *Folkways*, notes:

"Probably Heaven and Earth are the most ancient of all Vedic gods, and from their fancied union, as husband and wife, the other deities and the whole universe were at first supposed to spring." "The whole earth is embodied in the woman…. Women are gods. Women are vitality" says the Vedic Scriptures. In Manu "the self-existent God is described as dividing his own substance and becoming half male and half female."[13]

The Vedic-espoused god was able to separate itself into male and female entities, i.e., immaterial or energy became material and distinct life forms. The two sexual entities of life were represented by male *lingam* (male sex organ, or phallus) and female *yoni* (female sex organ), each occurring alone or together. The word *lingam* also means "symbol." It was a symbol of Lord Shiva which represented the eternal reproductive power of nature, unending cycles of creations and destructions, and births and deaths of all life. Sumner continues: "The dualism of male and female, spirit and matter is essential to all creations. To one imbued with these dualistic conceptions the lingam and yoni are suggestive of no improper ideas."[14] Consequently, in its most primal forms, an imaginative individual can picture the male *lingam* arising from a mound located in the center of the female *yoni* represented by a bowl defined by four markers in a grove.[15] Smaller scaled-down versions of an elongated rock in a bowl representing male and female constituent sexual parts, respectively, were and are still common in India. A *yoni* is similar to an early British and continental European peoples' cauldron in its physical shape and representations of life and regeneration. A *lingam* protruding through a *yoni* gives the trident symbol, regarded as a powerful guard against evil. This symbol is still seen on the foreheads of Indian holy men. This trident symbol was demonized by Christians to discredit the pagan gods of the early British and Continental European peoples.[16] This further reinforces the philosophical idea that a modern baseball infield with its mound and four markers could harken back to representing male and female sexual components as practiced in early Britain and continental Europe and in ancient Indian religious services.[17] Sun-worshipping and principles of duality of life and nature with their beginnings in religious expressions were entrenched in all aspects of Indian and early British and European peoples' societies and philosophies.

In further support of the widespread nature of these practices and beliefs in ancient India, Pupul Jayakar in *The Earth Mother: Legends, Goddesses, and Ritual Arts of India* writes:

> The antiquity of the worship of the *lingam*, the phallus, and the *yoni*, the female sex organ, and their active rituals are evident from the presence of large numbers of phallic stones and circular stones found at Harrapan culture sites. Through the centuries primitive man has sought the phallic symbol of divinity in river-smoothed pebbles alive with color in water—in the *bana lingams*—in fragments of ancient stone carvings, and in rocks with suggestive forms rising immovable from the earth.[18]

Harrapa and Mohenjodaro are two of the most well-known sites of archaeological excavations which portrayed life and civilization in ancient India.[19] The idea of a phallic symbol to represent divinity is old.[20] Bhattacharyya in *Ancient Indian Rituals and Their Social Contents* writes:

> At Mohenjodaro we come across the models of *linga* and *yoni* which were probably used as life-bestowing-amulets, while at Harrapa a number of conical *lingas* representing the male organ, and large undulating ring stones, thought to represent the female principle, have been recorded.[21]

The *yoni* cult was also very old.[22] The foundations were laid a long time ago in ancient India for religious and dualistic philosophical (male-female, living-lifeless, birth-death, material-energy, darkness-light etc.) principles which later became integrated into early games.

This concept of a union of a female Mother goddess with a male god occurring within a sacred square, which itself eventually became the "baseball diamond," was introduced earlier. It is believed, as Bhattacharya notes: "Primarily the *linga* was the symbol of cultivation while the *yoni* represented Mother Earth."[23] He points out that several of the old figurines found at Harrapa portray the Mother Goddess and were colored red. One of the old seals discovered at Harrapa showed a nude female figure with head facing downwards and legs upwards with a plant protruding from her womb. This is viewed as primitive prototype of the Earth Mother *Sakambhari*, mentioned in the *Markanya Purana*, another sacred Indian text. This Mother goddess concept was an old and cherished one in ancient India.

Sumner further enlightens us:

> The Sakta worshippers are a sect who worships Sakta, the mighty, mysterious, feminine force recognized in nature, and which they personify as the Mother of the Universe, like the ancient Mother-goddess. This goddess is manifested, for Hindus, in natural appetites, in highly developed failures by which one exalts one's self and defeats one's enemies.[24]

The last sentence of this quotation is pertinent to an understanding of the need for events such as war and games. Goddesses, like their male counterparts, had appetites and victors offered the sacrificial victims of war and games on altars at dedicated sites. Sacred and sacrificial sites such as temples became blueprints for the physical and philosophical foundations of baseball. Widespread worshipping of various goddesses in ancient India facilitated the survival of these practices with their accompanied rites and rituals.[25]

More modern works have referred to the Mother goddess of ancient India as *Shakti*. Besides *Shaivism* (followers of Lord *Shiva*) and *Vaishnaivism* (followers of *Vishnu*) there is still a cult called *Shakti* devoted to a female energy concept. Chatterjee and Chatterjee in *Sacred Hindu Symbols* also point out that the doctrines and philosophies of *Shakti's* believers endorse more than one *Shaktis* or "Creative Energies."[26] W.J. Wilkins in *Modern Hinduism* (1887) writes: "It is estimated that of the Hindus in Bengal about three-fourths are devoted to the worship of Sakti; i.e., the power or energy of God as represented in many female forms."[27] He mentions the devotees of the goddesses believed goddesses produced gods; whereas, the devotees of gods think gods produced goddesses. Both sets of devotees recognized divine beings express themselves as either sex, since both gods and goddesses die and are reborn in different forms.

Various gods and goddesses were propitiated with sacrificial offerings of the conquered after war or games when heroes were exalted and enemies humiliated. Gods and goddesses were offered human tributes, especially those selected as most beautiful or brave. Sacrifices were generally performed to awaken and appease the Earth Mother on sacred temple sites. Wilkins mentions a mythological rationalization for the presentation of blood to the goddess, *Durga* or *Kali*:

> When the Goddess [Kali] was weary in her conflict with the demons she came to destroy, she drank the blood of her slaughtered foes. By the sight of blood the satisfaction she had when refreshed by that draught is brought to mind, and, being in a benignant mood, she bestowed blessings upon her worshippers. It should be noted that it is only to the consort of Siva, not to himself, that animal sacrifices are offered.[28]

As noted by Wilkins and others, blood and life refreshed the goddess *Kali* or *Durga*. Offerings were also symbolically representing the replenished blood after menstruation by the Earth Mother. For example, there were two main divisions of the sects involved in *Sakti* worship; these were *Dakshinas*, or the right-hand worshippers, and *Vamacharis* or the left-hand worshippers.[2930] The *Dakshinas* worshipped the female deities, openly observed the Puranic rituals, and made no blood offerings. The *Vamacharis* worshipped in accordance to the *Tantras*, and their rites and rituals were performed in secret and only the initiated were allowed to participate in such ceremonies. In addition to these major two sects, there were also the *Kiratis*. Members of this *Kiratis* sect were worshippers of the goddess *Devi*, who in her form as *Kapalika* was propitiated with human sacrifices. When human-sacrifice practices became illegal, devotees offered their own blood, or mutilated or tortured their own bodies as propitiations to the goddess. (Further details are given in the work of W.J. Wilkins.[31]) Sacrificial offerings to the goddesses were seen as necessary and made on appropriate altars within the sacred confines of holy grounds or temples. The most suitable places to make these sacrificial offerings were on the sacred mounds in the centers of squares or circles, where each central mound represented the *yoni* of a named goddess. These ancient sacrificial traditions and practices continued with the migrating Indo-European peoples.

It was previously mentioned that early British and continental European peoples buried sacrificial or votive offerings under the centers of the sacred mounds and squares. Whether the mound is a phallic symbol or a representation of a *yoni*, the net effect was the same in that sacrificial offerings were made there. This equivalency of male and female concepts fits well with ancient Indian philosophy, since male and female identities of life were just another of their many duality concepts. The sexual and social aspects evident in early British versions of this game were in keeping with its ancient Indian origins. Sexual unions were often associated with religious sacrificial offerings (*Yajna*).[32] Bhattacharyya mentions: "In the *Satapatha Brahmana* we come across numerous passages in which sexual union is identified with sacrifice."[33] He also cites rituals where the goddess-queen and priest-king were ceremoniously raised in the air in a ritual which became known as the *Asvamedha* sacrifice. These offerings were perceived as economic necessities for survival of the group. In the same work, Bhattacharyya states the life of a priest or king was limited when productivity went down, as they were sacrificed for the good of the community.[34]

This ancient Indian practice likely survived as the old British and European practice of *heaving* or *lifting* previously seen in connection with Easter as a remnant of ancient fertility rites. This old and noble concept of willingly sacrificing oneself for the communal good in a sacred ceremony and being witnessed by the community has a long entrenched history in ancient India. Such ancient concepts of sacrifice were endorsed by their philosophical teachings. Prabhupada points out a few relevant sections with regards to the importance of sacrifice:

> 30. All these performers who know the meaning of sacrifice become cleansed of sinful reactions, and having tasted the nectar of the results of sacrifices, they advance towards the supreme eternal atmosphere....
>
> 31. O best of the Kuru dynasty, without sacrifice one can never live happily on this planet or in this life: what then of the next? ...
>
> 5. Acts of sacrifice, charity, and penance are not to be given up; they must be performed. Indeed, sacrifice, charity and penance purify even the great souls.[35]

This value of sacrificial principles survived and came to North America via the British and continental European peoples. Such ancient practices of self-sacrifice for the communal good were incorporated into these peoples' strategies of games and war.[36] Early British and European peoples' heroic self-sacrificial strategies have survived in this their ancestral-based game of baseball. One can envisage an individual sacrificing himself by drawing his enemies' attention to create a distraction while others of his clan or tribe take advantage of this opportunity to breach defenses.

The best way to prove an individual's heroic worth for sacrificial offering was through wars or games. Sacrificial offerings of priests or kings later gave way to the substitution of others, especially defeated war opponents, prisoners, and criminals. Later animals were sacrificed as substitutes for humans. Males of the species were preferred choices, these being bulls instead of cows, stallions instead of mares, and rams instead of ewes. Relics and rumors of past human sacrificial practices have survived in India. Sir Charles Eliot in *Hinduism and Buddhism* (1921) mentions seeing well-educated Indians beheading goats in sacrifices to Mother Goddess *Kali*.[37] He also mentions that "[u]ntil recently the Khonds of Bengal used to hack human victims in pieces as a sacrifice to the Earth Goddess and throw the shreds of flesh on the fields to secure a good harvest."[38] Sir Charles Eliot also notes that in the chief sanctuary of *Saktism* at *Kamakhya* there is a shrine in the deep center which consisted of a rock with a cleft, and this is revered as the *yoni* of the goddess, where goats were sacrificed to the goddess, *Kali*. There are also references to human and animal sacrifices during *navarathra* in which "nine nights" of the bright moon considered sacred to the goddess *Durga* or *Dash Mahavidha* were observed.[39] In time, human and animal sacrifices were replaced by clay and metal images; or, by fruits such as coconuts and mangoes with flowers and incense. Vedic sacrificial formulas, mantras and rituals were also performed or recited before fire-altars. With this background, it is easier to understand the concepts of sacrifice and sacrificial altars in British and European rituals that led to baseball.

The basic foundational designs of "baseball diamonds" as shrines incorporating squares, circles and mounds began in ancient times with religious roots. Such practices are recorded in India, and other places, as Jayakar states:

> The primordial sense of the sacredness of sites, a sacredness that survives the changing gods, is evident also in tribal people, the main servitors of important holy Hindu shrines. At Jagannath Puri in Orissa, the Savaras Tribe have free entry to the *garbha ghra*, the sanctum sanctorum, where, the Blue God, is worshipped as Jagannath, the Lord of the world; .... At the ancient Guruvayur temple in Kerala, there is a small Sakti shrine beyond the temple walls. The shrine consists of four walls around an *Asoka*, at the base of which the goddess, as an iconic stone, is installed. The shrine is believed to be of great antiquity. Nayar women circumambulate the tree and shrine before they enter the precincts of the Guruvayur Krsna Temple.[40]

The above quotation shows ancient sacred sites and temples which survived in India had an inner sanctum, *garbha ghra*, or womb house. The great Earth Mother was worshipped from time immemorial. This female or mother principle was recognized as the pervading cosmic force, and identified with Earth or Nature. Jayakar writes with respect to the Earth Mother, that she enters into the lives of the communities via their fires and plants, being sacrificed and rising again. The goddess is therefore an indestructible energy source. In addition, Jayakar leaves no doubt about the role of the Earth Mother and the necessity for performing sacrifices in a mysterious circle (*Sri Chakra*) or cauldron.[41]

Hindu temples were built with an inner sanctum or shrine room, *garbha ghra*, or literally "womb house," a place where an image of a god or goddess was placed. This inner sanctum was surrounded by four pillars, one at each corner of a square. Naturally, such an important sacred site was on elevated ground or a mound, with any *yoni* representation aligned in an east-west direction. In cases where a goddess, Mother Earth, was worshipped the mound represented the womb, a symbolic entry or exit place for life and regeneration. This mound became a sacred consecrated place of worship and veneration. The dead were also placed here for rebirth and regeneration. Bodies of dead children under two years of age were not cremated, but were returned to the Mother Goddess, guardian of the dead. The general word for funeral ceremonies was *Shradda* which indicated a dignified act in veneration and honor of the dead. A verse in the *Rig-Veda* (x. 18.) states:

> Open thy arms, O Earth, receive the dead:
> With gentle pressure and with loving welcome
> Enshrouds him tenderly, even as a mother
> Folds her soft vestment round the child she loves.[42]

In Vedic times, both burial and burning of the dead occurred.[43] Cremations are now common in India, but evidently in earlier times the dead were also buried.[44] Earlier, sacrificial or votive offerings were also placed in or made on a mound. Some Indian burial mounds evolved as *stupas* which were later much admired by Gautama Buddha, the founder of Buddhism.

It was recognized that in life, unions of both female and male principles were essential for the production of crops, cattle, children, and other offspring. The worshipping of male sun with female earth was presided over by the priesthood. Priests and priestesses became the new mediators between gods and goddesses and mortals. In the Oraon tribe of India, a ritual has survived which reenacted the symbolic marriage of the Earth Goddess with *Suraj Deota*, the Sun god. Such a ritual reenactment was similarly performed by other peoples such as the early British in their Bovine Bardic enclosures, where three bulls, representing the sun, ritually mated with three cows, representing the earth. (Discussed in Chapter 10.)

A. L. Basham in *The Wonder That Was India* writes: "The stupa began as an earthen burial mound which was revered by the local population."[45] Gautama Buddha had asked his faithful disciple, *Ananda*, and followers to build stupas over the various fragments or ashes of his cremated body in the traditional Indian way. The basic plan of Buddhist and Jain temples followed the old and established Indian pattern.[46] Each of the renowned Buddhist stupas consisted of an elevated centrally located dome which housed a sacred relic of the revered Buddha or a Buddhist Saint. Each central projection was surrounded by four pillars or gateways (*torana*) at cardinal points. This area was fenced to separate sacred from ordinary. Such ornamental rails used to surround a terrace with its sacred tree, relic, etc., were called *sucakas*. Repeated footsteps of worshippers with their clockwise circumambulations (*pradaksina*) created a pathway around each fenced area. These clockwise movements of the faithful were a way of paying reverence to the holy relics at these sacred sites.[47] This reverence was reminiscent of older Indian beliefs in which a sacred tree, itself thought to be a resident deity or housed one was enclosed to protect it from the trampling feet of faithful worshippers.

From the above descriptions, it is easier to picture how early British and continental European "baseball diamonds" were patterned after ancient and sacred Indian places such as temples and stupas. Such places and practices were later adapted by Buddhists and became more widely renowned as Buddhism and its non-violence philosophy spread. In effect, the high central mound (stupa) of the defined infield square where a sacred relic was previously buried became the pitcher's mound; the infield (sacred area) within four cardinal points (gateways or *torana)* were likewise marked by four bases (altars); the base paths defined pathways on which the players run (circumambulations); and the white lines (ornamental rails, *sucakas)* separate in-play (sacred) areas from out-of-play (non-sacred) areas. These Buddhist adaptations re-enforced the wider impacts of earlier Indian structures. Early British and continental European migrants likewise maintained their religious roots and traditions with regards to sacred places, groves, and places of worship. Buddhism was essentially reabsorbed by Hinduism in India, but before this happened, Buddhism became a force in many Asian countries including Sri Lanka, China, Tibet, Korea, Mongolia, Vietnam, Laos, Nepal and Japan. Buddhism influenced their arts, philosophies, scholarships, and everyday lives.[48] Both Hinduism and Buddhism believed in the "Law of Karma," or as expressed in the Biblical quotation "As ye sow, so shall ye reap," but not only in this life but in other lives as well, in the form of re-incarnation. Analogously in this game the performance of a player in one inning not only influences his impact in the current inning, but also how he is treated in successive innings by his opponents.

*   *   *

As mentioned previously, early British and European games incorporated religious and mystical features of mandalas into their outdoor design and defensive strategies. The game's foundations in this stage of development in ancient India included rites and rituals to secure the safety of the local community from ever-present hostile and evil spirits or supernatural forces. This was necessary since it was believed every living being had a spirit, or a spirit resided within it, which could be good or evil. Consequently, any fortification for physical defense of the community included protection against even more powerful and dangerous evil spirits. The sacred square was viewed as an energy-charged space to be defended against intrusion by outsiders. The four gateways in the cardinal directions, or astronomically aligned positions, were guarded by spirit entities. Analogously, modern baseball players recognized the importance of defending against the entry of any outside force into their defended square. Similarly, each of the four bases is guarded by a specialist player as part of a coordinated effort to prevent entry to any seeking to breach the defenses of the infield-square. (Illustrations of early games of baseball have the basemen in contact with the base, as if still on guard duty or bound by some invisible force as noted in the work of Spalding.[49]) Entry occurs by a superior or luckier entity. Once the intruder enters this square, equilibrium is disturbed and havoc created within the perimeters, if the intrusion is not judiciously controlled. The magician-priest was usually in the center of the square and controlled the defensive forces from the mound which represented the domains of the Mother Goddess or the fusion of the female and male energy principles. Similarly, the modern pitcher is the player who initiates the defense against intrusion and coordinates the attack on any successful intruder.

In baseball, players complete a circle to score a run, the only major modern game in which such circumambulations are seen. In addition to other occasions for circular movements, sadhus (Indian holy men) Jnaneshwardas and Mukundcharandas in *Hindu Rites and Rituals, Sentiments and Sacraments* write:

> In ancient times, man used to dance in a circular motion around his favourite friend to show respect and joy on meeting him. Similarly, the chosen leader of a group would be placed in the centre of a circle and the others would dance around him. We witness this even today.[50]

Since humans did this to show love and respect to friends, then in ancient times there was no hesitation to doing these circumambulations (*pradakshina*) to honor their favored gods and goddesses, who were at the center of their lives. In one ritual prayer, these two sadhus mentioned above states:

> In the *Shatapatha Brahmana*, the circumambulation (*pradakshina*) represents the daily march of the sun, rising in the east, travelling south and then setting in the west. When the Brahmin priests perform *pradakshina* they utter the sentiments, "Sunwise, let this sacred work of ours be accomplished," and then walk three times around sunwise....
>
> Incidentally, circumambulation in the reverse direction is called *prasavya* in Sanskrit, i.e., walking anti-clockwise, which is considered unholy.[51]

Ancient Indian sunwise circumambulations were also practiced by other cultures, notably ancient Greeks, Romans, Celts and Gauls. Likewise, other people walked around any individual considered holy or saintly. The Roman Catholic Church similarly included circumambulations in their consecration ceremonies of bishops and churches. The Irish, in their funeral ceremonies, walked around a graveyard three times in a sunwise direction. Christian pilgrims similarly walked around the Holy Sepulchre in Jerusalem. W. Crooke in *An Introduction to the Popular Religion and Folklore* mentions the importance of the magic circle in folklore as a protective amulet or device in India.[52]

Circumambulation movements are found in many cultures associated with early or post-sun religious worship and devotion or respect to a friend. Earlier the direction of running in this game was likewise clockwise. As time progressed the non–Christian or pagan connotation was removed and running in an anticlockwise direction was permitted and survived in early games.[53] In baseball, runners similarly move in a circular pattern, i.e., around the central mound of an inner square, touching the four bases to complete a circular process.

Baseball contains numerous rites, rituals and inferences which originated in or show Indo-European based and ancient Indian roots. It was noted that religion and consequently religious ceremonies and associated rituals pervaded every action of Hindus from birth to death, and even beyond by the deceased's survivors. In Hinduism, ceremonies began even before a child was born, e.g., the *garbha-dhana* (gift of the womb) ceremony facilitated conception. Most of these religious ceremonies were carefully detailed and included the three basic elements of Vedic worshipping. These were: (1) sacrifices were placed in a fire with accompanying prayers, (2) magic as evident by mystical symbols, and (3) incantations. Some ceremonies (e.g., *Garbhadhana*) have fallen into disuse. One ceremony, the *Punsavana,* celebrated the birth of a child. Such ceremonies were divided into three parts: *Jatakarma,* for physical birth, *Medhajanana*, birth of intelligence, and *Ayusha Vardhana,* boon of long life. (This is also the prayer of many modern baseball players: superior inherited athletic ability, extraordinary intellectual endowment, and an injury-free long career.) Stanley Rice in *Hindu Customs and Their Origins* (1937) mentions the rites and rituals of a ceremony called *Medhajanana*, in which a child was "baptized" and blessed on invocation of the Earth Goddess. Rice writes:

> In many of these ceremonies the position is most carefully described.... Then again the man must face west, the woman east and so on. The east is of course the direction of the rising sun and if the woman, who is the most important participant in ceremonies of childbirth, faces east the man who faces her must turn towards the west. On the other hand, the south is always carefully avoided. The south is the abode of Death and the kingdom of Yama, and so there is a custom that a man should not lie down with his head to the north because he would then be facing south, with his feet ready to start the last journey. But a corpse is laid out with its face to the south because that is the way the soul must go. The north on the other hand, is an auspicious quarter. Wherever you are in India the Himalaya is to the north of you and the Himalaya is the abode of the gods; obviously if you want to propitiate them, you must do so in an attitude of adoration, for they, like Jahveh, are jealous gods.[54]

The above quotation gives an idea of the importance of observing the four cardinal directions entrenched in ancient Indian religious ceremonies. This description shows an additional ancient rationale for facing the North (Himalaya, the home of the gods). In this game of baseball, the four directions are likewise marked by four bases (previously sites for altars). The pitcher in this ritual faces home plate, and similarly strides toward the home of the gods. The hitter in this ritual strides toward the south, home of Yama, god of death. The pitcher is successfully rewarded more often than the hitter; or alternatively, Yama welcomes those who step toward him in this ritual.

*   *   *

Many geometric abstractions such as angles, filled and open circles, cross, diamonds, lines, squares, triangles (∆ or simply ∧) and inverted triangles (∇ or ∨), and combinations of these which have special religious meanings and significances can be found on the "baseball diamond." Often these have hidden meanings, the right-facing swastika (卐) form or its mirror image left-facing (卍) form also represented a union of Sun god and Earth Mother in perpetual motion.[55] This symbol was usually viewed as two lines joining the four altars of opposite cardinal directions thereby producing a cross with the point of intersection being in the middle; the ends of each line were bent at a ninety-degree angle in keeping with ancient Indian magical formulae. The ninety-degree-angle precision was later made important in the construction of their sacred fire-altars. The swastika, right (卐) or left-facing (卍) form, points in a sunwise or antisunwise (clockwise or anticlockwise) directions, respectively.[56] Since the underlying philosophy was one of the duality of nature (life and death, male and female, etc.).

Before the birth of Buddhism and Jainism in India (500–600 BCE), Indo-European peoples had already moved northwestward continuing with some of their inherited ancestral Indian beliefs and practices. A more recent analogous migration and strong retention of ancestral ways is that shown by people of Indian descent who continued their Indian traditions even two centuries later in Indian enclaves of the Caribbean, Guyana, Surinam, Fiji, and in parts of Africa.[57] In all likelihood, there were initially periods of weak, strong, or sporadic contacts between migrants and their ancestral homeland. In such overseas Indian societies, traditional ways and practices were so entrenched that even though these Indian migrants, or Diaspora, have lived for generations in these foreign places, they maintained some traditions which reflected their roots and old identities of ancient village life in Mother India. This cultural identification was so strong that they were often viewed as foreigners and made the scapegoats for whatever ill befell their adopted host country. Other cultural groups have the same experience.[58] Some early British peoples such as the Scots have managed to maintain their traditions (e.g., bagpipe music, dancing and highland games) wherever they live.

Indo-Europeans in their migration northwestward into old Europe, including Britain, encountered others who already occupied these terrains. They conquered, co-existed with, and assimilated or absorbed local inhabitants. They found in old Britain and Europe that worshipping of the Mother Goddess was just as prevalent or even more so, even though she was known by other names. Certain symbolisms were similar, for example, red, the color of blood, retained its significance as the color of life and regeneration.[59] Black became the color of fertility as represented by dark rich earth, whereas white represented death and exposed bones.[60] Whether marking sacred areas of the worshipping of their gods and goddesses or death, the net effects of defining special territories with white lines were the same.

With the abovementioned background knowledge in mind there are several pieces of information supporting the proposition that the basic religious and philosophical foundations that were incorporated into early versions of baseball, had their origins in ancient India. This accounts for the various rites and rituals observed before, during, and after a game. It explains the roles of the mound, bases, symbolisms and circular movements (circumambulations). Beliefs in Mother Earth or Earth Mother are embedded in baseball along with concepts such as the duality of nature, winning and losing, rising and falling, and living and dying. It teaches the interconnectedness of matter and energy, living and non-living, human and animal, male and female, and gods/goddesses and mortals. It endorses sacrifices for the communal good, since doing this elevates one's position in the hierarchy of the living toward reaching godhood or nirvana, where the endless cycle of births and deaths end.[61] We are reminded of the words of Lord Krishna as he views this rhythmic play of creation, as cited from the *Bhagavad Gita* by Fritjof Capra in *The Tao of Physics*:

> At the end of the night of time all things return to my nature; and when the new day of time begins I bring them again to light.
>
> Thus through my nature I bring forth all creation and this rolls around the circles of time.
>
> But I am not bound by this vast work of creation. I am and I watch the drama of works.
>
> I watch and in its work of creation nature brings forth all that moves and moves not: and thus the revolutions of the world go around.[62]

Each game is an unfolding drama of creation and dissolution.

At games, festive and religious atmospheres are invoked and participants and onlookers can appreciate their ancient invocations. These urges to reconnect with the past are just as strong as any of yesteryear's calls to the ancients.

Appendix F

A Brief Background of the Early Germanic and Scandinavian Peoples

Chapter 5 mentions that an old German variant of baseball was known as *das deutsche Ballspiel* or the "German ball game." More importantly, Block states that in 1796 Gutsmuths, a German expert in the field of education and recreation, compared the then British and German versions of baseball. There were certain common elements in both versions, but Block notes that in one instance the German version was ahead by fifty years, since a runner could also be put out by tagging the base ahead of the runner, or when the runner overran or missed stepping on the base. A revival and improvement was being sought by educator Gutsmuths.

In America both Irish and German immigrants excelled in early American baseball and were thought to have a natural affinity and ability for the game. German boys and young men who played baseball learned the game here in America.[1] Many players of German ancestry have also subsequently excelled at baseball and added their contributions. Baseball superstars with German heritage in their roots include George Herman "Babe" Ruth, and legendary manager Charles Dillon "Casey" Stengel.

In pre–Roman times, the Germans were similar to the tribal peoples who settled in early Britain with regards to some of their major cultural beliefs and practices, which included their warrior attitudes and codes, and love for games or sports (often to prove their manhood). Both were peoples of Indo-European origins. The peoples of Germanic and Scandinavian origins, generally referred to as "Teutonic," had similar mythologies. After the withdrawal of the Romans from Britain, several Germanic Tribes (Saxons, Angles, Jutes, and Frisians), Danes, and Normans raided and ruled parts of Britain. As these Teutonic invaders settled they added their cultural contributions including religious attitudes, sports and games to those of the people of old

Britain and its surroundings. (In some earlier writings, for example from Addy, the people who lived in Britain refer to any foreigner who came later as Teutons or Teutonic.)

In England there are surviving names of places, for example, *Punre leah* meaning "grove, or forest clearing of Thunder" that show the Anglo-Saxon influences.[2] Groves were similarly held as sacred places by Teutonic peoples. The Thunder God Donar (Thor's predecessor) was associated with the great oaks of the forests. The myths mention that a perpetual and sacred fire burned in the temple of the Thunder God within an oak tree sanctuary. Groves were also affiliated with sacred springs. In such places sacrifices were likewise made to Odin, God of War, by burning, strangling, and stabbing with a spear. Odin was also father of the gods, "All-Father," and ruler of Asgard, home of the Aesir gods.[3] Sacrifices were also made by hanging men and beasts on trees. One such special occasion was held every nine years and some festivals lasted nine days. Captives of war were likely to be put to death by hanging as a sacrificial offering to Odin. H.A. Guerber in *The Norsemen* writes about the sacrifices to the god Tyr, also patron God of the Sword: "These sacrifices were made on rude stone altars called Dolmens, which can still be seen in Northern Europe."[4] Tyr, the equivalent of Saxon god Saxnot, was considered as the Sun god and his shining sword as a ray of the sun. Sacrificial offerings were likewise part of a sun-worshipping ritual.

Mounds were regarded as sources of inspiration, rebirth and regeneration. Teutonic mythology tells of Sigrun, a Valkyrie or Valkyr, joyfully entering the burial mound of her dead husband, Helgi Hundingsbani, where both were reborn. This was thought to have occurred at least three times. In another instance the myth tells of the Vanir god, Freyr, being laid for three years in a burial mound with a door and three holes in the sides through which gifts of gold, silver and copper were placed by priests. The Icelandic *Kormaks Saga* mentions a sacrifice being made to the elves for the healing of wounds, the process involved the killing of a bull consequently turning the mound red.[5] Sacrifices of oxen, sometimes referred to as *Fröblod* in Denmark and Sweden, were also made to the male god, Freyr, who dispensed peace and plenty to humans and was also invoked in the blessings of marriages. Both Freyr and the elves were connected with the sun.

The standard practice before a war involved a contest between two selected champion warriors, or two small bands of men, from each side with the remaining warriors on both sides looking on, cheering for their hero or heroes (i.e., man-to-man or team-to-team combat). This was an attempt to settle disputes and prevent further war and destruction between clans, tribes or kingdoms of related peoples with kindred ties. As seen in various stories passed down, Teutonic peoples loved and glorified individual man-to-man combats involving sword-wielding warriors or hand-to-hand fighters. Teutonic myths describe the dueling battle between Thor, God of Thunder, and his opponent Hrungnir, the giant. Thor, armed with thunder and lightning, hurled his hammer, *Mjollnir*, at Hrungnir while the giant simultaneously hurled a whetstone at him. The hammer of Thor smashed the whetstone of Hrungnir to pieces with one small piece being embedded in Thor's head. This mythical dueling confrontation can be seen as analogous to "bat and ball" games, Thor being the hitter and Hrungnir the thrower. This individual or team combat involving a hero and sometimes his faithful followers also became the norm in sports and games. This approach became a way of settling friendly or not so friendly rivalries and disputes, and to the victors went the prizes or "spoils of war" such as land, homes and women. Both wars and sports provided opportunities for individual and team glory, heroism, bravery and sacrifice.

Teutonic myths tell of Odin, flinging his spear toward his opponents before the start of combat. An act of hurling a spear over the enemies was executed to bring good luck, show a determination to fight to the death or end of war, and declare an intention to sacrifice captured warriors. (This act is reminiscent of the throwing out of the first pitch before a modern game of baseball, usually by someone associated with the home team.) Grimm, *Teutonic Mythology*, mentions that the old Teutonic gods were credited with stupendous feats of building and stone-throwing.[6] In Teutonic myths, mention is often made of rock or spear-throwing contests between rivals.[7] The name *Germani* assigned by the Romans to their German opponents was thought to mean "people of the spear or loud, noisy men."[8] The Teutonic people were expert rock- and spear-throwers, swordsmen and hand-to-hand combat fighters. Some, for example, the Franks, held yearly martial contests to honor and show respect for their weapons, such as the sword. Oaths were taken on the sword. Guerber writes:

> Tyr, whose name was synonymous with bravery and wisdom, was also considered by the ancient Northern people to have white-armed Valkyrs, Odin's attendants, at his command, and they thought that it was he who designated the warriors whom they should transfer to Valhalla to aid the gods on the last day.[9]

The god Tyr rewarded excellence in swordsmanship of valiant warriors with them being sent to Valhalla where they were recruited into the services of Odin to be involved in *Ragnorok* (the final battle between the Aesir and the Vanir gods).[10] Wielding a club or a sword requires manual dexterity and finesse which are similar to the skills acquired in the wielding of a bat in the striking a moving object. The art and science of club-wielding and swordsmanship were preserved in ballgames such as the early forms of baseball in old Germany. What better approach to train young warriors for combat than involvement in games such as an early form of ball game without injury, or death. (The Teutonic god Tyr, like the early British hero Finn, was a prototype of the expectations from a ballplayer, that is, skilled with weapons and possessing the right attitude and intelligence.)

In Teutonic as in early British myths, the numbers three and nine are also of special significance since they are mentioned several times with regards to major events and personalities. According to the ancient cosmology of the Teutonic mythical world, there were nine worlds with three levels of existence.[11] The god Odin hung upside down for nine days and nine nights on the central evergreen World-Tree, *Yggdrasil*, which linked the nine worlds. During this period Odin learned nine powerful songs.[12] The World-Tree and Well of Wyrd, *Urdabrunnr* (also called Urda's or Urth's well), were integral to the lives of the gods and various occupants and the multi-verse world. The Three Norns (or Nornir) were three mighty women related to past (named Urd, Urda, Urth or Wyrd), present (Verdani) and future (Skuld) who sat at the base of the World-Tree and decided the fate of everyone, including the gods and goddesses, and everything. In all worlds. There were groups of nine or thirteen women, *volvas* or seeresses, constituting a special unit who travelled around and performed divinatory rituals similar to the roles performed by priestesses of the goddess cultures of old Europe, the Mediterranean and the Near East. Ralph Metzner further adds that the *volvas* or seeresses performed ceremonies called *seidrs*, interpreted runes, and foretold outcomes of battles, hunts, expeditions and alliances. These women therefore played integral roles in pre-combat activities.[13]

J.A. MacCulloch in *The Celtic and Scandinavian Religions* describes the Valkyries:

> The Valkyries are Odin's war-maidens or choosers of the slain, just as Odin himself and Freyja are said to choose those who have fallen in battle, half chosen by the god, half by the goddess. One of Odin's names was Val-father, "father of the slain," as he received the warriors whom these choosers of the slain brought to Valhall. They were "battle-maids" or "helmet-maids" or "wish-maidens"— fulfillers of Odin's wishes. While they are minor goddesses, mortal maidens might be raised to their rank, like Brunhild. Sent by Odin, they rode forth to battle wearing helmets. There they called men's fates and give victory, but the slain they brought to Valhall. There they, Herjan's maids (Herjan is Odin) attend the service to the table, bring the horn of wine to Odin, and serve the warriors with ale....
>
> The Valkyries are described as wearing swords, carrying spears, their byrnies red with blood, riding over air and sea. Sometimes they go in groups of nine.

In the Eddic poem *Helgakvitha Hjorvarthssonar* Helgi saw nine Valkyries riding.... In another poem Helgi saw Sigrun (who is Svava, a human Valkyrie,
reborn) riding through the air with eight other Valkyries when he was at sea in
great storm, which now abated. Three groups of nine are also spoken of. One
of them rode before the others.[14]

The myth of the Valkyries or Valkyrs likely originated from the fact that
women of Scandinavian tribes went out to battle and in one poetic Edda,
Atlakvitha, are called *skjaldmeyer*, "shield-maids."[15] It is likely that they similarly went out to fight in groups, with each unit likely consisting of nine
women. This grouping of nine was embedded in Teutonic mythology and
culture (including war) and therefore likely to be continued and expressed
in competitive team-games. One tale mentions that three Valkyrs (Olrun,
Alvit and Svanhit) while bathing were caught by three brothers (Egil, Slagfinn
and Völund or Wayland the smith) who then made them their wives, but
after nine years they escaped by flying away from their husbands. The relationships were terminated; the number nine therefore marked a new beginning and an end. The number nine was therefore deeply embedded in
Teutonic practices and likely contributed to the basis of the philosophical
choice of a modern ball team consisting of nine players and involved in nine
rounds of battles.

An understanding of the basic Teutonic mythologies and beliefs is essential to comprehend the Teutonic attitudes toward war and sports. Galina
Krasskova, in *Exploring the Northern Tradition*, writes:

> Within Heathenry, the soul is conceived of not as a single, undivided entity but
> as a composite of parts, a microcosm of the immense and varied microcosm of
> the multi-verse in which we live. The soul constitutes a matrix of interrelated
> and interdependent sections, each with its own impact on one's life. To be hale
> and hearty, and whole, the entire matrix must be kept strong, and in balance....
>   Typically, the soul may be seen as having between nine and 12 parts (some
> denominations combine several of the soul sections listed).[16]

According to Krasskova, the constituent parts of the heathen soul were the
Lik/Lich: the Physical Body; Ond/Aedem: the Divine Breath; Hamingja: Luck;
Maegen: Vital force; the Willa: the Will; Hugr/Hyge: the Intellect; Mynd/
Minni: Memory; Odr/Wod: Passion, Ecstasy, and Inspiration; Fylja/Faecce:
Guardian Spirit; Orlog/Orlaeg: Personal Wyrd or the interrelationship of a
being constantly changing; Hamr/Hama: Etheric Soul Skin; and Mod: Self-
Consciousness.[17] This further shows a complex belief system and gives
another possible underlying rationale for the importance of the number nine
in their beliefs. It also accurately implies that a person's entire totality must
be involved for success to occur in any worthwhile endeavor. The total

involvement of the nine components of oneself is necessary for success in modern baseball.

Heimdall, called the White God, was regarded as the son of nine maidens. He was the warden of the rainbow bridge Bifröst, which spanned the divide between heaven (Asgard, the home of the Aesir gods) and earth (Midgard, home of mortals), and guarded against the entry of the giants (from Jotunheim). This idea of Heimdall guarding against the undesired entry to the home of the Aesir gods beautifully defines the analogous role of the pitcher on the mound and his battle with opponents seeking entry into his domain.

The treasures of the Aesir gods included a gold ring, *Draupnir*, which produced eight other rings every ninth night. In addition, Guerber writes:

> This mythical Odin cut himself nine times in the breast,—a ceremony called "carving Geir Odds,"—and told them he was about to return to his native land Asgard, his old home, where he would await their coming to share with him a life of feasting, drinking, and fighting.[18]

Such symbolic acts of Odin, God of War, being carved into nine portions or battles, and nine warriors battling another team of nine, mirrors baseball.

One saga tells of the friendship of two warrior friends, Halfdan the Viking and Njorfe, king of the Uplands in Norway. These two friends forged a close bond of friendship and swore blood brotherhood and allegiance to each other. Each had nine stalwart sons who were jealous of one another and prone to inter-family quarrelling. In a ball game a team of nine brothers faced the opposing team of nine brothers. They played very roughly resulting in broken arms and bruised or maimed limbs. The game deteriorated and one participant was struck with a dangerous and serious blow. Retaliation after the game resulted in the death of the vengeful striker. The revenge and counter-revenge blood-feud that ensued resulted in the destruction of the nine young men from both sides.[19] (Exactly what the ball game was we do not know.)

Similar to early British, the Teutonic peoples had an underlying belief that life continues after death in some form or another. As seen before, for example, in old Ireland, such beliefs bolstered the ferocity and commitment of the hero Finn and his band of famed warriors, a competitive attitude that was also prevalent in their sports and games. Similar ferocity and attitudes with regards to Teutonic peoples especially their warriors were likewise seen. Metzner writes:

> Odin's dedicated warriors were called the *berserkirs,* meaning "those wearing bearskins." ... They wore pelts to acquire the animal's power and ferocity. There was also the *ulfhedner,* the "wolfskins," who identified with the wolf to obtain

its hunting prowess.... These berserk and wolf-coat warriors were said to be in a kind of ecstatic stance, a holy rage, when they rode into battle, howling eerily, disdaining shields, and inspiring terror in their enemies. As Snorri describes them in the Ynglinga *Saga,* "His [Odin's] men went without armor and were mad as hounds or wolves. They bit their shields, and were as strong as bears or bulls. They slew men, but neither fire nor iron had effect on them. This is called "to run berserk." Similar stories of warriors seemingly transformed into wild animals fighting with superhuman strength and ferocity are found in Irish tales of Cu Chulainn and of Finn and his *fian* warriors....

The warriors believed that if they were slain in battle they would be taken by the Valkyries, Woton's [Odin's] battle maidens, to Valhalla, the warrior's paradise. They would spend the night drinking mead and feasting, only to resume fighting the following day, their wounds miraculously healed. Only those killed in battle, the *Einherjar,* would go to Valhalla.[20]

The above descriptions give insights into the Teutonic warrior ethics, codes and attitudes expected from those involved in war and games.[21] Such a mind-set creates an atmosphere and feeling of fearlessness and invincibility.[22] The similarities between, for example, the Fianians of Ireland and *Berserkirs* of Teutonic Odin's dedicated warriors are striking and likely results from a common ancestry of Indo-European peoples.

During combats, women were nearby bringing food to the combatants, removing and attending to the wounded. They urged their men to fight without fear since a worse fate, including enslavement, awaited them and their children should their men lose. Women galvanized their warriors to greater efforts, especially when defeat seemed imminent.

Besides bravery and fearlessness during battles, some Teutonic warrior groups showed imperviousness and indifference to personal pain and suffering. They blackened their faces, bodies and shields to strike terror before they advanced like demon-possessed beings in their night attacks on opponents. Their warrior codes included a mindset that it was more honorable to die on the battlefield than to lose and live on to old age. The attitudes and reputations of these determined and ferocious warriors deterred opponents and helped to achieve victories. Warfare or training for war was a rite of initiation of young men into the tribe and social order of the society. Games provided safer venues for the acquisition and testing of the desired attitudes, skills and techniques necessary to earn the respect of other warriors, be favored by the gods and their agents, and pursue a place in Valhalla. Today, modern baseball players hope to gain entry into the Baseball Hall of Fame, the equivalent of the mythical Teutonic Valhalla, awarded only to select few.

Another view of Valhalla, besides being with Odin and the Valkyries as a reward for the brave who died in battle, is that of its being a place of eternal battle, a warrior's paradise. Davidson writes:

> The true place of conflict of dead warriors is surely neither in heaven or earth, but in the underworld. This is where Saxo's hero Hadding watched the everlasting battle when he was conducted to the land of the dead. He saw two armies fighting, and was told:
>
> These are they who, having been slain by the sword, declare the manner of their death by a continual rehearsal, and enact the deeds of their past life in a living spectacle. *Gesta Danorum*, 1, 31
>
> Another story, from *Flateyjarbok* (1, 206) sets such a conflict inside a burial mound. Here two companies, one in black and one in red, fight without ceasing.[23]

The calm on the outside did not tell of the conflicts raging within the mound between the two teams of adversaries. These continuous daily battles parallel the scenarios seen in modern baseball where heroes are expected to perform and returned recharged for the next game. Moreover, most Baseball Hall of Famers would love to be back in the battle just one more time. Most fans of the game would be glad to see the great ones playing again.

Old European heathens, before their conversion to Christianity, built burial mounds (each called a *howe*) over the graves of their ancestors where offerings were made. They believed that their ancestors could be communicated with whereby wisdom, guidance and blessings gained, for example, by spending the night at a *howe*. Each *howe* therefore provided a doorway or portal between the realm of the deceased ancestors and the world of the living. It is therefore not surprising that mounds occurred in sacred and dedicated places where warriors and the community assembled to participate in commemorative rituals, festivals and games. Davidson writes:

> In the fertility religion, the emphasis is not so much on a world of the gods to which man attains after death if he fulfils certain conditions as on the veneration of dead ancestors, and the need for the living to remember them at various feasts and festivals, to visit their graves, and perhaps to sit on their burial mounds for wisdom and inspiration.[24]

The burial mounds of the deceased, besides being held in high regards, were also visited by descendants, relatives, friends and admirers on festive and religious occasions. Therefore on and near the mounds, tributes, such as games or sports, and reenactments of significant events, like battles, were dedicated to their gods, honored ancestors and deceased heroes. After death, the burial mounds of close friends were placed near each other so that the friends could easily continue communication.[25] In such cases the mounds were well-kept and accessible for honoring the ancestors and gods on festive occasions. Over time it is easy to envisage these areas evolving as sites for sacred games. As time passed the reasons for these games were lost, but the games and accompanied rituals and festivities remained, however modified.

Teutonic mythology tells of two races of gods, the Aesir (to which Odin and Thor belonged) and the Vanir (to which Njord, Freyr, and Freyja belonged). The Vanir gods were associated with the mounds or earth. (Freyr's death and burial in a mound was kept from the people for three years.) Human sacrificial offerings were also practiced by the cults of the Vanir gods. Rulers, such as kings and other headmen, were often regarded as husbands to a fertility goddess (such as Freyja or Nerthus) and each underwent a real or symbolic death. Davidson writes: "Although the Vanir were not gods of battle, the protection which they offered would no doubt extend into time of war."[26] It is therefore likely that sacrificial offerings were also made to the Vanir deities on the mounds in order to secure food, prosperity and protection. In addition to having similar warrior codes and practices, the myths of the Teutonic were similar to those of the early British peoples. The mythologies of these Indo-European peoples in turn were similar to those recorded of the even more ancient Indians.

Numerous rectilinear places called *viereck-schanzen* were found in Germany. The likely uses of such places for sacred religious and fertility rituals (with accompanied sacrificial offerings) lasted a few centuries longer in Germanic and Scandinavian countries. The Germans and Scandinavian peoples were converted to Christianity much later than the peoples of early Britain. Many of the Teutonic myths and beliefs were considered heathen and therefore likewise condemned, stopped, and adapted or modified to harmonize with those of the Christian Church.

The Vanir goddess Freyja was concerned not only with passionate and sensual love, but also with magic. Freyja had some authority in the world of death. Davidson writes: "In Grimnismal [poem in the Edda, the utterance of Grimnir, Odin in disguise] it is even stated that Freyja receives some of those who die in battle; she has half the slain who fall each day, while half go to Odin."[27] Freyja had an exquisite golden necklace, *Brisingamen*, that became her prized possession and wore it constantly around her neck. A necklace is usually found associated with a mother or fertility goddess from the earliest of times. With regards to the significance of a necklace, Davidson writes: "It illustrates the familiar tendency to represent the sexual parts of the body by others higher up, and by ornaments worn on these."[28] Many early cultures regarded a grove as feminine, whether Freyja was specifically worshipped in a grove is unclear, but seems likely.[29] Modern baseball players of various cultural backgrounds have taken to the wearing of necklaces during the games as their ancestors likely did in ancient rituals in tribute to a mother goddess. It should be noted that the sun was viewed as feminine in old Germany, therefore any rituals performed in the worshipping of the sun would not be a contradiction.

In addition to the rituals of sun gods and sun goddesses, Teutonic mythology also tells of *Ragnarok,* the dusk or twilight of the Aesir gods, in which a battle between two powerful rivals, Aesir and Vanir deities, was fought. The early expressions of this game in Teutonic cultures may well have also been based on a reenactment of the battle between the Aesir and Vanir deities across a divide spanned by the bridge Bifröst. Baseball is fought with intensity and attracts the religious and the secular with equal fascination and may reflect groundings with a Teutonic heritage. In any MLB's World Series game, we are watching an analogous battle of two rival teams of gods, with us cheering for our favored ones.

The observed air of expectancy and "religious fervor" at important modern baseball games seem reminiscent of past practices where we await the wills of the gods and goddesses. Often the outcomes of games are affected by chance or unlikely events. It seems that despite the best human intentions and efforts, supernatural entities such as the mythical Teutonic "Three Norns or Three Fates" still write the scripts of the games and decide: who wins or loses, becomes hero or scapegoat, rises to stardom or fades into oblivion, and lives to fight another day or rides into the night.[30] It is easy to picture nine Valkyries picking up fallen heroes and various gods and goddesses as well as minor deities and ancestral beings lining the battlefields to watch and be entertained.

Teutonic myths, as with those of the early British, likewise offer further understanding and appreciation for the underlying philosophical, religious and cultural foundations of baseball.

Chapter Notes

Introduction

1. A. L Basham, *The Wonder That Was India*, "Speculation and Gnosis," 249–250 (Rig Veda X. 129.1–129.7). Translations vary, but the meanings are the same.

Chapter 1

1. Expressions that involve throwing include "Throw one's lot in," "Throw someone out," "Throw in the towel," "Throw someone a bone," "Throw the book," "Thrown game" and "Throwing tantrums."

2. In ancient Mexico, Quetzalcoatl was a powerful creator, god of the Toltecs and Aztecs. He had a nemesis called Tezcatlipoca, which tranlates as "the Treacherous One." Tezcatlipoca caused the death of many people and was stoned, but he survived and continued to scheme against Quetzalcoatl (Leeming and Page, *God: Myths of the Male Divine*, 102–103).

3. The classic case of personal courageousness is the Biblical story of young David in his battle with the armed giant, Goliath.

4. This is the earliest instance of playing a simple game of throwing with someone else. The child is developing his arm strength and throwing skills. Later on the simple game of throwing and catching will be played.

5. The time frame seemed to be much earlier, from one to two million years for preceding or precursor and related species. Readers are referred to, for example, the second edition work of Chris Stringer and Peter Andrews's *The Complete World of Human Evolution* (2012). Chris Stringer in *Lone Survivors: How We Came to Be the Only Humans on Earth* (2012) and *The Origins of Our Species* (2012) delves into a variety of fields on this subject of our human origins.

6. Such sports include cricket, baseball, softball, rounders, rugby, and American, Australian or Canadian football, as well as sports that involve throwing objects, such as the javelin, hammer, and discus throws, and shot-put.

7. This advantage is still used today by modern pitchers who throw from a mound ten inches above the level field.

8. With the realization of the military importance and strategic advantages of good distance throwers in warfare, better methods and devices (bows, sling-shots, and catapults) to throw objects were eventually developed. Through the use of these artificial power arms, spears and bigger rocks were thrown at greater distances more accurately. This was the beginning of the arms race that has yet to cease, today escalating into extreme weapons beyond all conceivable use or benefit.

9. Analogously, in this modern age, we still remember, watch re-runs, and hear about Nolan Ryan's, Randy Johnson's and Aroldis Chapman's un-hittable fastballs. These have now become the standard frames of reference for the highest velocity of the fastball in pitching. Leroy "Satchel" Paige's fearsome fastball of yesteryear has achieved forlkoric status and is still talked about at baseball camps, conferences, or wherever baseball aficionados congregate.

10. The interest in quantifying performance long preceded the Society for American Baseball Research (SABR). It was usually the "little ones" who talked and argued about what the "big" or "great ones" did, but it was the early statisticians who quantified the data and brought some order to heated disputes.

The use of statistics to quantify the effectiveness of modern hurlers is now more sophisticated, and is an important component in determining the Cy Young winner. The games of baseball (and softball) and cricket are natural training grounds for any budding or aspiring statistician.

There still exist some isolated communities, e.g., in Africa, where traders use their hands to exhibit complex accounting skills that are incomprehensible to the uninitiated.

11. With a simultaneous downpour of rocks it was more difficult for opponents to avoid getting struck. This strategy of rows of archers, javelin throwers, and later riflemen shooting and firing in successive turns survived into the nineteenth and twentieth centuries.

12. This seems to be the likely beginning of collecting prized rocks as weapons for war, or as former weapons of war.

13. These non-injurious objects included fruit balls, mud balls, dung balls, rolled-up animal-hide balls, or hide-wrapped or stuffed balls. This would be much like a game of Frisbee played today.

14. Incidentally, in the tomb of Egyptian Beni Hasan, ca. 2000 BCE, etchings were found on the walls that showed half-naked women throwing ball-like objects at each other. Several early societies and civilizations have records that show the throwing of ball-like objects in their games.

15. The continuation of these throwing and catching practices is still seen in numerous Little League Baseball (LLB) parks across North America.

16. In poorer countries in the Western hemisphere, the act of throwing is seen as a pathway to escape "the island" because of poverty and lack of economic opportunities.

17. Two cricket hopefuls, Rinku Singh and Dinesh Patel from India, a non-baseball country, began pitching in 2009 in the minor leagues with the Bradenton Pirates of the Gulf Coast League, a rookie developmental league. Singh is still with the Pirates organization. Patel was released in December 2010.

18. The Scots also have heavy hammer throws. The throwing of tree trunks may well have begun as a method of bridging a divide such as a trench or moat.

19. This game, called "bar throwing," was common among the Welsh. It is mentioned often in medieval verses. Churchyard bar-throwing contests were held during parish festivals. In Wales, there was an athletic contest called "feat-stone throwing," which was a display of strength and power. Contestants had to lift heavy stones above their shoulders and throw, and in some cases they threw the rocks backwards as far as they could. See Collins, Martin and Vamplew, "Bar Throwing (Wales)" and "Stone Throwing," *The Encyclopedia of British Traditional Rural Sports* (2005).

20. Ernst Guhl and Wilhelm Koner in *The Greeks: Their Life and Customs*, write:

> The balls were of various colours, made of leather, and stuffed with feathers, wool, or fig-seeds. With regard to size the distinctions were small, middle-sized, and very large empty balls. The game with the small ball (Μικρά) was again divided into three classes, according to smallest (Σφόδρα Μικάρ), the slightly larger (Ὀλίγω Τούόε Μεξου), or the relatively largest ball (Σφαιρίον Μεξου Τώνίε) was used. The chief difference between games with the larger and smaller balls seems to have consisted in the position of the hands, which in the former were not allowed to be raised above the height of the shoulders; while in the latter they may be lifted above the head…. The Ἀπόρραξισ was another game with small balls. In it the ball was thrown on the ground in an oblique direction, and was caught by the other player after having rebounded several times owing to its elasticity. These bounds used to be counted. The players altered their positions only when the ball is rebounding, had changed its direction [229: lines 2–12, 24–38].

Guhl and Koner also describe other ball games of throwing and catching, including one of Spartan origin called Ἐπίσκυροσ or Ἐφηβίκη, played between two teams of opponents. Some showed definite requirements with regards to throwing and catching the ball (230: lines 1–12).

Chapter 2

1. Today baseball bats are sometimes used as weapons because these objects are simple, inflict damage and intimidate.

2. Stick fighting with papyrus stalks was a sport in ancient Egypt at around 1350 BCE. It was also popular with nearby African peoples and countries, as in the case of the Nubians of the lower Sudan. The Egyptians used sticks, each with a knob at the striking end. Stick fighting is still a well-known martial-arts form and sport, and it has survived primarily in Africa, India, China, Korea, the Philippines and other parts of Asia.

3. While the Bronze Age preceded the Iron Age, in some cases the movement was directly due to the use of iron being developed independently. Likewise, in some cases, copper was used before bronze was introduced.

4. Some baseball players are still seen shaving the widths/circumferences of the handles of their bats.

5. Later a shield would be developed for blocking incoming attacks. Modern baseball hitters are reverting to various body-protective devices to "shield" themselves from potential serious injuries.

6. This is among the simplest of tools and based on the principle of the simple lever.

7. These are reminiscent of more recent practices of those who carried weapons in the days of the "Wild West."

8. These same primal and "savage" man-to-man battles are still evident within Western culture in mixed martial arts competitions such as the Ultimate Fighting Championships (UFC). UFC contests are a revival of such ancient sports as pankration (meaning "complete strength" or "complete victory") practiced in ancient Greece. In pankration contests, boxing, kicking, pressure locks, strangle holds and wrestling throws were all allowed.

9. The classic Biblical confrontation is between David, a "thrower" armed with rocks and a sling, and Goliath, a "club-wielder" armed with a sword.

10. In ancient Rome, in the gladiatorial arenas, contestants were often differently armed.

11. Home-team spectators are often tolerant when their own pitcher throws close to the head of the opposing batter (called a brush-back pitch) but are annoyed when an opposing pitcher does the same to the home team's batters.

Chapter 3

1. In some later cases, these undesirables became the outcasts or "untouchables" in places like ancient India.

These other primate rivals were not only *Homo Sapiens*, but may have also included *Homo Neanderthalensis*, i.e., Neanderthals. Bergounioux and Goetz in *Primitive and Prehistoric Religions* state:

Beyond this approximate date of twenty thousand years we cannot go, but it is certain that *Homo Sapiens* co-existed with the Neanderthal men whom they were ousting and who were rapidly becoming extinct [20: lines 3–7].

2. This is analogous to the Biblical story of Adam and Eve's banishment from from the Garden of Eden (Genesis 3).

3. In more modern times, for example, some isolated groups of indigenous peoples in, for instance, Asia, Oceania and South America have moved further into densely forested areas. These less accessible areas are chosen to avoid enemies and the introduction of new diseases, as well as cultural domination, assimilation and extinction.

4. For example, the apes and chimpanzees of Africa and the orangutans of Indonesia occupy formerly inhospitable and inaccessible places.

5. Kumaun was a district well within the higher mountain zone of the Himalayan tract. Bagwah is now often spelled *Phagwah*.

6. William Crooke, *The Popular Religion and Folklore of Northern India*, Vol. II, 321: lines 16–23. The same paragraph continues:

The people in some places attribute the increase of cholera and other plagues to its discontinuance. In the plains, the custom survives in what is known as Barra, when the men of two villages have a sort of Tug of War with a rope across the boundary of the village. Plenty is supposed to follow the side which is victorious.

The second part of the quotation is from 176: lines 8–11. The paragraph continues:

And anyone who was knocked down and fell into the hands of the other side was sacrificed to the goddess Kankeswari. The actual killing of the victim, as in the case of the sacrifices to the goddess Bachhlâ Devi, has now been discontinued under the influence of British officers. We shall meet later on in another connection other instances of mock fights of the same kind.

7. They had been engaging in these rock-throwing battles long before the British came. The British cleverly substituted cricket and it became the national game or obsession. These intense rivalries between two groups are still evident in the cricket matches between India and Pakistan.

8. Richard Holt, *Sport and the British*, 19: lines 19–34. Holt continues:

> Up until the middle years of the nineteenth century Harrovians were inveterate throwers of stone. "No dog," it was said, "could live on Harrow Hill," and "ponies frequently lost their eyes if they had to pull their owners' carts near the school." Fighting in its various forms was part of the everyday life of male youth whether done casually or according to the rites and competitive traditions of village or trade corporation.

9. Early humans were on the move in search of food and water. These natural meeting places included watering holes where animals gathered and rich fertile plains and valleys where edible plants grew.

10. These were the likely circumstances which gave birth to the ancient practice of "mooning" by young males.

11. The Maori warriors of New Zealand still perform intimidating pre-war rituals at their rugby games.

12. In baseball jargon, pitching well inside to the batter is referred to as "a brush back" or, if the pitch is elevated, "chin music."

13. The situation is much the same for bowling in cricket and pitching in softball.

14. The original uses of the early seeming "bunting" strategies were to stop incoming rocks for one's own use and to neutralize their harmful effect.

15. Such situations laid the foundation for the game of cricket, in which clubbers tried to hit incoming rocks back and forth into their enemy's camp. The Indians and Pakistanis are enamored with cricket.

16. This scouting of enemies' personnel for their strengths and weaknesses, so that appropriate counteractions or preparations can be made, is done at all competitive levels of baseball from Little League to Major League Baseball.

17. Sometimes evidence of this is still seen when pitchers throw before the hitter is ready to hit in the batter's box. This action is called a "quick-pitch." Since it is not safe, it is not legal.

18. The role of the guardians was to deny the intruder entrance.

19. A noteworthy example is Yankee Stadium, where busts and images of past great Yankees are on display.

20. For example, old forts are found in China, England, France, Ghana, India, Pakistan, Japan, and the United States. Some old Dutch fort structures, e.g., Fort Kyk-Over-Al, Fort Zeelandia and Fort Nassau, exist today in relatively obscure places like tropical Guyana (formerly British Guiana in South America), despite the harsh climate and neglect over the centuries. In some extreme cases, long defensive walls were built, e.g, the Great Wall of China.

21. It is easy to picture how mounds were formed and changed into sacred sites. Inside or outside of fortified communities, the dead might be burned or buried after battles. Over time, mounds formed from these accumulated remains of beloved, respected, or feared individuals, and the sites, first by function and then by shape, acquired special status. Such mounds were places around or on which children and youths also played. Games on sacred mounds included reenactments of past battles or tributes to honor fallen heroes and their deeds. On special occasions, games on sacred soils in such special areas involved religious leaders and the incorporation of sacred rituals. In time these game and battles became more sophisticated, incorporating societal, religious and philosophical beliefs.

This also accounts for the formation of stupas in ancient India where the remains of burned bodies were buried under markers.

22. Similar situations most likely also occurred elsewhere, e.g., among Indo-European peoples. The Hindu god Indra was a fort destroyer. The written record in Europe is more easily accessible and the documentation firmer.

23. Alice Bertha Gomme, *The Traditional Games of England, Scotland, and Ireland*, Vol. II, "Stones," 216: lines 25–36; and 217: lines 1–

16. The words Gomme cites are from Dublin, *Folklore Journal*, ii. 264–265.

24. This type of game is still seen in children's pre-game or practice, where a coach lobs balls in a circle for players to bunt or hit. This is usually done when one coach has several small children to pitch to.

25. The word *Celts* meant "high people" or "hill people," who were adept at slinging stones from vantage points, and the word *German* meant "people of the spear," or "spear men." Germanic and Scandinavian myths mention stupendous feats of stone-throwing. A battle began with a spear being hurled over the heads of opponents, signifying a determination to fight to the end. In such places, games such as stones would likewise be expected. The relevance of such peoples will be made clearer in later chapters.

Chapter 4

1. If the British had not recorded their observations of rock-throwing incidents among the people in India and neighboring Nepal, these practices may well have died out without being written about.

2. The first name of the editor was not given; she was instead referred to as "Mrs. Valentine." She was later identified as Laura Valentine. This extensive work received contributions from 35 writers.

3. Valentine, *The Girl's Home Companion...*, "Stool Ball," 117: lines 1–8, 11, 12, and 13.

Trap ball was an old British game. A trap was a device used to put the ball in the air, after which it was hit as far as possible. It was also called knur and spell; the knur was a hard ball made from knotted wood, and the spell was the staff used for striking the ball.

Runners moved in a clockwise direction. Valentine points out that in some places stool-ball was called "sun and planet," hinting at a religious connection.

4. It is tempting to suggest that rounders, as a variant of baseball or a baseball-related game, was played by the Puritans or Parliamentarians nicknamed "Roundheads." (In the 1630s, the Puritans had their hair cut short.) Various supporters (especially working classes) of the Puritans under Oliver Cromwell came from different enclaves all over the country. In Cromwell's army, during the English War, there would have been excellent opportunities to meld the various folk games of the different localities.

5. William J. Baker, *Sports in the Modern World*, 45: lines 26–39.

6. Sidney Oldall Addy in *A Glossary of Words Used in the Neighborhood of Sheffield* (1888) states:

> *Munshets* or *Munshits*, a boy's game.
>
> It is played by two boys in the following manner:–One of the boys remain at "home," and the other goes out to a prescribed distance. The boy who remains "at home" makes a small hole in the ground, and holds in his hand a stick about three feet long to strike with. The boy who is out at field throws a stick in the direction of this hole, at which the other strikes. If he hits it he has to run to a prescribed mark and back to the hole without being caught or touched with the smaller stick by his play-fellow. If he is caught he is "out," and has to go to the field. And if the boy at field can throw his stick so near to the hole as to be within the length or measure of that stick, the boy at home has to go out to field. A number of boys often play together; for any even number can play. I am told that the game was common fifty years ago. In principle it resembles cricket, and looks like the rude beginnings of that game [322].

Addy describes a game called *hittera ball*, played in Eyam, Derbyshire. This game was similar to the game of "knur and spell" (1888 Supplement, 29).

The "ball" is hit with a stick. No throwing is involved and the hole would likely be at a marked position which appears to be an early "home plate."

7. Valentine, *The Girl's Home Companion...*, "Rounders," 23: lines 1–4.

8. Stow-ball and stobball are also thought to be analogous to stool-ball, with the lower part of a tree trunk or stump being used as a base. Details can be found in Block, *Baseball Before We Knew It*, 119–122.

9. Joseph Strutt, *The Sports and Pastimes of the People of England*, "Stool Ball," 165–166.

10. The "cat," a ball made with rubber, yarn and leather strips, was the object thrown

that the batter tries to hit. In the game old-cat, the number of cats depended upon the number of players available. One-old-cat had a striker and thrower; two-old-cat a striker, a thrower and a fielder; three-old-cat a striker, a thrower, a catcher and a fielder. As the number of cats increased, the game moved from running back and forth to a traingular, and then to a square form. For further discussion, see David Block, John Wood and Harold Seymour.

11. F. W. Hackwood, *Staffordshire Customs, Superstitions and Folklore*, "Tutball," second column on 173 and both columns on 174.

12. Alan S.C. Ross in *Proceedings of the Leeds Philosophical and Literary Society*, Literary and Historical Section (1968), XIII, Part II. "Pize-ball," 55–77 and 55, line 1 for quotation.

13. Addy, *A Glossary of Words*, 269. Addy defines pize as "to strike, to knock (*Pize* him over), a blow; and pize-ball as a game at ball" (176).

14. Addy, *A Glossary of Words*, Pize-Ball, 176. It seems here that one out means all out. This use of the term "burnt" and others like "soaking," "plugging" and "wounding" will be further discussed in later chapters.

15. Alan S.C. Ross, "Pize-ball" (Ref., Note 12), 56: lines 15–16.

16. Whit Monday is the Christian religious holiday commemorating the appearance of the Holy Spirit to the disciples. This suggests the game had some religious affiliation. Tutball was also associated with Ash Wednesday. Many of these early baseball games were associated with religious holidays, perhaps as people were home with more spare time for games and recreational activities.

17. Don Morrow, et al., *A Concise History of Sport in Canada*, 128: lines 8–11. Morrow mentions in the very early twentieth century, leagues were formed in Western Canada, for example in the provinces of British Columbia (e.g., New Westminster and Vancouver) and Alberta (Calgary and Edmonton) (128: lines 11–15).

18. *Ibid.*, 109: line 29.

19. *Ibid.*, 109: 31–32; and 110: lines 1–2. The paragraph continues:

> No one wore gloves; the score was kept by notches on a stick; and games lasted from 6 to 9 innings. Games played

earlier than 1838 (so Ford suggested) were declared finished when one team reached 18 or 21 runs first. Finally the players—Ford noted that the number per team varied between 7 and 12–ranged in age from 15 to 24. Ford named them all.

His [Ford] letter establishes baseball as one of the earliest team sports in Canada. Moreover, it underscores the village roots of the game. Vestiges of the 1838 rules—namely the use of 11 players and 4 bases and a common striker's box/home bye—remained in the Woodstock-Ingersoll area until at least 1860 [110: lines 2–14].

N.B.: The Ford referred to is Adam E. Ford (1831–1906), who wrote about the Beachville game of June 4, 1838, a holiday, Militia Muster Day, between players (Beachville Club versus the Zorras) of two neighbouring townships.

"Plugging" was made illegal with the introduction of what is now generally regarded as the New York Knickerbocker Club's rules in 1845. The undue credit given to this group and its members would be later commented upon and corrected by, among others, John Thorn in *Baseball in the Garden of Eden: The Secret History of the Game* (2011).

20. If the pizer took too long, there were taunting chants:

> "Pize your neighbour while you are able,
> While the donkey's in the stable!" (Alan S.C. Ross, "Pize-ball," 59: lines 14–15).

21. The Old English word for town was *tūn*, which meant an area of land enclosed by walls or a fence, similar to the *tuts* used as markers. This would suggest "town ball" took place in a dedicated area. The term "British baseball" is used to distinguish early baseball in Britain from the later American developed baseball.

22. Appendix C has full quotes and descriptions of these games.

23. Viscountess Wolseley, *In a College Garden* (1916), 236: lines 10–14. The paragraph continues:

> But it seems probable that the first [stowball] is a kind of golf and that the last two [stool-ball and bittle-battle] denote what was no doubt an ancestor of cricket, handed down in a somewhat altered form to the Sussex women of today....

A tradition exists that it was originally played by milkmaids using their milking stools as bats, but the name of "bittle-battle," which is also given to the game, leads one to think that these young women used their "bittles" or wooden milking-bowls as bats, and that the milking stool was the wicket. This might account for the peculiar appearance of the "targets" that are now used as wickets, for they consist of either square or round boards, about one foot in diameter, and fastened to an upright post fixed in the ground [236: lines 14–18 and 27–33; and 237: lines 1–4].
The first name of the author was not given.

24. (1) Derek Birley in *A Social History of Cricket* (1999) writes:

English cricket was born at sometime in the later Middle Ages, of uncertain, though bucolic parentage. Amongst its near relations, now defunct, are folk-games like stool-ball (a unisex affair); the hardball, stowball; and the cat family (tip-cat, kit-cat, cat and dog, cat-in-the-hole) which used bits of wood as the missile [3: lines 1–5].

(2) Frederick Gale in *Echoes from Old Cricket Fields* (1871) writes:

Assuming that there was an interregnum between the days of tip-cat and cricket, and that club-ball intervened, no one can well doubt but that cat-and-dog, tip-cat, rounders, club-ball, and cricket are all, so to say, blood relations [10: lines 18–22].

(Gale's work was re-published in 1972.)

25. The game and flavour of old-cat is given by American educator Frank J. Lowth in *Everyday Problems of the Country Teacher, a Textbook and a Handbook of the Country-School Practice* (1926):

(b) *One Old Cat*: This is a fine game for girls as well as boys. A soft playground ball is used. Four or more can play at the game. The players comprise the pitcher, the catcher, the batter, and as many fielders as desired or available. The batters do not run bases. When the pupils come out on the playground at intermission, one cries out "my first bat," and is the first batter. In the same way others become a catcher, pitcher, first fielder, second fielder, and thus down the line. In

playing, if a ball is caught, if the ball is caught on the third strike, or if a foul ball is caught on the fly, or on the first bound, then the batter is out. If a third strike is not caught, then the batter is given three more strikes. When a striker is out, the catcher becomes batter, the pitcher becomes catcher, the first fielder becomes pitcher, and so on. The batter who goes out becomes the last fielder. Sometimes the game is varied by having the batter run to a base and back to home plate when he strikes fair ball. In making the run, the batter is out if the pitcher or catcher or some other player reaches the home plate when he strikes a fair ball. In making the run, the batter is out if the pitcher or catcher or some other player reaches the home plate with the ball before he does. One old cat is lots of fun, and children rarely tire of it [149].

26. See Appendix C for further details of rounders, bittle-battle and stool-ball.

27. The game of bittle-battle can also be mentioned here. The "bittle" was thought to be the bat and the "battle" the ball. Wolseley in her 1916 work (*In a College Garden*) mentions that "bittles" were the wooden bowls used as bats, and the milking stool as the wicket.

28. Francis Willughby in David Cram, Jeffrey L. Forgeng and Dorothy Johnston's edition of *Francis Willughby's Book of Games: A Seventeenth-Century Treatise on Sports, Games and Pastimes* writes:

The players being divided according to their skills, they lay a stool down on one side, so as the seat or board of the stool is perpendicular to the ground....

Instead of a stool they have sometimes a great stone at D and another at C....

D or C is sometimes called a Tut & and the game Tutball [178: lines 1–3, 30 and 34].

29. Cram, Forgeng and Johnston in *Francis Willughby's Book of Games,* 283, lines 111–4.

30. David Underdown, *Revel, Riot and Rebellion*, 76: lines 9–23, 27–28, 30–32; and 77: lines 1–3. At the end of the paragraph, Underdown has a note that states:

There were two variants of stoolball: a primitive form played with a paddle or the hand instead of the bat, and the more elaborate Wiltshire form played with a hard ball and a wooden staff resembling a modern baseball bat. I suspect that the simpler form was the one popular in other parts of the country, being played, for example, at village revels for a tansy and a Banquet of curds and cream.

Appendix C continues the quotation.

31. *Ibid.* Underdown writes: Stoolball was not confined to the cheese country: it was being played at Ombersley, Worcestershire between 1608, and was known in pasture and clothing districts of Lancashire between 1680 and 1715, as well as in Bedfordshire, Hertfordshire, and Norfolk a century earlier.... Stoolball was played at Broad Hinton, on the northern fringe of the Marlborough Downs in 1613.... Stoolball's heartland was in the region near the Wiltshire-Gloucestershire border. Colerne Down was the "place so famous and frequented for it." People were presented for playing it on Sundays at Tetbury and the nearby village of Rodmarton in 1609 and 1610, and at Castle Combe forty years earlier. It surfaces at Slaughterford Magna, and Broughton Gilford, all cheese country villages, in the same period [76: lines 27–28, 30–32; and 77: lines 1–3].

32. The cheese-producing country villages referred to were the regions of Wiltshire, England.

33. John Newbery, *A Little Pretty Pocket-Book,* 88 and 90, respectively (taken from a facsimile with an introductory essay and bibliography by M.F. Thwaite, Oxford University Press, London, 1966).

34. *Ibid.,* 87 and 91, respectively.
Cricket.
This Lesson observe,
When you play at *Cricket,*
Catch All fairly out,
Or bowl down the *Wicket.*
Trap-Ball.
Touch lightly the *Trap,*
And strike low the ball;
Let none catch you out,
And you'll beat them all.

35. Peter Roberts, *The Cambrian Popular Antiquities; or An Account of Some Traditions, Customs, and Superstitions of Wales,* 123: lines 4–13; and 124: lines 8–17.

36. David Block, *Baseball Before We Knew*

It: A Search for the Roots of the Game, discovers that Frederick Louis (son of George II, heir to the throne and Prince of Wales and the Earl of Middlesex) played the game on what is now Ashley Park, Walton on Thames, as reported in "Baseball: Prince of Wales Played 'First' Game in Surrey," 10 June 2013, BBC News (http://www.bbc.com/news/uk-england-22840004); and "The Birth Place of Baseball Was in Britain!" 12 June 2013, *Daily Mail* (http://www.dailymail.co.uk/news/article-2340053/U-S-baseball-expert-proves-baseball-played-England-royalty.html).

37. Arnold Bennett, *Anna of the Five Towns,* 124, lines 8–10. The author continues:
Within half an hour the treat was in full career; football, cricket, rounders, tick, leap-frog, prison-bars, and round games, transformed the field into a vast arena of complicated struggles and emulations [124: lines 10–13].
Appendix C has the complete quotation from Bennett's work.

38. Hackwood in *Staffordshire, Customs, Superstitions and Folklore* states that the poorer children of Staffordshire played tutball because no expensive equipment was used except the barely affordable natural rubber ball [173: second column, lines 43–49].

39. At that time, there were some who frowned upon participation in games, and there were others who saw games as a vehicle for teaching moral and ethical codes of behaviour and conduct.

40. This description fits right into what has been previously mentioned by several writers about stool-ball, tut-ball or baseball being enjoyed at Easter time.

41. "Ch" is an abbreviation of "Church." Quotation taken from an article titled "Diary Entry May Offer Proof That Baseball Came from England," published on SportsIllustrated.com, 11 September 2008. This news item was also widely reported on the radio, television, magazines and newspapers around the same time.

42. David Block, *Baseball: Before We Knew It,* 140: lines 31–33.

43. *Ibid.,* 140: line 36; and 141: lines 1–16.

44. In particular the English-speaking peoples of modern Britain and former British colonies (except the U.S. and Canada); the vestiges of the former empire are now members of the British Commonwealth of nations.

45. The wicket is akin to the strike zone in that it must be protected from the ball, and the distance between the wickets is about the same as the distance between the pitching plate and home plate in baseball.

46. There is also LBW (leg before wicket) where the batter's leg is struck by the ball on its path to hitting the wicket. This prevents the batter from deliberately blocking the ball with his legs from hitting the wicket.

47. A British gentleman was someone of financial means and social respectability in the community (1). Richard Holt in *Sport and the British: A Modern History* writes that the first set of written cricket rules were compiled by the Duke of Richmond in 1727. The early cricket teams received patronage from the ruling landowner. Cricket was an early spectator sport as people showed up to watch games between their Clubs and others (25: lines 33–37; and 26: lines 1–9). Supported by: (2) William J. Baker, *Sports in the Western World,* 85: lines 91–6.

48. Tony Collins, John Martin and Wray Vamplew, *Encyclopedia of Traditional British Rural Sports*, 233: 1st column, lines 16–21.

49. The working class environment in Liverpool and South Wales continued as also documented by Martin Johnes in his article "Poor Man's Cricket: Baseball, Class and Community in South Wales ca. 1880–1950," *International Journal of the History of Sport*, 17, no. 4, (December 2000): 153–166.

50. In cricket the bowling and batting creases takes up about six feet of the cricket pitch, so the distances between batter and bowler is about the same as the net distance of 60 feet and six inches in baseball. In baseball, the pitcher can further cut down this distance of 60 feet and six inches by maximizing his pitching stride.

51. Alice Bertha Gomme, *The Traditional Games of England, Scotland, and Ireland,* "Rounders" 145–146, "Stool-Ball" 217–220, and "Tut-ball" 314. Appendix C shows quotations from the 1894–1898 work.

52. This is the same Henry Chadwick, sportswriter and authority of baseball in America, who was later called the "father of baseball."

53. Devonshire or Devon is in the Southwest of England, to its west lays Cornwall and to its east are Somerset and Dorset. Devon-

shire would have fallen mainly within the former early British enclave of the tribal *Dummonii* in pre-Roman Britain.

54. For example, the English-speaking Caribbean and Guyanese communities have been radically changed with massive migrations to Britain, the U.S. and Canada.

55. Chadwick, *The Sports and Pastimes of American Boys…*, 9: lines 17–21.

56. Chadwick mentions "our manly National game of base-ball." The manly Bostonian version was already fading from memory. Chadwick had also never seen the game of Welsh football being played. This is described in Note 98.

57. The Rev. J.G. Wood, *The Boy's Modern Playmate. A Book of Sports, Games, and Pastimes*, Preface v: lines 7–9.

58. James Otis, *Mary of Plymouth: A Story of the Pilgrim Settlement*, 99–102.
William J. Baker, *Sports in the Modern World*, 83–84; and John Thorn, *Baseball in the Garden of Eden*, 59.

59. Appendix C has a quotation from James Otis, *Mary of Plymouth: A Story of the Pilgrim Settlement,* 99–102.

60. Games, like religion, language and culture, have evolved over a long period of time. Analogously, Hinduism, Buddhism, Judaism, Christianity and Islam have national and regional variations, and these in turn may have localized variations, giving rise to "cults" and "sub-cults." Languages have regional variations and dialects. Over time, variations are a natural result of any evolving process.

61. Otis in *Mary of Plymouth: A Story of the Pilgrim Settlement* (1910) writes about the first settlers from Plymouth England who came on the *Mayflower* in 1620:

> The first thing done was to build a high platform, where the cannon that had been brought from England could be placed, so that the Indians might be beaten off if they came to do us harm [22: lines 13–22].

62. Further recommended reading on why Europeans conquered certain regions of the world is found in Jared Diamond's *Guns, Germs and Steel.*

63. Robin Carver, *The Book of Sports,* 2: lines 1–8. Carver must have arrived in America in the late eighteenth century.

64. *Ibid.*, 37: lines 1–2, 9–10; and 38: lines 1–2.

65. Carver also gives descriptions of British games of cricket, football, and prisoner's base. The description of cricket was longer than that written for base ball.

66. Gambling was also associated with early cricket before the game was standardized and gentrified to promote acceptability and the spread of the game. Likewise early cricket was played by ordinary people and was known for its fighting and gambling, but gentrification helped in the cleaning up of the game and its elevation as a game for the rising middle class, and those who require a more leisurely paced game.

67. Cricket made its appearance in early colonial America, as did other sports from old Britain. Melvin Adelman in *A Sporting Time* documents "The Failure of Cricket as an American Sport," Ch. 5, pp. 97–119. Within the British heterogeneous group were variations with regards to culture, class, economics, games, sports and recreational pursuits. Steven Riess, in the first chapter of *City Games,* "Urbanization and Sport in the Walking City," outlines the various problems, possibilities and preferences that the sporting fraternities and cultures faced by the various identifiable groups (such as the Irish, Scots and Welsh) of early colonial times in America (13–48).

The British had legal copyright and therefore a say to any adoption of their professional cricket and football rules. Americans did not want to be seen as adopting a British game with its rules and cultural trappings. The same sense of national pride prevented baseball development in South Wales, where the American improvements were not accepted. (Martin Johnes' article "Poor Man's Cricket" is mentioned in Note 49.)

68. This is similar to the situation in which any individual or club inside or outside the U.S. must first apply to Little League Baseball (LLB) of America for permission to play using LLB's rules and then pay annual dues. An analogous situation exists for new MLB clubs.

69. Thorn, *Baseball in the Garden of Eden.* Thorn also outlines the rules of the 1845 New York Knickerbocker Base Ball Club and comments on them on pages 69–77.

70. In 1891, the rules still allowed for hitters to call for what pitches they wanted. Wood in *The Boy's Modern Playmate* writes:

Section 5.—The batsman on taking his position must call for either a "*High Ball*," a "*Low Ball*," or "*Fair Ball*," and the umpire shall notify the pitcher to deliver the ball as required; such call shall not be changed after the first ball delivered.

Section 6.—A "*High Ball*" shall be sent in above the belt of the batsman, but not higher than the shoulder. A "*Low Ball*," shall be one sent in at the height of the belt, or between that height and the knee, but not higher than his belt. A "fair ball" shall be one between the range of shoulder high and the knee of the striker. All the above must be over the home base, and when fairly delivered, shall be considered fair balls to the bat [51: Sections: 5 and 6, lines 11–20].

In another example, any pitch delivered by an overhand throw was called a "foul baulk." Wood in Sections 3 and 4 writes:

Section 3.—Should the pitcher deliver the ball by an overhand throw, a "foul baulk" shall be declared. Any outward swing of the arm, or any other swing save that of the perpendicular movement referred to in Section 2 of this rule, shall be considered an overhand throw.

Section 4.—When a "foul baulk" is called, the umpire shall warn the pitcher of the penalty incurred by such unfair delivery; and should such delivery be continued until *Three Foul Baulks* have been called in one inning, or six in the entire game, the umpire shall declare the game forfeited [50, Sections: 3 and 4, lines 8–17].

71. Thorn, *Baseball in the Garden of Eden,* 47–48.

72. This explains why overhand pitching is far more common, though there is still the occasional sidearm or underhand pitcher in the MLB. These pitchers change the viewing perspective of the batter, forcing them to track the ball from a lower point of release.

In early cricket, according to Vernon Bartlett, *Past of Pastimes,* "bowling was underhand, and along the ground" (50: lines 32–33).

73. Thorn, 47: lines 24–25, 35–37; and 48: lines 1–10.

74. Bartlett in *Past of Pastimes* (1969) examines the claims that Abner Doubleday invented baseball in 1839. Bartlett shows the falsity of these claims as debunked by *Ency-*

clopaedia Britannica, an American publication. Evidently baseball was being played before 1839 as Bartlett also mentions Thurlow Weed, an American, writes about a baseball club founded around 1825; and Oliver Wendell, another writer, mentions that he played baseball at Harvard in 1829. Bartlett also describes a game called "old cat," or "cat" that was similar to rounders and baseball. See Chapter 4, "From Pall to the Cricket Pitch," 42–55.

75. *Ibid.,* 44: lines 13–16.

76. David Voigt, *American Baseball: From Gentleman's Sport to the Commissioner System,* Vol. 1, states:

> Nurtured in the critical method of enquiry, historians naturally find fault with the Doubleday origin; indeed, Spalding must have doubted it himself since his own ghost-written history of the sport records accounts of games played prior to 1839 which would not support his evolutionary hypothesis. But in seeking a motive for Spalding's deliberate myth making, one finds him unscrupulous in his chauvinistic determination to "prove" the American origin of the game. In his history he repeatedly argues that Baseball is wholly American [5: lines 26–33; and 6: line 1].

77. In Britain, individuals were questioning the pervasive authority of the state. In the English Civil War (1630s to 1640s), the Puritans and Parliamentarians, led by Oliver Cromwell, fought against the British crown. It was in Britain that the once dominant idea of the "Divine Right of Kings" was dispelled, and where the English Bill of Rights was adopted in 1689. The pursuit of the freedom of religious worship drove many from Britain to America.

78. The early baseball games in America and Canada were often associated with unsavoury characters (e.g., oil-slick gamblers as promoters) and undesirable behaviours (e.g., drinking and fighting).

79. Colin D. Howell documents the emergence of baseball as the dominant summer sport in Canada, at the expense of cricket and lacrosse. See his *Northern Sandlots: A Social History of Maritime Baseball* and *Blood, Sweat, and Cheers: Sport and the Making of Modern Canada.*

80. Similarly, other European settlers likely introduced their early precursor or variant versions of their baseball game in their colonies around the world. For example, the Germans and Dutch had their own versions of baseball.

81. The British introduced many other children's games, such as hopscotch, marbles, and sing-along games throughout their colonies in the Caribbean. Many of these same British games are mentioned in the 1894–1898 work of Gomme, *The Traditional Games of England, Scotland, and Ireland.* Some readers may recall the popular "Old MacDonald" sing-along song from childhood days.

82. In many of these early British or European colonies, the management personnel were all from the educated middle or upper class. The colonizers played cricket and the colonized learned their masters' games. The British did not need British labourers or unskilled workers in the plantations, so many were not brought to the colonies. The skilled tradesmen (e.g., carpenters, shipbuilders) and craftsmen were brought and these likely carried their football to the colonies. Soccer was a well-established game of the working class in Britain. Baseball on the other hand was already being considered quaint and most likely too few among the working class were around to play the game in their colonial outposts. In addition, the "whites" who went to the colonies would now have elevated social status and would join the game of the local white ruling elite. The emerging "new elite" took up cricket and gave up games like rounders to those of the female sex, except perhaps on social occasions. In the British colonies, the colonized copied their British masters so that they could also move up the chain of social acceptability. Cricket became the dominant male sport, with community and social life centered around the cricket clubs' membership and clubhouse facilities—dining, dancing, parties, card games, and so forth.

83. British citizens did go to South Africa, Zimbabwe, New Zealand and Australia. Other European nations went to other places in Africa, Far East and Central and South America.

84. The cricket clubs in the colonies were places with exclusive memberships for privileged colonials. Usually, a gentleman was

someone with money, property or from respected professions and ranking in the societal class structure or hierarchy.

85. Australia was formerly used as a penal colony. Other tropical places also harbour new diseases (e.g., mosquito and other fly-borne insect carriers) and hardships (e.g., heat and rain).

86. People from these English-speaking Caribbean countries (CARICOM), e.g., Barbados, Jamaica, Trinidad and Tobago, and Guyana on seeing baseball being played use rounders as their frame of reference to describe baseball to others.

87. Sir Winston Churchill, *A History of the English-Speaking Peoples: The Age of Revolution*.

88. Adam Freedman (op-ed contribution), "Independence British Style," *New York Times*, 2 July 2009.

Sir Winston Churchill in *A History of the English-Speaking Peoples: The Age of Revolution* (1957) writes with regards to the American constitution:

> It was based not upon the challenging writings of the French Philosophers which were soon to set Europe ablaze, but an Old English doctrine, freshly formulated to meet an urgent American need. The Constitution was a reaffirmation of faith in the principles painfully evolved over the centuries by English-speaking peoples. It enshrined long-standing English ideas of justice and liberty, henceforth to be regarded on the other side of the Atlantic as basically American [256: lines 16–23].

89. This occurred at least a century earlier, the 1728 set of principles were modified in 1744, 1774 and 1787.

90. Don Morrow in his chapter "Baseball" in *A Concise History of Sport in Canada* writes that this influence occurred with the willing participation of Canadians (128: lines 30–35).

91. *Ibid.*, 110: lines 17–18, 30–32, 32–35; and 111: 3–5, 12–13.

92. *Ibid.* Morrow writes that baseball fans in Toronto and the rest of Canada, during the winter months, were much interested in news, rumors and possibilities about the personnel and games of the upcoming season (131: lines 1–8).

93. A more recent and informative work on this subject is *Baseball Without Borders: The International Pastime,* edited by George Gmelch.

94. These wars are the Civil War, World War I, World War II, Korean War, Vietnam War, Cold War, Iraq Wars, September 11, 2001, terrorist attacks, and the current Afghanistan War. Other hardships include both economic depressions and recessions and natural disasters.

95. Except, perhaps, in Britain where cricket remains the game of choice. This intrusion would rekindle old nationalistic rivalries and culture wars.

96. Spalding in *America's National Game, 1839–1915* (1911), 2: lines 1–17.

97. The British could say the same thing about their game of "cricket, lovely cricket." British cricketers (military and civilian officers, businessmen, diplomats, scientists, explorers, etc.) went out to rule the world during the heydays of the British Empire. These same desired characteristics of the British were partly responsible for the setting up and dominance of the British Empire for centuries. (The British knew that the battles were won on the cricket and soccer fields of Britain.)

98. Spalding in *America's National Game, 1839–1915*, 7.

Spalding had likely never seen the game of Welsh football, which was most brutal:

> Numbers of players would be left here and there on the road, some having limbs broken in the struggle, others severely injured, and some carried on biers to be buried in the churchyard nearest to where they had been mortally wounded [Rhys Cox, quoted in Collins, Martin and Vamplew, *Encyclopedia of Traditional British Rural Sports*, 121].

The same can be said of the Scottish *ba* game.

99. This is well documented in the works of Joseph A. Reaves, *Taking in a Game: A History of Baseball in Asia* (2002) and *Baseball Without Borders: The International Pastime* (2006), edited by George Gmelch.

100. Former veteran MLB player, coach and manager Jim Lefebvre was hired to prepare the national Chinese baseball Olympic team for the 2008 Beijing Olympics.

101. MLB scouts are beginning to look for players (pitchers) in India. The Pittsburgh Pi-

rates had two Indian players in their farm system; only one remains.

102. One consequence and point of concern in recent years is the multitude of players exposed for using steroids and other performance-enhancing drugs.

103. Further information found in the articles in *Baseball Without Borders: The International Pastime* (2006), edited by George Gmelch, on baseball in Asia (Japan, China, Taiwan, Korea), the Americas (Cuba, Puerto Rico, Nicaragua, Brazil and Canada), Europe (Italy, Holland, and Great Britain) and the Pacific (Australia), Dan Gordon (Japan, Nicaragua), William W. Kelly (Japan), Joseph A. Reaves (China, Korea), Andrew Morris (Taiwan), Alan Klein (Dominican Republic), Tim Wendel (Cuba), Thomas Carter (Cuba), Thomas E. Van Hyning and Franklin (Puerto Rico), Carlos Azzoni, Tales Azzoni and Wayne Patterson (Brazil), Colin Howell (Canada), Peter Carino (Italy), Harvey Shapiro (Holland), and Josh Chetwynd (Great Britain).

Chapter 5

1. Melvin L. Adelman, *A Sporting Time: New York and the Rise of Modern Athletics, 1820–1870*, 13: lines 1–4, 20–26; and 14: 1–13.

Adelman continues:

> During the colonial period political and economic troubles had instigated the revival of ethnic and religious loyalties. For the most part, however, intermarriage among the families of English, Dutch, and Huguenot [French Protestants] leaders, the process of acculturation, and the relative ease of assimilation softened the effects of nationality on the city's social structure [14: lines 16–21].

2. John Taylor, *A Short Relation of a Long Journey Made Round or Ovall by Encompassing the Principalities of Wales from London*, London, 1652; later edited by James O. Halliwell and published as *A Short Relation of a Journey Through Wales by John Taylor, the Water-Poet* (London: Thomas Richards, 1859), 26.

The preceding paragraph reads:

> Of all the places in England and Wales, that I have travelled to, this village off Barnsley doth most strictly observe the Lord's day, or Sunday, for little children

are not suffered to walk or play; and two women who had been at church both before and afternoon, did but walk into the fields for their recreation, and they were put to their choice, either to pay sixpence apiece (for profane walking) or be laid one hour in the stocks; and the peevish wilful women (though they were able to pay), to save their money and laugh out the matter, lay both heelless merrily for one hour [25: lines 20–28; and 26: lines 1–3].

3. This is noted by Richard Holt in *Sport and the British: A Modern History*, where he comments that the educated classes began to view the amusements differently. The Puritans frowned upon the cruelties inflicted on animals in some sports. Puritans were against the disreputable behaviour (e.g., fighting, drinking and lawlessness) associated with some sports and alehouses, of course, they wanted the people in church on Sundays. Their views in some regards (e.g., with respect to animal cruelties and acceptable social behaviour) are now seen as right and acceptable standards today (29: lines 2–7, 22–33).

4. *Ibid.* Holt writes that with the decline of sports, people changed and the old hospitality norms were also changing. He mentions that the educated clergy of the church were losing their roots with the people and saw the sports of the common people as unproductive and dangerous outlets. Since the churches were linked to the local taverns and alehouses, these physical links were removed. Ball courts were removed from the churchyards and dances and sports on church properties ceased (46: lines 4–28, 31–32).

5. Noam Friedlander, *The Mammoth Book of Sports & Games of the World* (1999), "Welsh Baseball," 46–48. This work also states: "Supporters of this form of the sport claim that the American game came from Welsh baseball" (47: lines 4–5).

6. *Ibid.* Friedlander writes:

> The ancient game of ROUNDERS flourished in the West of England, and certainly led to the refinement building up in South Wales. It spread to isolated pockets, and nationals have been played between these two countries since 1908 [47: lines 4–8].

This can be seen as the earliest recorded

"world series," as separate countries (or nationalities),Welsh and English, were involved.

7. Collins, Martin and Vamplew, the editors of *Encyclopedia of Traditional British Rural Sports*, published an entry by Rob Light on cricket (79–86) and Emma Lile on Welsh cricket (86). Light states:

Cricket:

It is more than likely that the game that first came to be known as cricket was a variant of the numerous similar folk pastimes, such as stoollball, cat and dog, club ball, trap ball and tip cat, which were all based upon similar principles [79: second column, lines 3–9].

8. Block, *Baseball Before We Knew It*, 118: lines 27–33; and 119: 5–8.

9. Peter Roberts, then rector of Llanarnon and vicar of Madely in Wales, *The Cambrian Popular Antiquiities, or, an Account of the Traditions, Customs, and Superstitions of Wales*, 123: lines 4–13; and 124: lines 14–16.

10. Oliver Goldsmith, *The Deserted Village* (London: W. Griffin, 1770). Citation is from *Annotated Poems of English Authors*, edited by E.T. Stephens and D. Morris, *The Deserted Village by Oliver Goldsmith*, (London: Longmans, Green and Co., 1876). Google Books. Web. 10 April 2013.

Stephens and Morris wrote an essay giving some background on Goldsmith and his work, particularly this poem, *The Deserted Village*. These editors explained the meanings of the various terms or old language in the notes of the poem.

("RPO—Oliver Goldsmith: The Deserted Village, A Poem," 19 January 2016, Ian Lancashire for Representative Poetry Online, Department of English, University of Toronto, https://tspace.library.utoronto.ca/html/1807/4350/poem875.html.)

11. For example, Holt in *Sport and the British* adds some clarification:

The decline in traditional sports, especially those which involved fighting, was not simply a question of pressure from well-organized groups of evangelicals and business men; in addition to the abolitionists there was evidence of a gradual shift in public taste especially amongst the literate and highly skilled élite of working people themselves [43: lines 25–31].

12. These two counties North Wiltshire and North Gloucestershire would have likely fallen within the former early or pre-Roman Britain areas occupied by groups of various tribal identities such as the *Dobunni, Silures, Atrebates*, and *Belgae*. This reflects the diversity of the peoples involved in these games.

13. It was not only people in the South and Southwest who were heavily involved in games and sports, but also people in Northern Britain. The origins of golf are especially associated with the Scottish people. The then Duke of Hamilton writes in his chapter "Sport" in editor Henry W. Miekle's *Scotland: A Description of Scotland and Scottish Life* (1947):

Golf.

Of all the games played in Scotland in days gone by, three stand out as claiming Scottish origin and being particular Scottish in character—golf, curling, and shinty, and of these games golf has now achieved world-wide popularity. The frequent denunciations after the Reformation of golf-playing on Sunday, sometimes ending in prosecution of delinquents, bear witness to the centuries old popularity it has enjoyed [244: lines 26–31].

14. Erwin Mehl, "Baseball in the Stone Age," *Western Folklore* 7, no. 2 (1948): 145–161; and "Notes to Baseball in the Stone Age," *Western Folklore* 8, no. 2 (1949): 152–156.

15. Block, *Baseball Before We Knew It*, 67–79. Block mentions that Gutsmuth's work *Spiele Zur Uebung und Erholung des Körpers Und Geistes fur die Jugend, Ihre Erzieher und Alle Freunde Unschuldiger Jugenfreiden* bore a rather impressive title, which can be translated as "Games for the Exercise and Recreation of Body and Spirit for the Youth and His Educator and All Friends of Innocent Joys of Youth" (67: lines 17–21). Gutsmuth's work is written in old German and is accessible.

16. This was long before Spalding and others in America were even born, who were later championing the suitability of baseball as an excellent game to promote healthy attitudes in young people.

English Vicar Robert Crowley in his poem "The Scholar's Lesson" in *The Select Works of Robert Crowley* (1550), edited by J.M. Cowper (London: N. Trubner, 1872) points out the advantages of playing games as helpful to studies:

To shoote, to bowle, or caste the barre,
To play tennis or tosse the ball,
Or to rene the base, like men of war,
Shal hurt thy study nought at all [73: lines 33–36].

Block, *Baseball Before We Knew It*, comments that the last game ("Or to run the base, like men at war") being referred to may well be an early baseball game (230, lines 25–27).

The editor J.M. Cowper writes in his 1871 introduction to Crowley's 1550 work:

> The Scholar's Lesson is interesting as giving a glimpse of that muscular education which, as a nation, we are only now beginning to learn afresh. The scholar was to "recreate his mind" by fishing, fowling, hunting, hawking; while trials of strength, skill, speed—still to recreate his mind—were to be made in shooting, bowling, casting the bar, tennis, tossing the ball, and running base like men of war. The whole lesson contains good advice and is quite worthy of its author [xvi: lines 31–36; and xvii: lines 1–2].

In the note, Cowper adds:

> Base, or Prisoner's Bars, a game, success in which depended upon the agility and skill in running. The Game is still known in Kent under the name of Prisoner's Base. In the reign of Edward III, it was prohibited to be played in the avenues of Westminster Palace. A game exceedingly popular among the young men of this part of Kent, and known as "Goal Running," seems to be a modification of the ancient game of Base. For further information see Strutts's *Sports and Pastimes* [xvii: lines 33–39].

17. Block, *Baseball Before We Knew It*, 70: lines 23–33.

18. Steven A. Reiss, *City Games: The Evolution of American Urban Society and the Rise of Sports*, 22: lines 25–32. Reiss writes:

> The *Turnverein* or gymnastic society, a vital part of the cultural baggage brought by German immigrants, flourished in German neighborhoods, just like the German theater and choral societies…. The first turner societies in the U.S. were established in 1848 in Louisville and Cincinnati—two cities with large German populations—and others were soon organized in Baltimore, Brooklyn, Chicago, Milwaukee, New Orleans, New York, Newark, Philadelphia, St. Louis, and other cities with growing German communities…. The turners, highly regarded among sports-minded people, were described in the *American Journal of Education* in 1860 as "virtuous and accomplished, pure and active, chaste and bold, truthful and warlike" [23: lines 1–3, 7–12 and 16–19].

19. Adelman in *A Sporting Time*, 261: lines 24–29.

20. Mehl, "Baseball in the Stone Age," *Western Folklore* 7, no. 2 (1948): 145–161. "The Age of Batting Games," 151: lines 23–26.

21. David Levinson and Karen Christensen, *Encyclopedia of World Sport 1: From Ancient Times to the Present* (1996), 77–80. This game seems to be an imitation of early war scenarios whereby one group, tribe, or kingdom played against another. Each leader or "King" chose his own team and led it as he would be expected to do in battle.

22. Wood writes in *The Boy's Modern Playmate* (1891):

> Rule VI. The Umpire. Section 1.—The Umpire shall be chosen by the captains or officers of two contesting clubs, and he shall determine all disputes and differences between the contesting players which may occur during the game [55: lines 5–7].

23. David Levinson and Karen Christensen edition of *Encyclopedia of World Sport 1: From Ancient Times to the Present*, "Baseball, Finnish," 77–80.

This makes sense since the players could not stand on top of the stone or wood used as bases, and the circular area around the bases were therefore the designated safe areas.

24. *Ibid.*, 78: line 4.

25. Josh Chetwynd, *Baseball in Europe: A Country by Country History* (2008), 133.

John Leo, "Evil Umpires? Not in Soviet Baseball," in Dick Schaap and Mort Gerberg, eds., *Joy in Mudville: The Big Book of Baseball Humor* (1992), 39–42.

Bill Keller, "In Baseball, the Russians Steal All the Bases," *New York Times*, July 20, 1987.

26. It would have been easier and less costly for Russian immigrants to reach Western North America instead of going overland from Russia and then sailing westwards from other European ports. Many Russian émigrés

would have been unable to afford these higher costs. If they sailed West from Russia they would have ended up in South America first before sailing northwards. The chances of mass migrations of Russians to America were unlikely. Russia also had large land mass and Catherine the Great invited Germans to settle in Russia.

27. Ester Singleton, *Dutch New York* (1909) (republished in 1968), 290: lines 1–11.

28. William Rankin, a baseball writer for the *New York Clipper*, responded to Chadwick with regards to the origins of town ball. Rankin writes:

> Another thing he said: "This town ball was simply an Americanized edition of the English game of rounders—was in vogue until the decade of the 1800's when the Old Knickerbocker Base Ball Club, of New York modified the rules of play and forced a new game entirely." Oh, fudge! Cut that talk about town ball and rounders when talking about Manhattan Island. Base ball was invented by the Dutch and pray, what did they know about the English game of rounders? One might as well argue that Mr. Edison "modified" the old English candle and formulated the incandescent light in use now, as to say that base ball sprung from rounders or its "Americanized edition, town ball" [Mears Baseball Scrapbook, Vol. 8: *New York Clipper* Articles by Rankin, 1904–1912].

29. Washington Irving using the pseudonym Diedrich Knickerbocker in his satirical 1824 work, *Knickerbocker's History of New York from the Beginnings of the World to the End of the Dutch Dynasty*, gives us a glimpse of what some boys were doing to occupy themselves in the old city:

> Not but what there were some two or three youngsters who manifested the first dawning of what is called fire and spirit, who held all labor in contempt, skulked about docks and market-places, loitered in the sunshine, squandered what little money they could procure at hustle cap and chuck farthing; swore, boxed, fought cocks, and raced their neighbor's horses; in short, who promised to be the wonder, the talk, and abomination of the town, had not their stylish career been unfortunately cut

short by an affair of honor with a whipping post [107: lines 13–22].

30. Ross, "Pize-ball," in "Proceedings of the Leeds Philosophical and Literary Society," Literary and Historical Section, XIII, Part II, 55–77, Nov. 1968 (mentioned in Chapter 4, Note 13) states:

> The reason for the presence of these Dutch words in Yorkshire—and, In England, only in Yorkshire—is not far to seek: surely it must lie in the 17th c. Dutch "immigration" connected with the drainage of the Level of Hatfield Chase, an area not very far from Doncaster. The best account of the Drainage, and of the events consequent upon it, is still that given by Joseph Hunter in his South Yorkshire (1828–31) [67: lines 6–11].

More information given in Notes 128–131 on pages 76–77 of Ross's article.

31. Barbara and Henri Van der Zee in *A Sweet and Alien Land: The Story of the Dutch in New York*, 37: lines 9–19 and 24–25.

The preceding paragraph of the quoted text reads:

> America had seized the imagination of the British, and fantastic schemes were proposed. A certain Captain Riley went so far as to suggest the making of a plantation "by which the Kingdom may annually be rid of 3000 poor … the prisons be emptied, and much blood saved as well as relief given by sending them thither" [37: lines 3–8].

32. Robert C. Ritchie, *The Duke's Province: A Study of New York Politics and Society, 1664–1691*, 4: lines 30–38; and 140: lines 12–14 and 22–29.

33. Russell Shorto in *The Island at the Center of the World: The Epic Story of Dutch Manhattan and the Forgotten Colony That Shaped America*.

34. Don Morrow in Chapter 6, "Baseball," in *A Concise History of Sport in Canada*, edited by Don Morrow *et al.*, 109: lines 1–3.

35. William Bennett Munro in *Crusaders of New France: A Chronicle of the Fleur-De-Lis in the Wilderness* (1921) writes:

> The chief festivities occurred at Michaelmas, Christmas, Easter, and May Day.... Sunday was a day not only of rest but of recreation. Clad in his best raiment, everyone went to Mass, whatever the distance or the weather. The parish

church indeed was the emblem of village solidarity, for it gathered within its walls each Sunday morning all sexes and ages and ranks. The habitant did not separate his religion from his work or his amusements; the outward manifestations of his faith were not to his mind things of another world. The whole countryside gathered about the church doors after the service…. The crowd then melted away in groups to spend the rest of the day in games or dancing or in friendly visits of one family with another….

Dancing was by all odds the most popular pastime….

The inhabitants love to sing, especially when working with others in the woods or when on the march…. But the popular repertoire was limited to a few folksongs, most of them songs of Old France. They were easy to learn, simple to sing, but sprightly and melodious… [218: line 9–10, 23–26; 219: 1–10, 16–19; 220: lines 3–4, 9–10, 12–16].

Munro further emphasizes that impacts of folklore from their old country of origin were strong and how superstitions were helped by their active imagination in a vastly unknown environment (221: lines 3–8).

36. *Ibid.* Munro gives a good idea of how people worked and socialized:

Especially popular among young people of each parish were the *Corvées Récréatives,* or "bees" as we call them nowadays in our rural communities. There were the *Épuchlette* or corn-husking, the *Brayage* or flax-beating, and others of the same sort. The harvest-home or *Grosse-Gerbe,* celebrated when the last load had been brought in from the fields, and the *Ignolée* or welcoming of the New Year, were also occasions of good will, noise and revelry [219: lines 20–26; and 220: 1–3].

37. Block, *Baseball Before We Knew It,* 147–150.

38. Eric Richards, in *Britannia's Children: Emigration from England, Scotland, Wales and Ireland,* documents the migration from Britain. Richards states:

Commerce may have been the main engine of emigration, but religion (especailly dissenters) gave colonisation a strength and ideology that is easily un-

derestimated. Religious fervour girded migrant soldarity and fed millenarian expectations. Most of all, it provided the leadership and resolve vital to pioneriing colonisation [45: lines 19–23].

Chapter 6

1. The people of early colonial America, consisting of 13 English-speaking colonies, rebelled against British rule in the American War of Independence, 1776–1782.

2. Will Durant in *The Story of Civilization: Part III, Caesar and Christ: A History of Roman Civilization and of Christianity from Their Beginnings to A.D. 325* writes:

Normally the visitor [to the public baths] went first to a dressing room to change his clothes; then to the palestra to box, wrestle, jump, hurl the disk or the spear, or play ball. One ball game was like our "medicine ball"; in another two opposed groups scrambled for a ball, and carried it forward against each other with all the enterprise of a modern university. Sometimes professional ballplayers would come to the baths and give exhibitions. Oldsters who preferred to take their exercise by proxy went to massage rooms and had a slave rub away their fat [375: lines 17–25].

3. The Puritans were trying to complete the work of the early Reformation of the Christian Church by implementing a stricter code of religious, moral and social norms on the whole society.

4. This was in line with Biblical writings that on the Seventh day the Lord rested after working the previous six days creating heaven and earth and everything therein. Some subgroups (e.g., among the British) or people were not observing the Sabbath Day, but were associated with the three "F's," these being feasting, fighting and fornication.

In addition, many of these "sporting" events involved gambling, cruelty to animals and danger to life, limb and property.

Stephen Miller in *The Peculiar Life on Sundays* gives details of the Lord's day and the Sabbath.

5. David W. Anthony, *The Horse, the Wheel and Language* (2007).

Historians agree that the pre-Christian British were a people of Indo-European origins who spread as far and wide as they possibly could into Europe and the British Isles.

The British peoples from Britain or Britannia were known as Britons and those from Brittany (northwestern part of France) as Bretons.

6. Vanessa Collingridge in *Boudica: The Life of Britain's Legendary Warrior Queen* states that modern Wales encompasses the former British inter-tribal or inter-kingdom areas of *Demetae, Ordovices,* and *Deceangli.* Collingridge also shows a map on page vi with the "Tribal Boundaries of Early Roman Great Britain." She mentions tribes and kingdoms: *Caledonia, Brigantes, Parisi, Coritani, Iceni, Deceangli, Cornivii, Ordovices, Dobunni, Catuvllauni, Trinovantes, Demetai, Silures, Atrebates, Belgae, Regnenses, Cantiaci, Durotriges* and *Dumnonii.* These tribal boundaries covered the whole of Britain. Constant inter-tribal or inter-kingdom rivalries most likely resulted in shifting borders and allegiances.

There were at least 17 groups. More details can be seen in the map of pre-Roman Britain in the work of Anne Ross and Don Robins, *The Life and Death of a Druid Prince: The Story of Lindow Man, an Archaeological Sensation.* The authors state: "Celtic tribal names in Britain and Ireland, with the sites of Lindow Moss, Llyn Cerrig Bach, and place names incorporating *Nemet-,* meaning 'grove' or 'sanctuary'" (80).

7. James MacKillop, *Myths and Legends of the Celts,* 25: lines 23–24.

8. Ireland was never conquered by the Romans, but later came under Christian control. Only part of Scotland was under Roman control, the Hadrian and Antoinne walls were reputedly built as defensive measures against invading or defending Scottish tribes.

9. Block in *Baseball Before We Knew It* mentions that batting ball games were known (273: lines 34–38; and 274: lines 12, 9–18).

10. Throughout history, it is not unusual for a conquering power or religion to establish its own sacred places over the sites of the sacred places of the conquered. These practices have often led to some of the world's continued political and religious-based conflicts over sacred ancestral sites, as seen in India (Hindus and Muslims) and Jerusalem (Jews and Muslims).

11. Bards were the early British poets who passed on oral histories and traditions through verse. They were held in high esteem and ranked just below the priests of early Britain. Sometimes the terms bards and Druids were interchangeable. The bards inspired warriors before battles and celebrated or consoled their people thereafter.

Numerous British triads contained the distilled and accumulated folk wisdom of the various British peoples. These triads were presented in a poetic and easily memorized oral format.

12. The Otherworld was the realm where deities, powerful spirits and honoured ancestors resided. This invisible place was believed to be somewhere over the seas, underground, and alongside them. It was paradise, a place of happiness and comfort. At certain times of the year, beings were thought to be able to move from one world to another and *vice versa.*

13. Isabel Elder, *Celt, Druid and Culdee,* 53: lines 26–30.

Hu Gadarn (alias "Hu the Mighty") was credited with leading Celts to Wales, and was later synonymous with the sun god. This request of Hu Gadarn promoted respect for dissident views to be freely aired in public without recriminations and likely laid the foundations for freedom of expression as a tradition in Celtic realms.

Elder also wrote that under Hu Gadarn the educational system was formalized and intellectual, artistic and cultural pursuits (including writing Ogham characters) were encouraged and thrived. The standard of Hu Gadarn included the depiction of an ox (53: lines 10–25).

14. In Hindu society this inter-relationship still exists since all aspects of life are interwoven. In daily life religion cannot be separated from culture, music, dance, philosophy, folklore, and lifestyle.

Chapter 7

1. Deanne Westbrook, *Ground Rules, Baseball and Myths,* "Baseball and the Sacred," continues:

> This ubiquitous modern quest need not surprise us, for it has been argued that the Enlightenment, with its guiding scientific light resulted in historical discon-

tinuity that not only marked the boundary of the modern era but actually produced a mutant species of the sacred, its forms subsumable under the term "uncanny" [42, lines 27–36; and 43: line 1].

2. C.M. Bowra in *Primitive Song* (1963) writes:

A myth is a story whose primary purpose is not to entertain but to enlighten primitive man on matters which perplex him and cannot be made intelligible as they can to us, by analysis or abstraction, since they are beyond his linguistic and mental resources. He is presented instead with a story which attempts to illuminate obscure subjects by providing a kind of historical antecedent or parallel to them. ... They try to appeal to half-conscious and unconscious elements in human nature. To grasp their relevance we must not think logically of cause and effect but try to capture a mood or an atmosphere or an emotional frame of mind, in which individual images count for everything and must be allowed to make their full impact with the echoes and implications and associations which they evoke [217: lines 1–24; and 218: lines 1–4].

3. This is still seen in Scottish communities around the world where those of Scottish descent participate in the Highland games at the annual gathering of clans. Holy days were days designed to be primarily religious and "holi days" more festive, merry and celebratory. The distinction is often blurred and the eventual outcome was the joining of two words to give holiday.

4. Roman soldiers commented that the Celtic women of Britain were ferocious fighters and not to be tangled with.

The relevance of the participation of both sexes in this game will be stressed in the later chapters.

5. Cram et al.'s edition of *Francis Willughby's Book of Games, a Seventeenth-Century Treatise on Sports, Games and Pastimes*, 283, "Stoolball, Tutball," lines 30–32.

6. Robert Herrick, *Poetical Works of Robert Herrick*, 32, Number 691.

7. Stool-ball was called tut-ball in some places, Gomme writes. Tut-ball, he wrote, was now only played by boys, but half a century ago by adults on Ash Wednesday,

believing that unless they do so they would fall sick in harvest time. This is a very ancient game, and was elsewhere called "Stool-Ball," indulged in by the clergy as well as the laity to avert misfortune....

Addy (Sheffield Glossary) says this game [tut-ball] is the same as "pize ball" [314: lines 26–30, 32–33].

Appendix C has the full quotation.

8. Ramsey MacMullen in *Christianity & Paganism in the Fourth to Eight Centuries*, points out how hard it is to cast aside traditions especially those long entrenched in religion involving, for example, burials. At the funeral of Pope Pius IX, even those high ecclesiastics were not immune to the continuation of pagan practices, since a bag of coins were placed on Pius IX's deceased body in the sarcophagus to pay Charron for his services of ferrying the souls across the rivers Styx and Acheron which separated the world of the living from the underworld (109: line 36; and 110: lines 1–18).

9. Roberts, *The Cambrian Popular Antiquities,* 123: lines 5–13; and 124: lines 15–17.

10. Robert W. Henderson, *Ball, Bat and Bishop: The Origin of Ball Games*, Chapter 10, "Stoolball," 70: lines 11–16.

11. *Ibid.*, 71: lines 13–18; 73: lines 14–16.

After the first paragraph, Henderson continues:

This is shown in D'Urfey's *Pills to Purge Melancholy,* a collection of rather *Risqué* poems, including one from a play *Don Quioxte*, acted at Dorset Green in 1694. The First verse reads:
Down in the Vale on a Summer's Day.
All the Lads and Lasses Went to Be Merry,.
A Match for Kisses at Stoolball to Play,.
And for Cakes and Ale, and Cider and Perry.
Chorus: Come All, Great Small,.
Short Tall, Away to Stoolball [71: lines 18–27].

12. *Ibid.* After the second paragraph of the quotation, Henderson writes in the rest of the paragraph:

An English clergyman, Henry Bourne, writing in 1725, tackled the problem of the origin of the curious Easter ball games. Why the ball games were so popular at the Easter season instead of other games puzzled him. But he did come to the conclusion, although without presenting evidence, that "it will be readily granted that the twelfth century Easter ball ceremonies in the Churches of France, and decried by some theologians of the time, were the origin of our present recreations and diversions on Easter Holy Days, and in particular the playing of ball for a tanzy cake, which at this season is generally practiced; and I would hope practiced with harmlessness and innocence. For when the common devotions of the day are over, there is nothing sinful in lawful recreation" [73: lines 16–29].

The work referred to is that of Henry Bourne in *Antiquitates Vulgarares: Or, the Antiquities of the Common People* (1725). This work was republished by John Brand in *Observations on Popular Antiquities* (1777).

13. Adelman, *A Sporting Time*, 98: lines 22–30. Adelman states in the next paragraph:

By medieval times ball games were tightly interwoven with life in rural England, being associated with Christian holidays, parish feasts, and other religious activities. Some opposition always existed to these games, ... but not until the beginning of the early modern period did a vigorous reform movement, led by dissident Puritans, "present a powerful challenge to the customary practices of popular recreations." Their emphasis on a strict Sabbath and their fears that amusements distracted people from their basic religious and social duties shaped the Puritan view of sport. They also objected strongly to traditional recreations because they were rooted in pagan and popish practices....

Adelman points out there was this necessity for these pastimes since these rituals provided a vital connection with the people's ancestral past and with the broader community (99: lines 1–8).

14. Henderson, in *Ball, Bat and Bishop*, states:

There was nothing to prevent the playing of stoolball at other times than Easter, and although the Easter customs persisted, the game, naturally popular with young people, particularly those amorously inclined to "co-ed" pastimes,

was played occasionally throughout the year. Nevertheless the Easter stoolball in many country places in England was the time above all times for love making, which undoubtedly led to a permanent pairing of many ball-playing couples [75: lines 22–29].

15. Violators of these church prohibitions were threatened with financial penalties or other punitive measures.

W.W. Grantham in *Stollball and How to Play It* (1931) states:

1572 *Freke*. "Item, whether that there be any common pastimes or plays used in your parish in time of Common prayer, or Sermons; whereby, the people or youth be, is or hath been drawn away from their church at unlawful time, as hooping ... football ... stoolball. or any other unlawful game or exercise."

1586 *Essex*. A young man was brought into the court of the archdeacon of Essex on the charge of: "plaieinge at stol-bawle on holie Thursday last service time." Sentenced to pay 12d to the poor.

1634 *Bristoll*. "The whole churchyard is made a receptacle for all ydle persons to spend their time in stop-ball ... the time of Divine Service not excepted."

1670 *Wilson*. "I have seen ... stoolball ... and many other sports on the Lord's Day."

1704 *Bunyon*. "His son's sins being drunkenness ... and unbecoming actions about stoolball."

1720 *Lewis*. "All games where there is any hazard of loss are strictly forbidden ... not so much as a game of stoolball for a tansy ... upon pain of damnation" [14–16].

16. These were the days of the "spare the rod, spoil the child" mindset, the church officials therefore did not have to use the threat of fines to deal with children. Sound thrashings given to child offenders by church-zealots would have been most likely effectively used as a deterrent.

It was mentioned earlier that women were placed in stocks for violations of the Sunday prohibitions in rural Wales (Chapter 5, Note 2).

17. Grantham states:

1640 *J. Smyth* in *Hundred of Berkeley*, "Doe Witness that gentry, Yeomantry, rascality, boys and children doe take in a game called stoball."

1660 *Charlemayne.* "The common people will endure long and hard labour insomuch that after twelve hours hard work they will go in the evening ... to stockball" [15].

18. The game's religious and social aspects coupled with the use of terms such as "burning" and "wounding," particularly in early British-controlled areas, provide additional insights into the game's early roles and functions. Other terms that will be added to this list in the next chapter includes "stabbing" and "soaking."

19. Pre-Roman peoples include pre-Celtic and Celtic; Germans include Saxons, Angles, Jutes and Frisians; Scandinavians include Danes, Norwegians, Swedes and Vikings; and Normans a mixture that included North Germanic Norse Vikings, Danish, Swedish, Icelandic and French.

20. These old Gaelic words for athletic exercises, *guiftal,* and public meetings, *sonachs* or *acoutheach,* are from William Shaw's *A Gaelic and English Dictionary* (1780).

21. Elder, *Celt, Druid and Culdee,* 53, lines 10–14; 56: lines 8–10; and 58: lines 2–6.

The historian being referred to is Dr. Robert Henry, "History of England," *The History of Great Britain* (1793), published posthumously.

22. Roberts, *The Cambrian Popular Activities,* writes:

The ancient Britains, being naturally a warlike nation, did, noe doubt for the exercise of their youth in tyme of peace, and to avoid idlenes, devise games of activitie, where ech man might shewe his natural prowes and agility, as some for strength of the body, wrestling, lifting of heavie burdens; others for the arme, as in casting the barre, sledge-stone, or hurling the bowle or ball, others y' excelled in swiftness of foote, to wynne praise therein by running, and surely for the exercise of the partes aforesayd, this Knappan was prudentlie invented [332: lines 10–24].

23. T. Sharper Knowlson, in his 1972 updated work, *Origins of Popular Superstitions and Customs,* of John Brand's 1841 text, *Popular Antiquities,* "Easter Holidays," 32: lines 23–32; 33: lines 1–8; and 35: lines 9–12.

24. John Brand, "Lifting on Easter Holidays," *Popular Antiquities of Great Britain,* states:

Lifting was originally designed to represent our Savior's resurrection. The men lift the women on Easter Monday, and the women lift the men on Tuesday. One or more take hold of each leg, and one or more hold each arm near the body, and lift the person up, in a horizontal position, three times. It is a rude, indecent, and dangerous diversion, practiced chiefly by the lower class of people. Our Magistrates constantly prohibit it [97: lines 26–34].

25. Knowlson, "Easter Holidays," 35: lines 9–12.

26. Analogous fertility rites and ritual sacrifices such as *heaving* and *lifting* practices run deep within our human psyche as revealed in examinations of the struggles for survival of most tribal, ethnic or national communities. Since such similar sacrificial or symbolic ritual practices were almost culturally universal, and in many instances relics of such acts survived, this meant that these fertility rituals were perceived as playing pivotal roles in the success of the group's own health and welfare including progeny and food. For example, similar practices were seen in ancient India (Asvamedha sacrifice), where the queen and priest were raised by men into a position for sexual union which itself was identified with sacrifice for the benefit of the local community.

The similarity of these *heaving* and *lifting* practices with those of ancient India are apparent, but it is clearer in the Indian case that they were a part of fertility rite or ritual sacrifice. This is reminiscent of the fertility rituals of the high priest's union with the queen, which Narendra Nath Bhattacharyya, *Ancient Indian Rituals and Their Social Contents,* describes. He raises the question as to why sexual union and states that intercourse was identified with sacrifice as seen in the Asvamedha sacrifice. The various parts of a woman's body were compared to the essential components in a sacrificial practice (9: lines 11–19 and 19–28; and 10: lines 1–10).

27. The older meanings of these acts are easily found in an examination of British peoples' historial roots. The sexual socialization aspects evident in these rural or folk

games of early Britain with older pre-Christian Easter traditions (*heaving* or *lifting*, stool-ball, eating, drinking, dancing and making merry) were in keeping with their early Indo-European's fertility rituals and roots. In ancient India, sexual unions were often associated with religious sacrificial offerings (*Yajna*). Bhattacharyya, *Ancient Indian Rituals and Their Social Contents*, writes: "The queen is raised up high by a few men, and so is the priest. And in that condition they make sexual intercourse as the ritual demand" (9: lines 11–12). Bhattacharya observes: "In the *Satapatha Brahmana* we come across numerous passages in which sexual union is identified with sacrifice" (9: lines 16–17). This idea was mentioned previously by Bhattacharya, who wrote that the priest and queen were tossed into the air, analogously to the early British practices of *heaving* and *lifting*. These practices were continued in secret by the *Vamacharis* sect in their worship of *Sakti* (17: lines 12–19, 33; 17: lines 26–32; 34; and 20: lines 15–18).

28. Other celebratory activities were occurring. For example, Ronald Hutton in *The Stations of the Sun: A History of the Ritual Year in Britain* writes:

> [On Easter] All across England and Ireland in the same century [eighteenth] smaller communities engaged in dancing, Athletics, racing of horses and dogs, feasting, and a variety of local games. The tradition persists to the present day in the scheduling of fun-fairs and professional sports. What has perished is any sense of a celebration of communal identity [205: lines 43–44; and 206: lines 1–4].

29. German philosopher Hans-Joachim Schoeps, *The Religions of Mankind: Their Origin and Development*, writes:

> Procession, too, is basically a form of dance, aimed at mobilizing the religious community. "Every procession is as it were sacramental, in that it places something sacred in motion and spreads the power of the holy thing over a certain area. In the sacramental procession, such as is practiced by the Roman Catholic Church, the blessing locked within the sanctuary spreads out over village and town, over field and meadow"

(Gerard van der Leuw) [37: lines 36–37; and 38: lines 1–5].

30. Ronald Hutton in *The Stations of the Sun: A History of the Ritual Year in Britain* writes:

> The most decorous form of the custom was in Wales and its borderland, where groups of young people went from house to house upon the appropriate day, carrying a chair decorated with greenery and ribbons. They would place willing members of the opposite sex in this and raise them up three times before being rewarded with money, food, drink, or kisses…. In part of Wales the lads processed with a fiddler playing before them. In Hertfordshire and around Ludlow in Shropshire, the "lifters" carried a bowl of water and a posy of flowers as well, using them to sprinkle the feet of the person in the chair. Hertfordshire parties were sometimes mixed gender, and they sang "Jesus Christ is risen again" before they perform the lift [211: lines 27–31 and 33–38].

The practice was moving away from its roots to becoming Christianized. His chapter on Easter (20) gives more details.

31. In times when and where activities associated with religious practices were prohibited, leading practioners and their faithful either disguised their practices or took them underground as they moved from community to community. Hence the practices of the Druidic priesthood continued even without their ancestral or special places. It was mainly the ordinary people who most likely maintained and continued the traditions. Ward Rutherford, *Celtic Mythology*, writes about this in Roman times and the Elizabethan periods, where the Druidic priiests and bards, and Catholic priests respectively went underground. This is supported by Gildas a sixth-century British historian (39: lines 24–39).

32. For example, Chapter 1 in Sir James George Frazier's *The Golden Bough: A Study in Magic and Religion*, Vol. 1, 1–108.

33. Special lit fires were used as a medium whereby messages or souls were taken to the gods or abodes of the gods. In the latter case it was thought that fires accelerated the release of the soul from the body so that the spirit of the dead can get there faster as seen

in ancient Hindu, Buddhist and early European Celtic (Britons and Bretons), Germanic and Scandinavian practices, or, that it can begin its journey in another form such as reincarnation as in Hindu, Buddhist, Jain and Celtic beliefs. Sacrificial offerings, for example, humans, animals and food (grain and fruit), were made to appease or feed the gods to ensure continued health and prosperity of individuals or their communities. Early British, e.g., the Britons of Britain, communities set ablaze large wicker structures with their human or animal sacrificial offerings. The fires used in sacrificial practices or ceremonies were regarded as sacred.

34. Brand in *Observations on Popular Antiquities* (1841) writes:

> The Sixth Council of Constantinople, A.D. 680, by its 65th canon (cited by Prynne in his *Histriomastrix*), has the following interdiction: "Those Bonefires that are kindled by certaine people on the New Moones before their shops and houses, over which also they are ridiculously and foolishly to leape, by a certain ancient custom, we command them from henceforth to cease. Whoever therefore shall doe any such thing; if he be a clergyman, let him be deposed; if a layman, let him be excommunicated."
>
> Upon this Prynne obseves: "Bonefires therefore had their originall from an idolatrous custome, as this Generall Councell hath defined; therefore all Christians should avoid them." And the Synodus Francica under Pope Zachary, A.D. 742, cited *Ut Supra*, inhibits "those sacrilegious Fires which they call Nedfri (or Bonefires), and all other observations of the pagans whatsoever" [172: lines 1–8, and 12–17].

The church would later copy these same burning processes to put people (heretics, pagans, and witches) to death. "*Nedfri*" meant "need fires" and "*bonefires*" "bone fires (burning of bones)." These fires were thought to be essential in sacrificial rituals.

35. In Biblical times as recorded in Genesis: 22:1–12, Abraham was prepared to sacrifice his own son on a bundle of wood to be lit to comply with the request of his god.

The King James Bible mentions (1) the prohibition of having children being sacrificed to gods with fire on altars (Deuteronomy: 12: 31; Jeremiah: 32: 35; and Ezekiel: 20: 26) and (2) the comdemnation of sacrificial offerings under trees, in valleys, and in the clefts of rocks (Isaiah: 57: 4–5).

36. Parts of these old practices survived in England, Scotland and Ireland. Addy in *A Glossary of Words* has the relevant information on pages xx: lines 15–17, 22–25, 34; and xxi: lines 1–6 and xxi: lines 9–10.

Addy mentions that the "needfire, *Nedfir*" were common to both early Brtish and Germanic peoples (xxi: lines 9–10).

37. William Boralse in *Antiquities of Cornwall* (1754) writes:

> Of the fires we kindle in many parts of England at some stated times of the year we know not certainly the rise, reason, or occasion, but they may probably be reckoned among the relics of the Druid superstitious Fires. In Cornwall, the festival Fires, called Bonfires, are kindled on the Eve of St. John the Baptist and St. Peter's Day: and Midsummer is thence, in the Cornish tongue, called Goluan, which signifies both light and rejoicing. At these Fires the Cornish attend with lighted torches, tarr'd and pitch'd at the end, and make their perambulations round their Fires, and go from village to village carrying their torches before them; and this is certainly the remains of the Druid superstition, for *Faces Praeferre*, to carry lighted torches, was reckoned a kind of Gentilism, and as such particularly prohibited by the Gallick Councils: they were in the eye of the law *Accensores Facularum*, and thought to sacrifice to the devil, and to deserve capital punishment [130: lines 34–41; and 131: lines 1–7].

Apparently, church officials thought that the Cornish people like other early Brtish peoples elsewhere were offering sacrifices to the devil. Their practices were considered "gentilism" that is non-Christian. This festival was revived recently and is now celebrated every June as the Golowan Festival in Cornwall, Great Britain.

William Borlase, author of *Antiquities of Cornwall* (1754), was an antiquarian, geologist and naturalist, who also did pioneering work in archaeology investigating the barrows of Cornwall. Barry Mardsen, author of *The*

Early Barrow Diggers, comments on the work of William Borlase on pages 82–83.

Addy writes about the celebration of the festival of Beltein, which was observed until as the eighteenth century on the first of May in every village in Scotland. In this celebration of a rural sacrifice, the community pleaded for the health of their crops and livestock with token sacrificial offerings to local deities. They cut a square on the ground so that they could all fit and in the central position a fire was made on the turf. The dish made and offered had nine knobs and one for each local deity or putative protector (lii: lines 21–28; and liii: lines 1–29).

38. Knowlson writes about an old tradition about dancing around a coal fire. Participants of such traditional activities include high public and judicial officials (50: lines 31–33; and 51: lines 1–12).

39. Medieval Christians demonized the early British and Continental European god Cerunnos, giving him horns thereby associating him with the Devil. The pagan god like others was then discredited.

40. Addy mentions that people gathered to perform ceremonies that were meant to placate the preserver and destroyer of their crops and domesticated animals. Others (for example, Knowlson, *Origins of Popular Superstitions and Customs*, 43–53) have indicated that this ritual sacrifice was likely a relic of a human sacrifice. Brand had commented on such observations in his 1841 work.

41. Addy writes:

Places called *Bell Hagg* and *Burnt Stones* were places where in former times, balefires were kindled, and where, the rites of these late instances are survivals were practiced.

In both cases the rites were initiated by Churchmen, the one being a laybrother of the Cistercian order, and the other a parish priest. It is highly probable that similar rites were practiced down to a comparatively late period; indeed, when we consider that plays were acted in churches even after the Reformation, we shall see how tenaciously the people cling to their old customs and superstitions [xx: 22–26, 35; and xxi: lines 1–6].

Addy also gives more details about the places called *Bell Haag* and *Burnt Stone* located on higher ground where fires were lit and cattle driven through. Addy thinks that these traditions were wider than early British since they were also practiced by early Germanic peoples (see li: lines 31–34; and lii: lines 1–20).

42. Knowlson writes:

The ancients passed their children through the fire, and the villagers at Whalton used to jump over and through the flames. Moreover, as will be seen from the historical references to be given shortly, there is further ground provided for the establishing a genuine fire worship.... The same site for the fire is chosen year after year, and it has never been changed. The village turns out *En Masse* to see the bonfire built. The children join hands and dance around the stack of wood and branches until they are tired; youths and maidens also dance a little distance away.

At dark a cry is raised: "light her!" Soon the whole village is illuminated by a huge blaze, and the Baal fire is at its height. No ceremony follows, but tradition says people jump over the fire and through it, a tradition which is well founded, for we have strong evidence of such practices in Scotland and Ireland [43: lines 24–29; and 44: lines 8–20].

43. The Reformation is usually viewed as beginning in the early sixteenth century under Martin Luther. The Puritans started to gain ascendancy in the late sixteenth century and eventually gained power in the seventeenth under the leadership of Oliver Cromwell (1653–1659). The Puritans advocated and lived according to a strict religious code. Hackwood also gives supportive evidence of the suppression of May Day revelry that included sports.

44. Sir Thomas Randolph in *An Eclogue on the Noble Assemblies Revived on Cotswold Hills by Master Robert Dover*, in *Poetical and Dramatic Works of Thomas Randolph. Now First Collected and Edited from the Early Copies from MSS with Some Account of the Author and Occasional Notes* by Carew Hazlitt, writes:

These teach that dancing is a Jezabel,
And barley-break the ready way to hell;
The morrice Idols, Whitsun Ales, can be.

But profane relics of a Jubilee:
These, in a zeal t' express how much
they do.
The organs hate, have silenc'd bagpipes
too;
And harmless Maypoles, all are rail'd
upon,.
As if they were the towers of Babylon.
Some think not fit there should be
any sport [Vol. II (London: Reeves and
Turner, 1875), 621–626: lines 53–61].

N.B.: Jezabel, a Phoenician princess, was
the wife of the Biblical king Ahab. In her capacity as queen of Israel, she led Ahab and
Israel from the worship of their own true god
to the worship of Baal, meaning Lord. Jezabel
as queen facilitated the state to allow other
pagan rites contrary to Judaism (1 Kings: 18).
She had many of the Jewish prophets killed
and sought to kill Elijah the prophet who had
likewise condemned her actions. After the
death of Ahab, Jezabel continued her influence on the Hebrews through her sons, first
Ahaziah and then Jehoram, until her death.
Jezabel was thrown out the window by
her eunuchs and her body left in the street to
be eaten by dogs. Her death fulfilled the
prophecy of Elijah.

Some are now thinking that Jezabel as
queen in a highly patriarchal society should
be viewed more sympathetically and that
she was a faithful wife, mother and grandmother who looked out for the rights of her
people.

The "barley-break" mentioned in the
poem was a game played by children or
young people of both sexes. Each team had
three pairs of mixed couples.

45. Addy mentions bonfires being associated with the god Baal (Notes 40 and 41). In
some cases, Baal was thought to be the name
of the sun god, or planet Jupiter, but the con-
sensus seems to be Baal generally meant the
title of lord or master, as given to a local deity.
The Gallick Council, that is, the Christian
Church authorities of Galatia, was very familiar with early British and Continental
European practices. St. Paul (New Testament)
had spoken out about the worship of the
sun in Galatia. St. Patrick did the same in Ireland.

46. Sir Thomas Randolph, *An Eclogue on
the Noble Assemblies Revived on Citswold
Hills*, continues:

Some think not fit there should be any
sport.
I' th' country,'tis a dish proper to th'
Court.
Mirth not becomes 'em: let the saucy
swain.
Eat beef and bacon, and go sweat
again,.
Besides, what sport can in the pastimes
be,.
When all is but ridiculous foppery?
[623: lines 6–11, or lines 61–66 of the
poem].

And yet their sports by some controll'd
have been.
Who think there is no mirth but what
is sin [624: lines 5–14 or lines 85–94].

47. Schoeps in *The Religions of Mankind*
writes:

Procession may evolve into religious
drama. In the festival calendar of the ec-
clesiastical year, the Christian Church
relives again and again the life and death
of its Lord. It presents the events of salvation and redemption in its services as
symbolic drama. The Greek Orthodox
Church does this with a particular im-
pressiveness. So also the death and resurrection of the vegetation god in Baby-
lonia and Syria, or the sham battles
fought between the adherents of the god
and his adversaries in the Egyptian cult
of Osiris, or the mystery of the sacred
wedding in Eleusis and elsewhere, were
intended as real, ritual links between
the believer and the deity. Of course,
magical notions also entered in as, for
example, among the ritual ball games
of the Aztecs; it is thought that the imi-
tative action will actually create what is
represented and thus permit man to participate in salvation [translated from the
1961 German edition *Religionen: Wesen
Und Geschichte*, by Richard and Clara
Winston, 38: lines 6–20].

48. *Ibid.*, 93: lines 26–31.

49. J. Krishnamurti, *The Awakening of
Intelligence*, 472: lines 10–14; and 481: lines
26.

50. Jesus in the New Testament, the
Gospel of Matthew: 18: 20. "For wherever two
or three are gathered together in my name,
there am I in the midst of them."

St. Paul in New Testament, Book of Hebrews: 10: 25. "Not forsaking the assembling of ourselves together, as the manner of some is; but exhorting one another: and so much the more, as ye see the day approaching."

51. Jacob Grimm in *Teutonic Mythology* (1844) writes about this ancient human need to gather together forcing the Christian Church to be tolerant of old practices and adapting them to serve the new roles:

> Oftentimes the Church and I have specified sundry instances either was from the outset or gradually became, tolerant, and indulgent. She prudently permitted, or could not prevent, that heathen and Christian things should here and there run into one another; the clergy themselves would not always succeed in marking off the bounds of the two religions; their private leanings might let some things pass, which they found firmly rooted in the multitude. ... Churches often rose precisely where a heathen god or his sacred tree had been pulled down, and the people trod the old paths to the accustomed site: sometimes the very walls of the heathen became those of the church, and cases occur in which idol-images still found a place in of the porch, or were set up outside the door, as at Bamberg cathedral there lie Slavic-heathen figures of animals inscribed with runes. Sacred hills and fountains were re-christened after saints, to whom their sanctity was transferred; sacred woods were handed over to newly founded convent or the king, and even under private ownership did not altogether lose their long-accustomed homage [Vol. III, XXXV: lines 3–10, 16–34; and XXXVI: lines 1–4].

Chapter 8

1. If they did keep written records, these were probably on bark, leaves, or staves which would more readily decay. In the Time-Life Book series *Myth and Mankind*, the writers Fergus Flemings, Sharukh Hussain, C. Scott Littleton and Linda A. Milcor state in *Heroes of the Dawn: Celtic Myth* that Caesar writes about this and offer their own comments:

> The Druids believe that their religion forbids them to commit their teachings to writing." Possibly the druids feared that their wisdom would be corrupted and vulgarized if it was available to the masses in written form. However, the ban may partly have been for political reasons: written records would have greatly reduced the druids, prestige as the sole repositories of all religious and cultural knowledge [11, second column, lines 28–36].

2. Horik Svensson in *The Runes* writes: Runes are an Ancient form of writing that was likely used widely for thousands of years in the lands of northern Europe. A great deal of mystery surrounds their origins and use. According to Viking tradition, the word "rune" means a whispered secret. The Concise Oxford Dictionary informs us in somewhat drier fashion, the word "rune" means "any of the letters of the earliest Germanic alphabet used by the Scandinavian and Anglo-Saxons from the third century BCE and formed by modifying Roman or Greek characters to suit carving [8: lines 1–12].

3. The old Gaelic word *dur*, meaning fortress, has survived as the basis for the word *durable*. This and all other old Gaelic words mentioned herein were taken from William Shaw, *A Galic and English Dictionary* (1780), unless otherwise noted. Shaw used the old word "Galic"; in modern times "Gaelic" is used.

4. Old Gaelic: "*Bas, Ceal, Eug, Teimhe, Gus, Etfeachd, Bann, Bano, Meilg, Cro,* and *Nas,* meant death"; and "*Cogadh, Grim, Duchon, Gliad, Cofnamb, Doicheadfaidh Combuaread, Crioch,* warfare." The word *Crioch* was also used to mean gatherings.

5. The ancient Hindus (recorded in the Vedas, about 800–600 BCE) produced the Sulbasutra text describing the construction of right angles, squares and circles. These rules were necessary for the production of precise sacrificial fire altars (Kim Plofker, *Mathematics of India* in V.J. Katz, ed., The *Mathematics of Egypt, Mesopotamia, China, India, and Islam*). The Brahmins who constituted the Hindu priesthood of ancient India

were equivalent to, for example, the British and European Druids.

6. Examples: In old Africa, most villages had a sacred grove and only priests were allowed to enter. In ancient India, almost every village temple was usually built around or near a grove. The Khonds of Bengal, ancient India, kept groves as temples and did not use buildings.

A list of Biblical groves is given by Alexander Porteus in *The Folklore of the Forests, Myths and Legends* (1928), 45–47.

7. Alexander Porteus, *The Folklore of the Forests, Myths and Legends*, 48, lines 41–45; 49, lines 1–4, 13–25. Porteus continues:

When temples of stone were first begun to be erected an opening was left at the summit of the roof as reminiscent of the holy grove to the sky.... Celts unroofed their temples once a year [49: lines 333–6; and 50; line 1].

8. *Ibid.* Porteus writes:

In Central and Northern Europe dark Groves composed of ancient trees, and situated in the midst of gloomy forests, were, as said previously, the only temples, but these had been rendered holy by awe and reverence with which they had inspired each succeeding generation. An invisible deity dwelt in them who made his powers felt in storms which swept over them, or in the sunshine which flooded the woodland glades....

Many of the smaller forests or woods of Germany are considered to have been holy groves where in ancient times sacrifices were made under certain trees, and in which the bards were inspired to prophesy. Thus we find Odenwald or Odinswald, the grove sacred to Odin....

Throughout the whole of ancient Germany the groves dedicated to certain deities were forbidden to be entered by anyone except the officiating priests or soothsayers, and the gods were believed to sit enthroned on the trees of these sacred groves [48: lines 23–30; 50: lines 9–13; and 51: lines 3–8].

9. Fergus Flemings, Sharukh Hussain, C. Scott Littleton and Linda A. Milcor in *Heroes of the Dawn: Celtic Myth* (*Myth and Mankind*), 40: first column, lines 25–27.

The Gauls are the people of ancient Galatia, now France.

10. James G. Frazer in *The Golden Bough: A Study in Magic and Religion* (1958), Chapter IX, "The Worship of Trees," 126, and Chapter X, "Relics of Tree-Worship in Modern Europe," 139.

11. Anne Ross, *Everyday Life of the Pagan Celts*, "Temples, Shrines and Sanctuaries," 136–140.

Lines cited are from 137: lines 11–13; and 138: lines 1–3.

12. *Ibid.* Ross, Fig. 40, "Plans of 'viereck-schanzen,' pagan earth precincts," 137.

13. No one knows the actual old British names for these square enclosures. The Old Gaelic word *drud* means enclosure. Note that this word for enclosure bears the same root as the word for the British and Continental Celtic priesthood, i.e., the Druids, suggesting a possible religious connection for small enclosures where they presided. Alternatively, it could refer to an area ringed with sacred oak trees.

14. Ross, *Everyday Life of the Pagan Celts*, 139: lines 4–7, 29–31; and 140: lines 1, 3–9.

The MLB's San Francisco Giants current home, AT&T Park, follows this ancient plan. Balls hit beyond the right field wall end up in San Francisco Bay.

15. Ross, *Everyday Life of the Pagan Celts*, writes that the Celts had places, where deities were invoked by the priests on behalf of the community. These same places were also used on their sacred and festive occasions (136: lines 12–15).

These occasions were accompanied with entertainment, games and sports, and sacrificial animal or human offerings. It should be noted that their calendar was measured by night (15: lines 24–35).

16. This poem "Stool-Ball or the Easter Diversion" was published by an anonymous author in The *London Magazine, or Gentleman's Monthly Intelligencer*, 2 (December 1733), 637–638. Lines cited: 15, 19–24.

The letter "s" was substituted for the letter "f." For an easier read, readers may refer to Block's *Baseball Before We Knew It*, 114–118; the line numbers cited are similar.

Stocks were instruments where a person's head or limbs were placed to restrict movement, and a pillory post was where a person was shackled or manacled. Both were instruments of public punishment for minor offences.

17. *Ibid.* People met in the same place for sports and pleasure (also meaning social, courtship and sexual interactions). The relevant lines are quoted from the same above-mentioned poem (Note 16), lines 12 and 13, respectively.

18. Porteus, *Folklore of the Forests, Myths and Legends*, writes:

> There are still dug up, the ancient Mona's Isle great Trunks of Oak, which are the relics of the Holy Groves of the Druids there. Tacitus says a garrison was established in that Island to overawe the vanquished, and destroy the groves dedicated to sanguinary superstitions [80: lines 30–35].

19. Roman temples would in turn be replaced by Christian churches.

20. Ross, *Everyday Life of the Pagan Celts*, 96 and 97, Fig. 33. This figure is captioned: "Part of a ritual crown from Hock-wold-cum-Wilton, Norfolk, Pottery mould from Kettering, Northamptonshire."

21. *Ibid.* Ross writes that the Celts like others were head hunters which were displayed as trophies often hung on hill-forts. The severed heads were thought to hold special powers of divination, brought luck and served as talismans against evil (155: lines 6–18).

22. The 1773 poem, "Stool-ball, or the Easter Diversion," full citation details given in Note 16, pages 136–137: lines 60–68.

Block, 115: lines 32–36; and 116: lines 1–6. Block cites this 1733 poem and modernizes the language.

23. Samuel Hibbert, *A Description of the Shetlands Islands Comprising An Account of Their Scenery, Antiquities, and Superstitions*, 232: lines 13–18 and 23–25.

Perthshire was officially the local government county of Perth in central Scotland (1890 to 1930).

24. In most religions, places of worship such as temples were considered holy and there was usually an area that was only open to priests or high priests.

25. Such a central location was evident in the gladiatorial contests in the arenas of Rome. Such arrangements allowed for more mass participation in the spectacles before the spectators or audience.

26. This is analogous to what is seen in many religions where the major holy or altar area is set apart at one corner or end and generally accessible only to the priests. Christian churches and cathedrals, Hindu temples and Jewish synagogues follow this plan. In some of these places there are sections where only the holiest of the holy are allowed to enter.

27. Early pictures of baseball fields show the players, officials and spectators very close to the action. Spectators are also shown in the outfield areas.

This seating accommodation now works best for those seated in the arc between first and third bases. This primary dueling area is where the television cameras are also focused. Modern baseball diamonds are being designed to bring the fans closer to the game's actions.

In the supposed class-conscious game of cricket the observers are away from the action; whereas, in the democratic game of baseball the seating allows the privileged to be closer.

28. This infield arrangement alters the dynamics of the two modern versions of baseball and cricket. For example, in cricket, the ball that would be over the boundary to give six runs would likely be caught in fair territory in baseball. This is one explanation for higher scores in cricket.

29. Diagrams in Chadwick's 1884 work (*The Sports and Pastimes of American Boys*) titled: "Diagram of a Baseball Field with the Lines of Measurements," and "The Diamond Field," 33 and 34, respectively; an illustration is seen on 37.

30. For example, pictures in G.S. Ward, and Ken Burns, *Baseball An Illustrated History*, pages 10, 15 and 62–63.

31. Derek Berkley in *A Social History of English Cricket* states:

> The game of cricket, presumably because it was obscure and relatively innocuous, was not mentioned in the King's Book of Sports. But in 1611 it at last surfaced as an adult activity, albeit a somewhat inglorious one [7: lines 20–22].

"The Declaration of Sports" was first issued by King James I in 1617 and re-issued by King Charles I in 1633.

Secondly, Vernon Bartlett in *The Past of Pastimes* points out that cricket was also a rural game and besides being viewed in Britain as a manly game had similar problems with regards to drinking and betting:

But cricket was for a long time a rural game, and one of very little importance if it was played by the sons of the gentry at their schools. It was abandoned by them when they grew up. Betting which has ruined so many games, may be said to have saved cricket. How and Why?....

They arranged matches with other villages, and thus found new excuses for betting. Village cricket became, and has remained, one of the most typical features of English rural life. In 1748, the legal authorities decided that cricket was a "very manly game, not bad in itself, but only in the ill-use made of it, but that is against the law." There was also a good deal of drinking, the licensing laws being less eccentric in previous centuries than they are now, and it being then "very manly" to drink oneself under the table [53: lines 27–36; and 54: lines 1–20].

British cricket, like early baseball, had similar problems with regards to drinking and betting but was also thought to be a "manly game." Like baseball, a player may now prove his "manliness" by hitting and throwing prowess.

32. Arthur Croome in *Fifty Years of Sport at Oxford, Cambridge and the Great Public School* (1886) writes:

One of my best friends at Cambridge was E.B. Fawcett, a very tall man—he must have been 6 ft. 2 in. at least, who was famed for having made the record in throwing the cricket ball at Brighton College when a boy at school. I forgot the exact distance, but fancy it was over 126 yards. [The distance is recorded as being 126 yards, 6 in.] And there were usually quite a number of men in the university who could throw 100 yards or more. In my last year at the University Sports on Fenner's, I was second with 94 yards, the first being a man named Mellor, who threw 96. I remember this was universally noted as bad and unusual. I was playing with the Warwickshire Knickerbockers *V.* Cheltenham College, who captained by the excellent sportsman, R.T. Reid, now Lord Chancellor of England. Our eleven was a weak one, almost its only distinction being its col-

lective ability to throw a ball a terrific distance [Vol. I., 98: lines 35–47].

Arthur Croome shows throwing was an essential and valued skill in cricket.

33. The terms infield and outfield were known in cricket. From W.J. Lewis's *The Language of Cricket, with Illustrative Extracts from the Literature of the Game*:

OUT-FIELD, to. To act as fieldsman in the out-field; OUT-FIELDER. A fieldsman stationed in the out-field; a "long-field." OUT-FIELDING. 1. Fielding in the out-field, especially at the more distant positions in the field of play. 2. The field of play outside the specifically ground of pitch: now usually called the "outfield." OUT-FIELDSMAN. A man who fields in the deep field; an out-fielder [180].

Besides the given meanings of these words, each definition is accompanied by citation in early literature (eighteenth, nineteenth or twentieth century) where the word was used.

34. Elder, *Celt, Druid and Culdee,* 61: lines 25–31; and 62: line 1.

Elder added that the chambered barrows and cairns of Britain were used as places for religious assemblies and worships, especially when the sun was high over the horizon. It was pointed out that the fireplaces had exits for smoke (details on 62: lines 6–12; and 63: lines 11–13).

35. These priestly roles were also played by the Brahmins of ancient India in similar clearly defined sacred areas, which contained fire altars.

36. James Mackillop, *Myths and Legends of the Celts*, gives more information about the Celts.

37. In modern baseball, these permanent upright structures are absent. These fixed stone slabs or wooden posts were removed for a variety of reasons, the most important rationales being: a safety issue, an upright stone or wooden pole will cause more injuries to players on collision; and secondly it removes the past religious or burial associations. But this situation presents visibility problems, since a sunken stone, especially when obscured by dirt, can be difficult for an umpire to see. In addition, modern bases or simple substitutions allow children and older players to easily transform non-dedicated areas for baseball and related activities.

38. Ralph Blum, *The Book of Rune: A*

Handbook for the Use of and Ancient Oracle, the Viking Runes, writes:

> The Runes. Older than the New Testament, The Runes have lain fallow for more than 300 years. Akin in function to the Tarot and the Chinese *Book of Changes,* the Runes were last in current use in Iceland during the late Middle Ages. In their time they were as the *I Ching* of the Vikings.
>
> The wisdom of the Rune Masters died with them. Nothing remains but the sagas, and far-flung fragments of runic lore and the Runes themselves....

There is no firm agreement among scholars as to where and when runic writing first made its appearance in Western Europe. Before the Germanic peoples possessed any form of script, they used pictorial symbols that they scratched onto rocks. Especially common in Sweden, these prehistoric rock carving or *Hällristningar* are dated from the second Bronze Age (ca. 1300 B.C.[E.]), and were probably linked to Indo-European fertility and sun cults. The Carvings include representations of men and animals, parts of the human body, weapon motifs, sun symbols, the swastika and variations on Square and circular forms [17: lines 2–9; 18: lines 1, 26–27; 19: lines 1–10].

39. *Ibid.,* 19: lines 16–18.

40. *Ibid.,* 19: line 21; and 20: lines 1–2.

41. Carver, *The Book of Sports,* 38: lines 4–5.

42. Wood, *The Boy's Modern Playmate: A Book of Sports, Games, and Pastimes,* 49: Section Rule: III. "The Pitcher," lines 4–6.

In the 1830s, the bases were called "byes" in Canada. Morrow, *Baseball,* in Morrow and Keyes, ed., *A Concise History of Sport in Canada,* 109: lines 28–30.

43. For example, the traditions of a spiritual journey in yoga involve four traditions or paths. The number four is thought of as symbolizing perfection in many of the major world religions such as Judaism, Christianity, and Islam, and is thought to be even more significant in Hinduism and Buddhism. In Hinduism, for example, the Vedas are divided into four sections, and the priesthood into four types.

The ancient Indians, Europeans and others believed that the earth was a square, hence the familiar survived expression "the four corners of the earth." In old Indian and European (both insular and continental, British, Germanic and Northern European) beliefs the four major directions were north, east, south, and west, and the four elements were "earth, air, fire, and water." (A fifth element called "ether" is also mentioned). The early British and European calendar year was also divided into four distinct seasons; the arrival of each was clearly marked and celebrated with its own particular festival. They recognized the moon had four phases (quarter, half, three-quarters, and full), and viewed it as a shape-changer.

Much later, the importance of the number four was embedded in old British culture as seen in the renowned tale of "The Grail Castle." This story features (1) the four Grail treasures: dish, sword, spear and grail; (2) the four functions of the human psyche: sensation, thinking, intuition, and feeling; (3) the four personality archetypes: king (pentacle of sensation), warrior (sword of intellect), magician (wand of intuition), and lover (cup of feelings). The story is thought to be grounded in imaginative British folklore and mythology.

Some believe this story of "The Grail Castle" later influenced the myth of the Holy Grail. Others had pointed out that officials of the Roman Catholic Church were never comfortable with the myth because it owed its origin to pagan beliefs rather than Christian. The grail was thought to be a magic cauldron, a common theme in old British stories, always full of refreshing and regenerative food, i.e., a cornucopia. The cauldron was also thought to bring life to the deceased and hence called the cauldron of rebirth. In K. Wilkinson's edition of *Signs & Symbols:* "Symbolically, the origins of the Holy Grail are thought to have an association with the cauldron of Celtic mythology. Central to pagan ritual, the cauldron is a symbol of fertility and abundance." This also brings to mind the ancient symbol of the *Trident* which was used to fight evil, but Christianity later associated it with the Devil to discredit pagan gods, beliefs and practices.

More details can be found in the works of: (1) Kenneth Johnson and Marguerite Elsbeth, *The Grail Castle.*

(2) Robert Moore and Douglas Gillette,

King Warrior Magician Lover: Rediscovering the Archetypes of the Mature Masculine.

(3) K. Wilkinson, *Signs and Symbols*, "The Holy Grail: Nature of the Grail," 209, first column, lines 9–13.

44. Such deep-rooted common British and Continental European beliefs about directions, human qualities, elements and personality types were all represented by the four corners of a sacred square. Originally, home plate like the other bases was marked by a circular or squared altar. In early British times, this marker represented a cauldron which was symbolic of living (famine and plenty), regeneration (injury and healing), fertility (birth) and rebirth (endings and beginnings).

45. Newbery, *A Pretty Little Pocket Book* (1744), 90: lines 1–4:

Base-Ball.
The *Ball* once struck off.
Away flies the *Boy.*
To the next destin'd Post.
And then Home with joy.

46. If two triangles are cut off the squared plate, a five-sided figure is produced. The pentagon-shaped plate is an ancient one. A five-headed depiction of the god Shiva is often seen and Shiva is manifested as the five elemental substances, these being the old British four (air, water, earth, and fire) and ether.

47. Addy, *A Glossary of Words*, 177: *Plate*: line 5.

According to *The Druidic Handbook: Ritual Magic Rooted in Living Earth*, an "upright" pentagram represents the oak, and the "inverted" pentagram, the heather, underlying the reverence paid to trees in the past in old British and other related cultures. A tree with its crown can be similarly represented with the pictogram of a house or home. John Greer in *The Druidic Handbook, Ritual Magic Rooted in Living Earth* states:

A pentagram is a star made of five equal lines meeting at five equal angles. Since the time of Pythagoras, who brought sacred geometry to the Western world in the sixth century BCE, it has been one of the core symbols of Western magic and spirituality. It has many meanings through the years. Modern Pagans who think of it as a purely Pagan symbol, for instance, may be startled to find it in the

medieval poem Sir Gawain and the Green Knight as an emblem of Christian virtues! [51: lines 15–23, and Figures 2 and 3 of the Pentagram, "Upright" (Oak) and "Inverted" (Heather)].

48. Analogously, Hindus had long regarded the banyan tree as sacred. Under this tree, god Siva (or Shiva) was often depicted with his Rishis (Holy Men) sitting at his feet. The tree is often mentioned in Buddhist literature. James Forbes (*Oriental Memoirs: A Narrative of Seventeen Years Residence in India, Vol. 1*) was the first Westerner to note and describe the tree and its significance: "The Hindus are particularly fond of this tree; they consider its long duration, its outstretched arms, as emblems of the Deity, and almost pay it divine honours" (15: lines 19–23). It was planted near Hindu temples. Brahmins found solitude under these trees, as groves, for their religious contemplations. The similar roles and functions of the oak and banyan tree are strikingly obvious. Each tree was thought to be a living being or home to a supernatural entity.

49. Elder, 41. The oak tree was also sacred to devotees of Mars and Jupiter (Romano-Gaul), Hesus (Gaulish), and Thor (Germanic). Jesus Christ used the oak as a metaphor in his teachings noting that the mighty oak was once a tiny seed.

50. *Ibid.*, 52: lines 4–6. Elder adds that members of the priesthood, besides being associated with the oak (Drus), were also servants of the truth (druthin) (52: lines 3–9).

51. *Ibid.*, 66: lines 21–29.

This is another basis for the old British cross. The cross represented God in the shape of a man with outstretched arms. The god represented by the cross was the father of mankind and this tree symbol was revered. The circle on the cross probably represented the whole canopy of the oak tree and this being symbolic of the universe.

The revered oak tree would be used to represent or teach about the sun god. In some cases, the roots of a sacred tree were thought to represent the head of the god or goddess, the trunk the body, and the branches and limbs the reproductive genitalia exposed to the elements.

The middle branch about the center of the tree was the tallest and received the lightning strikes or thunder bolts, and was therefore thought to be favored by the god of thunder and lightning, *Taranis*.

Elder also states that mistletoe was another representation of their *Jesu*, who was the messiah. This set the stage for the acceptance of Christianity, since they also believed in the resurrection of the dead (66: lines 30–31; and 67: lines 1–5).

Cornish folklore tells of this King of Glory, *Yesu*, coming to save mankind (68: 7–14).

It was pointed out that ancient people of Britain never had to change the name of their god *Yesu* who they and their forefathers had worshipped before the arrival of Christianity (68: line 1–3). Note that *Yesu* easily became *Jesu* or Jesus.

52. The Hindu's Lord Shiva, also god of weather, was depicted or viewed as controlling thunder and lightning, thereby being similar with the Celtic god of thunder, Taranis. The Trimurti Hindu god of Brahma, Vishnu and Shiva was similarly described as Creator, Sustainer and Destroyer, respectively.

Worshippers of the rising sun are associated with Brahma, the meridian sun with Siva, the setting sun with Vishnu, and all phases of the sun with the Trimurti (The Rev. E. Osborn Martin's *The Gods of India*).

53. Elder states the people of Britain were well-prepared for the acceptance of Christianity (68, lines 15–23) and likewise their religious institutions and places of worship were readily adapted, when Christianity was introduced (68: lines 24–32; and 69: lines 1–3). (This idea of Elder is in keeping with what was later seen in the New World where the native populations initially thought that the arriving Europeans were their expected retuning gods as prophesied in their religions.)

54. Anne Ross in her chapter "Material Culture, Myth and Folk Memory" in *The Celtic Consciousness* (edited by Robert O'Driscoll), 203 and legend of plate 8 (source: J. Roberts, 85 Glenfield Avenue, Bitterne, Southampton). This is analogous to the same overview given by a modern baseball "diamond."

55. John Davies, *The Celts,* 79: line 29–31; and 84: lines 8–9.

Lucan, cited by both John Davies and Ward Rutherford, was a noted Roman historian of his time.

Proinsias Mac Cana in *Celtic Mythology* writes:

> Teutates, Esus, Taranis: "Mars," "Jupiter." In the first century A.D., Lucan mentions three deities by their Gaulish names (*De Bello Civili* I, 444–6):
>
> "Cruel Teutates propitiated by bloody sacrifice, and uncouth Esus of the barbarous altars, and Taranis whose altar is no more benign than that of Scythian Diana." …
>
> According to one of the sources cited by the later writer the victims of Teutates were asphyxiated by being plunged head foremost into a full vat, those of Esus, were suspended from trees and ritually wounded, and those from Taranis were burned, numbers of them together in cages of wood…. The sacrifice to Taranis echoes Posidonius (as followed by Caesar and others), who reported in the first century BC that the Gauls burned numbers of human victims in huge wickerwork images. The Sacrifice to Esus is not clearly defined, but it may be the remnant of a myth similar to that of the Germanic Odin who hung on the World Tree for nine days and nine nights and whose victims were likewise left hanging on trees [25: third column, lines 1–4, and first column, 27: lines 1–4; 27: first column, lines 16–23, 28–40].

Mac Cana comments that the scene from the Gundestrup cauldron was likened to being drowned in a container of a drink such as mead, wine or beer. He mentions the three-fold deaths (wounding, burning and drowning) of Irish chieftains at the Samhain festival that marks the end of summer (27: first column, line 40–58; 27: second column, lines 1–9; and 28: first column, lines 1–2).

56. Ward Rutherford in *Celtic Mythology: The Nature and Influence of Celtic Myth— From Druidism to Arthurian Legend,* 86, lines 28–30. Ward continues:

> At least one king, Muirchertach mac Erca, is known to have died in this way and Lindow Man, who is not a king was certainly an aristocrat, underwent such a death. Post-mortem examination shows that he was first stunned with two blows from an axe, then garrotted with a ligature so tight that it broke his neck. Finally his throat was cut. It has been

suggested that this was to let blood flow, but there can, of course, have been no blood flow after death as circulation would have ceased, though the custom of cutting the throats of victims to allow this to happen—presumably as a ritual fertilization of the earth—is known from other contexts.

Tolstoy suggests that the death of Lleu described in "Math son of Mathonyw," in which he is stabbed with spear while standing with one foot on a bath of water placed on a river's bank, may contain relics of a Triple Death. The same writer discusses a reference to it in a manuscript in the British Library which refers to Merlin being pierced with a stake, stoned, and then drowned [86: lines 30–40; and 87: lines 1–5].

The Lucan mentioned here is the same Roman historian mentioned in Note 55 above.

In support of this triple death sacrificial possibility, Anne Ross and Don Philips (*The Life and Death of a Prince ...*) have made a strong case for the Lindow Man having undergone the triple death in a ritual sacrifice to make propitiations to their Celtic gods for help in dealing with Roman invaders. The Lindow Man refers to the body of a man recently discovered (1983) in a swamp in Britain. The body is thought to be about 2000 years old.

57. The Rev. C. Arthur Lane in *Illustrated Notes on English Church History*, Vol. 1 writes:

They [Druids] sacrificed in open-air temples, surrounded by groves of oak trees or circles of immense stones.... On great occasions human victims were offered as vicarious propitiatory sacrifices. The objects of fire, earth, and water, vegetation, &c. were additional objects of veneration [Vol. 1, 3: lines 1–3, 4–5].

58. Elder writes about the religious services being held at midday:

Druidic services were held while the sun was above the horizon; the performing of ceremonies at any other time was forbidden by law [63: lines 11–12].

59. In early British and Continental European mythology, the Otherworld can be reached through water which goes underground. The third-base position could have originally been a sacred well or spring and was later substituted for by a pail or bucket of water.

Elder writes that there were sacred central stones (*Maen Llog*) which received water from the clouds. Rivers and waters of certain rivers (Dee) were regarded as sacred and were used in religious practices (63: lines 17–18, 20–25, 29–31).

This means that sacred waters from sacred rivers, or wells and springs, were part of the religious rituals of the peoples of early Britain.

The famous Gundestrup cauldron of Denmark shows a scene where armed warriors are carrying a tree, and a person is being immersed into a cauldron either as a sacrificial victim or for rebirth or regeneration. The sacrificial practices involved the four elements of earth, air, water and fire. The gods needed these sacrifices for their own well-being and immortality.

Further, many sacred places and groves had or were near sacred wells or springs. A bucket of water was placed near modern third base for players, hence the term "stepping towards the bucket" when a hitter strides towards third on swinging.

These practices of sacrificial offerings (including children) were known in Biblical times as described in the Old Testament by the prophet Isaiah, Chapter 57: verses 5–8:

5. Enflaming yourselves with idols under every green tree, slaying the children in the valleys under the clifts [sic] of rocks?

6. Among the smooth stones of the stream is thy portion; they are thy lot; even to them hast thou poured a drink offering, thou hast made a meat offering. Should I receive comfort in these?

7. Upon a lofty and high mountain hast thou set thy bed: everything thither wentest thou up to offer sacrifice.

8. Behind the doors also and the posts hast thou set up thy remembrance: for thou has discovered thyself to another than me, and art gone up; thou has enlarged thy bed, and made thee a covenant with them; thou lovedst their bed where thou sawest it.

Norman Cohn in *Cosmos, Chaos & the World to Come* writes: "The prophet Isaiah lived in the eight century [BCE], but it is generally accepted that at least half of the book that goes under his name in the Hebrew Bible was composed much later" (151: lines 16–18).

60. For example, Ross, *Pagan Celtic Britain,* 103, Fig. 31, "Sacrificial scene from the Gundestrup cauldron, Denmark" and Mac Cana's *Celtic Mythology,* 28 and 29 Fig. *Opposite.* This scene from the Gundestrup Cauldron portrays a prominent figure being carried by soldiers and immersed into a vat either as a sacrificial victim to the God *Teutates* or to gain immortality.

61. The mounds of the old world are well known, but the practices of building mounds were also known in North America. For example, mound building in North America by the editors of Time-Life Books, *Mound Builders & Cliff Dwellers,* Richard B. Johnston, *Archaeology of the Serpent Mounds Site,* and Walter A. Kenyon's *Mounds of Sacred Earth, Burial Mounds of Ontario.*

62. Sir Cyril Fox in *Life and Death in the Bronze Age: An Archaeologist's Field Work* writes on the mounds in Wales, Britain:

> The barrow- or cairn-digging with which this book is mostly concerned, however was my own work, wholly in South Wales, carried out during my tenure of the Directorship of the Museum: firstly, two barrows on land purchased by the War Department under a 1937 Defence Scheme–Simondston and Pond Cairns at Coity, near Bridgend, Glamorgan— and thereafter six on air fields under construction during the Second World War, from the autumn of 1939 onwards– Six Wells 271....
>
> All these barrows (earth mounds) and cairns (stone heaps) were described in various archaeological journals, in the years 1926, 1936, and 1941 to 1943, shortly after the field-work on each of them was completed... [XIV, lines 34–37; and XV, lines 1–7 and 17–20].

Fox writes that after he took up his appointment in 1925 at the National Museum of Wales at Cardiff that many farmers were bringing in their finds (potteries, urns or bronzes) to be evaluated.

Ibid., XIV: lines 21–32.

Fox's Figures 1: "Offa's Dyke and Ysceifiog Barrow and Circle. Holywell Race Course," and 2: "Ground-plan of Ysceifiog Barrow, showing the Circular Trench and the Central Pit-Grave with their respective Entrances." An attempt has also been made to show the areas of the floor of the grave, the burial deposit, and of the cairn on 2 and 4, respectively.

Fox writes about the antiquity of the peoples of early Britain (xvii and xviii).

63. E. O. Gordon, *Prehistoric London, Its Mounds and Circles...* (1946), writes about the mounds of London:

> "The history of a nation is the history of its religion, its attempts to seek after and serve its God," says an old writer. Of no nation or country is this more true than of Great Britain, where the standing stones of Stennis in Orkney, to the Maen Ambres in Cornwall—the prehistoric remains of open-air sanctuaries,—artificial mounds and scientifically constructed astronomically circles, bear witness to the vigour and vitality of a national religion, which has already passed from the primitive into the metaphysical stage, and embodies abstract ideas, astronomical observations and a high and pure code of morals [1: lines 1–11].

64. R. Hippisley Cox in *The Green Roads of England* notes that the situation was similar across England and writes on, for example, Tumuli (Round Barrow):

> Both long barrows and round barrows, especially the latter, are quite common objects of the wayside in the course of the green roads, and are often placed at the junction of the branch road, or on the conspicuous point of a hill, as if to serve as a guide or direction post. Long barrows are mostly found singly.... In appearance they look like a bank of earth, measuring some sixty to a hundred yards long, with one end wider than the other, and the broad end usually pointing to the east. Skeletons of a long-headed race have been found in these chambers, definitely proving these barrows to belong to the Stone Age. Round barrows occur both singly and in groups the latter frequently arranged as if in deliberate relationship to each other, both as regards size and position.... The round barrows or tumuli are simple mounds of earth varying greatly in size, sometimes surrounded by a ditch, and sometimes by a bank and

ditch, the ditch being placed either within or without the bank [4, lines 12–37].

65. Barry M. Mardsen in *The Early Barrow-Diggers* documents in details what happened at these early archaeological sites, for example, Wiltshire, Dorset, Derbyshire, Cornwall and Yorkshire. In the summation Mardsen writes:

> Barrows have been an integral part of the English landscape from time immemorial. It is sad therefore to close this book with the thought that these minor field monuments so vital to the study of the prehistoric past, are at present suffering such wholesale destruction, that despite the numbers they in a few decades cease to exist....Yet at present their existence as a coherent group of monuments is threatened by the ever-growing of building and cultivation, and the increasing destruction by modern farming methods. ... Modern bulldozing and deep ploughing have completely erased sites as though they never existed [114: lines 28–32; and 115: lines 4–7 and 10–11].

Mardsen in his Chapter X, "Cornwall," cites the 1872 work *Naenia Cornibiae* of W.C. Borlase which gives us a feel for what happened at some of the sites investigated by early amateur "archaeologists" and the desecration of thosands of barrows etc. In addition there was reclamation of waste lands for housing and mining (82: lines 1–12).

W. C. Borlase, a country gentleman and a Cornish MP, did his investigations of the barrows in the nineteenth century. Unfortunately, W. C. Borlase himself did the same as others to some extent, and his records were incomplete. (One of the earliest recorded investigations in Cornish history was done in 1584 by John Norden in his survey of Cornwall. Another researcher named William Borlase presented his work in *Antiquities of Cornwall* in 1754.) The barrows caught the attention of others over the years, but even in the cases with well-intentioned amateurs, the excavations, preservations and documentations of these historical sites were not done properly or satisfactorily.

66. P.V. Glob, Director General of Museums and Antiquities in Denmark, in *The Mound People: Danish Bronze-Age Man Preserved*, writes about the dominant mounds in Denmark namely, those of Borum Eshøj, Muldbjerg and Bredhøj.

Glob writes that the Mound People's mounds of Denmark were constructed to take advantage of Bronze Age landscape and local conditions and moreover turf was used:

> The Bronze Age landscape had a spacious park-like quality with scattered groups of trees and great expanses of pastureland where sheep and oxen grazed in great numbers... In the positioning and design of the mounds the Bronze Age people showed a unique capacity for working hand in hand with nature. The mounds are not placed exactly on the highest point of the hill but a little to one side where the hill begins to slope, and that in itself gives them a distinct appearance....
>
> That the Bronze Age mounds have preserved their original shape so well is because they were not made of heaped-up earth and gravel but carefully built of turfs, and also supported by stones placed in a ring or wall under the base. Originally, some of these stone circles were free-standing. In other mounds, the stone-circle was replaced by a wattle-fence made by driving in stakes and weaving twigs between them [131: lines 7–10, 12–17 and 19–27].

Glob then states in the next paragraph that to build such mounds would take an enormous amount of organization and labor (131: lines 28–36).

67. Porteus, *The Folklore of Myths and Legends*, Chapter IV.

68. Gordon, *Prehistoric London, Its Mounds and Circles,* 16, lines 27–28. In addition, there are several words (*ton, tot, tor, twn,* and *tyn*) used in combination with others that attests to the existence of these sacred mounds, for example, "*tor,* a sacred mound," as in Crokerntorre, and *ton* in Kennington, Wellington and Winton. In towns, the addition of local words for mound to their names meant they either occurred naturally or were artificially graded and terraced. Silbury Hill in Britain is the tallest and one of the largest artificially made mounds in the world. Many places were named simply as, for example,

Whitfield Mound or Parliament Hill or with *ton/tor* in their names signifying a circle, mound or hill. Gordon mentions numerous circles, mounds or hills in his work, affirming that they were present everywhere people settled in old Britain. He points out that large or small, the circles, mounds or hills were all built on the same general plan with a main or central area and a real or symbolic encircling trench with mere remnants or traces of these surviving in some cases.

69. Ross (*Pagan Celtic Britain*) states that sacred wells, springs, trees and burial mounds were associated with hallowed sites where religious rites were performed. She also mentions:

> Grave mounds may likewise, to a certain extent, be considered to have been in a sense sanctuaries, and one may bear in mind the constant Celtic emphasis on a continued physical existence beyond the grave, their obvious cult of ancestors (expressed by Caesar in terms of Dis Pater), and like the great Boyne tumuli, the alleged homes of the Tuatha Dé Danaan. It is inevitable that ancient tombs should be regarded as the dwellings of the departed.
>
> The *Viereckschanzen*, presumptive ritual enclosures, suggest a wealth of religious sites in central Europe, and are a timely reminder that similar, and so far unrecognized enclosures may exist in Britain. Ritual sites such as those found at Libernice near Kolin [Slovakia], while unusually complex, may perhaps approximate to the site recorded at Winterborne Kingston in Dorset, and to others from Denmark [85: lines 21–34].

See also "Cult of Graves," 65–78.

70. Jan Filip in *Early History and Evolution of the Celts: The Archaeological Evidence* in *Celtic Consciousness* (edited by Robert O'Driscoll) states:

> In the region stretching from France, through southern Germany as far as Bohemia, unusual sites have been found, dating from the time of the oppida; known as *Viereckschanzen*, they are from 70 to 100 meters long, surrounded by a low earthen mound and ditch. In some of them sacrificial pits have been discovered, and the signs of some of construction inside; it has therefore been

suggested that they may have been late Celtic ritual sites, the forerunners of the late Gallo-Roman temples [49: lines 27–34].

71. Hilda Roderick Ellis Davidson, *Myths and Symbols in Pagan Europe: Early Scandinavian and Celtic Religions*, 26: lines 22–30, 35–40; and 27: 1–2.

72. Ross, *Everyday Life of the Pagan Celts*, 138: lines 3–20, and figs. 40 and 41 on 137 and 138, respectively. Ross also writes that the priesthood carried out sacrificial rites and rituals in these open spaces, such as groves, wells, tops of hills, burial grounds, etc., which were associated with particular patron gods. Ross points out that such places were found in early Britain and Continental Europe (136: lines 26–38; and 137: lines 1–3).

73. *Ibid.*, 138, Fig. 41 "Ritual Shaft, Holzhausen, Bavaria."

74. *Ibid.*, 140: lines 23–32.

75. Elder, 62: lines 6–13.

76. Chadwick, Fig. "Diagram of a Base Ball Field with the Lines of Measurement."

77. Wood, *The Boy's Modern Playmate*, 49: Section–Rule III. "The Pitcher," lines 1–4.

78. Noam Friedlander, ed., *Mammoth Book of Sports and Games of the World*, 46–48.

79. Ross, *Pagan Celtic Britain*, "Cult of Graves," 65: lines 14–20, 27–30.

80. Grimm, *Teutonic Mythology*, Vol. III, Preface, XXXV: lines 30–31. Full quote is given in Chapter 7, Note 51. Grimm continues:

> Law-usages, particularly the ordeals and oath-takings, but also the beating of bounds, consecrations, image-processions, spells and formulas, while retaining their heathen character, were simply clothed in Christian forms. In some customs there was little to change: the heathen practice of sprinkling a newborn babe with water closely resembled Christian baptism, the sign of the hammer that of the cross, and the erection of tree-crosses the irmensûls and world-trees of paganism. Still more significant must appear that passage where Völuspa and the Bible coincide; in the far later Sôlar-lio traces of Christian teaching are discernible [XXXVI: lines 4 to 15].

81. Such practices run deep in our human history. James Fergusson in *Tree and Serpent Worship; Or, Illustrations of Mythology and Art in India in the First and Fourth Centuries After Christ* (1868) mentions the use of symbols in which a square represented earth, a circle water, a triangle fire, a crescent wind, and a cone ether (106).

82. For example, the Rev. C. Arthur Lane in *Illustrated Notes on English Church History*, writes of Britannic religion: "[It is] said to have comprised belief in a supreme deity; and the immortality and transmigration of souls; but the number of classical deities mentioned by Julius Caesar shows that they worshipped a plurality of lesser divinities besides" (Vol. 1., "Profane History and Religion," 2, lines 24–26; and 3, line 1).

Joseph Campbell in "Peripheries of the Indo-European World, Indian Reflections in the Castle of the Grail" in *Celtic Consciousness* writes:

> Sometime around 1000 BCE, the people of what is known to historians as the Hallstart Culture began spreading both eastward and westward, out of the lands that are now of Austria and southern Germany. By 500 BCE, those of the westward migration had developed in France and Northern Switzerland a new and brilliant culture, known as La Tène. It was these Celts who, in that period, invaded Rome. They entered the British Isles about the second century BCE with their priests and magicians, the Druids, and they there became assimilated to the earlier Bronze-Age inhabitants, the people of that wonderful cosmic image of the great heartbeat of the universe, which have already shown, was known as well to India as to Europe: its cycles of 432, 000 years being a feature of both the Indian *Puranas* and the Icelandic *Grimmismol* [16: lines 13–23].

83. Cassandra Lorius, *Mandalas & Meditations for Everyday Living* (13, lines 1–2, 7–8, 10–12, and 19–20).

84. In which the four Grail treasures dish, sword, spear and grail were sought after.

This story has old British origins, with the dish replacing the cauldron. It can be interpreted as the search for the meaning of life and the major obstacles which one en-counters in such a pursuit; it also shows the inter-connectedness of several aspects of human existence. The complex interrelated themes of the *Grail Castle* can be illustrated by using squares, circles and lines. Mythologist and philosopher Joseph Campbell in his chapter "Peripheries of the Indo-European World, Indian Reflections in the Castle of the Grail" in *The Celtic Consciousness* discusses the analogies of the *Grail Castle* with the mystical traditions of ancient India (see Note 82). A few scholars point out that this most celebrated and renowned British-based philosophical story was indeed mandala-like in concept, as Kenneth Johnson and Marguerite Elsbeth in *The Grail Castle* writes:

> The Grail Castle is clearly a mandala. Because it is surrounded by a moat, it is enclosed by a circular motif, precisely like the mandalas of India and Tibet…. A typical mandala is circular in form, though it usually includes a square or some other fourfold figure as well…. The mandala unites the circle and the square…. The Celtic Grail castle represents an experience of mystical unity [9: lines 20–22, 8–9, 19 and 4; diagram, *The Grail Castle Mandala*, 11].

Johnson and Elsbeth also give more details about mandalas showing their linkage to the beliefs of various cultures (9: lines 4–24).

David Leeming writes on "The Arthurian Legacy and Christianity":

> As St. Patrick and the stories surrounding him represent the coming of Christianity to Ireland, similarly the Arthurian story gradually became a central part of the central aspect of the whole Christian mythological system as it applied specifically to Great Britain…. At the fringes of all this national mythology is the Arthurian Fisher King, whose wounds must be cured before Britain can cease to be a wasteland [*The Olympus in Camelot: The World of European of Mythology*, 97: lines 24–27; 98: lines 1–7; and 99: lines 4–6].

85. Many ancient cultures begin their morning prayers standing on the banks of holy rivers. Note the words "With my face to the rising sun" in the hymn "Let Us Break Bread Together."

1. Let us break bread together on our knees.

When I fall down on my knees
With my face to the rising sun,
Oh, Lord have mercy on me.

86. Anne Ross, *Pagan Celtic Britain*, 71: lines 14–16 and 19–20.

87. With regards to Scandinavian symbols, Horik Svensson, *The Runes, Divine the Future with This Ancient Norse Oracle*, writes that the diamond is a male rune called *Ing*, but it is a partner to *Lagu*, a female rune associated with fertility. Any rune when turned upside down has the opposite meaning, but in this particular case the diamond-shaped figure remains the same.

Horik Svensson, in *The Secret of the Runes: Divine the Future with This Ancient Norse Oracle*, writes:

This is a primal rune whose symbolism is clearly that of female genitalia....

Since Ing was a fertility god and this rune is, at least symbolically, sexual,....

On a spiritual level, this rune shows that the querent is soon to reach a state of inner peace and quiet, of inner balance. In all cases time will tell whether this happy state is lasting or simply transitory, and the accompanying runes will give strong suggestions as to the eventual outcome [67: lines 1–2, 12–13, 20–24].

88. A most interesting philosophical interpretation is given in the supposed *Barddas* manuscripts which can be applied to the any baseball diamond. The Rev. John Williams Ab Ithel, *Barddas: Or a Collection of Original Documents, Illustrative of the Theology, Wisdom, and Usages of the Bardo-Druidic System of the Isle of Britain*, Volume 1, 1862, Google Books. This author states on "Bardic-Druidic Theology":

There are three Circles of existence: the Circle of *Ceugant*, where there is nothing but God, of living or dead, and none but God can traverse it; the Circle of *Abred*, where all things are by nature derived from death and Man has traversed it; and the circle of *Gwynvyd*, where all things spring from life, and man shall traverse it in heaven [171: # 12, lines 1–6].

In this regards, Rutherford in *Celtic Lore* writes that these supposed three circles are in line with old Druidic teachings with regards to reincarnation and its circles of existence:

The concentric circles of *Ceugant, Abred*, and *Gwynvyd* stand respectively for: infinity where animate and inanimate as we recognize them do not exist; the place of rebirth where the spirits awaiting reincarnation sojourn; and perfection (or "whiteness"), where life reasserts itself and the individual develops through the impact of experience [121: lines 21–26].

Ward rightfully points out that the Barddas manuscripts with its limitations with regards to the British Druidic religion and beliefs must be carefully viewed (120: lines 36–39; and 121: line 1).

89. John Branch in "Groundskeepers Display Artistry on the Diamond," *New York Times*, October 1, 2008.

It has often been seen before in modern times that despite the passage of centuries and generations, the indigenous art of a suppressed people eventually finds expression and reconnection with ancestral traditions and cultural heritages. It is often as if these hereditary expressions lie dormant like a seed springing forth when the conditions and opportunities are ripe. Examples are seen in the revival or resurfacing of art from several First Nations of the West Coast of British Columbia, Canada.

An example of the intricacies of Celtic art is given in the work of Courtney Davis in *Celtic Designs and Motifs*.

Chapter 9

1. In cricket, the dueling area, called the pitch, though level is slightly elevated above the surrounding field. Both ends of the pitch are used alternatively for bowling and batting. In baseball there is no such interchange of pitching and hitting ends.

In more recent times in some cases, sunken pits were used and the seating/standing accommodations elevated.

2. Holt in *Sport and the British* writes:
Traditional sports were rooted in the territorial as well as in the conjugal order. During the seasonal pattern of amusements that reached their height between spring sowing and summer harvesting

and in the dead months of midwinter, the young men not only organized themselves for mating and for work, they asserted the identity of each generation of village inhabitants. Deep attachment to the land and a fierce local patriotism were part and parcel of popular recreations. Inter-parish fights were commonplace... [15: lines 35–36; 16: lines 1–7].

3. Ramsey Macmullen, *Christianity & Paganism in the Fourth to Eight Centuries* (112: lines 25–32). The preceding sentences of the first cited paragraph are:

The identical nature of the Christian and non-Christian cult of the dead appears not only in its physical details themselves, all of those just reviewed being of the third century and so at the earliest end of the chain of information that we possess; but they are clear as well in the impossibility, sometimes of determining which religion is represented by a given piece of evidence: for example, in the line of a third-century epitaph from Mauretania, where the dedicants recall how "We decided we would add on this stone table," *Mensa*, to their mother's grave. For various reasons, none of them decisive, this epitaph and burial may be judged Christian or not; but it hardly matters. Sarcophagi with symbols and reliefs made for pagan customers were used by Christians [111: lines 13–22].

4. *Ibid.*, 112: lines 25–31.

The scenes being referred to include: favorite food of the deceased provided at these memorial feasts; pouring of wine into the tomb; family coming together to dine around a tomb covered with a tablecloth; and the custom of holding meals in churchyards. (For example, see details in MacMullen's *Christianity & Paganism in the Fourth to Eight Centuries*, 111–112.)

5. For example, in Teutonic mythology mounds were sources of inspiration, rebirth and regeneration (Appendix F), and in ancient India mounds were likewise prominent (Appendix E). For example, W. Crooke in *The North-Western Provinces of India, Their History. Ethnology and Administration* writes:

The Buildings of the Buddhist period have been classified by Dr. J. Ferguson

as–Lâts or pillars; Stûpas or sepulchral mounds; Rails: Chaityas or assembly halls; Vihâras or monasteries. Of all of these numerous interesting remains exist in the Province. We have pillars of Asoka already enumerated–Stupas at Sarnath near Benares; Kasiya in Gorakhpur; Sahet Mahet in Gonda and many other places; the Buddhist cave at Pabhosa, near Allahâbâd; the Vihâra at Sarnâth; the Jatavana; the fragments of the Buddhist railing found at Mathura [79: lines 26–36].

The above quotation attests to the prevalence of stupas in ancient India.

6. Jacob Grimm, *Teutonic Mythology, Vol. III* writes:

The festivals of a people present a tough material, they are closely bound up with its habits of life, that they will put up with foreign additions, if only to save a fragment of festivities long loved and tried. In this way Scandinavia, probably the Goths also for a time, and the Anglo-Saxons down to a late period, retained the heathenish Yule, as all Teutonic Christians did the sanctity of Eastertide: and from these two the Yule-boar and Yule-bread, the Easter pancake, Easter sword, Easter fire and Easter dance could not be separated. As faithfully were perpetuated the name and in many cases the observances of Midsummer. New Christian feasts, especially of saints, seem purposely as well as accidentally to have been made to fall on heathen holidays [Preface, xxxv: lines 17–36; and xxxiv: line 1].

7. Ross, *Everyday Life of the Pagan Celts*, writes that as people travelled they carried along the remains of their dead and where these were finally buried became respected places for commemorating rituals (78: lines 3–7).

Rutherford in *Celtic Lore* writes that people of the Hebrides gathered at graveyards where they circled and danced, and where sham battles were fought as late as the fourteenth century (92: lines 22–30).

8. Ross, *Pagan Celtic Britain*, in Chapter 1, "Cult of Graves," 65: lines 18–21, 28–30, 32–34; and 66: lines 11–12.

A variety of holy places such as trees, wells and grave mounds were found (66: lines 16–22).

9. For example, the tradition of commemorating the death of someone by sports. Addy in the 1888 supplement to his 1838 work, *A Glossary of Words Used in the Neighborhood of Sheffield*, mentions a curious custom called *hock-tide* where to commemorate the death of a person there was an annual event in which games were played by his neighbors near to the home where the deceased had lived (page 29 of the 1888 Supplement, ebook).

10. Morris, *A Game of Inches*, 23: lines 22–25.

Morris adds:

Incidentally, softball incorporated a peculiar rule in 1908 by which the leadoff hitter could choose to run the bases clockwise or counter clockwise. The other base runners were then obliged to follow the leadoff hitter's cue (Lois Browne, *Girls of Summer* [1992 publication] 15) [23: lines 32–35].

11. Edward Burnett Tylor, *Religion in Primitive Culture* (1873), with an Introduction by Paul Radin (251: 1–2; and 252: 21–30).

Tylor shows how far back this practices of seting up stones in a pattern goes:

Not only were stones, especially curious ones and such as were like men or animals, objects of veneration, but we learn that they were venerated because mighty spirits dwelt in them…. The remarkable groups of standing stones in India are, in many cases at least, set up for each stone to represent or embody a deity. Mr. Hislop remarks that in every part of southern India, four or five stones may often be seen in the ryot's [peasant cultivator] field, placed in a row and daubed with red paint, which they consider as guardians of the field and call the five Pândus; he reasonably takes these Hindu names to have superseded more ancient native appellations. In the Indian groups it is a usual practice to daub each stone with red paint, forming as it were a great blood-spot where the face would be if it were a shaped idol [248: line 30; 249: lines 11–13, 28–29].

Edward Burnett Tylor. *Primitive Cultures: Researches into the Development of Mythology, Philosophy, Religion, Language, Art, and Custom*, 2d ed, 2 vols. Vol. II, John Murray, Aber-

marle Street, London, 1873, Google Books, Web, 10 April 2013.

12. *Ibid.*, Tylor writes:

The ethnographic argument from the existence of stock-and-stone worship among so many nations of comparatively high culture seems to me of great weight as bearing on religious development among mankind. To imagine that peoples skilled in carving wood and stone, and using these arts habitually in making idols, should have gone out of their way to invent a practice of worshipping logs and pebbles, is not a likely theory. But on the other hand, when it is considered how such a rude object serves to uncultured men as a divine image or receptacle, there is nothing strange in its being a relic of early barbarism holding its place against more artistic models through ages of advancing civilization, by virtue of the traditional sanctity which belongs to survival from remote antiquity [253: lines 18–32].

13. Jane Ellen Harrison in *Ancient Art and Ritual* (1913) writes:

Anthropologists who study the primitive peoples of to-day find that the worship of false gods, bowing "down to wood and stone," bulks larger in the mind of the hymn-writer than in the mind of the savage. We look for temples to heathen idols; we find dancing-places and ritual dances. The savage is a man of action. Instead of asking god to do what he wants done, he does it or tries to do it himself; instead of prayers he utters spells. In a word he practices magic, and above all he is strenuously and frequently engaged in dancing magical dances. When a savage wants sun or rain, he does not go to church and prostrate himself before a false god; he summons his tribe and dances a sun dance or a wind dance or a rain dance. When he would hunt and catch a bear, he does not pray to his god for strength to outwit and outmatch the bear, he rehearses his hunt in a bear dance [30: lines 1–26; further details on 31: lines 2–14].

14. Grant Allen, *The Evolution of the Idea of God: An Enquiry into the Origins of Religion* (1904), 100: lines 29–31.

Ibid. Allen writes:

Among the Semitic peoples, always especially interesting to us from their genetic connection with Judaism and Christianity, the worship of stakes usually took the form of adoration paid to the curious log of wood described as an *Ashera*. What kind of object an *Ashera* was we learn from the injunction in Deuteronomy, "Thou shalt not plant an *Ashera* of any kind beside the altar of Jahweh." This prohibition is clearly parallel to that against any hewn stone or "graven image." But the Semites in general worshiped as a rule at a rude stone altar, beside which stood an *Ashera*, under a green tree,–all three of the great sacred objects of humanity being present together. A similar combination is not uncommon in India, where sacred stone and a wooden image stand under the shade of the same holy peepul tree [135: 28–37; and 136: 1–5].

The worship of sacred trees is almost as widely diffused over the whole world as the worship of dead bodies, mummies, relics, graves, sacred stones, sacred snakes, and stones or wooden idols [138: lines 18–21].

For further details (143: lines 12–19).

15. Similar practices existed elsewhere, Sir James Frazer, *The Golden Bough,* Vol. 1, Chapter 1, "Tree-Worship" and "Tree-Worship in Antiquity," 56–108.

16. For example, the work of (1) Sir James Frazer, *The Golden Bough*, Chapters IX, *The Worship of Trees*, 126–138; and X, *The Relics of Tree-Worship in Modern Europe*, 139–156.

Frazer points out that it was natural that the peoples of Europe should worship trees since the primeval Forests of Europe dominated the then landscape from Insular Britain to Continental Europe. People thought spirits resided in these impressive trees and that they themselves were children of such trees. The worshipping of trees was therefore easily explained (126: lines 12–18 and 23–27).

And (2) Ross (*Pagan Celtic Britain*), "Sacred Trees and Groves," 59–65.

17. Sir James Frazer, *The Golden Bough*, Vol. 1, 59: lines 8–12; 60: lines 6–7, 23–25: and 64: lines 10–11, Google Books, Web, 10 April 2013.

18. *Ibid.* Frazer gave examples of the importance of such celebratory unions in India and Germany to promote the growth of shrubs and increased production of fruits (see 60: lines 6–15).

19. Authors: (1) Grant Allen in *The Evolution of the Idea of God* proposes that sacred places were once burial sites, and thereby provided a link between tree-worship and serpent-worship. Allen writes:

Now, in this typical and highly illustrative myth—no doubt an ancient and well-known story incorporated by Virgil in his great poem [Third Æneid]–we see that the tree which grows upon a barrow is itself regarded as the representative and embodiment of the dead man's soul, just as elsewhere the snake which glides from the tomb of Anchises is regarded as the embodied spirit of the hero, and just as owls and bats which haunt sepulchral caves are often identified in all parts of the world with the souls of the departed....

Now, how did this connection between the tree and the ghost or ancestor grow up? In much the same way, I imagine, as the connection between the sacred stone or the sacred snake and the dead chief who lies buried beneath it. Whatever grows or stands upon the grave is sure to share the honours paid to the spirit that dwells within it. Thus a snake or other animal seen to glide out of a tomb is instantly taken by savages and even by half-civilized men as the genius or representative of the dead inhabitant [139: lines 21–29; 140: 31–37; and 141: 1–2].

(2) William Crooke, *An Introduction to the Popular Religion and Folklore of Northern India.*

(3) John Deane, *The Worship of the Serpent Traced Throughout the World*, writes:

There was a remarkable superstition in regard to *A Serpent of Enormous Bulk Which Girded the World,* current in the mythology of almost every nation where ophiolatreia prevailed; nor was China exempt from the general credulity. This idea, perhaps, originated in the early consecration of the serpent to the sun; and the subsequent conversion of a *Serpent Biting His Tail,* into an emblem of the Sun's path. This hierogram was again considered as typical of *Eternity*, partly from the serpent being a symbol of *Deity*; partly from the *Perfect* figure of a *Circle* thus formed, without beginning or end; and partly from an opinion of the eternity of matter... [71: lines 12–25].

Deane comments on "Dragons and Serpents in Ancient China and India" on 72: 9–23 and 73: lines 1–2, respectively.

(4) James Fergusson, *Tree and Serpent Worship or Illustration of Mythology and Art of India in the First and Fourth Centuries of Christ from the Topes at Sanchi and Amravati*.

(5) E. Washburn Hopkins in *Origin and Evolution of Religion* provides further insights into the rationales for such practices. Hopkins writes:

> Serpents are among the earliest and most widely worshipped creatures. No one who has seen a boa constrictor, a cobra, a python, or a rattle snake can question that such a being would be the object of devout regard on the part of any man who worshipped any animal. But any snake's beauty, sinuous motion, mysterious habits, power of fascination, its association with tombs and trees, at the roots of which it is apt to live, its suggestive shape, are enough to make it respected as a being having occult and obscene powers. Its abode and cunning give it a reputation for wisdom; its wisdom helps its reputation for evil; its hole makes it a guardian of treasure; and when it is honoured with a temple, where treasure is stored, this reputation is increased. Because it lives about the altar and the house, where it gets food, and perhaps especially because it lives in tombs, it is regarded as the re-embodied spirit of the dead, coming up out of the under-world for its meals. Aeneas regarded the serpent at the altar as the local genius of the place or spirit of his father. The old Germans thought that snakes and mice, also coming out of the ground, were peculiarly apt to be re-incarnated spirits. The Pied piper and the Bishop of Hatto had to deal with such spirits [36: lines 27–34].

Washburn writes about the world-wide importance of the serpent in various countries, cultures, and myths including those of Babylon, China, Germany, India, and Lithuania. Snake-worship was also known to be practiced by ancient Chinese, Hebrew, Hindu, Dravidian or Mongolian and Scandinavian cultures. Washburn, like others writers mentioned above, concluded that this worship of trees, sun, phallus and serpent led to a "heliolithic culture" (37: lines 1–33; and 38: lines 6–19).

20. Frazer, *The Golden Bough* 70: lines 18–28; and 72: lines 23–29.

21. *Ibid.* Frazer writes that like others the oldest sanctuaries of the ancient Germans were natural woods. The Scandinavian peoples, e.g., Swedes, believed that each tree of a sacred grove in Uppsala was divine. Some Slavic peoples revered the sacred trees so much that they considered it wrong to even break a twig (57: lines 28–29; 58: lines 1–14; and 64: 18–25).

22. Bartlett in *The Past of Pastimes* writes:

> The most famous pagan celebration of the return of spring was, of course linked with the May-pole, which was condemned during the commonwealth as "a heathenish activity, generally abused to superstition and wickedness"... [59: 19–23].

23. (1) Ross, *Pagan Celtic Britain*, Chapter 1, "Sanctuaries, Temples and Cult Sites," "Sacred Trees and Groves":

> As with many other peoples, certain trees and groves of trees were sacred to the Celts and treated with veneration [59: lines 31–32].

And (2) Frazer in *The Golden Bough*, Chapter 1, "King of the Wood, Tree-Worship" writes:

> From an examination of the Temple words for "temple"; Grimm has made it possible that amongst the Germans the oldest sanctuaries were natural woods. However this may be, tree-worship is well attested for all the great European families of Aryan stock. Amongst the Celts the oak-worship of the Druids is familiar to everyone. Sacred groves were common among the ancient Germans, and tree-worship is hardly extinct among the descendants at the present day. At Uppsala, the old religious capital of Sweden, there was a sacred grove in which every tree was regarded as divine.

Amongst the ancient Prussians (a Slavonian people) the central feature of religion was the reverence for the sacred oaks, of which the chief stood at Remove, tended by a fire of oak-wood in the holy grove....

The old Prussians, it is said, believed that Gods inhabited high trees, such as oaks, from which they give audible answers to inquirers; hence these trees were not felled, but worshipped as the homes of divinities. The great oak at Remove was the especial dwelling place of the god; it was veiled with a cloth, which was, however, removed to allow worshippers to see the sacred tree [57: lines 29–29; 58: lines 1–14; and 64: lines 18–25].

24. Ross, *Pagan Celtic Britain*, 60: line 39; 61: lines 1–6; and 63: lines 21–23; and 64: lines 11–19.

25. The famous silver Gundestrup Cauldron of Denmark shows a scene where a line of soldiers are depicted carrying a tree in a likely sacrificial or resurrection scene. This scene also shows three persons, each carrying a raised serpent.

Ibid., 63: Fig 9.

26. (1) Proincias Mac Cana, *Celtic Mythology*, photograph on 42–43.

And (2) Ross, *Pagan Celtic Britain*, 117: lines 27–29, 32–38; 182: lines 16–28, 3113–3–4. 183: lines 1, 5–6, 9–11, 24–32 and 34–38; 215: lines 10–23.

Ross, 201–210, "The Horned God of the Brigantes," "The Horned God as Mars," "The Horned God as Mercury," "The Horned God as Silvanus," and "The Horned God as a Head." Chapter 3, "The Horned God in Britain" (172–219).

Ross, 198–201, "The great serpent as keeper of treasure," and "The Celtic serpent as an attribute of the war god."

Ross, 203: lines 31–32, 38–39; 204: 1–4, 31–33; and 203: lines 25–28.

27. Ross, *Pagan Celtic Britain*, 211: lines 23–24.

28. *Ibid.* For example, "The Ram-Headed Serpents, Snakes and Dragons," 430–434, "The Great Serpent as Keeper of Treasure," 198–199, and "The Celtic Serpent as an Attribute of the War God," 199–201.

29. *Ibid.*, 434: lines 17–25.

30. John Bathurst Deane, *The Worship of the Serpent Traced Throughout the World* writes:

For the paucity of the remains of the ancient Ophiolatreia in Ireland, we are perhaps indebted to the renowned St. Patrick, whose popular legend may not, after all, be so ridiculous or so groundless as Englishmen and Protestants are accustomed to imagine. It is said and believed by the lower order of Irish to this day, that St. Patrick *Banished All Snakes* from Ireland by his prayers. May not this imply that St. Patrick, in evangelizing that country, overthrew the superstition of the SERPENT-WORSHIPPERS? [254: lines 1–18].

31. *Ibid.*, Deane writes:

V. Western Europe.

1. Britain. Our British ancestors, under the tuition of the venerable Druids, were not only worshippers of the solar deity, symbolized by the serpent, independent of his relation to the sun, in peculiar veneration. Cut off from all intimate intercourse with the civilized world, partly by their remoteness, and partly by national character, the Britons retained their primitive idolatry long after it had yielded in the neighbouring countries to the polytheistic corruptions of Greece and Egypt. In process of time, however, the gods of the Gaulish Druids penetrated into the sacred mythology of the British, and furnish personifications for the different attributes of the dracontic god HU. This deity was called "THE DRAGON RULER OF THE WORLD." And his car was drawn by SERPENTS. His priests in accommodation with the general custom of the ministers of the Ophite god, were called after him, ADDERS [240: lines 1–21; and 241: lines 1–8].

32. Jacob Bryant in *A New System of Analysis of Antient Mythology,* Vol. I (1807), writes:

As the divine honours paid to the Sun, and the adoration of fire, were at one time almost universal, there will be found in most places a similitude in the terms of worship. And though this mode of idolatry took its rise in one particular part of the world, yet, as it was propagated to others far remote, the stream, however widely diffused, will still savour of the fountain. Moreover, as people were determined in the choice of their holy places by those preternatural phænomena, of which I have before taken notice; if there be any truth in my system, there will be uniformly found some analogy between the name of the temple, and its rites and situation: so that the etymology may be ascertained by the history of the place. The likes will appear in respect to rivers and mountains; especially to those which were esteemed at all sacred, and which were denominated from the Sun and fire [235: lines 1–6; and 236: 1–13].

In Vol. II, "OB, OUB, PHYTO, Sive De OPHILATRIA," Bryant writes:

It may seem extraordinary, that the worship of the serpent should have ever been introduced into the world: and it must appear still more remarkable, that it should almost universally have prevailed. As mankind are said to have been ruined through the influence of this being, we could little expect that it would, of all other objects, have been adopted, as the most sacred and salutary symbol; and rendered the chief object of adoration. Yet so we find it to have been. In most of the antient rites there is some allusion to the serpent [1: lines 1–9].

33. *Ibid.*, Vol. II, plates VII and VIII for illustrations. The serpent was now winged, carried or encircled a globe which represented the sun.

34. In places such as India (where the population is diverse and subsets often isolated) there still are communities where stone-, tree-, serpent- and sun-worshiping religious beliefs and practices exist, despite the millennia or centuries of Hinduism, Buddhism, Islam and Christianity and modern philosophical teachings.

35. William J. Baker in *Sports in the Western World* writes:

Old pastimes brought from the fields and villages of England had a difficult time surviving in the frigid Puritan atmosphere of New England. On Christmas Day in 1621 Governor William Bradford came across some newly arrived colonists in the streets of Plymouth "at play, openly, some pitching the bar and some at stool-ball, and such-like sports." He voiced his disapproval, but they countered that it was against their conscience to work on Christmas Day. He informed them that it was against *his* conscience to allow them to play. Idleness was not his only concern. His stern stance was directed as much against the recognition of Christmas, that old pagan, Catholic holiday, as against mere play.

Far more than games in the street, youths "dancing and frisking together" distressed the Pilgrim Fathers. In their minds such frivolity smacked of the old May Day festivities; sexual indulgence ("bastardy") was one of their fears. In 1627 a lively character named Thomas Morton erected an eighty-foot pole that served as a maypole at Merry Mount, near Plymouth. He then invited neighboring colonists and Indians to join in the festivities of wine, dance, and song. Horrified, the puritan governors sent a group of elders to investigate, and they promptly put an end to that "pagan merriment" by cutting down the maypole. Such imports from Stuart England had no place in the "ordering, & preservation & furtherance" of the Puritan theocracy in Massachusetts [83: lines 7–27].

36. Notes 19 and 30–33. Additional information can be found in:

(1) Hodder M. Westropp and C. Staniland Wake, *Ancient Symbol Worship. Influence of the Phallic Idea in the Religion of Antiquity*, Broadway: J. Bouton, 1875, republished Escondida, CA: The Book Tree, 1999.

(2) Hargrove Jennings. *Ophiolatreia or Serpent Worship: An Account of the Rites and Mysteries Connected with the Origin, Rise and Development of Serpent Worship in Various Parts of the World, Enriched with Interesting Traditions and a Full Description of the Celebrated Serpent Mounds & Temples, the Whole Forming An Exposition of the Phases of Phallic, or Sex Worship* (privately printed), 1889, Google Books, Web, 10 April 2013.

(3) Edward B. Tylor, *Primitive Culture, Researches into the Development of Mythology, Philosophy, Religion, Language, Art, and Custom*, Vol. II (London: John Murray, 1889).

37. Phillip Gardiner in *Secret Societies: Gardiner's Forbidden Knowledge, Revelation About the Freemasons, Templars, Illuminati, Nazis, and the Serpent Cults,* writes:

The sword [Medieval snake sword] first appeared around 4,000 years ago and immediately became a preeminent weapon, preferred by the warrior class. Recent metallurgical studies have shown how complex piled structures or layers improved the sword from as early as 500 BCE in Celtic artefacts. Little wonder that the smithy was an important part of legend and folklore, as the skill implied in the making of these swords is substantial....

The inclusion of the serpent in the blade was eventually replaced with iron inlaid letters and symbols, and Christian phrases such as In Nomine Domini ("In the name of the Lord"). The remarkable archaeological fact of serpents appearing in the designs of the 5th century swords links perfectly with the time of Arthur. As the Pendragon or Head/Chief Dragon Lord, he would certainly have been seen with such device, and in the stories mentioned previously, there are textual links in the legend. Could it be that the tales of Arthur and his serpentine or dragon swords were based upon reality? [79: lines 16–21; 80: lines 1, 37–38; and 81: lines 1–8].

38. The serpent is sometimes depicted as forming a circle with its tail in its mouth. This circle so formed was thought to symbolize eternity. (Dragons and serpents played important roles in ancient Chinese and Indian cultures. In Hindu mythology, the serpent Asootee encircles the world.)

39. Balaji Mundkur, *The Cult of the Serpent: An Interdisciplinary Survey of Its Manifestations and Origins,* 47: lines 4–6, 29–33; and 49: lines 1–15.

He writes in the next paragraph:

The abhorrence of venomous creatures in general is epitomized in a medieval Northern European prayer attributed to the Apostle John:

My God and father our Lord Jesus Christ, through whose word Heaven has been fortified, who reigns over everything and whose might is feared by every creature, therefore we call upon

thee for help in order that, upon hearing thy Name, the serpent should be still, the dragon take flight, the viper be silent, the scorpion be annihilated. The toad called the frog repose benumbed, the basilisk be conquered, the venomous spider cause no harm [and] in the end, that all venomous creatures, and even more, all wild reptiles be pierced through. Thus I beseech thee, destroy its venom, destroy their death-dealing ways, remove their strength. And give them eyes to see, ears to hear, and hearts to comprehend thy might [49: lines 16 to 26].

40. Ernest Bloch, *Atheism in Christianity,* in "Second Thoughts About the Serpent: The Ophites," states:

These [serpent] associations were not forgotten, though they were continually distorted. They were taken up again after the time of Christ by the Ophites (*Ophis*: snake), a Gnostic-Christian sect active in the third century.

We know the teachings of this sect almost solely from the writings of their opponents. The age old cult of Ophis came down from matriarchal times or even earlier. It can be found in a positive or later, mostly negative sense in many religions, though not with the edge it has in the Bible....

For hanging from the Tree of Knowledge as the "larva of the goddess Reason," he had taught the first man to eat of its fruit... [167: lines 27–30; 168: 1–5; and 169: lines 1–3].

41. See also the work of Weston La Barre, *They Shall Take Up Serpents: Psychology of the Southern Snake-Handling Cult,* which discusses serpent worship from ancient times through Biblical times to Christianity.

42. Frazer, *The Golden Bough: A Study in Comparative Religion,* Vol. 2 (1890), 246: lines 20–27; and 247.

Frazer writes that the bonfires were usually made in springtime and midsummer, but in some places also on Hallow E'en (October 31st) and Christmas (247: lines 13–16). Fire-Festivals were held on Easter Eve being the Saturday before Easter Sunday. It was the tradition in Catholic countries that all fires be extinguished and a new fire was made from which the Easter candle was lit. This new fire (from the Easter candle) was used to re-start other lights and fires in the church. In Germany, many of the bonfires were held in an open space near the church (251: lines 12–21).

43. *Ibid.* 254: lines 22–27; and 255: line 1.

Frazer specifically mentions that in Holland the fires were lit on highest grounds and the people likewise danced around these fires. In Germany the Easter fires were visible from miles around since they were lit in mountainous areas (253: lines 15–19, 21–23.)

In Sweden, these fires were likewise lit on the first of May visible on hills and knolls (258: lines 1–7).

44. *Ibid.* 255: lines 10–13 and 24–28.

45. Ross in *Everyday Life of the Pagan Celts* writes about the pervasive roles religious beliefs and practices played in the everyday lives of early British and Continental-related European peoples (133: lines 18–19, 23–33, and 35–38).

Besides the similar preoccupation or analogous religious dedication to the modern game, there were the same high expectations from its venerated "Gods" and "heroes." Heroes were expected to embody the best of the society and those placed upon the pedestal had to be among other things intellectuals, warriors, poets, etc. (133: lines 11–17).

46. Ross, *Pagan Celtic Britain*, writes about the central figure on the Gundestrup cauldron, where a stag god is depicted in this classical Buddha-like pose (182: lines 16–22, 30–36).

Mac Cana, *Celtic Mythology*, on Cernunnos, writes:

> One of the more obvious similarities between insular mythology and Gaulish iconography is their rich profusion of zoomrphic imagery. In sculpture the gods are often accompanied by animals or birds associated with the cult, or in some cases no doubt, with deities conceived in animal form, as in the Paris relief of Esus and the bull. In other instances the animal actually appears as part of the deity, and of these the most notable is the "horned god," who bears the horns of stag, ram or bull upon his head. These horn-bearing figures have a long history which extends back far before the emergence of the Celts as a recognizable socio-cultural grouping, but in the course of time they apparently

became an integral part of religious thought of the Celtic people [39: lines 1–22].

(More details on the horned god, Cernunnos striking a Buddha-like pose. 39: 23–29, 41–65.)

C. Walter A. Fairservis, Jr., in *The Roots of Ancient India* (1971) discusses the artefacts found at Mohenjo-daro (built ca. 2600 and abandoned ca. 1900 BCE) of the Harrapan civilization of ancient India and mentions:

> This [seal] shows what appears to be a deity wearing a buffalo-horn headdress, numerous bangles, bracelets, and V-shaped necklace collar or necklace.... On either side, however are wild animals [275: lines 7–10, 12–13].

This may be a prototype for Shiva.

47. Traces of the usage of older terms survived long enough (1744) to be recorded in cricket. W.J. Lewis in *The Language of Cricket* writes:

> OUT PARTY or the OUTS. The side that is fielding; the "out side," as distinguished from the "in party" or the "ins" [*Obsolete.* 1801, 1823, 1853].
> OUT-PLAY. Fielding: = "out cricket."
> OUT SIDE. The side that is fielding, as distinguished from the "in side," the side that is batting.
> IN PARTY or the INS (Obsolete terms), now the IN SIDE. The side that is batting as distinguished from the "out party."
> 1744–55 Laws § 6: Laws for ye Umpires.... They are the sole judges of all outs and ins, of all fair or unfair Play, [etc.] [181, 135 and 288].

James L. Steele, the *Outing* magazine describes a baseball game at Hoboken, N.J., in 1859:

> Baseball differs from cricket, especially in there being no wickets. The bat is held high in the air. When the ball has been struck, the "outs" try to catch it, in which case the striker is out; or if they cannot do this, to strike the striker with it when he is running, which likewise puts him out [James L. Steele, *How the National Game Developed, Some Baseball Reminesces,* in "Outing," an Illustrated Monthly Magazine of Recreation (1885–1906, Published June 1904, Vol. 44, First—number 333, lines 28–34)].

(Spalding, *America's National Game*, also cites Steele's work, page 69, lines 9–13).

This shows that the side on the field was called the "outs." The idea of the game was to get the "ins" out as quickly as possible.

48. According to the Hindu Vedas, Yama is the ruler of the realm of all departed spirits. Sometimes he is described as ruler of a realm that departed spirits seek to avoid (Ref: Radhakrishnan and Moore). Princess Savitri impressed God Yama (also the son of the sun god, Surya) with her devotion, strength and quick-wit that he (*Yama*, Lord of Death) released her husband, Satyavan, back to the land of the living (Shakrukh Hussain, *Demons, Gods & Holy Men from Indian Myths and Legends*, "Savitri: the perfect wife," 116–117).

49. Rutherford in *Celtic Lore* describes the inherent dualistic nature of religions including those of Hinduism and (old) Druidism and mentions the cosmic battles between two forces vying for supremacy such as the Tuatha De Denaan and the Fomors (121: lines 32–39).

50. Ross, *Everyday Life of the Pagan Celts*, 54: lines 1–4.

51. *Ibid.*, Ross mentions the boyhood deeds of Cú Chulainn as being typical of the time (55: lines 17–21).

52. *Ibid.*, 56: lines 19–29. Ross also states that Celts like to fight from chariots and be engaged in the respected tradition of single combat between two warriors (58: line 41; and 59: lines 1–4).

53. Ross, *Everyday Life of the Pagan Celts*, writes their proclivities to be engaged in single combat, especially when intoxicated, led to intra- and inter-tribal fighting (74: lines 31–35). Internal dissentions were counterproductive and therefore laws were passed to limit the self destruction that was occurring (77: lines 6–11).

54. Ross, *Everyday Life of the Pagan Celts*, 63: lines 18–22.

55. *Ibid.*, 63: lines 29–31, and 32–34.

56. Chadwick in *The Sports and Pastimes of American Boys* writes:

Fair Play in Games.

The most marked feature of true manliness of character is a love of fair play. … Without referring to any other line of sports, sufficient examples can be found in the arena of the American game of base-ball to illustrate the nature

of fair play and its opposite. When two contesting nines enter upon a match game of base-ball, they do so with the implied understanding that the struggle between them is to be one in which their respective skill in handling the ball and the bat, and in running of the bases, is alone to be brought into play, unaided by such low trickery as is comprised in the acts of cutting into the ball, tripping up of base runners, hiding the ball, willful collision with fielders, and other specially mean tricks, of the kind characteristic of corner-lot loafers in their ball games. All these so-called "points" are beyond the pale of fair and manly play, and rank only as among the abuses of the game. While strategic skill is a legitimate feature of a contest on the diamond, it includes only such points of play as are shown in a skilful outwitting of the batsman in the delivery of the ball and in out-manoeuvring opponents in base running [12: lines 8–29].

57. Such practices were expected in militaristic or warlike societies. Will Durant in *The Story of Civilization: Part III. Caesar and Christ* writes:

3. The Games.

Now that was seemed banished, the great games were the most exciting event in the Roman year. They took place chiefly in celebration of religious festivals—of the great mother, of Ceres, of Flora, of Apollo, of Augustis; they might be the "Plebian Games" to appease the plebs, or "Roman Games" in honor of the city and its goddess Roma: they might be offered in connection with triumphs, candidacies, elections, or imperial birthdays; they might like the *Ludi Saeculares*, commemorate some cycle in Roman history. Like the games of Achilles in honor of Patroclus, those of Italy had originally been offered as sacrifice to dead men. At the funeral of Brutus Pera in 264 BC his sons gave a "spectacle" of three duels; at the funeral of Marcus Lepidus in 216 BC twenty-two combats were fought; and in 174 BC Titus Flaminus celebrated his father's death with gladiatorial games in which seventy-four men fought.

The supreme events were combats

of armed men, in duels or en masse. The contestants were war captives, condemned criminals, or disobedient slaves. The right of victors to slaughter their prisoners was generally accepted throughout antiquity, and the Romans thought themselves generous in giving captives a chance for their lives in the arena... [381: 30–39; 385: lines 25–29].

Durant mentions that these games, preceded with solemn procession, were part of the state religion with the vestal virgins, priests and emperor (high priest) being involved (388: lines 1–4).

58. Spalding in *America's National Game* writes:

Cricket is a gentle pastime. Baseball is war! Cricket is an Athletic Sociable, played and applauded in a conventional, decorous and English manner. Base Ball is Athletic Turmoil, played and applauded in an unconventional, enthusiastic and American...

Base Ball, I repeat is War! And the playing of the game is a battle in which every contestant is a commanding General, who, having a field of occupation, must defend it; who, having gained an advantage, must hold it by the employment of every faculty of his brain and body, by every resource of his mind and muscle [7: lines 24–28; and 9: lines 11–16].

59. For example, Michael Gershman, *Diamonds, The Evolution of the Ballpark.* Chapters 1, 2 and 3; and Chadwick's *The Sports and Pastimes of American Boys*—diagrams on 32 (Diagram of a Baseball Field with the Lines of Measurement) and 33 (The Diamond Field).

60. Chadwick, *The Sports and Pastimes of American Boys*, writes on "fair play" in games:

The most marked feature of true manliness of character is a love of fair play. It is a jewel in the crown of manhood of the first water, and without it all sports degenerate into low and dishonest struggles to win by trickery and deception instead of by honorable efforts to excel. A love of fair play is inherent in the breast of every man worthy of the name, and all such detest to see unfair play exhibited on any field whatever, but especially

in games where athletic skill is the chief attraction, for on such fields it is that fair play shines out at its brightest... [12: line 9–15].

Note 56.

61. Morris, *A Game of Inches,* Chapter 3, "Pitching," 100: lines 17–23.

62. The "unfairness" of the competition between hitter and pitcher are evident in the 1891 work of Rev, J.G. Wood, *The Boy's Modern Playmate*.... Rule III. "The Pitcher," and Rule IV. "The Batter," 49–52.

63. David Quentin Voigt in *American Baseball: From Gentleman's Sport to the Commissioner System,* 1. writes in Chapter 1, "The Amateur Era":

But more dominant American values, such as fierce competition and creeping commercialism, disrupted the climate of sportsmanship....

None of the ingenious attempts to keep the game exclusive prevented the working classes from participating. To be sure, the long working day posed a problem for many men, but one team was so dedicated to the game that its members turned out for practice at five in the morning. The rise of such teams posed a "vulgarizing" threat to the gentlemen, but the post–Civil War era stimulated their increase....

During the Civil War, Baseball was played among Union troops, thereby threatening the gentlemanly monopoly [10: lines 11–13, 21–27; and 11: lines 9–10].

64. Morris, *A Game of Inches* writes about overhand pitching (59: lines 38–40; and 60: lines 1–25). Relevant information is found in Chapter 3, 100.

65. Examples:

(1.) Daniel Petersen in *Life's Little Mysteries,* "Why Is There a Pitcher's Mound in Baseball?" 02 July 2010. Web. 10 April 2013.

(2.) Authors: The Writers at Life Little Mysteries. *Life's Little Mysteries: Answers to Fascinating Questions About the World.* TechMediaNetwork, 2011.

(3.) Harold Friendin in his (suite101.com) article titled: "Why Offense Has Increased: Part 1. The Lowered Pitching Mound."

66. Morris in *A Game of* Inches, Chapter 3, "Pitching," describes the innovations made by the pitchers and the difficulties faced by

the rule makers and umpires in judging the legality of a pitch. 101: lines 5–13:

    67. *Ibid.*, Morris writes:

      11.2.3 Mound Building. Until 1950 the rules specified that the pitchers' mounds could be no more than fifteen inches high, but did not require a standard height. ...

      Altering the height of the mound gradually developed into an art form... [482: lines 10–12, 13, and 22–24].

On December 3, 1969, the height of the mound was lowered to 10 inches from 15 inches.

    68. The concepts: of 30 yards, i.e., 90 feet was already in vogue in the old game called "Prison Base"; chalk or paint (clay) was also previously used to mark the boundaries; and the use of "dens," i.e., "dugouts" for the players were old practices. Appendix D has more details of "Prison Base."

    69. Peter Morris in *A Game of Inches: The Stories Behind the Innovations That Shaped Baseball* writes:

      a. Ninety Feet. The Knickerbocker's fourth rule used paces to set the distances between the bases, and there is dispute as to how to convert these. Some experts believe the initial distance was about ninety feet while others think it may be shorter.

      John Thorn, for example, believes that until the mid–1850s the bases were only seventy-five feet apart. Still others, such as Fred Ivor-Campbell, have suggested that paces were used to produce "scalable" dimensions: adults could use something close to ninety feet while children would use a shorter distance. Support for either of these views may be derived from the *1864 American Boy's Book of Sports and Games*, which reprinted the official rules and observed "the boys should reduce the distances there set down about one-sixth" (*1864 American Boy's Book of Sports and Games, 83*) [Section 1.16., 37–38].

    70. Hackwood, *Staffordshire Customs, Superstitions and Folklore*, describes the game of "Prisoner Bars" and points out the origins of this running game were lost in the mists of time. He mentions that: 20 to 30 yards were used as the measured distances between the stakes or stones, the boundaries were marked by paint or chalk (171: lines 40–56).

Chalk was naturally abundant in Britain. This game seems to have similarities with the ancient Indian game of *Kabbadi*, still played in some South Asian countries, Japan and Iran. It is also played in Indian ethnic communities in Ontario and British Columbia, Canada.

Joseph Strutt (1838) and Robin Carver (1834) also mention the games of prisoner's base or bars. Carver mentions that in base or goal ball "four stones or stakes are placed twelve to twenty yards asunder" (Joseph Strutt, *The Sports and Pastimes of the People of England*, 144: lines 21–24; and Robin Carver, *The Book of Sports*, 38: lines 4–5).

The in-fields have therefore ranged from 20 to 30 yards in length (from Little League Baseball to Major League Baseball dimensions).

    71. C. Smith in *Games and Games Leadership* (1932) describes this game of "Capture the Flag," as well as that of "Prisoner's Base."

    72. Strutt, *The Sports and Pastimes of the People of England*, Book II, 143: lines 35–36; 144: lines 1–2, 3–5, 21–24; and 145: lines 6–13.

Strutt also states:

      The first mention of this sport that I have met with occurs in the Proclamations at the head of parliamentary proceedings, early in the reign of Edward III, where it is spoken of as a childish amusement, and prohibited to be played in the avenues of the Palace at Westminster, during the sessions of Parliament, because of the interruption it occasioned to the members and others in passing to and fro as their business required. It is also spoken of by Shakespeare [Cymbeline, Act 5, and Sc. 3] as a game practised by the boys:

        He with two striplings, lads more like to run.

      The country base, than to commit such slaughter.

      Made good the passage.

      It was, however, most assuredly played by the men, and especially in Cheshire and other adjoining counties, where formerly it seems to have been in high repute [Book II, 144: lines 5–20].

73. Hackwood, *Staffordshire Customs and Folklore*, 171: second column, lines 46–55, 60–63. Hackwood mentions that the game was so popular that the gatherings obstructed members of Parliament from entering or leaving the building (172: first column, lines 1–2, 4–5).

Edward III (born 1312) was then king of England, 1327 to 1377 CE.

74. *Ibid.*, 172: lines 46–66 (or second column, lines 1–6).

75. *Ibid.*, 172: lines 2–20. See also the rest of the section for further information as regards to the popularity of this game. Running was popular in Britain in Shakespearean times as Forbes Sievering records in Ch 9, "Games" of Ed. Onions, C.T, Lee, Sidney and Walter Alexander Raleigh's *Shakespeare's England: An Account of the Life & Manners of His Age, Volume II* (1916):

> Shakespeare, with charcteristic brevity, gives a picture of runners exhausted at the end of their course:
>> Forspent with toil, as runners with a race,.
>> I lay me down a little while to breathe
> (3 Hen. VI, II, iii, 1–2)
> (454: lines 39–40).

Sievering quotes Samuel Rowlands, *The Letting of Humours Blood in the Head-Vaine* (1600):

> To wrastle, play at stooleball, or to runne [452: line 38].

N.B.: The games of stool-ball and running are mentioned together. Both games were played at Easter.

76. Carver, *The Book of Sports*, Ch 5– "Sports of Speed," Sub-heading: "Prisoner's Base," 55–56; 55: lines 1–3.

77. Chadwick, *The Sports and Pastimes of American Boys…*, 15: lines 1–3.

78. David Quentin Voigt, *American Baseball: From Gentleman's Sport to the Commissioner System,* Vol. 1, 4: lines 24–34; and 5: lines 1–3.

Chapter 10

1. Olwen Brogan in *The Coming of Rome and the Establishment of Roman Gaul* in Piggott et al.'s *France Before the Romans* writes:

> Such knowledge of reading and writing as the Gauls possessed was ascribed to the influence of the Druids … [who

were] responsible for the longest document in Gaulish that has survived, the Calendar of Coligny (Ain)…. This is a list of lunar months and their associated ceremonies [219: second column, lines 46–53].

This means at least some continental Celts had a written language.

2. *Ibid.*, Brogan notes that while the Romans "respected Celtic religion," they did appropriate the native gods, giving them Latin names, but they did not tolerate the Druids, who had both religious and political influence. Augustus appears to have aimed squarely at the Druids in forbidding Roman citizens to take part in "foreign cults"; Tiberius issued an edict against "magicians and the like"; and Claudius was responsible for their outright suppression, citing their "bloody practices," driving the Druids underground (219: Column 1, lines 11–18; Column 2, lines 23–41, 44–46).

3. For example, John Rhys in *Welsh People* (1848) writes:

> We have already hinted that The Welsh are well endowed in the matter of imagination and fancy. This faculty has sometimes played a great role when it was found combined with a certain kind of faith…. From this combination there sprang up among the Brythons of yore a spirit of romance which held the Europe of the Middle Ages bound, as it were under a spell. There is no great literature of the Continent which does not betray the influence of the Brythonic hero Arthur, whom his people as late as the time of Henry II expected to see returning from the Isle of Avalon hale and strong and longing to lead his men and country men to triumph over the foe and oppressor… [592: lines 11–14, 19–27].

The great Arthurian legends of British and Continental literature were Welsh.

4. Many of baseball's expressions have been and are used in everyday language and idiomatic expressions, e.g., reaching home, touching base, three strikes and you are out, and in the ballpark.

5. The late Reverend Shaw had 205 contributors from some of the pillars of then–British society. Shaw's 1780 work is *A Galic and English Dictionary: Containing All the*

Words in Scotch and Irish Dialects of the Celtic That Could Be Collected from Voice, and Old Books and MSS.

6. *Britons* are the inhabitants of *Britannia*, and *Bretons* those of *Brittany*, now Southwest part of France.

7. "Bowling" is the term used to describe the action of a person who delivers the ball to a batter in the game of cricket. The bowler may vary not only location of his deliveries, but also speed (fast and medium) and spin (breaking balls, e.g., leg-break and off-break). In cricket, no artificial mound is on record of being used. Bowling from a mound (natural or artificial) had to exist for another game. (This recalls at least a throwing game from a higher elevation as described by Francis Willughby in an early form of stoolball.)

Early baseball and cricket both had underhand delivery of the ball in some versions of these games (Morris, *A Game of Inches*, Chapter 3: "Pitching: (i) *Deliveries*, 100–107).

8. James Bonwick, *Irish Druids and Old Irish Religions* (1894), section on "Sun-Worship" 195: lines 7–9. *Open Library*. Web. 10 April 2013.

9. In baseball, the game begins when the home-plate umpire says: "Play ball!" Frederick Gale, *Echoes from Old Cricket Fields* (1871), in the Appendix mentions:

The Laws of Cricket in 1870.

Rule XIV: At the beginning of each innings the Umpire shall call "Play." From that time to the end of each beginning no trial ball shall be allowed to any Bowler [107: line 12; and 108: lines 36–38].

(Hence the concept of "warm-up" pitches before an inning was established.)

10. In the modern times, the game as well as the ball is called "baseball," umpires are "base-umpires," and the four markers "bases."

11. Shaw in *A Galic and English Dictionary*, 253: lines 9–16, 23–29.

Beal, as mentioned before, is one of the many names of the Sun god.

12. *Ibid.*, Shaw writes:

Bealteine. The first of May. Teine Beil, or fire of the god Belus, i.e., Mayday in Irish, so called from the fires which the Druids, lighted on the summits of the highest hills, into which they drove the four-footed beasts, using at the same time certain ceremonies to expatiate for

the sins of the people. This pagan ceremony of lighting those fires in honour of the Asiatic God Belus, gave its name to the entire month of May, which to this day is called *Mios Na Bealteine*, in the Irish language. Dr. Keating says the design of it was to keep off contagious disorders from them for the year, and that all the inhabitants of Ireland quenched their fires on that day, and kindled them again out of some part of that fire [5: lines 1–18].

Dr. Keating, who wrote *History of Ireland*, was a distinguished Irish historian and a contemporary of Shaw.

13. Ward Rutherford in *Celtic Lore*, 92: lines 8–15 and 22–25.

In addition, Bonwick in *Irish Druids and Old Irish Religions* (1894) writes:

But what was St. Patrick's teaching?

The Saint [Patrick] is recorded to have said of the sun. "All who adore him shall unhappily fall into eternal punishment." In his *Confessio*, he [St. Patrick] exclaimed, "Woe to its unhappy worshippers for punishment awaits them. But we believe in and adore the true Sun, Christ!" [192: lines 17–22].

The circular dance in honour of the sun was derived from the East. Lucian says "it consisted of a dance imitating this god" (the sun). The priests of Baal indulged in it. A Druid song has this account—"Ruddy was the sea-beach while the circular revolution was performed by the attendants, and the white bands in graceful extravagance" [195: lines 20–26].

At the *Lucaid-Lamh-Fada*, or festival of love, from, Aug. 1 to Aug. 16, games were held in honour of the sun and moon (195: lines 33–34; and 196: line 1).

The sun god of the pagan Celtic and Druidic-led peoples were effectively replaced or substituted for by Jesus Christ. It was also easier to move from "Esus" (or Hesus) to "Jesus."

14. There are several names for the same sun god. Often there is a variant of the same name; or, there may be a different name for the sun god depending on the position of the sun overhead.

15. For example, the *Old Galic and English Dictionary* records: "*Troghain*, sun—rising";

"*Turgabhail Greine*, the course of the sun"; "*Tur,* journey"; "*Tuis, Tus,* a beginning, origin"; "*Fuin,* the end or termination of a journey"; "*Fair* meant the rising or the setting of the sun"; "*Grianach,* sunny"; "*Eirghe Na Greine,* sunrise"; and "*Luidhe Na Greine,* sunset."

16. Bonwick in *Irish Druids and Old Irish Religions* writes:

> A stone was dug up in the road from Glasgow to Edinburgh, on which was an inscription to *Grannius,* the Latin form of *Grian,* the sun. Enclosures in the Highlands were called *Grianan,* the house of the sun. On Harris Island is a stone circle, with a stone in the centre, known as *Clack-Na-Greine,* the stone of the sun. At Elgin, the bride had to lead her husband to the church following the sun's course [192: lines 1–8].

17. *Ibid.,* Bonwick (197: lines 16–28).

The Martin referred to is Martin Martin, the 1753 author of *A Voyage to St. Kilda, the Remotest of All the Hebrides, or Western Isles of Scotland.*

Similar observations were recorded by the Lancashire and Cheshire Antiquarian Society, "Transactions," Vol. IV., 322: lines 1–7.

The Hindus similarly offer milk in their religious services. Small amounts of milk are placed on the worshipper's cupped hands, from which the milk is drunk.

18. The word "globe" has different connotations now. The world then still believed that the earth was flat. In 1597–1598, the Globe Theater was built. This was made famous by William Shakespeare whose plays were performed there.

19. The Hindu women still use a red rounded spot or mark in the center of their foreheads to indicate that they are married.

20. The red-round cylindrical bases could have well been phallic symbols similar to the Indian *Lingams.* The color red is symbolic of blood, a life-giving force or renewal of life. Sacrificial altars were colored red in Indian cultures.

21. The Sun-god had various names as mentioned earlier. The Scots have maintained a traditional "Ba" game. The word "Ba" referred to both the game and the ball. There is both a lad's and men's version. The ferocity of the players ("Uppies" and "Downies") involved in this game is unmatched anywhere.

It is however consistent with their warrior traditions. The origins of this old handball game are unknown and probably lost in antiquity. For the Norse and the Saxons, "Baldur" was the name of the "white god," or "sun."

22. In ancient Egyptian mythology, "Ba" was the human soul that remained with the deceased. This soul was often portrayed as a winged creature, the "Ba-bird," represents the ascension of the soul after death. Recently, there was a popular tributary song to God: "In His hands, He has the whole world..."

23. The British novelist, Arnold Bennett in *Anna of the Five Towns* (1902) writes:

> Another diversion which he (Titus Price) always took care to organise was the three-legged race for boys. Also, he usually joined in the *Tut-Ball,** a quaint game which owes its surprising longevity to the fact that it is equally proper for both sexes.

The editor, Margaret Harris, of the 1995 edition of Arnold Bennett's *Anna of the Five Towns* writes in the notes: "**Tut-Ball*: a game like rounders, but played with no bat. The field is marked out by 'Tuts,' or brickbats, round which a player who has hit the ball with his or her hand must run" [124: lines 6–10; and 225: note # 124, lines 18–21].

Appendix C has more information. There are several modern versions of baseball for children and also for adults. In modern baseball and or softball, there are adaptations for different ages, levels, circumstances, and preferences, e.g., T-ball, Coaches pitch, Little League, Junior League, Senior League, College Ball, and Professional Ball.

24. Bonwick in, *Irish Druids and Religions,* writes:

> A scotch writer observes:—The hearty Celts of Ireland say, "The top of the morning to you." Are these expressions to be regarded as remnants of the Dawn-worship? It may be so, for many similar traces of the worship of the sun and moon, as givers of good fortune, are still to be found [196: lines 7–12].

Daily greetings (Good Morning, Good Day, Good Afternoon, Good Evening) are based on the position of the sun overhead.

25. The Hindu *Rig Vedas* portray *Indra*

primarily as a deity of the thunderstorm. A.L. Basham in *The Wonder That Was India* writes:

> From the point of view of the Aryan warrior the greatest god was *Indra*, who fulfilled the dual function of war-god and weather-god. Though his name was different he had many of the characteristics of the Greek Zeus and the Germanic Thor. As Indra tonans he was at the Head of the Aryan host and destroyed the fortresses of the Dasas; as Indra pluvius he slew the dragon Vrtra who held back the waters, and thus he brought rain to the parched land. Indra was associated with storm and thunder, and like Zeus and Thor his hand bore the thunderbolt (*Vajra*), with which he destroyed his enemies. He was a rowdy amoral deity, fond of feasting and drinking....

Two of Indra's traits connect him with Indo-European mythology, for they were applied to various gods and heroes throughout ancient Europe, and a wild rider of the storm [235: lines 41–43; and 236: lines 1–8, 35–38].

In old British Germanic and Scandinavian languages, *Taran* meant "thunder" and "*Taranis*, the God of Thunder."

Radhakrishna and Moore in *A Source Book of Indian Philosophy* state:

> To *Indra* [primarily a deity of the thunderstorm].* (*Indra is the most prominent of the gods of the gods in the Rg Veda. He is most frequently praised for his power and heroism, as the god of battle.)
>
> 1. I will extol the most heroic *Indra* who with his might forced earth and sky asunder; ....
>
> 2. *Surya* is he: throughout the wide expanses shall Indra turn him, swift as car-wheels, hither,
>
> Like a stream resting not but ever active: he destroyed, with light, the black hued darkness [5: lines 36–38; and 6: lines 1–4].

26. The Indian Vedas portrays "Agni" as "the God of fire" (Ref. in Note 25, 7–8, 9).

27. Possibly the expressions: "Good Morning," "Good Day," and "Good Night," to you, had similar origins, that is invoking the blessings of the particular sun god.

28. Shaw, *A Galic and English Dictionary*, 340 (Solas and Solus).

29. Two ideal distances for such a representation are the lengths of a side and the diagonal of the baseball square, or a right angle triangle.

30. Different balls were used for different purposes. In the Clarendon Press's republication, A. Forbes Sieveking in *Shakespeare's England: An Account of the Life & Manners of His Age*, Vol. 11, in Chapter 9, "Games" states:

> The balls are described as being smaller than the wind-balls (or balloons) and harder—being made of white leather, and "stuffed" not with wool torn from rags, but chiefly dog's hair, the ball being struck not with the palm of the hand but with a net (i.e., a racket) [460: lines 13–18].

Julian Marshall in *The Annals of Tennis* writes:

> The civic authorities, meanwhile, were not behind the legislature in forbidding Tennis among "unlawful games" practiced to the detriment and neglect of "Artilery" shooting. At the same time, however, or shortly afterwards, we find it warmly commended by Richard Mulcaster in the following passage, taken from a chapter wholly devoted to the Ball, hand-ball, foot-ball, and arm-ball (= Balloon, or Pallone)... [70: lines 22–31].

Anyone who has coached youth baseball knows that the players naturally make these "rainbow throws." These improper throws have to be corrected.

Steve Craig in *Sports and Games of the Ancients* writes:

> The Yanoama tribes in North West Brazil form a circle and keep hitting the ball (a monkey bladder ball) upward. One tribe ascribes to the form of play with magical and spiritual qualities; therefore it is played only by men. To the Yanoama this game represents the repetitive appearance and disappearance of the sun and moon, a common theme to *Tlachtli*, the Aztec version of the great rubber ball game [137: lines 33–39].

Also mentioned were similar games played by the Paressi, who used a hollow rubber ball and their heads to hit the ball; the Arawaks had a head ball game, the ball was made with an extract from the gum tree; and the Mayan and Aztec had a game where the hips were used to hit the ball (137: lines 40; and 138: lines 1–8).

31. The Colin B. Mark's Gaelic to English online dictionary also gives *Solas* as meaning light and knowledge. This best describes the philosophical concepts that the *Solas* game sought to teach the young people.

32. The spectators of baseball games include people from all walks of life—academics, professionals, semi-professionals, laborers, etc. One MLB president, Dr. A. Bartlett Giamatti, was a former Yale University's president. Several academics, e,g,. the late Dr. Stephen J. Gould, writes on baseball. Many writers, poets, novelists, etc., are seen at the games. Many examples of such writers are given by John Thorn's (Ed.) in *The Armchair Book of Baseball*.

33. In Little League Baseball, anyone who runs in a clockwise direction is called out. In the modern game of baseball, players run in a counter-clockwise direction. This suggests that in one earlier version of the game, players ran in a clock-wise direction after hitting the ball. This was previously mentioned as the case for some earlier games.

34. John Brand, *Popular Antiquities*, Vol. 1. 134: lines 19–27; and 47.

In addition, John Jamieson, in *An Etymological Dictionary of the Scottish Language*, Volume IV, writes about these rooted ancestral traditions (Gaelic and Gaelic druidic) in everyday life in magical cermonies, weddings and baptisms, dances and travellings that involved doing things the right way in respect to following the direction of the sun. It was thought that failure to do so invites disaster (792: second column, lines 33–36, 60–64, 66–67; and 793: first column, lines 5–10, 21–42).

35. Bonwick (*Irish Druids and Old Irish Religions*) mentions that the bride led her husband to the church following the course of the sun, in Elgin, Scotland. Bonwick writes about two dances: the *Reel* which maintained the traditional circular movements of early British peoples, and the *Deisol* which likewise imitated circular movements of the sun and simultaneously blesses the sun. These circular dance movements are in keeping with others of the past (191: lines 22–26).

Bonwick also mentions other examples of the movement in the sun-wise direction. In some cases, it was taboo to go against the face of the sun.

In Hindu wedding ceremonies, the direction of circular movement of the couple being married around the sacred fire (representing the "Radiant One") is also clockwise, with male and female taking turns in leading. Hindu devotees still make their religious prayers at sunrise and at sunset. An Indian custom has survived the ages, this being that one must be up before sunrise so as to avoid the displeasure of the gods.

36. Other old Gaelic words for the eye were: *Suil, Rofg, Cais* and *Dearc*.

37. Old Gaelic, *Ogh* means "entire, whole."

38. Old Gaelic, *Totta* means "shaft"; *Sollus* "light;" and *Dearfa, Riodha*, and *Gath Greine* "sunbeam."

39. Some old words: "*Sollus, Dearfa*, light from the sun," and "*Suil, Dearc*, the eye," are also similar (Notes 36 and 38). Other old Gaelic words: "*Suilghoirt* eye-sore;" "*Solafda* brightness, luminous"; and "*Suilach* having eyes."

40. This scene was intellectually pleasurable and beautiful to those believers who worshipped the sun. This would have been analogous to their studying the reflection of the moon using the "sacred" or "holy wells" as telescopes.

41. Rutherford, *Celtic Lore*, 92: lines 14–15.

42. Old Gaelic, *Fal* meant "circle;" "*Leath* half apart, separate;" "*Leathchearcal* semicircle"; and "*Leathchruinne* a semicircle, hemisphere."

43. For example (1) Ross in *Pagan Celtic Britain* describes and discusses the former sacred sites of early British Peoples.

and (2) Stuart Piggott in *The Druids* shows details of former early British sanctuary sites, 54–78 including figures 28–58.

44. *The Anti-Jacobean Review and Magazine: And Protestant Advocate*: or Monthly Political and Literary Censor from August to December (Inclusive), Vol. X (The Anti-Jacobin Press, London, 1801) 236: lines 11–19. *Google Books*. Web. 10 April 2013.

Seems as if *Sol-Bheim* (sunbeam) is a possible origin for the expression being "beamed" meaning being struck down with an object like "a bolt of lightning."

45. Bonwick (*Irish Druids and Old Irish Religions*) also has an extensive list of words used throughout his book.

46. Addy, *A Glossary of Words*, vii: lines 3–5.

47. *Ibid.*, vii–ix.

Addy mentions that he got the benefit of the work of the late Rev. Joseph Hunter who had intended to publish his manuscript in 1821, but it was never published for unknown reasons.

48. In addition, as James Bonwick points out, many were in denial that their ancestors were sun-worshippers (chapter on "Sun Worship," 189–198).

49. Charles Squire, *Celtic Myth and Legend*, 42: lines 4–9, 26–29; and 43: line 1.

Squire continues:

> In other cases, what is obviously the same personified power of nature is found in various places with the same attributes, but with a different title. Besides these, there must have been a multitude of lesser gods, worshipped by certain tribes alone, to whom they stood as ancestors and guardians. "I swear by the gods of my people" was the ordinary oath of a hero in the ancient Gaelic sagas. The aboriginal tribes must also have had their gods, whether it be true or not that their religion influenced the Celtic Druidism. ... These local beings would in no way conflict with the great Celtic nature gods, and the two worships could exist side by side, both even claiming the same votary [43: lines 1–20].

50. Peter Berrisford Ellis in *The Druids*, writes about *Lugh*:

> Among the names of the Celtic gods which appear most frequently is that of Lugh in Irish, Llew in Welsh and Lugus in Gaulish. The inscriptions to him are more numerous than to any other Celtic god... The name appears in place names in many former Celtic territories: Lyons, Léon, Loudan and Laon in France; Leiden in Holland; Liegnitz in Silesia; and Carlisle (Luguvalum in Roman times) in England... At Lyons (Lugdunum) the Gaulish Celtic celebrated an ancient feast of Lugus... The same feast occurs in insular Celtic tradition. In Ireland it was known as Lughnasadh, held on 1 August. It was one of the four major

pre–Christian festivals and basically an agrarian feast in honour of harvesting of crops. The name still survives as Lúnasa (August) in Irish, in Luanistyn (August) in Manx, and in Lúnasad for the Lammas Festival in Scottish Gaelic [124: lines 38–39; and 125: lines 1–5, 11–14, and 16–22].

Ellis gave further details about Lugh on 125–127. Lugh was also regarded as the "Fair one," and thereby shows some of the Indo-European connections.

51. *Indra* was portrayed as the god of war in the *Vedas*, the Indian Epic meaning the "Ultimate Knowledge."

52. Shaw, 241.

Shaw writes:

> *Leice, Leug,* a precious stone, a diamond. In the highlands a large crystal of the figure somewhat oval, which priests kept to work charms by. Water poured upon it at this day is given to cattle against diseases. These stones are now preserved for the same purposes by the oldest and most superstitious in the country [241–242].

53. George Frederick Kunz, *The Mystical Lore of Precious Stones*, 70: lines 23–25.

54. *Ibid.*, Kuntz continues:

> A curious fancy, prevalent in regard to many stones, attributed sex to the diamond, and it is therefore not surprising stones were also supposed to possess reproductive powers. In this connection, Sir John Mandeville writes:
>
> "They grow together, male and female, and are nourished by the dew of heaven; and they engender commonly, and bring forth small children that multiply and grow all the year. I have often times tried this experiment that if a man keeps them with a little rock, and waters them with May dew often, they shall grow every year and the small will grow great" [72: lines 11–21].

55. Lewis Spence in *The Mysteries of Great Britain*, Chapter X—"The Writings of Morien," writes:

> Moreover, the sources from which Morgan drew his Druidic material are only occasionally indicated throughout the volumes, and although the origins of some of them are obvious, we are left absolutely in the dark as the source of others. This notwithstanding, these works

are of primary importance in such a quest as ours, because of the great and varied acquaintance they reveal with the faith and mythology underlying the British Secret Tradition, and an endeavor will be made in these pages to summarize the system of which they treat [215: lines 22–28; and 216: lines 1–5].

Lewis writes of Owen Morgan ("Morien"), author of *The Light of Brittania* and *The Royal Winged Son of Stonehenge and Avebury*:

Are certainly extraordinary storehouses of Druidic lore, but the facts they contain are so inextricably mingled with classical and Eastern mysticism that it is frequently difficult to disentangle them [215: lines 18–22].

56. *Ibid.*, Spence in his continued summation of Owen Morgan's work wrtes:

All titles of the sun except Hu Gadarn, are comprehended in a Triad known as Plennydd, Alawn, and Gwron. The earth, for its part, was known as the three queens of Arthur, spring, summer, and winter [217: lines 4–8].

The negative or evil principles were three males Avagddu, Cythraul, and Atrais which signified Darkness, Pulverizer, and Soddener, and the three female principles, Annhras, Malen, and Mallt, or Graceless, Grinder, and Soddener [217: lines 8–12].

57. *Ibid.*, Chapter X—"The Writings of Morien, 218: lines 34–36; and 219: lines 1–9 (some words are italicized for emphasis).

Spence adds:

The three bulls are the aforesaid Plennydd, Alawn, and Gwion, and the three cows, Morwyn, Blodwen, and Tynghedwen-Dyrraith., who are found later as the three sister-spouses of Arthur, personifications of the earth at the three stages of the year [219: line 6—10].

The sun was often represented by a bull which in old Gaelic was called *Tarbh,* and in Welsh—*Tarw, Buwch,* hence *Taurus the Bull.*

Bonwick in *Irish Druids and Old Irish Religions* (1894) writes about the Sacred Cow or magical cows (*Glas Gaibhne* or the Grey Cow) in Old Irish traditions, thereby recalling traditions of India. This respect was so strong since it was mentioned that King Diarmuid

MacCearbhail killed his own son for his destruction of a Sacred Cow (see page 62: 1–13).

Hindu myths also tell of the Heavenly Bull (*Parjanya*) mating with Mother Earth (*Aditi*). Hindus still hold cows as sacred and purely white ones are even more revered as deity.

N. B. Owen Morgan ("Morien") 1894 work, *Light of Britannia*, Chapters IV.–V., 34–59.

Morgan sheds some light on his work, he writes:

The sun in three principal stations, viz., at the vernal equinox, summer solstice, and the winter solstice, is personified in each, and is named in reference to the three stages by the Druids, Alawn, Plennydd, and Gwron (beginning at the vernal equinox)… [17: lines 27–31].

58. Hu Gadarn ("Hu the Mighty") the mythical figure who reputedly brought the early British to Wales. He has also been identified as a Welsh horned god, and others have identified him with the early British god, *Esus*.

In addition, Ross (*Pagan Celtic Britain*) provides some insights as to the validity and relevance of bulls and cows in the culture. Britain was thought to be protected by three bulls (386: lines 29–30; 387: 1–4, 23–30; 388: 1–2, 20–28; 388: 37–39; and 389: lines 1–5; and 389 to 390).

Other relics of sun worshipping and sacrificial practices did exist until recently. Knowlson in *the Origins of Popular Superstition* writes that earlier on the festival of Beltain held on the first of May, many workers gathered in the fields to celebrate the occasion. The activities included making and sharing a meal (which included milk and eggs) likely an offering to some deity of earlier times (45: lines 20–28).

The work was cited from Sir John Sinclair's earlier *Statistical Account of Scotland* (1794), 620.

59. Morgan in *Light of Britannia* writes:

Any circular stone temple of the Druids is named Buarth Beirrd–Cattle Pen of the Bards; not "Oxen" of the Bards: for *Bu* (e sound to the u) signifies the same thing as the Latin *Bovis*, and implies the cattle genus. For "oxen" we are to understand bulls. Bulls being too dangerous to meddle with, and to be used in the religious symbolic rites of the Druidic bards, the more easily managed oxen came to be used instead, as substitutes for bulls. Thus evidently there were three cows and three bulls employed as symbols by the Druids, in their cattle pen or circle. In reference to the sacred oxen, styled as being of, or belonging to, "many hills," the expression, we think, refers to the "many hills," upon which stood the many Druidic sanctuaries to which sacred oxen belonged [49: lines 21–31; and 50: lines 1–4].

Ibid., Morgan writes:
The Druids used three bulls to match the three cows in their religious system, as they did three apples to symbolize the sun at the three stages in his annual course, as seen from the horizon. They are referred to in the Welsh Triads as three regal bulls or sovereigns of Britain. Three consort cows are also mentioned in the Triad [50: lines 19–24].

These ideas are not too far-fetched as documented in studies of ancient India. Walter A. Fairservis, Jr., *The Roots of Ancient India. the Archaeology of Early Indian Civilization.*

60. Both Owen Morgan and E.O. Gordon provides further information on this "*Buarth Beirdd*, or the *Bovine Bardic Enclosure*," a "scared *Cattle Pen* or *Circle*," and the rationales for the choices of "three cows and three bulls."

(1) Gordon in *Prehistoric Mounds of London: Its Mounds and Circles* writes:
The Druidic symbol of the name of the Deity is three rods or pencils of light [/|\]. Of these three lines in various conjunctions was framed the first or Bardic Alphabet. Knowledge and religion cannot be separated. In public transactions the Ogam or Bardic Characters were employed; in transactions with foreigners, Bardic or Greek.

Hu Gadarn's successor, Ædd Mawr, BCE 1000, is the reputed founder of the Druidical Order in Britain. He is said to have founded within his dominion three wise men, called Plenydd, Alawn, and Gwron, and to them he trusted his organization [28: lines 16–26].

(2) Owen Morgan mentions that this same triadic symbol, /|\, and if turned upside down, \|/, had different meanings such as male, female, good or evil.

Morgan in *Light of Britannia* writes:
As we have already pointed out, the Druids personified the sun's emanations at three distinct stages of the solar year, March 21st, June 21st, and December 20th, and they symbolized the three stages by the strokes \|/, usually shown in the form /|\ …

When the figure for the middle hole was inserted the three symbols would appear thus \|/. The middle stroke would be the Linga, implying the sun's virile power in spring. The two side strokes are referred to by the chief Bard Taliesin, in his Càd Godden, as "The Royal Knees," the Said or Linga being between them [43: lines 25–29; and 44: lines 5–10].

61. Peter Gelling and Hilda Ellis Davidson in *The Chariot of the Sun* writes:
The belief that it is possible to influence the fertility of the land and abundance of crops by sexual intercourse on the part of human beings is too familiar to need elaboration. As far as the rock engravings [of Sweden] go, it looks as if more attention was paid to its effect on animals…. If he [man in the rock engraving] could plausibly be regarded as the sun-god, he would not only be warding off evil but actually bestowing a positive blessing on the occasion [sacred wedding ceremony]; but it would be just as plausible to regard the male participant in the marriage as representing the god. The part would be played, perhaps, by a priest, who would be considered for the occasion to embody the deity [68: lines 12–15, 19–25].

In Figure 31 (page 69), the Rock carving from Bohuslän (Gelling and Davidson), is depicted a human figure about to mate with an animal.

Gelling and Davidson writes:
Although it is probably true that the southern group of Scandinavian rock engravings reflects the needs and desires of an agricultural population, the religion which they embody seems to have been primarily concerned with the fundamental principle of life, and specific references to the farmer are common. Some of the sacred marriage scenes have revealed a concern for livestock, and as

a natural counterpart there are a few engravings which show the plough....

The bulls in the Aspeberger group have already been mentioned. The three animals in line look at first glance as if they represented a herd being driven by a herdsman, but all are clearly distinguished as a male, so it seems that religious feeling here is concentrated on the bull.... These engravings seem to show a closer connection between the bull and the sun than that which would arise from a general association to ensure the former's fertility....

The most spectacular evidence for a rite in which the bull was involved was discovered by Dr. Åke Fredsjö at Torsbo, south-west of Kville, in Bohusän. It shows three men, each raising one arm with a large three-fingered hand, which recalls the sun-gesture. Above and to the right of them are four bulls with large horns, three of them in very lively attitudes. The fourth is in a less active pose, but is the center of interest, for behind one of its horns, and probably holding it, is a man [79: lines 1–7; 81: lines 1–5, 18–20, 82. lines 16–20; and 83: lines 1–3].

62. John Rhys and David Brynmor-Jones in *Welsh People* (592: lines 11–31; and 593: lines 11–13 and Note 3.

63. Walter A. Fairservis Jr. in *The Roots of Ancient India: The Archaeology of Early Indian Civilization* states that in Mohenjo-Daro, India:

One is struck by the number of scenes in which attitudes or acts of adoration or sacrifice occur....

The animal most often depicted [on the Harappan seals] is a bull-like creature with horns thrust forward....

One of the most intriguing of all the scenes depicted among the seals and sealings is that which shows individuals apparently bull-leaping in the Cretan fashion, that is, somersaulting from the horns of the animals into the air—both forward and back....

The depiction of cattle is seemingly to emphasize the power and strength of the bull rather than the more useful products and service which are derived from cattle....

The best candidates for "temples" are those structures which are raised high on platforms in which drains, baths and fire pits of one kind or another are found. Ceremonial ablution, ritual purification, fire sacrifice, possible ritual drinking, and the priestly offering of animals and humans are suggested by the evidence. Yet we have little suggestion as to whom or to what such rites were devoted. After some twenty field campaigns we have barely a clue as to the Harappan pantheon: no images, icons, texts, or proof of a temple [274: lines 31–33; 274: lines 14–16; 276: lines 30–35; 277: lines 34–37; and 301: lines 11–19].

There was precedent in ancient India for what the Celts, an Indo-European people, were doing in Britain.

64. Ross, *Everyday Life of the Pagan Celts*, describes Dagda, the "Good God" who was equivalent to the "Good Striker" (159: lines 36–41; and 160: lines 1–4).

65. (1) Rhys and Brynmor-Jones, *Welsh People,* writes with regards to the old agricultural practices of the Welsh:

In the laws yokes of four different lengths are mentioned:–The *Ber-Iau,* or short yoke of three feet, for two oxen; the *Mei-Iau,* or field yoke of six feet, for four oxen; the *Ceseil-Iau,* or auxiliary yoke of nine feet, for six oxen; and the *Hir-Iau,* or long yoke of twelve feet, for eight oxen. The Welsh farmer seldom, however, yoked less than four oxen to the plough [249: lines 19–25].

(2) In addition to Spence, *The Mysteries of Great Britain*, who discusses triplicate forms of gods and goddesses, Davies in *The Celts* mentions Celtic goddesses were more often portrayed in triplicate and there was a need for balance between these two opposite, but essential forces:

Consistent with the delight in triadism, goddesses, even more than gods, are frequently portrayed in triplicate. There are three cloaked figures from Housesteads on Hadrian's Wall, the three mothers on the stone relief from Vertillum in Burgundy and the triad of deities on a plaque found at Bath. In Irish literature, the story of Cu Chulanin features three mother goddesses, Morrigan, Mache, and Bodh, battle furies with an uncanny resemblance to Macbeth's three witches…. Irish mythology suggests a dualism between the male deities of the tribe and the female deities of the land. Assuming that the Celtic pantheon is susceptible to coherent interpretation, perhaps the most convincing is Cunliffe's suggestion that gods represented war, the sky and the tribe and the goddesses represented fertility, the earth and the locality, and that it was constructive tension between them which produced balance, harmony, and productivity [83: lines 6–11, 18–23].

This need for harmony between male and female divinities is also held by, e.g., Hindus, Buddhists and Taoists.

66. These strong predilections for three and triplicate representations of some divinities are supported by Ross, *Everyday Life of the Pagan Celts*, 157: lines 13–22.

67. Examples are: "*Triur*, three, the number three"; "*Teoir*, three, thrice"; "*Teorinneach*, three-fold, three-footed"; "*Teora*, three, thrice"; "*Teorchan*, the space of three hours"; "*Teorlaethan*, three days"; "*Teorchafach*, three-footed"; "*Troifte*, a three-footed stool"; "*Tredeinas*, three days"; "*Trearcheann*, three heads"; and "*Cumal*, the price of three cows."

68. In addition, Ellis in *The Druids* writes:
As in the Greek world, so among the Celts, who saw the *Homo Sapiens* as body, soul and spirit; the world they inhabited as earth, sea and air; the divisions of nature as animal, vegetable and mineral; the cardinal colours as red, yellow and blue, and so forth. Three was the number of all things. Most of their gods were three personalities in one. Combinations of the figure three occur often in Celtic tales such as nine (three times three) and thirty-three.

Ireland itself is represented in the female triune goddess–Éire, Nanba and Fótla. There were three Celtic earthly gods–Goibhniu, Luchta and Creidhne. The Goddess of fertility, of smiths and of healing and poetry, even the Dagda himself were worshipped in triune form. The most famous war goddess was the Mórrígán, sometimes Mórrígú, "great queen," and she also appears interchangeable as Macha, Badh and Nemain. She embodies all that is perverse

and horrible among the supernatural powers [128: lines 5–19].

69. A three-headed and four-arm statue of Shiva exists (second century BCE) at Gandhara, India. In Hinduism, Brahma (creator), Vishnu (maintainer or preserver), and Shiva (destroyer or transformer) represent the three primary aspects of the divinity known as the *Trimurti*. The Vedic God of fire, *Agni*, was depicted as two-headed to indicate his destructive and benevolent qualities, and he was also seen as the force of trees and plants (Wilkinson's *Signs & Symbols*. Early British and Continental European beliefs and representations were in line with those of others who shared similar values, philosophies, etc.)

70. For example, Ellis in *The Druids* writes:
Many Celtic gods were worshipped in triune or triplicate form. The concept of a three personality god seems to have its roots in Indo-European expression. In Hindu belief the Trimurti consist of Brahma, the Creator, Vishnu, the Preserver, and Shiva, the Destroyer. Pythagoras saw three as the perfect number of the philosophers—the beginning, middle and end—and used it as a symbol of deity. Indeed, the ancient Greeks saw the world ruled by three gods–Zeus (heaven), Poseidon (sea) and Pluto/Hades (underworld). Three permeates Greek myth: the fates are three, The Furies three, the Graces three, the harpies three, the Pythia or Sibyl (the Delphic oracle) sits on a three-legged stool, the Sibylline books are three times three, the Muses are three and so on [127: lines 32–39; and 128: lines 1–4].

71. Block in *Baseball Before We Knew It* writes:
Long before the advent of the Knickerbocker Base Ball Club, three-strikes-yer-out was an indelible feature of the game. In fact, the feature may actually derive from some of baseball's earliest ancestors….

J.F.C. Gutsmuths, the author of the 1796 rules for *Das Englicshe Base Ball*, specified that "the batter has three attempts to hit the ball while at home plate." … In the half century preceding the Knickerbocker rules of 1845, every published description of early baseball embraced some variant of the three-strike rule as a fundamental tenet of play [85: lines 25–27; and 86: lines 4–6, 10–12].

72. *Ibid.*, Block discusses Rule 15: "Three hands out, all-out," 88–90.

73. Artifacts (seals) showing the swastika and solar cross were found in the ancient city of Mohenjo-Daro of the Harappan Civilization of Ancient India. Walter A. Fairservis's work, *The Roots of Ancient India*, 275.

The swastika is also thought to represent two crossed snakes, a relic of earlier snake worship.

74. Readers will recall that the path of the sun at various times of the year, the coils of a serpent and the cross-section of a tree can all be represented by a spiral.

The Trident in ancient Hindu and Greek religions was regarded as a weapon against evil. Christians associated this symbol with the Devil and this was used to discredit pagan gods.

(1) Wilkinson's edition of *Signs and Symbols* states: "In most cultures the spiral is regarded as a feminine shape" (285: first column, lines 7–9).

And (2) Mark O'Connell and Raje Airey, *The Illustrated Encyclopedia of Signs and Symbols*, states:

Spiral: The clockwise spiral starts from the middle, symbolizes water, power, independent movement and migration. One of the most important and ancient symbols; most common of all decorative motifs throughout cultures. As an open and flowing line it suggests extension, evolution and continuity.

Spiral of life: Found in the Bronze Age in Ireland, this sign is drawn in one single line without beginning or end [243: first column, lines 1–17, 27–32].

75. There are various representations of these three legs with regards to knee angles and orientation of spins. Some rotations are in a clockwise and others in an counter-clockwise direction.

76. The Indian Vedic literature refers to the sun as the most beautiful creation. The motivation for the migration likely included following the path of the sun westwards.

77. Cielo in *Signs, Omens and Superstitions* (1918) writes:

Every nation had its lucky and unlucky numbers that occur in their mythology and history. Greeks believed in the sacredness of the number *Nine*. They had nine muses, nine principal deities, nine oracles etc. [103].

The Druids like the Brahmins were a numerate people. Curiously, there is an old Gaelic word "*Cuntas*, algorithm."

The number nine is thought to hold special significance in many cultures. The number nine if multiplied by whole numbers except zero will produce digits whose sum will be nine or multiples of nine. Examples: (1) $3 \times 9 = 27$, and $2 + 7 = 9$; (2) $9 \times 9 = 81$, and $8 + 1 = 9$; (3) $24 \times 9 = 216$, and $2 + 1 + 6 = 9$; (4) $132 \times 9 = 1188$, and $1+1+8+8 = 18$, and $1+8 = 9$ (Ref. of Cox and Foster).

78. Rutherford, *Celtic Lore*, 109: lines 3–5.

79. *Ibid.*, 91: lines 33–36.

80. Davies, *The Celts,* 91: lines 16–17.

81. Ross, *The Folklore of the Scottish Highlands*, 78: lines 32–36; 84: lines 31–36; and 85: lines 1–4.

82. Sandra Kynes, W*hisperer from the Woods. the Lore and Magic of Trees*, 11–12.

83. Dagda's special club can be compared to Thor's hammer and Indra's thunderbolt.

84. Old Gaelic, "*Naoi, Naonar,* nine"; "*Naoidho,* ninth"; "*Naochad, Deich, Ceithair Fichad,* ninety"; and "*Naoi Uaire,* nine-fold." Ninety feet as the distance of one side of the infield square shows this old British and Continental European influence.

85. Knowlson, *Origins of Popular Superstitions*, 45: line 33; and 46: lines 1–22.

Sir John Sinclair in *Statistical Account of Scotland* (1794), Vol. II writes:

The people of this district have two customs, which are fast wearing out, not only here but all over the Highlands and therefore to be taken notice of while they remain. Upon the First of May, which is called *Beltan* or *Bál-Tein*-day, all the boys in a township or hamlet meet in the moors. They cut a table in the green sod, of a round figure, by casting a trench in the ground of such circumference as to hold the whole company. They kindle a fire, and dress a repast of eggs and milk in the consistence of custard. They knead a cake of oatmeal, which is toasted at the embers against a stone. After the custard is eaten up, they divide the cake into so many portions, as similar as possible to one another in size and shape, as there are persons in the company. They daub one of these portions all over with charcoal until it be perfectly black. They put all the bits of the cake into a bonnet. Everyone, blindfolded, draws out a portion. He who holds the bonnet is entitled to the last bit. Whoever draws the black bit is the devoted person who is to be sacrificed to *Baal*, whose favour they mean to implore, in rendering the year productive of man and beast. There is little doubt of these inhuman sacrifices having been once offered in this country as well as in the East, although they now pass from the act of sacrificing, and only compel the *Devoted* person to leap three times through the flames; with which the ceremonies of this festival are closed... [620: lines 17–28; and 621: lines 1–13].

Similar descriptions are in the 1769 work of Thomas Pennant which is cited by Addy in *A Glossary of Words* (1888) Introduction, lii–liii.

86. Shahrukh Husain, *The Goddess: Power, Sexuality, and the Feminine Divine* (51: lines 21–29).

This goddess, Morgan the fate, was known by other similar names, the meaning is the same.

There are other popular goddesses. Morrigan, the early British (Irish) goddess of war, fertility, and vegetation, was also known as Macha, Melb or Maeve, Tara, Badb, Eriu, Fodla, Nemain and Rhiannon. She was worshipped from prehistoric times to Christianization (CE 400). Carvings and stone pillars bear her name (M. Jordan, *Dictionary of Gods and Goddesses*).

87. Rutherford, *Celtic Lore*, mentions a reenactment of a battle scene, one team representing the May Queen (Spring) and the other the Winter Queen (Winter) (92: lines 22–30).

Note 13.

88. The Norsemen once ruled Britain. These exposures would have reinforced their own beliefs. Norse and Icelandic mythologies also indicate the significance of the number nine (Havamal, a poem of the *Elder Adda*). The god Odin hung upside down from an ash (Yggdrasil) tree over a spring:

I know that I hung.
on the windswept tree,.
for nine full days....
I learned nine mighty songs....
(Mentioned in: (1) David Leeming's *The World of Myth*, 162; and (2) J. A. MacCulloch, *Celtic and Scandinavian Religion*, Section on Valkyries, 123–126).

89. Bhatttacharyya, *Ancient Indian Rituals*, writes that a wedding ceremony in Madras included acts where a mixture of nine different kinds of seeds were sown in a earthen pots and watered for four days before these seedlings were thrown into a river (see 106: 31–34).

This suggests that the number nine had a fertility connection in ancient India. The ancient Hindus also had ceremonies where nine plants were gathered to form the body of the goddess Gauri; and similarly a clay image of the goddess, Durga, and a bundle of nine plants were worshipped for nine days. The birth of a child is celebrated on the ninth day. Likewise on the ninth day, special rituals are performed after the death of a loved one. Appendix E provides further information.

90. Kenneth Johnson and Marguerite Elsbeth, *The Grail Castle*, 29: lines 2–18. more details on Finn MacCool on found on 195–196.

91. *Ibid.*, Johnson and Elsbeth write:
The Code of the Fenians clearly differs in many respects from the belief system of today's "macho man." ...

One of the secrets involved with being a Warrior is this: there is *Power* in helplessness, in recognizing one's vulnerabilities, frailties, and limitations. Only when the Warrior reaches inward to do battle with the darkness of his own shadow can he begin to assess the weaknesses of his true enemy. The Warrior needs to hone his mental and emotional faculties as well as his physical body if he is to survive in the chess game of life... [29: lines 19–20, 29–35].

92. Elder, *Celt, Druid, and Culdee* (57: lines 3–8, 19–24).

93. The selection process was also rigorous. Elder states that these restrictions were stringent with regards to parentage in that one had to show for nine successive generations his fore-fathers were free men. This was an effective way to keep out those of uncer-

tain paternity and retain a kind of hereditary priesthood (57: lines 9–18).

94. Approximately, one in fifteen players drafted make it to the Majors. Staying there is another matter.

95. Years of toiling, dedication and sacrifice are no guarantee of appropriate rewards. Those who cry there is no justice in this game may now seek comfort, as others of yesterday, by taking water from a place where three streams meet and beseeching a blessing from the sun at a high place with the invocation of earlier times. In one invocation, for example, they washed themselves in the nine rays of the sun. Ross, *The Folklore of the Scottish Highlands*:

> Another invocation, where the desired result is believed to be brought about by chanting the correct lines, and having highly-pagan sentiments, occurs in the beautiful *Ora Ceartais*, "Invocation for Justice." According to Carmichael, a person seeking justice used to go down at dawn where three streams met—always a magic place according to Celtic belief. When the sun shone on the very tops of the hill the man must cup his hands and fill them with water from the point where the streams met. He then dipped his face into his hands, and repeated the invocation [53: 10–27].

N.B.: Some major aspects (sun, serpent) of God are covered in the lines that followed (54: lines 1–9).

96. Rutherford, in *Celtic Lore*, mentions an aged Hebridean Islander, South Uist going up a local mound at sunrise to sacrifice a lamb. Uist is an island of the Outer Hebrides, Scotland (92: 16–17, 19–21).

There is precedent for similar survival of traditions and culture, etc., in India, there were Hindus who fled the advance of the Islamic invaders and dispersed in other places further into the countryside and more isolated places.

Similarly, despite the centuries and influences of the British, practices such as child infanticides, burning of widows (*Sati*), child brides, caste system and sacrifices (human and animal) to some deities continued in India. Some practices continued even after being prohibited by the British in the eighteenth and nineteenth centuries.

Chapter 11

1. The empirical observations are that the more religious a people are the more likely they are to be more superstitious. This does not imply that religions and superstitions are the same.

2. This belief of each inanimate object and animate being having a soul was once widespread in many cultures. Everything was therefore treated as the dwelling place of a spirit and therefore accorded proper respect.

Ancient Indians held similar beliefs, and some of these beliefs and practices have survived in India.

3. Shaw has the Old Gaelic word "*Saobhchrabhadh*, superstition." Julius Caesar writes in *Commentaries on the Gallic War* that the priests of the early British made vast figures (e.g., wicker men) which they filled with living men and then set on fire. This was an apparent sacrifice to appease a god such as *Taranis*. (The picture by Jenny Greenteeth in the work, *A to Z of the Occult*, by S. Cox and M. Foster, shows such a scene.) Caesar writes that they covered their altars, in their sacred groves, with blood of their sacrificial victims. He also mentions that they consulted their deities through human entrails (cf., the Romans used the entrails of chickens). Caesar describes these early British practices as inhuman superstitions. Gaius Paulinus in 61 CE had the priests killed and the sacred groves burned at Anglesey, called Mona, of the British Isles, the center of early British priests.

4. Hackwood summarizes the situation with regards to superstitions in *Staffordshire Customs and Folklore*, where he writes that superstitions continue long after knowledge has advanced and continue to influence our decisions (146: first column, lines 1–6, 7–10, 25–36).

5. The "superstitions" discussed herein do not include personal idiosyncrasies, ingrained peculiar habits, or possibly compulsive behaviors.

6. Baseball players in both America and Japan, two of the most highly technologically advanced and university-educated societies on the planet Earth show their own superstitions.

7. This is similar to the Hindu belief of predestination or karma, and that the wills of the gods can be changed with the appro-

priate rituals on the fire altars mediated by the Brahmin priests.

8. Preventative actions here would mean full planning, preparation and training for the upcoming battles. It would also include votive offerings and appropriate sacrifices to the gods. The Hindus similarly performed sacrifices or made votive offerings at their fire altars to ward off any portending mishaps or misfortunes foreseen by the sages.

9. Some individuals and societies are still struggling with the general acceptance of Darwin's ideas on evolution of species.

10. Knowlson, *The Origins of Popular Superstitions*, 1: lines 1–16.

11. This probably laid the foundations for their concerns about the natural environment, e.g., trees have their own spirits or that the spirits of the departed dwell in the trees, hence trees were not to be willfully destroyed. For example, the Irish believed in *Fairies* and *Leprechauns*, and the Scottish in *Brownies* and *Kelpies*. Likewise the English believed in *Fairies* and *Hobgoblins*, Scandinavians in *Elves*, Teutonic peoples in *Fairies*, *Trolls*, *Gnomes*, and *Dwarves*, and the French in *Goblins*, *Lutins* (a type of hobgoblins), and *Fées* (fairies). A four-leafed clover was thought to mark the spot where fairies gathered; hence the four-leafed clover brought good luck (Astra Cielo, *Signs Omens and Superstitions*).

12. This knocking on wood was supposed to be done three times to be effective. It was thought that "knocking on wood" kept evil or malicious spirits away.

13. Raymond Lamont Brown, *A Book of Superstitions*, 8: lines 1–8.

14. *Ibid.* Brown writes:

Today, as it has been from the dawn of time, man's superstitions have taken three definite forms. The first of which is prohibition, or taboo, in which it is believed that actions will provoke evil spirits, or in a more modern sense ill-luck will ensue....

The second form of superstition is the ritual in which a sequence of events brings about desired effects. The third concerns omens—the portents and forewarnings by which, it is claimed, a specific result may be expected [8: lines 9–16, 34; 9: lines 1–3; and 10: lines 15, 16–22].

In addition, Anne Ross in *The Folklore of* *the Scottish Highlands* writes: "Lucky signs were known as *Rathadach;* unlucky omens were called *Rosadach*" (99: lines 12–13).

15. *Ibid.*, 10: lines 15, 16–22.

16. It must not be assumed all superstitions had negative implications or consequences.

17. The early British festival of Beltane is still celebrated by thousands every year, e.g., on Calton Hill, Edinburgh, Scotland.

18. McNeill, "A Scottish Calendar" in *Scotland: A Description of Scotland and Scottish Life*, writes about the Beltane festival which included bonfires, dancing, roasting eggs and rolling bannocks down the hillsides. This celebration was done in nineteenth century in the village communities (Henry W. Meikle, ed.: 255, lines 18–30). McNeill continues:

In early times the Celtic year began in the winter, and Hallowe'en was thus the Celtic New Year's Eve. As at Beltane, great fires burned on the hilltops; but whereas those of Beltane, were lit at dawn, the Hallowe'en fires were lit at dusk. These fires have burned down the centuries to our time in an unbroken chain. In the sixties of the last century [nineteenth], an Edinburgh man, travelling from Dunkeld to Aberfedy, counted no less than thirty bonfires on the hills, each having a ring of people dancing round it. Shortly before the First World War, "On a crisp autumn night, in a remote part of the Highland," writes a correspondent to a Scottish newspaper, "we were looking over to where the dark mountains were silhouetted against the rising moon. For miles the landscape was dotted at wide intervals with bonfires that blazed against the dark hillside. The date was 31st October, and these bonfires were the direct descendants of the fires lit each year by the ancient Druids" [258: lines 17–32].

19. Analogous or almost identical beliefs and practices are still held by Hindus and Hindu-impacted areas of the world. It underlines the idea that the early Brtish and Continental European peoples were of Indo-European origins. Astrology still plays a significant role in the lives of the Hindus of India. It is said that no major business or personal decision is made without consulting the stars via astrology.

These bonfires as indicated before were for the burning of sacrifices, except now animals or humans were not used. The Hindus have a similar custom of burning the Holi at the Phagwah festival.

20. These eastern centers of learning were influenced by Buddhism, which in turn was influenced by Hinduism. This explains the likely connection between early British teachings and that of other eastern philosophy impacted by Buddhism and Hinduism (Appendix E).

21. Old Gaelic, *Leug*, "a diamond or Gem"; and "*Leug* or *Lugh*, name of triune sun-god;" and "*druichd, cruiniog, druichdan, ceobrin, dealt* dew." Note that some of the old words for "dew" were close to the word "druid" suggesting a religious connection. On May Day (May 1) celebrations in honor of the sun god, *Beal*, women bathed their faces with dew from the grass; the dew was thought to have special properties of making a person beautiful. Dew is analogous to the holy Christian or consecrated water.

22. George Frederick Kunz, *The Mystical Lore of Precious Stones*, Vol. 1, 79: lines 22–29.

23. The widespread belief of the ancient world was that one person, by merely looking at another, has the power to jinx or affect and so bring bad luck, illness, or misfortune on another. It is mentioned in the Bible (e.g., Proverbs 23:6 and Mark 7: 21–22.) Ref., Simon Cox and Mark Foster, *An A to Z of the Occult*, Sub-heading "Evil Eye," 70–73.

24. A diamond engagement ring was thought to bring good luck. It is thought that the first diamonds discovered by Europeans in South Africa were found in a sorcerer's bag. The Hindus wear a diamond on the forehead as a guardian against misfortune and also as a bringer of good luck. Other cultures similarly venerate diamonds (Kunz, *The Mystical Lore of Precious Stones*, 81).

25. An Indian salve for use on the eyes included powdered antimony compounds in the mixture. Modern baseball players commonly wear shoe polish or lamp-black to reduce the glare of the sun.

26. Brown, *A Book of Superstitions* (13: lines 4–10).

Stones were placed on rings. Rings were often used in divinations. A gold ring was thought to bring good luck, and silver, peace.

27. Indian craftsmen and jewellers did the same for their people. Indian women are dressed with intricately designed jewelry especially on special and festive occasions.

28. Certain stones were thought to possess remarkable magical powers and protective properties. This led to both a continuation and reinforcement of beliefs in the special talismanic properties of crystals. The tradition of wearing stones as jewelry is still seen, as Ross in *The Folklore of the Scottish Highlands* indicates:

> Some charms were incanted for specific types of evil magic, others to counteract enchantment in general. One of the latter type, much used in the Outer Isles, is associated, like so many, with the beloved saint, Brigit or Bride, once a powerful Goddess invoked widely over the pagan Celtic world and in Christian times venerated as Saint Brigit of Kildare, where, in true pagan fashion, nine virgins perpetually attended her fire, which was never allowed to be extinguished.
>
> Deeply-rooted and ancient traditions underlie the widespread belief in this evil power; it filled people with dread, and many people feared it so much that their lives were hemmed in and affected by taboos connected with it [78: lines 29–36; 84: lines 31–36; and 85: lines 1–4].

Hackwood in *Staffordshire Customs, Superstitions and Folklore* defines "charm":

> The charm, the amulet or the talismanic, that magic object the possession of which brought the owner good luck or in some way influenced the fates to his own advantage might consist of almost anything, not the least curious form being that of a word or phrase [148: first column, lines 45–51].

Chapter XXXVI—"Popular Superstitions," 146–152.

29. The word oval comes from ova, an egg. Astra Cielo in *Signs, Omens and Superstitions* writes:

> Eggs have many mystic meanings, and in olden times were supposed to symbolize the world. The yolk represented our earth, the white our atmosphere, and the shell was the firmament. ...
> The druids used eggs in their religious

festivals and considered it the symbol of fecundity. Every Druid wore an egg about his neck, encased in gold, as symbol of his priestly authority. …

Eggs laid on Good Friday are revered in Catholic countries as bringing good luck, and carefully kept all the year as talismans. They are supposed to keep the house free from fire.

In Scotland an "eirack's" egg, that is, the first egg that is laid by a young hen is gathered as the principal ingredient of Hallowe'en charm [31: lines 1–4, 19–22, 25–31].

Ross in *The Folklore of the Scottish Highlands*, cites a poem by Alexander Carmichael, an expert in the folklore of the Scottish Highlands. In this work, charms were made with Brigit invoked as protector against misfortune, evil beings and malicious persons that would bring harm to crop, livestock and self (78: lines 37–38; and 79: 1–5). Alexander Carmichael (1864–1929) "collected a huge body of folklore" of the Highlands and other areas of Scotland (Ross, 84).

Old Gaelic: "*Olcas*, evilness;" and "*Aidhbhram, Cronaithan, Fulradharcam*, to bewitch" (Shaw, *A Galic to English Dictionary*).

30. The priests, later called conjurors and magicians after the arrival of Christianity, casted spells and curses on Roman invaders before their battles. In Addy's work the remnants of the earlier Druidic priesthood before Christianity were called "wise men."

31. Lug was regarded as one of the "Tuatha De Danaan," or "People of The Goddess Danu." J.A. MacCulloch in *The Celtic and Scandinavian Religions* writes:

They [The Tuatha De Danaan] came from heaven says one account, which fits in well with their character. They know magic; they possess magic treasures, e.g., inexhaustible cauldron of Dagda, the matchless spear of Lug, and the unconquerable sword of Nuada... [41: lines 21–25].

The Formorians were the indigenuous peoples of early Britain.

32. Currently, it seems that lavish jewelries have been displaced by tattoos; their original roles were also as lucky charms and protection from evil. Tattoos were a popular early British practice. The Lindow man found in the bog was heavily tattooed. This body-art

form is back in style. The Hindus still practice tattooing of the body using henna dye.

33. Kunz, *The Mystical Lore of Precious Stones*, Vol. 1, 77: lines 5–13.

Kunz adds: "Reuss calls it [diamond] 'a gem of reconciliation.' As it enhanced the love of a husband and wife" (77: lines 13–15).

Marbodus, Bishop of Rennes, France, wrote a poetical treatise on the virtues of precious stones thought to be written near the end of the eleventh century. His work was later printed in 1531 (Kunz 15 and 16).

Most recently, Robert Simmons, *Stones of the New Consciousness, Healing, Awakening & Co-Creating with Crystals, Minerals & Gems*, outlines the rationales for the usage of diamonds in meditation, healing and everyday life.

34. The crucifix is also said to be an old British and Continetal European pre-Christian symbol.

35. That is, the sun-god, *Beal*, or the triune sun god, *Leug.*

36. Kunz, Vol. 1, 76: lines 23–29; and 77: lines 1–2.

37. Steve Roud, *The Penguin Guide to the Superstitions of Britain and Ireland*, Section, "Stones: Holed," 437: column two, lines 6–11.

38. This traditional design is still seen on the MLB Detroit Tigers' diamond.

39. Ross, *The Folklore of the Scottish Highlands*, notes one incantation for a charm, from the Outer Hebrides in which the name of Mary was invoked in the charm as protection from all harm who harbours ill will and thought to possess an "Evil Eye" (64: lines 20–25).

As it was with folks of yesteryear in the Scottish Highlands, many of those who wear jewels as charms seem to be adherents of the Roman Catholic faith. Many individuals similarly make the sign of the cross before batting or pitching, or after getting a hit or achieving a strikeout.

40. The color blue was used as a talisman in amulets against the "Evil Eye." In India, babies are adorned with a necklace consisting of a cord with blue beads (Ref. of Cox and Foster has details).

41. Players would deny that they are superstitious, because in doing so they may invite opponents, rivals or fans to take counteractive actions to undo the magic or fear others would make fun of their player's beliefs.

42. The British had "no spitting in public places" in their health advisory information, "The Laws of Health," that was promoted in their colonies. This became a universal code of conduct with regards to personal hygiene in the British Commonwealth Countries. It dealt with washing of hands, turning your face aside from others and used a handkerchief when sneezing or coughing etc.

The old British health authorities got that code right, especially now when viewed in the light of the modern understanding of the spread of communicable viral diseases, e.g., HIV-AIDS and SARS influenza.

Now in baseball, this needless and unsightly spitting is overly exaggerated. Or most likely, the old British standards of personal hygiene were not taught in some of their colonies.

It should be noted that in old films of the Wild West, a symbol of manhood or toughness was one who cold spit the most and furthest. This was done especially before a fight.

43. Brand, *Popular Antiquities*, section on "Saliva or Spitting" (723: lines 1–5; and: lines 26–33).

44. Rabbi Dr. R. Brasch in *How Did It Begin? Customs & Superstitions and Their Romantic Origins* writes:

> The habit of spitting on things for luck has a sacred origin. It leads back to belief in magic and the story of the Gospels.
>
> Ancient man regarded spittle as representative of his soul. To expectorate, therefore, was like making an offering to the gods who, in return, would extend protection to the spitter....
>
> Human saliva served as a charm against witchcraft and enchantment and was considered a potent antidote against every type of poison. The magical rite of spitting thus found its place in primitive medicine, especially in treating the eyes.
>
> In pugilistic bouts in ancient days, fighters spat on their hands, expecting that this would magically increase the strength of their blows [18: lines 36–37; and 19: lines 1–3, 10–16].

45. Roud, *The Penguin Guide to the Superstitions of Britain and Ireland,* 430: column two, lines 45–47; and 431: column one, lines 30–32. Several other examples are given on 430–431.

46. Hitting successfully is valued and once a player can hit well, he will find his name on the line-up card of professional baseball teams before game time.

47. The spitting of black tobacco juice would certainly disgust any self-respecting spirit who may be lurking around watching the game. The fairies would certainly move away, since they were reputed to appreciate and reward cleanliness. In the olden times, tobacco was not known. The practice of smoking or chewing tobacco originated from North America. The Hindus were chewing betel leaves and spitting the black liquid thereby produced.

48. The visiting team would spit to avoid misfortune, while the home team crowd wishes that they fail miserably. The home team knows that the visiting team's supporters elsewhere are wishing that they fail.

49. We are reminded of where Cielo in *Signs, Omen and Superstitions* mentions one superstition of Orthodox Jews: "Evil Eye.—To avert the curse of the evil eye, spit three times on your finger tips and make a quick movement with your hand through the air" (93).

50. Pitchers may do likewise. Some look towards the heavens acknowledging the presence and power of the devine. On cold days, the umpire may allow the pitcher to blow on his hands.

51. For example, Knowlson, *Origins of Popular Superstitions* (59: lines 8–12, 19–21, 27–29, 31; and 168: lines 1, 6–10).

52. Chalk was common in Ireland, cliffs to the east of Portrush in County Antrim, Northern Ireland were called the "White Cliffs." In England, there are the famous "White Cliffs" of Dover, Kent.

Lime is calcium oxide, CaO; slaked lime, quick lime or hydrated lime is calcium hydroxide, $Ca(OH)_2$; and chalk is calcium carbonate, $CaCO_3$. Underground caves are found in Britain where chalk was mined. These were reputedly used for pagan rituals by possibly latter day British Druids in the seventeenth to nineteenth centuries.

53. Michael Edwardes, *Everyday Life in Early India*, 54: lines 9–13.

54. During the Second World War, the stereotyped image of an American soldier overseas was one who was chewing gum or tobacco.

55. Bonwick in *Irish Druids and Old Irish Religions* (1894) writes about the chewing of

the thumb to discourage evil. For example, the Irish hero Fionn chewed his thumb and the attractive woman next to him was forced into her true form, that being an old hag with evil intentions. If one is sufficiently astute, one can ward off bad spirits by chewing on one's thumb when the occasion arises. This old chewing of the thumb was just as effective as making the sign of the cross (50: lines 13–23).

56. The new NY Yankees stadium was opened for the 2009 baseball season, but the old traditions continues in the new stadium.

This is more so for the rookie players.

57. Ross in *The Pagan Celts*, 154: lines 33–37; 155: lines 5–14, 40–41; 156: lines 1–9; and 157: lines 3–7, 10–12.

Ross in *Pagan Celtic Britain*, Sub-section titled: "Documentary Evidence for the Cult of the Head," 155–161.

58. The high intellectual output of that area of New England is probably a reflection of the relatively high number of the early Brtish leadership and descendants who initially settled in that area. The witch trials in Salem began in 1692; this suggests a possible re-emergence of early pre–Christian pagan rituals, or paranoia by overzealous Puritans.

59. If a former Boston Red Sox player signs with another team that offers more financial incentives, he is forgiven; but, if he signs with the hated Yankees, this is seen as a sign of "betrayal." This "betrayal" is viewed as the worse thing a former Red Sox player could possibly do.

As mentioned before, war, sports, culture and religion were inter-related; and so were the associated rites and rituals. This situation is similar to the society of the Hindus of India, where religion, culture, and philosophy are intertwined.

60. No other modern voice, except that of the late Ms. Kate Smith, at any baseball game has ever so stirred the "soul" or evoked such emotions.

Lugnasad was also known as Lammas Eve, celebrated on 1st August.

61. Some baseball parks have introduced "speed dating," thereby giving single young people a chance to meet in a non-threatening atmosphere. For example, this is now an annual feature at the "Skydome" of the Toronto Blue Jays.

Rutherford (*Celtic Lore*) writes:

> In pagan times weddings were solemnized nearby. Until recently, young men and women would pledge themselves to a trial marriage here, and should it prove a failure, return the following year to dissolve them [95: lines 2–4].

Rutherford describes the trial marriage practices of young men and women at the Lammas fair at Kirkwall and Orkneys (95: lines 7–10).

Old Gaelic, "*Lurag* meant young pretty female;" "*Ogun*, a young man;" "*Ogh* whole, entire;" "*Ugh*, an egg;" and "*Ughamhuil*, oval." This similarity of the old words indicates a connection with the people and their oval place.

62. Kunz notes:

> Reuss calls it "a gem of reconciliation," as it enhanced the love of a husband for his wife…. A curious fancy, prevalent in regard to many stones, attributed sex to the diamond, and it is therefore not surprising that these stones were also supposed to possess reproductive powers…. If, however, the diamond (or turquoise) were offered as a pledge of love or friendship, the spirit was quite willing to transfer its good offices from one owner to another [77: lines 13–15; and 79: lines 11–14].

Chapter 12

1. Nicholas Copernicus's (1473–1543) heliocentric work was published just before his death. Galileo Galilei championed Copernicanism (from 1610 onwards) and consequently had to face the wrath of the Catholic Church's inquisition (1632).

2. Spirals that were tightly wound represented the winter sun and the less tightly wound, spirals the summer sun.

3. The planet Earth is spinning or rotating at the rate of 1,031 miles per hour or 1,667 kilometers per hour. This rotational velocity is at a maximum at the equator and reduces towards zero as the poles, North and South, are approached.

4. This was first worked out by the French physicist Gustave-Gaspard Coriolis (1792–1843) in 1835. Hence this effect is called the *Coriolis* Effect.

5. More details are given by, for example, John Lynch in *The Weather*.

6. A tilt of 23.5° degrees is responsible for the different hemispheres (north and south) to be at different angles to the sun at different times of the year.

7. The formal study of these biological temporal rhythms in response to the daily, tidal, weekly, seasonal, and annual rhythms is called chronobiology.

8. Strictly speaking, the water from geothermal and hydro-electrical sources is influenced by the sun's impact on cloud formation and movement etc.

9. John Lynch, *The Weather*, 14: column 2, lines 5–17.

10. Old Gaelic, "*Cuidhal Fhniomh* meant spinning wheel." In some cultures the sun god traverses the sky in his wheeled chariot—often with 4 spokes. Appendices E and F.

11. "Red sky at night, shepherd's delight. Red sky in the morning, shepherd's warning."

12. Several myths acknowledged the importance of weather in wars and struggles. Some stories mention that the early British high priests, Druids, were able to raise fog, mists, and storms in battles or cause these to disappear. This shows that early commanders and soldiers, like others, desired weather conditions to be in their favor whenever they went to war. Priestly incantations and sacrifices were made to ensure favorable conditions for their own side. For example, early British priests in their battles with the Romans at Anglesey, Wales, in 61 CE sought to invoke foul weather and curses on their invaders. These invocations of weather (and sun or moon) in warfare were not confined to only insular British and Germanic peoples.

The Hindu God, Indra, used lightning to destroy the fortifications of his opponents.

Brahmin priests of India also had incantations which were directed to affect weather conditions.

In Biblical times (Old Testament, Book of Joshua, 10: 12–14), Joshua commanded the sun to stay up so that his soldiers could continue their battles with the enemy. This impact of weather on war has continued in modern times, for example, the timing of the historic D-Day invasion of Normandy in World War II was influenced by weather conditions. German High Command thought an invasion by Allied Forces was unlikely because of bad weather conditions.

13. Hindus still continue old traditions in which they greet the sun in their daily puja rituals at dawn, seeking to invoke his blessings for the day. Appendix E has further details in the similarities between Indian and early British religious rituals.

14. Wood, *The Boy's Modern Playmate*, 159: lines 1–2, 15.

15. Ross in *The Folklore of the Scottish Highlands*, writes:

> The very names of the quarters of Celtic year are pre–Christian. *Earrach*, "Spring"; *Sambradh*, "Summer"; *Foghara*, "Harvest"; *Geambrach*, "Winter." And in the main, the ancient pagan quarterly festivals, for purification and good fortune, have continued to be practised at the same calendar seasons [118: lines 3–7].

16. Exceptions now occur in some tropical countries. Some countries in which "winter ball" is played include Mexico, Puerto Rico, and Venezuela. Games are played there during times when Northern countries are experiencing winter.

17. There is precedent for this lighting of the arena. The Roman Coliseum (amphitheater) was at times lit for evening games and entertainment during special occasions. Will Durant in *Caesar and Christ, A History of Roman Civilization from Their Beginnings to A.D. 325. Part III,* writes:

> On occasion the entire multitude might be fed by the order and bounty of the emperor, or dainties and presents might be scattered among the scrambling crowd. If as sometimes occurred, contests were presented at night, a circle of lights could be lowered over the arena and spectators. Bands of musicians performed in the interludes and accompanied the crises of the combats with exciting crescendo strains [384: lines 16–21].

Workers of the laboring classes and freed slaves in America of the recent past were able to attend evening games (often played by visiting "barnstorming" teams) after work in well-lit fields. The advent of electrical lighting made this possible.

The same pattern is seen today where both light and music enhance the dramas of the battle unfolding on the diamond.

18. Old Gaelic, "*Niomhdha*, bright, shining;" and "*Niomhan*, to shine, glitter."

19. Old Gaelic, "*suilbhirachd*, smiling."

20. Sea level is the reference point for atmospheric pressure measurement. The old units of measurement of standard atmospheric pressure (atm.) were 14.7 pounds per square inch and 760 mm or 76 cm of mercury. The new unit of reference for standard atmospheric pressure is 101.325 kPa (kPa—kilo Pascal). As height increases, one bears less weight of air on one's body. The barometric pressure therefore falls in proportion to the height reached.

21. The electromagnetic radiation that reaches earth makes it warm.

22. The air is being heated directly by the sun and also receiving energy from the heated earth.

23. Water vapor is an aggregation of water molecules. This aggregation of water molecules makes the air less dense. The water molecules (H_2O, Relative Molecular Weight, RMW, of 18) replace, e.g., the heavier oxygen (O_2, RMW, 32), nitrogen (N_2, RMW, 28) and carbon dioxide (CO_2, RMW, 44) molecules. Hence moist air is less dense than dry air and will tend to rise above the dry air. This explains why clouds are formed high above our heads.

This is based on Avogadro's law which basically states that equal volumes of all gases at the same temprature and pressure contain the same number of molecules.

Moist air is less dense than drier air at the same temperature and pressure for the same volumes.

24. This is the same observable effect as one running (or biking) with the wind and against the wind.

25. The effect is smaller because of the shorter distance between the mound and the home plate.

26. Two excellent references on these topics are the works of (1) Robert K. Adair, *The Physics of Baseball*, and (2) Robert G. Watts and A. Terry Bahill, *Keep Your Eye on the Ball*.

27. Faster outfielders are best suited to cover the extra distances.

28. The composition of air percentage (%) by volume: Nitrogen (N_2), 78.09%; Oxygen (O_2), 20.95%; Argon (Ar), 0.93%; Carbon Dioxide (CO_2), 0.038%; others gases (less than 0.002% each), Neon (Ne), Helium (He) Krypton (Kr), Hydrogen (H_2), and Xenon (Xe). In the atmosphere can also be found trace amounts of other gases (Carbon Monoxide (CO); Sulfur Dioxide (SO_2); Nitrous Oxide (N_2O); Nitrogen Dioxide (NO_2); Methane (CH_4); Ozone (O_3); and Ammonia (NH_3). The atmosphere also contains variable amounts of water vapor (H_2O), dust particles, pollen, and other solid particles; the variation is dependent on time and place.

The breathed out air, from a person's lungs, contains, by volume, about 14% oxygen and 4.4% carbon dioxide.

29. The average adult at rest breathes about 12 to 20 times per minute, and the exercising adult about 35 to 45 breaths per minute.

Chapter 13

1. The then Major League Baseball Detroit Tigers president John McHale said of the old Tiger Stadium: "There is real sense of communing with the gods of baseball in a building like this." The last game played in the old Tiger stadium was in 1999. The home of the Detroit Tigers is Comerica Park (2000 to present) which maintains some of the charms of the old Tiger Stadium.

Bill Klem, an umpire, on "Bill Klem Day" in 1949 said: "Baseball is more than a game to me—it's a religion." Paul Dickson, *Baseball's Greatest Quotations* (225).

2. *Ibid.*, Ebert Hubbard was quoted as having said: "The new definition of a heathen is a man who never played baseball" (192).

3. High definition (HD) television makes the action even more alive and the observer feels involved, and being right there and in the moment.

4. Bill Shea, a then Met executive, was widely quoted with: "Families go to ballparks and that is why baseball is still our national game" (Dickson, [391]).

5. *Ibid.*, Richard Gilman: "Baseball is a game dominated by vital ghosts; it's a fraternity like no other we have of the active and the longer so, the living and the dead" (159).

6. *Ibid.*, Ernie Harwell:
Baseball is ballet without music. Drama without words. A carnival without kewpie dolls.

Baseball is continuity. Pitch to pitch. Inning to inning. Game to game. Series to series. Season to season.

Baseball? It's just a game—as simple as a ball and a bat. Yet, as complex as the American spirit it symbolizes. It's a sport, busines and sometimes even religion [177].

7. For example, in one game (May 20th 2010, at Safeco Field) between Toronto's Blue Jays (25–17) and Seattle's Mariners (14–26), in the bottom of the ninth, the score was 3 to 1 for Jays. The Jays' closer Kevin Gregg walked in two runs. The game was tied 3 to 3. Struggling and aging superstar Ken Griffey, Jr., came up as a pinch hitter. Fans were hoping for this match-up and picturing him being the local hero. Griffey drove in the winning run.

8. Bill James in Dickson, *Baseball's Greatest Quotations*:

Some years ago, it occurred to me that there must be dozens of ballplayers in each generation who leave a mark on the game in one way or another, and that when you go to a game you can therefore see the tracks of hundreds of players…

When you see the first baseman playing in front of the base runner, in his line of sight rather than standing behind him, who are you seeing? Willie Stargell [205].

9. The mid-seventh inning stretch and singing of "Take Me Out to the Ball Game" are designed to energize the home crowd to get them more involved in this particular game and time. The fans must enthusiastically cheer ("Make some noise!") for the home team. The crowd must be sent home feeling well as they did their part in this worship service. Dave Winfield wanted the participation of the fans in the stands during the 1992 World Series in Toronto vs. visiting Atlanta Braves. Fans responded to the call that "Winfield wants noise!"

10. Leo Durocher said, "I never questioned the integrity of an umpire. Their eyesight, yes" (Dickson, [120]).

Doug Harvey, after a member of his umpiring crew admitted to getting a call wrong: "That's what it means to be an umpire. You have to be honest even when it hurts" (176).

Kyle Garlett and Patrick O'Neal, *The Worst Call Ever! The Most Infamous Calls Ever Blown by Referees, Umpires, and Other Blind*

Officials, report that while at a ball game shortly after World War II, General Douglas MacArthur said: "It is wonderful to be here, to be able to hear the baseball against the bat, the ball against the glove, and to be able to boo the umpire" (front matter, epigraph).

11. Larry Goetz, a National League umpire, said: "It isn't enough for an umpire merely to know what he's doing. He has to look as though he knows what he's doing, too" (Dickson, 159).

12. The coach or manager may feel that his player is being squeezed. He therefore goes to the mound to talk with his pitcher and waits for the umpire to come and break up the meeting. The coach or manager then quietly voices his displeasure of the poor calls. In this way he avoids further alienating the umpire.

Warren Giles as National League president says that a corrupt umpire is not possible. He points out that tempers may be raised in the heat of the play and it is impossible to always make the correct call (*Ibid.*, 158).

13. Larry Goetz, an umpire on why managers should be thrown out instead of players, stated that people pay to see the players not the officials (Dickson, 159).

14. *Ibid.*, Eric Gregg said a manager ejects himself by his words or actions, since they know what is allowed (169).

15. *Ibid.*, Frank Robinson in a 1974 CBS's interview, after being hired as the first black MLB manager, said his color should make no difference to the game and public approval since people come to see the players and not the manager, who is only visible when he brings out the line-up card and when he behaves improperly (263).

16. This hostile crowd effect is regularly observed in Boston's Fenway Park and New York's Yankee Stadium, particularly when these two teams meet.

17. This was evident a few years ago in an important game of the Chicago Cubs at Wrigley Field. The youthful offender had to be escorted to safety by security officials.

18. Mudcat Grant said: "Those fans say things about your mother that makes you want to get up in the stands and punch a few of them" (Dickson, 167).

19. They are both the beleaguered under siege and the cavalry coming to the rescue of

their brethren. They are now doubly motivated.

20. Donald Hall writes: "We pretend to forgive failure: really we celebrate it. Bonehead Merkle lives forever and Bill Mazeroski's home run fades" (Dickson, 173).

21. Now the masses (including at home radio, television and Internet audiences) have an additional powerful effect on the game. Televised games cater not only to the crowds at the park, but also to other fans elsewhere—at home or in different states or time zones. The playing times of the games are usually chosen so that the games are on prime time television. This maximizes viewing audiences and consequently increases television advertising revenues. Times between innings and pitching changes provide ample opportunities for commercial advertisements. Late starts of games to accommodate prime time television often do not seem to take into account the best interests of the players, e.g., "Is this their peak time for best performance and less chances of being tired and becoming injured? Is this time too late for the home-team fans, especially the younger ones, who have to work or go to school the next day? Would the too tired fans be more likely to get into driving accidents on their way home?"

Chapter 14

1. Marshall McLuhan (1911–1980), Canadian communication theorist, was the author of the terms "Global Village," and "The Medium Is the Massage." Joseph A. Reaves, *Taking in a Game: Baseball in Asia* (12); and McLuhan, "Baseball Is Culture" in Humber and St James, *All I Thought About Was Baseball* (209–214).

2. This certainly applies to America, the center of baseball. It was said that anyone who wants to understand America must first understand baseball. The major issues of this society are reflected in the game, for example, the acceptance of African Americans in Major League Baseball.

3. Evolutionary struggles are usually over relatively longer periods of time, however, the end result of progression or termination is the same.

4. When good things happen, this is often called luck, good breaks, smiles, favors, or pleasures of the known or unknown gods;

similarly, when bad things happen, this is referred to as bad luck, poor breaks, or frowns and displeasures of the temperamental gods.

5. In this modern electronic and high technological age, the demise of baseball itself was predicted, yet it rebounds again and again.

6. Man-to-man duels were a way of settling personal differences or disputes across many cultures. Non-human primates also settle scores this way in their quests for dominance.

7. Early fighting clubs in America were too bloody and violent and were conducted in secret, away from the eyes of children, women and the law.

8. An analogous situation is the current emergence of Mixed Martial Arts (MMA) across North America.

9. The batter may also make a sacrifice for the good of his team.

10. Reaves, *Taking in a Game. A History of Baseball in Asia*. Chapter 4: *Japan's National Game*.

11. The saying of "one pitch at a time" is analogous to the often advocated survival strategy under adverse circumstances, where life is best lived "one day at a time."

12. Spalding, 9: lines 11–12 and 17–20.

Unlike baseball, other sports, such as Welsh football, in the eighteenth century were more warlike, as indicated by an observer, Rhys Cox, in the eighteenth century by Collins, Martin, and Vamplew in *Encyclopedia of Traditional British Rural Sports* writes:

> Numbers of players would be left here and there on the road, some having limbs broken, in the struggle, others severely injured, and some carried on biers to be buried in the churchyard nearest to where they had been mortally injured.
>
> Almost as fearful was a game, again in Anglesey, mentioned in a diary entry by William Bulkeley in April 1734, which showed that violence left no hard feelings, the sides parting as "good friends as they came, after they had spent half an hour together cherishing their spirits with a cup of ale … having finished Easter Holydays innocently and merrily" [121: Column one, lines 25–40].

Underdown, *Revel, Riot, and Rebellion, Popular Politics and Culture in England, 1603–1660*, writes that in England, Football was:

A more or less ritualized combat between communities often represented by virtually the entire male population parishes, it was an appropriate expression of parochial loyalty against outsiders, in which the identity of the individual was almost submerged in that of the group... [75: lines 11–15].

Rough play was already an established tradition in Britain, and the church was speaking out against it. Wales and England were sources of immigrants to America. The situation was very much the same for Ireland and Scotland, for example, the intense Scottish game called *Ba.*

13. British national pride came into play, it was said that the British would rather lose a war than a cricket test match to any of its then colonies, e.g., Australia, India, Pakistan, New Zealand, South Africa and the British West Indies (a term that included then British Guiana).

14. This quote appears in: *Devotions Upon Emergent Occasions, Meditation XVII.* Donne, who wrote the poem: "No man is an island," was a Christian, but this inter-connectedness of living things is shared by other established religions such as Buddhism, Jainism and Hinduism.

15. This pattern also extended to other smaller non–Christian communities, for example, in Vancouver, British Columbia, Canada, a Buddhist temple and baseball diamond (Oppenheimer Park) were constructed side by side. Vancouver was also once home to the locally- and West Coast–renowned pre–World War II Japanese Canadian Asahi Baseball Club.

16. This was in line with the pattern mentioned in England by solicitor William Bray and writer David Underdown in earlier chapters.

17. Spalding 4: lines 24–30; and 6: lines 20–24.

18. Underdown also mentions the playing of British football (or soccer) and its unseemly consequences such as drinking and fighting (74–77).

19. Earlier, in 1838, Carver, *The Book of Sports*, and in 1884, Chadwick, *The Sports and Pastimes of American Boys*, emphasized the usefulness of sports for young Americans.

20. Sacred places usually stood out in their natural surroundings, e.g., sacred groves, springs, rivers, mountains, and holy wells.

Now special features are incorporated in the construction of baseball stadiums to inspire and awe fans.

Special events are held there, examples of such events which have become historical and endeared are Lou Gehrig's farewell speech, Mickey Mantle's hit streak of 56 games, Ted Williams' batting average of 0.400, and Jackie Robinson's MLB debut.

21. Elder, *Celts Druids and Culdee*, 88: lines 20–21.

Williams Morgan in *St. Paul in Britain; Or, the Origin of British as Opposed to Papal Christianity* (1880) states:

It has been observed by the historian Hume, "that no religion has ever swayed the minds of men like the Druidic." The determined efforts of the Roman Empire to overthrow its supremacy, and, if possible, suppress it altogether, prove that its rulers had been made practically aware of this fact. A Druidic triad familiar to the Greeks and Romans was *"Three Duties of Every Man: Worship God; Be Just to All Men; Die for Your Country.**" It was this last duty, impressed by a thousand examples and precepts, and not its religious tenets or philosophy, which caused Druidism to be marked for destruction by an Empire which aspired to universal dominion and to merge all nationalities in one city. The edicts of the Emperors Augustus and Tiberius proscribed it throughout their dominions, making the exercise of the functions of a Druidic priest, as those of the Roman priest in the Reigns of the Tudor Sovereigns in England, a Treasonable Offence.

*There is touching beauty of the Druidic triads, as in the following:– "There are three men all should love: He that loves the face of his mother Nature; he that loves rational works of art: he that looks lovingly on the faces of little children" [60: lines 7–25].

The triad is simply an alternative version of the old battle cry "For God, King and Country." In the days of the divine "Right of Kings," when the king was God or God's chosen representative on earth, the battle cry was shortened to "King and Country."

22. I pledge allegiance to the Flag
of the United States of America,

and to the Republic for which it stands: one Nation under God, indivisible, With Liberty and Justice for all.

23. Americans pay great respect to their military personnel, and view those who suffer on behalf of the nation as genuine American heroes of unquestionable patriotism. Several former military personnel who served with distinction were elected to serve as presidents, congressmen and senators.

24. *Greek Lyrics* translated by Richard Lattimore. The ancient Greek poet, general and statesman, Tyrtaéus of Sparta (second half of the seventh century BCE) writes: *Courage: Heros Morteus: Heros Vivus* (14: lines 7–35; and 15: lines 1–16).

25. Many professional baseball players gave up baseball to serve in wars and some did not return.

Spalding (1911) writes: "Base ball, I repeat, is War! And the playing of the games is a battle" (9, lines 11–16).

26. Public Law 88–378, 78 STAT 325, which incorporated Little League Baseball, 07/16/1964. *National Archives*. Web. 10 April 2013.

27. Now the championship teams of other sports, e.g., football and hockey, also get the same opportunity to visit the White House and meet the president.

28. The tributes were made out of love or fear of powerful god(s). Religion influenced sports, more than one thinks.

29. The early British, European and other peoples believed that a spirit dwells in every living thing, analogously the genetic code "lives" within every organism. Each cell of every living thing carries its full genetic code (sex cells carry half the number). A human is made up of billions of cells, and each cell has 23 pairs of chromosomes. Each chromosome contains a long strand of a Deoxyribonucleic Acid (DNA) molecule with associated proteins. Each long DNA molecule contains a part or whole of the hereditary material or genes.

30. The successful warrior usually had the best choice of mates and better chances of siring his offspring.

31. In 1976, Bowie Kuhn, then commissioner of baseball said: "Baseball is beautiful … the supreme performing art. It combines perfect harmony the magnificent features of ballet, drama, art, and ingenuity" (Dickson, [231]).

32. Each knows, as Jon Davies in *Death, Burial and Rebirth in the Religions of Antiquity*, writes: "Of the approximately 100,000,000,000 people who have died since the Ice Age only a tiny fraction are remembered." See: Introduction—a concluding point, 19· lines 11–13.

The Poet mentioned is Thomas Gray, *The Works of Thomas Gray, in Prose and Verse*. Vol.1, London (1825), who writes:

Full many a gem of purest ray serene,
   The dark unfathomed caves of ocean bear:
   Full many a flower is born to blush unseen,
   And waste its fragrance on the desert air [229, lines 12–15].

N.B.: Several others including Milton and Pope have noted the ephemeral nature of life in their own works. Jane Austen in *Emma* (1816) cites this poem:

"Full many a flower is born to blush unseen,
   And waste its fragrance on the desert air."

33. In this age, it seems people are likely to be famous for "15 seconds," rather than Marshall McLuhan's fifteen minutes.

34. The ancient Greek poet, Semónides (of middle or late seventh century BCE) of Amórgos, writes in "The Vanity of Human Wishes" that the road ahead is full of uncertainty and chances of reaching our goals before old age are slim. *Greek Lyrics* translated by Richard Lattimore, 11: lines 25–37; and 12: lines 1–11. In addition, Max Duncker, *Story of Greece, from the Earliest Times to the End of the Persian War*. Vol. II., writes:

Up! Ye are the seed of Heracles, the invincible. Take courage, Zeus has not yet in wrath turned his face from you. Fear not the number of the enemy, nor flee. Let each man hold his shield firmly against his foe. The enemy of his own life, let him greet the dark lot of death as though it were the pleasant light of the sun. Well are ye skilled in the destroying work of Ares, who bringeth tears; ye have learned the wrath of cruel war; ye have been among the flying and the pursuers, ye young men; in both ye have had your fill. They who are bold to stand side by side in the conflict and advance against the foe rarely fall, and they protect the people behind them. The coward loses every virtue, and no man can tell you all the misery which overtakes him. Shameful are the wounds which fall upon the neck of one flying from the battle; shameful is the corpse which lies in the dust through the back. Close your ranks then, and each man plant both feet firm upon the ground; so stand, with teeth upon your lips [443: 6–25 lines; also 443–445].

35. Approximately, two to five out of a thousand high school children make it into any professional sports. In Major League Baseball about one of fifteen drafted players reaches the heights of the Majors.

36. Each family likewise hopes that someone will wave a magic wand and the transformation of their child would begin.

37. To dream the impossible dream of being a MLB player:

To give up other games of childhood,
To give up the fanciful pleasures of youth,
To live on unbelievable low wages,
To go on long rides on back roads,
To go to places few know,
To miss friends and family,
To be alone and always on the move,
To faithfully continue this quest till it hurts no more,
To be called in and told your day has come,
To be told to move up or down or out.
This is now the beginning of the end or the end of the beginning.

38. The Ancient Greek poet, Simónides of Ceos (556 to or about 468 BCE) writes in "The Comment of Simónides" about the uncertainties of life (*Greek Lyrics* translated by Richard Lattimore, 54: lines 25–30; and 55: lines 1–4).

39. The sun was thought by the ancient Hindus to see everything and therefore knows everything; and his supplicants prayed that he forgives and forgets all that he has seen and heard.

40. This is analogous to what the early British priests and teachers did in their temples and groves, preparing the next generation of priests and leaders. Like the British priests of old, each coach has his own formulations, incantations, and ideas of how to achieve his goals.

41. The Old Gaelic words describe it well: "*Turus*, a journey, voyage, expedition;" and "*Turna*, a furnace, a spinning wheel, a job of work." The baseball diamond is like a fiery furnace to prepare a skilled young man, or like a spinning wheel to weave a masterpiece of tapestry. Despite the numerous scientific analyses of various aspects of baseball, the game has not been made any easier.

42. The bar is set high, and we cut ourselves no slack. From this vantage point, baseball viewers have the answers for all that is ailing their team and players.

43. For example, early peoples such as British, Germanic and Scandinavian warriors' idea of heaven was a place where they fought all day and feasted at night. Night time was for the healing of injuries so that they can fight again the next day. Women were thought to be more dangerous and best to avoid. The myths of a race of the superior women warriors living on an island was of early tribal origins, such as the early British.

44. In Guyana (formerly British Guiana, South America) a legend exists that an Amerindian village was undergoing hard times because of a severe drought. After consultation between the village medicine man and elders, it was decided that the gods need a sacrifice to end the drought. The village chief offered himself and took his canoe and went over the waterfalls that still bears his name. Kaieteur Falls has a sheer drop of 741 feet, the highest in the world.

45. The Ghurkhas soldiers (also of legendary bravery) are of more recent vintage under the British flag and empire. They were commanded by British Army officers. Their written record before the arrival of the British is unknown.

46. Old Gaelic words, "*iodhbairt, ofrail, doibhre* meant sacrifice;" "*fear iodhbaras,* sacrificer;" "*naomh, feunta,* sacred;" "*naomhachd,* sacredness;" and "*feinmhort* suicide."

47. The sacrificial victim would be awarded a worthy place at the feasting table of one's honored ancestors. German myths tells of chosen fallen warriors in wars being fast tracked by the Valkyries to Asgard, home of the Asa-Gods, to share the joys of Valhal, feasting with Odin in eternal triumph and happiness (Donald A. Mackenzie's *German Myths and Legends,* previously [1912] titled: *Teutonic Myth and Legend,* x and xi in fore-

word by Donald Flanell Friedman in the 1985 edition).

48. Donald Flanell Friedman, in foreword to Mackenzie's *German Myths and Legends* x: lines 11–12.

49. In such cases, his story would be written about and be shown on television. In early British times, the bards would tell the tale of this hero.

50. The superstar player, 2016 Hall of Famer Ken Griffey, Jr., ran into walls numerous times in his efforts to make the catch, and had several serious injuries. Another similar fearless player, Jim Edmonds, was known to do everything humanly possible to make the out. These sacrificial efforts in some players just seem to come naturally.

51. Sacrificing his body is to get hit by the ball if that is what is needed to get on base, especially in critical situations. If he is badly hurt, he can be replaced at first base by a pinch runner. Reed Johnson did all that was necessary for his then team (Toronto Blue Jays). He was loved by the Jays' fans, and was the player one wants on his team. However in 2008, Johnson was not rehired by the Jays' management. On Johnson's return to Toronto with another team, the Toronto fans gave him a standing ovation.

52. Early in America, sacks (*sac*) were used as bases, hence the expression "the sacks are full," when all the bases were occupied or loaded. In this situation, a hitter is expected to bring in at least one runner by a sacrifice fly, bunt or suicide play.

53. The expression "heads will roll" probably originated from the British and European peoples, as they did not hesitate to decapitate their opponents.

In some ancient communities, the captain of the losing team, the entire losing team or the captains of both teams were sacrificed to the gods. Victims sacrificed to the god Odin, the all-father, were expected to bear their pains without complaining, as Odin.

Adrian Bailey in *The Caves of the Sun: The Origin of Mythology* writes:

One recurring theme along the routes of prehistory has been that of burial, heads in particular. Decapitation was an intrinsic part of solar rites. It featured in the medieval legends of Europe, especially among the Celts. In Arthurian romance, the victor of a combat or tour-

nament decapitated the loser. There is a distant parallel here with the curious ball games played among the Aztecs and the Maya of Central America, where decapitation had a long history. The game was played with a rubber ball between two teams, each of seven men including a captain (not unlike the team of Morris dancers), in a ball-court located at a sacred site. Fixtures may have been planned following a successful battle between warring tribes, for it has been suggested that one team was made up of prisoners of war, and the outcome was heavily loaded in favour of the victors. The captain of the losing team was beheaded, to join the skulls of previous victims displayed in rows on a *tzompantli*, or "skull platform" [236: lines 21–37].

54. Gannett, Blake and Hosmer (eds.), *Unity Hymns and Chorals...,* number 61, verse 2, 24 (this hymn has been modified by others and is published in other old works).

55. Spalding writes:

The genius of our institution is democratic: Base Ball is a democratic game. The spirit of our national life is combative; Base ball is a combative game. We are a cosmopolitan people, knowing no arbitrary class distinction, acknowledging none [3: lines 21–24].

See also Chapter 1: 1–9.

56. Few bards sung of the hardships of the ordinary people. Only the stories of the heroic warriors, nobles, kings, etc., were recorded and passed on.

57. In, for example, the work of Elder, Chapter VIII, 84–91, where some of the established Triads are cited.

58. There are usually three versions to every action: "the one planned, the one executed, and the one that one wished one did."

59. It is in such dire circumstances that the encouragement, love and support of others are most needed.

60. Some immature or emotionally distraught baseball players evidently cannot accept these personal failures; hence they throw tantrums throwing equipment, breaking bats, hitting walls and swearing at officials. In some cases, such distraught players attack other team-mates or injure themselves.

61. Incidentally, these were the same qual-

ities or treasures that were advocated by the Holy Grail Mandala.

62. One current MLB player looks skyward to acknowledge and seek the blessing of his grandmother before facing each pitch.

63. The carefully attuned can hear and picture the gods laughing at the human responses to their acts of "mischief."

64. The late Lou Gehrig made his memorable speech on July 4th, 1939, at Yankee Stadium.

Conclusion

1. Very often humans do certain things and maintain beliefs not because they are rational, but because habits or traditions held sway. In modern baseball in America, there are the American League (AL) and the National League (NL) of Major League Baseball (MLB). The difference between the AL and the NL is that the American League teams have the designated hitters (DH) and the pitchers do not bat; whereas, the National League teams do not allow designated hitters (DH) and the pitchers bat like other position players. The baseball purists or traditionalists are against the DH rule in the American League.

2. The Olympic games began in Athens, Greece, during each a truce was held between the various warring factions. Games were dedicated to the gods, chiefly Zeus. The modern games began in 1859 and became truly international in 1896. The sites of the original games were rediscovered by German archaeologists in the mid-nineteenth century.

3. The search for immortality had begun. This was also the dawn of religious beliefs.

4. In the first day of creation, according to the Bible in the book of Genesis (Chapter 1), after God created the Heavens and the Earth, He then created the sun to rule by day and the moon by night.

5. In this thinking mindset, one can easily visualize the beginnings of the duality principle of nature or philosophy, e.g., light and darkness, and good and evil being opposite sides of the same thing; or the emergence of the Ying-Yang principle where two absolutes merge.

6. They must have learnt the power of the "Dark Sun" since its darkness remained wherever emitted light from the "Bright Sun"

could not reach. They probably concluded: Light from the "Bright Sun" traveled in a straight line as so commonly evident whenever visible light was seen coming through the canopy of trees or their thatched-roof shelters or houses. The beams of light just managed to push the darkness aside. Since darkness was everywhere light could not bend to reach, then darkness traveled around curves and even into the furthest hidden corners. The unseen "Dark Sun" and its darkness were more powerful. Hence the "Dark Sun" was feared and had to be appeased. One strategy of appeasing the "Dark Sun" was to be friendly to the "Bright Sun," they hoped that the "Bright Sun" would protect them. Some early people embraced the darkness and counted their days by the nights passed in the daily cycles of darkness and light.

7. These earlier attempts to study, appease and worship the sun were their equivalent attempts to harness the energy of the sun to their own societal benefit. This is analogous to the current efforts of modern scientists and engineers who build solar panels and place these on buildings where the panels can best harness the emitted energy of the radiant sun.

8. The baseball "diamond" is in a fact a square.

9. In his letter to the Galatians, Chapter 3, verse 1, St. Paul in *The Living Bible Paraphrased*, writes: "What magician has hypnotized you and cast an evil spell on you?" The Galatians' beliefs were similar to the early peoples of Britain. This reference indicates how negatively the old tribal or inter-tribal priests, often called magicians or sorcerers, were viewed. It was thought the major centers of learning of all the early priests were in early Britain. Unfortunately, their magic or sorcery proved ineffective against the Roman legions.

10. The premise for this ruthless suppression of entertainment and non-wholesome activities were in all likelihood based on the letter that St. Paul writes to the Galatians, Chapter 5, verses 19 to 21:

19. But when you follow your own wrong inclinations your lives will produce these evil results: impure thoughts, eagerness for lustful pleasure,.

20. Idolatry, spiritism, hatred and fighting, jealousy and anger, constant effort

to get the best for yourself, complaints and criticisms, the feeling that everyone else is wrong except those in your group—and there will be wrong doctrine. 21. Envy, murder, drunkenness, wild parties, and all that sort of thing. Let me tell you again as I have done before, that anyone living that sort of life will not inherit the kingdom of God.

11. Block cites poems written years ago, for example, from the sixteenth to the eighteenth centuries CE, which indicate fun, entertaining and socializing aspects of stoolball. This practice has survived to some extent in that even today young people of both sexes do socialize in the playing of softball. Also in the summers at office outings or picnics, workers also play softball in their efforts to socialize and have fun.

In addition, Deanne Westbrook in *Ground Rules, Baseball & Myth* writes:

The dangerous connection between sex and batting is perhaps being suggested by [Thomas] Boswell [author of *Why Time Begins on Opening Day*]: both are expressions of the "desire for thudding force." The Anglo-Saxon word for intercourse originally meant "to strike" or "to hot" … It [batting] is safe, a satisfactory substitute not only for war but for sex… [122: lines 12–15, 20–21].

12. For example, the people of Cornwall lost their old language.

13. Joseph A. Reaves, *Taking in a Game. A History of Baseball in Asia.*

14. Fritjof Capra cites these words from the *Upanishads* with regards to particle and matter inter-conversion observations in modern physics:

It moves. It moves not.
It is far, and it is near.
It is within all this,
And it is outside of all of this.
[158: lines 5–8].

Appendix A

1. Davies, *The Celts*, 97, lines 37–39.
2. Ellis, *Celtic Dawn*, 29, lines 1–5.
3. Rutherford, *Celtic Lore*, 135, lines 13–19, 24–25.

Rutherford gives an example where an Armorican Druid and "Keeper of the Temple of Belenos" was given a teaching position at the rhetorical school of Bordeanx in the sixth century. He mentions that St. Gildas wrote letters denouncing the action of the British native princes who paid only lip service to Christianity (135).

4. Davies, *The Celts*, 97, lines 38–39 (Note 1).

Appendix B

1. John Rhys, *The Welsh People*, 596: lines 27–33; 597: lines 1–35; and 598: lines 1–4.

2. Hackwood, *Staffordshire Customs and Folklore*, VII, May Customs, 15: second column, lines 42–52; and 16: first column, lines 1–16, 27–64, second column, lines 1–3, 4–8.

3. *Ibid.*, 17, second column, lines 16–21, 22–26.

4. Sir Walter Besant, *London in the Time of the Stuarts*, 328–329.

5. *Ibid.*, 329–330.

Appendix C

1. Hackwood, 173: first column, lines 57–61, second column, lines 1–42.

2. *Ibid.*, 173: second column, lines 43–61; and 174 , first column, line 1–3, 15–19, second column, lines 1–19.

3. Bennett, *Anna of the Five Towns*, 123: lines 34–39; and 124: lines 1–3, and 7–13.

The editor of the 1995 edition of *Anna of the Five Towns*, Margaret Harris states in the notes: "Round-ball: games for any number of players, without sides or partners" (225: lines 1–2).

Harris states in the Notes section that "Bobby Bingo" was a game in which children danced around a ring (225: Note number 124, lines 3–19).

Harris notes that one version of "Bobby Bingo" played in Staffordshire is described *by Gomme* in *the Traditional Games of England, Scotland, and Ireland, Collected and Annotated (2 Vols., 1894-8).*

Harris explains in the notes: "*Tut-Ball*: a game like rounders, but played with no bat. The field is marked out by '*tuts,*' or brickbats, round which a player who has hit the ball with his or her hand must run" (225: lines 20–23).

Others, such as Gomme defines "Tut, a prominence" (Gomme 314, Note).

4. Gomme, "Tut-ball," 314: lines 10–34. Gomme gives her source as *Shropshire Folklore, 524.*

Addy, *A Glossary of Words*, "tutball," 269; "pize-ball," 176.

5. Delloyd J. Guth, *Late-Medieval England, 13771–485*, cites "Ross, Alan S.C. "Pizeball," *Leeds Studies*, XIII (1968), 557–7; and George R. Stephens in *Speculum*, XII (1937), 264—7" (numbers 1126, 1109).

6. Herrick,*The Poetical Works of Robert Herrick*, (1893), 32: lines 3–14.

The Editor, George Saintsbury, of *The Poetical Works of Robert Herrick* defines stoolball as "An early form of ball game, between cricket and rounders" (32, Note 1).

Saintsbury defines a tansy as "A pancake flavoured with that plant" (32, Note 2).

7. Underdown, *Revel, Riot, and Rebellion, Popular Politics and Culture in England 1603–1660*, defines stoolball:

> There were two variants of stoolball: a primitive form played with a paddle or the hand instead of the bat, and the more elaborate Wiltshire form played with a hard ball and a wooden staff resembling a modern baseball bat. I suspect that the simpler form was the one popular in other parts of the country, being played, for example, at village revels "for a tansy and a Banquet of curds and cream" [76: Note number 11, lines 1–5].

8. *Ibid.*, 76: lines 9–32; and 77: lines 1–3, 7–9. Chapter 4, Note 33 has the quotation.

9. Gomme, *The Traditional Games of England, Scotland, and Ireland*, 145: lines 7–37; and 146: lines 1–9.

10. *Ibid.*, Stool-ball, 217: lines 17–19, 23–24, 25–36; and 218: lines 1–4.

11. This sounds somewhat similar to modern baseball infields.

12. Editors, David Cram, Jeffrey L. Forgeng and Dorothy Johnston introduce *Francis Willughby's Book of Games: A Seventeenth-Century Treatise on Sports, Games, and Pastimes*, included their "Glossary of Games," the terms "Stoolball, Tutball," 283: lines 11–14, 16–22, and 30–32.

OED, abbreviation for "Oxford English Dictionary."

13. *Ibid.*, 178: lines 1–10, 30.

14. Otis, *Mary of Plymouth*, "How to Play Stoolball," and "On Christmas Day," 99: lines 23–24; 100: lines 1–22; 101: lines 24; and 102: lines 1–14.

Appendix D

1. Hackwood, *Staffordshire Customs, Superstitions and Folklore*, 171: first column, lines 40–59, and second column, lines 1–56.

2. Willughby, *Francis Willughby's Book of Games...*, "Prison Bars" 166–167.

3. *Ibid.*, "Prison Bars," 276. (They give several references to other works where Prison Bars are mentioned.)

4. *Ibid.*, "Running," 151.

Appendix E

1. For example, the eighteenth century British judge and pioneer Sanskritist Sir William Jones.

2. The geography of ancient India included modern Afghanistan, Bangladesh, India, Nepal and Pakistan. The religion then was essentially Hinduism, later came Buddhism and Jainism. Islam and Sikhism are newer arrivals on the religious scene. In India, Christianity was introduced by St. Thomas, but it never became a national religion.

3. Swami A.C. Prabhupada Bhaktiventa, in his translation of *The Bhagavad-Gita, Bhagavad-Gita as It Is,* Chapter 15. 12, 511: lines 7–9.

4. Alexander Cunningham, *The Ancient Geography of India*, 196: lines 18–23, 29–30; and 197: lines 24–27.

5. Jean Markale, *the Great Goddess, Reverence of the Divine Feminine from the Palaeolithic to the Present*, 5: lines 4–11; and 49: lines 10–14.

6. In many old cultures, the moon was regarded as the agent and controller of water, moisture, fertility, and reproduction. In Vedic times, the moon was thought to control the fertilizing waters, and this probably explains why the early British and others as well viewed the moon as masculine. The male-female roles were interchangeable.

7. Chhath means the number 6, a multiple of 3.

8. S.P. Sharma and Seema Gupta, *Fairs & Festivals of India*, 80: subtitle and lines 1–9 (Makar Sankranti Namahsavitre Jagdadeka Chakstushe Jagat prasatt sithithinaasa hetave).

9. William Crooke in *An Introduction to the Popular Religion and Folklore of Northern India* (1894) adds more light to choices of the worshippers:

> The general term for the great gods of Hinduism, the supreme triad—Brahma, Vishnu and Siva—and the other deities of the higher class which collectively constitute the Hindu official pantheon is Deva or "the shining ones." ...
>
> In the time of Sankara Acharya (1000 BCE) there were six distinct sects of sun-worshippers—one worshiped the rising sun as identified with Brahma; the second the meridian sun as Siva; the third the setting sun as Vishnu; the fourth the sun in all these places as Trimurti; the fifth class of worshippers of the sun regarded him as a material being in the form of a man with a golden beard and golden hair. Zealous members of this sect refused to eat anything in the morning till they had seen the sun rise; the sixth class worshipped an image of the sun in their mind. They were in the habit of branding circular representations of his disc on their forehead, arms and breast [1: lines 1–5; and 3: lines 6–17].

This worshipping of the sun in its various stages of the horizon was analogous to that seen with others, such as the early British and Continental European peoples.

10. Ref. of Nancy Wilson Ross, *Three Ways of Asian Wisdom, Hinduism, Buddhism, and Zen, and Their Significance for the West*, 18: lines 1–3.

11. Georg Feuerstein, Subhash Kak, and David Frawley, *In Search of the Cradle of Civilization, New Light on Ancient India*, 189: lines 10–18.

The *Vedas* are sacred Hindu books, and *Rig* or *Rg-Veda* means *Verse-Veda*. Mantra is the saying or thinking of an ideal that is repeated over and over again. The idea of repeating a desired saying is that the thought becomes entrenched and takes form, and a human becomes what he thinks. Vedantic philosophy or Vedantism is nonsectarian and not associated with any particular deity. Vedanta means the end of the Vedas. The Vedic age is regarded as about 3000–2000 BCE or earlier.

12. Early peoples sought to imitate the movement of their deity, serpent or sun, and also to looked to be like their god. This lends understanding to the idea that people want to choose a god which best resembles them, e.g., some Africans want a god who looks black, and feminists want a god who is a female or a goddess. Jean Markale (*The Great Goddess*) in the quotation above mentions that the sun, Grainne, was regarded as female (Note 5).

13. William Graham Sumner, *Folkways*, 544: lines 16–22.

14. *Ibid.*, 547: lines 5–9.

15. *Ibid.*, Sumner writes:

> Lingam and Yoni: The lingam symbol is to be seen all over India, alone or with the yoni. In some parts of India the lingam is worn as an amulet. The word "lingam" is said to mean "symbol." To Europeans the object seems indecent and obscene. If it is phallic origin, "the Hindus are no more conscious of the fact than we [are] of the similar origin of the maypole." It is no more erotic than an egg or a seed. It is a symbol of Siva, the eternal reproductive power of nature, reintegrating after disintegration. One form of Siva is androgyne [546: lines 28–31; and 547: lines 1–5].

16. E.S. Hartland in *Primitive Paternity* (1909) shows that phallic worship continued in France and Belgium into the middle ages, page 63.

17. The Siva Lingam of Achant arises from the ground and is said to rest on the yoni of a dancing girl. This Siva *Lingam* has three holes that are thought to represent the three eyes of Lord Siva.

18. Pupul Jayakar, *The Earth Mother, Legends, Goddesses, and Ritual Arts of India*, 9: lines 25–33.

19. These two major archaeological sites were about 400 miles apart on major trading routes of approximately northwestern ancient India (Ref., Walter A. Fairservis, Jr., *The Roots of Ancient India*).

Nancy W. Ross in *Three Ways of Asian Wisdom* writes:

> It has become increasingly plain to modern scholars that the population of India's remote unrecorded past was by no means composed of simple primitives. As far back as 2500 BCE—well over a thousand years or more before the

first Aryan invasion—these early Indians were already living in large well-planned communities. Three of the ancient cities in the Indus River region, Mohenjo-Daro, Harappa and Chanhu-daro, have been extensively excavated, and the diggings have yielded proof of an advanced state of civilization and a keen aesthetic sensibility revealed in sculptured human figures, animal models, children's toys and, in particular, many brilliantly carved seals [18: lines 16–25].

The cities of the Harrapan culture of India were thought to be destroyed around 1750 BCE.

20. The *linga* and phallic worship are thought to be derived from the idea that a pillar represents the axis of the universe and is a universal cosmic supportive force through time and space. The origins of *linga* worship are controversial. One proposal was that it was derived from the worship of a tree; after the tree stump rotted it was replaced by a stone pillar that looked like a *linga* (ref. of Chatterjee and Chatterjee).

21. Narendra Nath Bhattacharyya, *Ancient Indian Rituals and Their Social Contents*, 100: lines 4–8.

Sometimes salagrams, ammonite fossils of Cephalopoda class from about 425 million years old, were used as the yoni, the symbol for female regenerative principle. There were many subclasses of Cephalopods, they were more common during the Jurassic and Cretaceous periods. The salagrams are usually black in color and appear curved or with spiral grooves. These fossils are viewed as resembling the chakra or wheel of the Hindu god, Vishnu. The Salagram Shilas were thought to originate from different body parts of the god, Vishnu. These salagrams (i.e., fossilized molluscs) are found on the bed of the Gandaki River, a tributary of the sacred Ganges.

22. *Ibid.*, Bhattacharyya writes that the *Yoni* cult is very old and the search or its prehistoric origins should be found in the ruins of Harappa and Mohenjodaro. He reminded us that the primitive hoe (*langala*) was designed to resemble the male sex organ (*linga*). The underlying ideas of the cults of *yoni* and *linga* contributed to a duality in their philosophical outlook (100: lines 9–20).

23. *Ibid.*, 100: lines 12–13 (Note 22).

24. Sumner, *Folkways*, 545, lines 29–33; and 546: line 1.

25. Nancy W Ross, *Three Ways of Asian Wisdom*, writes:

Yet even so, the religion of India's early inhabitants was never entirely lost. It disappeared underground and stayed alive among the people, emerging in due course to make its special contribution to the manifolds subtleties and facets of Hinduism. Some of the recognizable elements of pre–Aryan Indian beliefs are the ritual use of water, veneration of the holy *lingam* (phallus) as the symbol of divine creativity, the worship of trees, serpents, bulls and other animals. The powerful idea of god as mother, the age-old mother Goddess in her many aspects, dates back to Dravidian cults. So too, it is generally believed, does the great god Shiva, whose flame-circled bronze figure in the role of cosmic Dancer (an icon created in southern India) gives magnificent expression to Hindu belief in the eternal dualistic creation-destruction rhythm of the universe [18: lines 31–37; and 19: lines 1–6].

26. Gautam Chatterjee and Sanjoy Chatterjee in *Sacred Hindu Symbols* writes:

Shakti—The Mother Goddess.

Apart from Shaivism and Vaishnavism there is another cult called Shakti which personifies a female energy concept. According to the Shakti School of thought its doctrines and practices are one or more Shaktis or "Creative Energies." …

Daughters of Shakti.

Lakshmi and Saraswati are the two daughters of Shiva-Parvati. These two daughters [not only] further the shakti or "energy" concept, but show a positive direction to the life of the devout [23: lines 24–27; 24: lines 31–32; and 25: line 1].

27. W.J. Wilkins, *Modern Hinduism, An Account of the Religion and Life of the Hindus of Northern India*, Chapter V. "The Saktas—Those Devoted to the Worship of the Female Deities," 340: lines 1–4.

28. *Ibid.*, 342: lines 4–11.

29. This may be a basis for the two directions of running in worshipping services, one to the right (i.e., counterclockwise) and one to the left (clockwise).

30. O.L. Bahadur in *The Book of Hindu Festivals and Ceremonies* writes:

> The power of the Mother Goddess is perhaps greater than that of any other God. She is even worshipped by all the gods themselves. She is *Shakti*—the power of Brahma, Vishnu, and Mahesh…. She is worshipped all over India under different names and manifestations the most benign face of the Goddess is Durga [111].

It is possible that the Indian goddess, *Shakti*, later became the early British and European goddess, *Brigid*, on whom sainthood was later conferred by the Christians. We take our gods and religions wherever we go, as seen with modern immigrants to the West.

31. Wilkins, *Modern Hinduism,* Chapter V. "The Saktas—Those Devoted to the Worship of the Female Deities," 340–344.

32. This idea was mentioned previously, where the priest and queen were tossed into the air, analogously to the early British and European practices of *heaving* and *lifting*.

These practices continued in secret by the *Vamacharis* sect in their worship of *Sakti* (*Devi, Lakshmi,* and *Saraswati*).

33. Bhattacharyya, *Ancient Indian Rituals,* 9: lines 16–17.

34. *Ibid.,* 17: lines 12–19, 26–32; and 20: lines 15–18.

35. Prabhupada, *The Bhagavad-Gita as It Is,* Chapter 4: "Transcendental Knowledge," 162: lines 4–7, 25–27; and Chapter 18; "Conclusion—The Perfection of Renunciation," 562: lines 3–5.

36. Ross and Robins in *The Life and Death of a Druid Prince: The Story of Lindow Man, an Archaeological Sensation,* tells a story in which a Druidic prince suffered a triple death as a sacrificial offering to the gods for help to defeat the Roman invaders.

37. Sir Charles Eliot, *Hinduism and Buddhism,* Vol. II, Chapter XXXII:

> The Durgapuja is the greatest festival of the year in north-eastern India and in the temple of Kaligat at Calcutta may be seen the singular spectacle of educated Hindus decapitating goats before the image of Kali [286: lines 23–27].

38. *Ibid.,* 285: lines 23–26.

39. *Ibid.*

In front of the temple are two posts to which a goat is tied and decapitated daily at noon. Below is the temple of Bhairavi. Human sacrifices were offered here in comparatively recent times, and it is not denied that they would be offered now if the law allowed [288: lines 33–37].

W.J. Wilkins in his 1887 work (*Modern Hinduism*) mentions similar sacrificial blood offerings to goddess *Kali* (Note 37).

40. Jayakar, *The Earth Mother,* 11: lines 23–32; and 12: lines 1–9.

This is the origin of the word "juggernaut" (Nancy W. Ross, 50).

41. *Ibid.,* Jayakar, 53: lines 6–16.

Further information is given by Hussain in *The Goddess,* 97: first column, lines 26–43, second column, lines 1–2.

According to Hindu mythology, Brahma chopped the corpse of goddess Sati to make it lighter for the grief-stricken husband Lord Shiva to carry. The chopped off vulva fell on earth at Kamakhya, Assam. A temple was erected, and inside the temple the *yoni* is represented by a cleft-rock. An underground spring keeps it moist and the water that flows through appears red due to iron oxide.

42. This translation is published by Sir Monier Monier-Williams in *Religious Thought and Life in India: An Account of the Religions of the Indian Peoples Part 1, Vedism, Brahmanism, and Hinduism,* 280: lines 22–25.

43. Some non-human primates, e.g., chimpanzees, also bury their dead.

44. The real reasons for the switch to cremation from burial are unknown, but these would also have included a philosophical basis that the soul, the Spark of the Divine, needs a body to house itself as quickly as possible. The death of the parent is observed annually by his or her children. The *Rig-Veda* (X. 16.5) defines the role of the Agni (fire): "Again, O Agni, to the Fathers sends him who, offered in thee, goes with our oblations. *Wearing New Life,* let him increase his offspring: let him rejoin a body, Jatavedas" (Islamkotob's English Translation of *All Four Vedas,* Rig-Veda third book, Hymn XVI. Agni, 387: verse 5, lines 33–34).

The flame that starts each cremation on the banks of the sacred Ganges River is taken from a fire that has been burning for centuries, attended by the same families for countless generations.

45. A. L. Basham, *The Wonder That Was*

India: A Survey of the History and Culture of the Indian Sub-Continent Before the Coming of the Muslims, 351, lines 3–4.

The sentence continues: "and we have seen the cult of stupas was taken up by Buddhism, and that Asoka raised stupas in the Buddha's honor all over India" (351: lines 4–6).

46. Buddhism was founded by Gautama Buddha born about 563 BCE. The founder of Jainism, Mahavira, was born about 468 BCE.

47. Basham, *The Wonder That Was India*, writes:

> The stupa began as an earthen burial ground…. The core of the stupa was of unburnt brick and the outer face of burnt brick, covered with a layer of plaster. The stupa was crowned by an umbrella of wood or stone, and surrounded by a wooden fence enclosing a path for the ceremonial clockwise circumambulation (*Pradakshina*), which was the chief form of reverence paid to the relics within it [351: lines 3, 11–16].

48. Nancy W. Ross in *Three Ways of Asian Wisdom* discusses the importance for the iconic depiction of Shiva, and the brief explanations of Ananda Coomaraswamy are also cited, page 32.

49. For example, Spalding writes that James L. Steele in *Outing Magazine* had noted earlier that the first baseman was standing on the bag and the base runner on third was standing on the bag when the pitcher was ready to deliver the ball (69, lines 28–30; and 69: lines 35–39).

50. Sadhus Jnaneshwardas and Mukundcharandas, *Hindu Rites and Rituals, Sentiments and Sacraments*, 37: lines 4–9.

They stated that this circular motion was called *Pradakshina* and is a part of reverence in the prayer ritual.

51. *Ibid.*, 36: lines 33–38; and 37: lines 1–3.

52. W. Crooke in *An Introduction to the Popular Religion and Folklore of Northern India* writes:

> One of the most valuable of these protectives [Amulets] is the magic circle which appears in various forms throughout the whole range of folklore. We have seen how the Baiga perambulates his village and drops a line of spirits along the boundary to repel foreign ghosts. It is believed that evil spirits cannot pass a

line thus made. This accounts for the numerous European and Indian stone circles which in Ireland are the resort of fairies. We have constant references in the folktales to the circle within which the ascetic or magician sits while he is performing his sorceries…. In the tales of the Vetala we find the mendicant under a banyan tree engaged in making a circle, and Ksantisilia makes a circle of the yellow powder of bones, the ground within which was smeared with blood and which had pitchers of blood placed in the direction of the cardinal points [210: lines 12–21, 25–29].

53. It is also possible that a group of the early British peoples, who also counted the days in terms of nights, ran in the reverse direction in their mode of worship. The ancient Indian ancestry shows worship of opposite supernatural entities or dualities.

54. Stanley Rice, *Hindu Customs and Their Origins*, 164: lines 21–22, 25–38; and 165: lines 1–2.

Rice continues:

> Water plays a considerable part in these ceremonies, and it is not confined to cleansing properties. The placing of a water-pot near the mother is evidently symbolical. It may well just be taken that just as the sacrificial fire was, in some sense at any rate, an offering to Agni, the god of fire, so the water pot was meant to propitiate the water deities, especially Indra, though we need not suppose the Aryan deities of the rain were the first of their kind. In a country like India, where after a long, hot drought, a single shower will carpet the earth with green, and where so many things were thought to be obtainable by the exercise of charms and incantations, the primitive tribes could hardly have overlooked the value of water, which has been recognized in so many uncivilized parts of the earth. We are thus led once more to the cult of fertility in which so many of these ancient customs seen to have had their roots [165: lines 3–18].

55. Note that the Swastika was popular in India long before the Nazis usurped it and made it a symbol of evil. Walter A. Fairsevis in *The Roots of Ancient India* gives examples of the number of seals of each

kind found at Harappa: "Seals with a single symbol, such as the swastika (120), the endless knot (13), the multiple cross (14), or the grid (15) occur" (274: lines 23–26; and Figures 12–15 on 275).

56. Incidentally, the early British and others of neighboring places thought that movement in a clockwise direction was the right way and movement in a counter-clockwise direction was the wrong way.

This would be analogous to the previously mentioned *Dakshinas*, or the right-hand worshippers, and the *Vamacharis*, or the left-hand worshippers. In India, there are striking contrasts of beliefs and practices, e.g., meat eaters and vegetarians, and animal sacrifices to goddess Kali and all animal life held sacred (Jains).

57. These migrants were brought by the British Colonial power to fill specific labor demands of those places. The Colonial British moved significant amounts of Indians to places in Africa, for example, South Africa, Tanzania and Uganda.

58. A more well-known example is that of the Jewish Diaspora still preserving ancient traditions and bearing the brunt of repeated pogroms, discriminations and persecutions.

59. Marija Gimbutas in *The Living Goddess* mentions that special birthing rooms were found in Turkey (ancient Anatolia) painted red. In other places in old Europe, the insides of tombs were painted red, the color of the womb.

60. Curiously, in former tribal regions of Africa, black represented life, and white death.

61. It is probably not without significance that the three concentric circles (full or partial) of a baseball field similarly represent the areas of steady progression towards the center and ultimate goal. The analogy holds well in Little League Baseball, the bench and non-players want to get on the field, the outfielders want to get on the infield, the infielders want to get on the mound, and become the star of the show.

62. Fritjof Capra, *The Tao of Physics*, Chapter 13—The Dynamic Universe, 209: lines 8–17. In addition, this is given by A.K. Bhaktivedenta Swami Prabhupada, *Bhagavad-Gita as It Is*, Hymn 9, verses 7–10, 319–322.

Appendix F

1. George B. Kirsch, *Baseball and Cricket: The Creation of American Team Sports, 1838–72.*

2. H.R. Ellis Davidson, *Gods and Myths of Northern Europe*, 87.

3. *Ibid.*, Davdson notes: "They thought that he who is lord of war ought to be appeased by the shedding of human blood. To him they devoted the first share of the spoil, and in his honour arms stripped from the foe were suspended from trees" (87). Cited from *History of the Goths,* Translated by C.C. Morrow, Princeton University Press, 1915, Vol. 1V, 61.

4. H.A. Guerber, *The Norsemen*, 86.

5. Davidson in *Gods and Myths of Northern Europe* writes:

> In which dwell elves … and redden the outside of the mound with bull's blood, and make the elves a feast with the flesh; and you shall be healed. *Kormaks Saga*, 12 [156].

6. Jacob Grimm, *Teutonic Mythology,* Vol. 111, Gloucester, Mass, Peter Smith, 1976. First published in 1883. 1220–1221.

7. *Ibid.* Stones were often named after the gods who hurled them, for example, *Thunderstone* being named after the German god of Thunder, Odin. 1222: lines 10–15.

8. Ralph Metzner, *The Well of Remembrance: Rediscovery the Earth Wisdom Myths of Northern Europe*, 61: lines 10–11.

Metzner adds:

> In the year 9 CE, Spear and sword-carrying warriors, some wearing animal pelts and black body paint and howling ferociously in battle, beat back the Romans at the Teutoberger Forest in the Northwestern Rhine country. The Rhine became the natural border of the Roman Empire. The Romans called all people who lived outside the boundaries of the empire "barbarians," from a Greek word that once originally meant "stammerers," a condescending reference to what to the Romans thought were incomprehensible speech [61: lines 11–19].

9. Guerber, *The Norsemen*, 89.

Guerber writes:

> Tyr, Tiu, or Ziu was the son of Odin, and according to different mythologies, his mother was Frigga, Queen of the gods,

or a beautiful giantess whose name is unknown, but who was personification of the raging sea. He is the god of martial honour, and one of the twelve deities of Asgard. …

As the God of courage and of war, Tyr was frequently invoked by the various nations of the North, who cried to him, as well as to Odin, to obtain victory. That he ranked next to Odin and Thor is proved by his name, Tiu, having been given to one of the days of the week, Tiu's day, which in modern English has become Tuesday [85: lines 1–7, 14–20].

10. (a) Davidson in *Gods and Myths of Northern Europe* defines *Ragnorok* as the "Destruction of the powers," and is the "term used to describe the end of the world, when the monsters slay the Gods, and Midgard and Asgard are destroyed" (236).

(b) Ralph Metzner in *The Well of Remembrance.* writes in Chapter 13, "The Twilight of the Sky Gods and the New Dawn of the Earth Goddess":

The Nordic eschatological myth of the *Ragnarök*, which is usually translated as "twilight of the gods" but more precisely means "final fate of the gods," has been given several different interpretations. Historians of religion … have pointed out that the myths of the world destruction related to the *Eddas* are not different from similar myths in other cultures, including those of India, Iran, and Israel and the apocalyptical biblical vision of *Revelation* [244: lines 1–8].

11. Galina Krasskova, *Exploring the Northern Tradition: a Guide to the Gods, Lore, Rites and Celebrations from the Norse, German, and Anglo-Saxon Traditions* writes:

In the end, the gods did not stop with the creation of just Midgard. They set in order nine worlds in all, which were connected by a gleaming rainbow Bridge called Bifrost:

1. Midgard, the home of men.
2. The pre-existing Muspellheim, the world of raging fire.
3. Niflheim, the other pre-existing world, of ice, cold and stillness.
4. Asgard, the shining home of the Gods.
5. Vanaheim, the home of the Vanir-Gods.

6. Jotunheim, the stormy realm of the giants.
7. Swartalfheim, the home of the dark elves.
8. Lightalheim, the world of the light elves.
9. Helheim, home of the dead (30).

Russian superstitions tell of nine sisters who plague mankind with fevers. They are chained in caverns and when let loose show no pity.

Grimm, *Teutonic Mythology*, Vol. III, writes: A Finnish song tells of a woman, Launawatar or Louhiator, become the "mother of nine sons: werewolf, snake, risi (?), lizard, nightmare, joint-ache, gout, spleen, and gripes. These maladies then are brothers of baneful monsters" [1161: lines 21–24].

12. On the tree, Odin, while hung upside down, chants:

I know I hung.
On the windswept tree,.
through nine days and nights.
I was stuck with a spear.
and given to Odin.
myself given to myself.
[Leeming *God, Myths of the Male Divine*: 92, lines 24–29, and *The World of Myth*, 162: lines 15–35; 163: 1–7].

In Teutonic mythology there are nine worlds and nine divisions of torture where wicked souls are punished.

In Hindu philosophy the body is thought to contain nine apertures or gates through which the spirit or soul may leave or enter.

In 1914, the Rev. E. Osborn Martin, a Wesleyan missionary in India and Ceylon for 13 years wrote (*The Gods of India*): "The Hindus worship nine planets or heavenly bodies. Two of these we have already noticed among the Vedic gods–Surya the Sun, and Soma (or Chandra) the moon" (295: 1–3).

13. Metzner, *The Well of Remembrance.* 156–158.

14. J.A. MacCulloch, *The Celtic and Scandinavian Religions*, 123: lines 37–39; 124: 1–12, 32–35, 39; and 125: 1–4. MacCulloch also writes:

One aspect of the Valkyries is that some of the heroines of the Eddic poems are so-called, whether myth raised them to their rank, or they were confused with Valkyries called by their names. Svava was one of these, and she was re-born as Sigrun, while a Valkyrie, Kara, is said to be a re-birth of Sigrun…

The Valkyrie belief was much developed in the north in Viking times, like that in Valhall. It may have come there from southern Germany, "the southern maid" being an epithet for a Valkyrie. It is also possible that the idea of mythical Valkyries may have originated from the fact that, among the Germanic tribes, actual women went forth to battle. These are mentioned in the Poetic Edda where, in *Atlakvitha* they are called *Skjaldmeyjar*, "shield-maids," many of whom perished in the temple of Atli. Saxo Grammaticus also speaks of such women more than once. They took part in the battle of Bravalla on the side of the Danes [125: lines 8–12, 28–38].

15. Guerber, *The Norsemen.* Chapter XVIII. "The Valkyrs."

16. Krasskova, *Exploring the Northern Tradition,* Chapter 5 "The Soul Matrix," 127: lines 1–7, 13–14.

17. *Ibid.*, Chapter 5, 127–140.

18. Guerber, *The Norsemen,* 39.

19. *Ibid.*, 298–307.

20. Metzner, *The Well of Remembrance,* 75: lines 17–32; and 78: lines 16–21.

21. Guerber, *The Norsemen.*

22. Davidson in *Gods and Myths of Northern Europe* writes:

Such fits of rage could be inconvenient in private life, and this is illustrated by a story from the private life of the famous poet, Egill Skallagrimsson. His father appears to have been a berserk in his youth, and when he had married and settled down in Iceland, he became over-excited one evening in a game of ball with his child. In a mad frenzy he killed the little boy's nurse, and came close to destroying his son Egill as well [68: lines 5–12].

23. *Ibid.*, Davidson, 152, lines 31–39; and 153: 1–2.

Saxo Grammaticus was a twelfth century antiquarian who wrote a history of the Danes, *Gesta Danorium.* H. R. E. Davisdon in *The Road to Hell: A Study of the Conception of the Dead in Old Norse Literature* discusses her work using *Flateyjarbok,* part of Old Norse literature.

24. *Ibid.*, 155.

25. Guerber, *The Norsemen* writes:

After [King Bele] giving his last instructions and counsel to his sons [Helge and Halfdan], and speaking kindly to his sons, and speaking kindly to Frithiof [Son of Thornsten], for whom he entertained a warm regard, the old king [Bele] turned to his lifelong companion, Thorsten, to take leave of him, but the old warrior declared that they would not long be parted. Bele then spoke again to his sons, and bade them erect his howe, or funeral mound, within sight of that of Thorsten, that their spirits might commune over the waters of the narrow firth which would flow between them, that so they might not be sundered even in death.

These instructions were piously carried out when, shortly after the aged companions breathed their last; and the great barrows having being erected [306: lines 6–19].

26. Davidson, *Gods and Myths of Northern Europe,* 99, lines 24–26.

27. *Ibid.*, 115: lines 33–36.

28. *Ibid.*, 116: Note 1, lines 2–4.

29. Freyja, was also a high Vanir priestess whose name was linked to rituals, *Seidrs,* in which the leading practitioner (*Volva* or seeress) sat on an erected platform or raised seat accompanied by others (musicians and a choir) in ceremonies. Her cult members, seeresses, travelled about to other places and events such as farms, feasts and festivals where they offered their services to those who asked. Such services included: divinations; answering of questions on relationships, marriages, war; proposing solutions to problems; advising preventative measures against disease and crop failures; and giving blessings. It is easy to see that special communal places, such as groves, were used to accommodate the needs of these travelling seeresses and their entourage belonging to the goddess Freyja's cult. The travelling seeresses and their entourages performed rituals and engaged local spectators in their communities.

In addition Davidson writes: "Every pagan settlement has thus paid some service to the fertility powers, who possessed the ultimate say as to its future, and the people of the north were no exception" (125: line 30–32).

30. Guerber, *The Myths of the Norsemen*, Chapter XVII: The Norns:

The Three Fates.

The Northern Goddesses of fate, who were called Norns, were in no wise subject to the other gods, who might neither question nor influence their decrees. They were three sisters, probably descendants of the giant Norvi, from whom sprang Nott (night). As soon as the Golden age was ended, and sin began to steal even into the heavenly homes of Asgard, the Norns made their appearance under the great ash Yggdrasil, and took up their abode near the Urdar Mountain. According to some mythologists, their mission was to warn the gods of future evil, to bid them make good use of the present, and to teach them wholesome lessons from the past.

These three sisters, whose names were Urd, Verlandi, and Skuld were personifications of the past, present and future. Their principal occupations were to weave the web of fate; to sprinkle daily the sacred tree with water from the Undar fountain, and to put fresh clay around its roots, that it might remain fresh and evergreen [166: lines 1–20].

Bibliography

Adachi, Pat. *Asahi: A Legend in Baseball, A Legacy from the Japanese Canadian Baseball Team to Its Heirs.* Etobicoke, ON: Coronex, 1992.

Adair, Robert Kemp. *The Physics of Baseball.* 2nd Ed. New York: Harper-Perennial, 1994.

Addy, Sidney Oldall, ed. *A Glossary of Words Used in the Neighbourhood of Sheffield, Including a Selection of Local Name, and Some Notices of Folk Lore, Games, and Customs.* Published for the English Dialect Society. London: Trubner, 1888.

_____. *A Supplement to the Sheffield Glossary.* Published for the English Dialect Society. London: Kegan Paul, Trench, Trubner, 1891.

Adelman, Melvin A. *A Sporting Time: New York City and the Rise of Modern Athletics, 1820–70.* Urbana: University of Illinois Press, 1986.

Allen, Grant. *The Evolution of the Idea of God: An Inquiry into the Origins of Religions.* London: Grant Richards, 1904.

Altherr, Thomas L. *Sports in North America: A Documentary History.* Vol. 1, Part 1 of *Sports in the Colonial Era, 1618–1783.* Gulf Breeze, FL: Academic International Press, 1997.

Anthony, David W. *The Horse, the Wheel and Language: How Bronze-Age Riders from the Eurasian Steppes Shaped the Modern World.* Princeton, NJ: Princeton University Press, 2007.

Austen, Jane. *Emma.* With an Introduction by Lionel Trilling. Boston: Houghton Mifflin, 1957.

Bahadur, Om Lata. *The Book of Hindu Festivals and Ceremonies.* New Delhi: UBS, 1994.

Bailey, Adrian. *The Caves of the Sun: The Origin of Mythology.* London: Jonathan Cape, 1997.

Baker, William J. *Sports in the Western World.* Revised Edition. Urbana: University of Illinois Press, 1988.

Bartlett, Vernon. *The Past of Pastimes.* London: Chatto and Windus, 1969.

Basham, A.L. *The Wonder That Was India: A Survey of the History and Culture of the Indian Sub-Continent Before the Coming of the Muslims.* 3d Revised Ed. New York: Taplinger, 1968.

Bennett, Arnold. *Anna of the Five Towns.* Edited by Margaret Harris. 1902. Reprint, Oxford: Oxford University Press, 1995.

Bergounioux, Frederic-Marie, and Joseph Goetz. *Primitive and Prehistoric Religions.* New York: Hawthorn Books, 1966.

Berra, Yogi. *The Yogi Book: I Really Didn't Say Everything I Said.* New York: Workman, 1998.

Besant, Sir Walter. *London in the Time of the Stewarts.* London: Adam and Charles Black, 1904.

Bhaktivedanta, A.C. Swami Prabhupada. *The Bhagwavad-Gita As It Is.* London: The Bhaktiventa Book Trust, 1997.

Bhattacharyya, Narendra Nath. *Ancient Indian Rituals and Their Social Contents.* Totowa, NJ: Rowman and Littlefield, 1975.

Bigelow, Robert. *The Dawn Warriors: Man's Evolution Toward Peace.* Boston: Little, Brown, 1969.

Birley, Derek. *A Social History of English Cricket.* London: Aurum Press, 1999.

Blaine, Delabere P. *An Encyclopaedia of Rural Sports; or Complete Account (Historical, Practical, and Descriptive) of Hunting, Shooting, Fishing, Racing, &c. &c. A New*

Edition (Revised and Corrected). London: Longmans, Green, Reader, and Dyer, 1870

Bloch, Ernst. *Atheism in Christianity: The Religion of the Exodus and the Kingdom*. New York: Herder and Herder, 1972; reprint, New York: Verso, 2009.

Block, David. *Baseball Before We Knew It: A Search for the Roots of the Game*. Lincoln: University of Nebraska Press, 2005.

Blum, Ralph. *The Book of Runes: A Handbook for the Use of an Ancient Oracle, The Viking Runes*. New York: Oracle Books, 1982.

Bonwick, James. *Irish Druids and Old Irish Religions*. London: Griffith, Farran, 1894.

Borlase, William Copeland. *Antiquities, Historical and Monumental of the County of Cornwall: Consisting of Several Essays on the First Inhabitants, Druidic-Supersition, Customs, and Remains of the Most Remote Antiquity in Britain, and the British Isles, Exemplified and Proved by Monuments now Extant in Cornwall and the Scilly Islands, with a Vocabulary by the Cornu-British Language*. London: W. Bowyer and J. Nichols for S. Baker and G. Leigh, 1769.

Borlase, William Copeland. *Naenia Cornubiae: A Descriptive Essay, Illustrative of the Sepulchres and Funeral Customs of the Early Inhabitants of the County of Cornwall*. London: Longmans, Green, Reader, and Dyer, 1872

Bourne, Henry. *Antiquitates Vulgaris; or, The Antiquities of the Common People*. Newcastle: J. White, 1725.

Bowman, John S., and Joel Zoss. *The Pictorial History of Baseball*. New York: Gallery Press, 1986.

Bowra, C.M. *Primitive Song*. Toronto: New American Library of Canada Limited, 1963.

Brand, John. *Observations on Popular Antiquities: Chiefly Illustrating the Origin of Our Vulgar Customs, Ceremonies and Superstitions*. London: Charles Knight, 1841.

Brasch, R. *How Did It Begin? Customs and Superstitions and Their Romantic Origins*. New York: David McKay, 1966.

Brogan, Olwen. *Roman Gaul*. London: Bell, 1953.

Bronson, Eric, ed. *Baseball and Philosophy: Thinking Outside the Batter's Box*. Chicago: Open Court, 2004.

Brown, Dale M., and Time-Life Editors. *Mound Builders and Cliff Dwellers*. Alexandria, VA: Time-Life Books, 1992.

Brown, Raymond Lamont. *A Book of Superstitions*. Devon, UK: Latimer Trend, 1970.

Bryant, Jacob. *A New System; or, An Analysis of Antient [Ancient] Mythology: Wherein an Attempt is Made to Divest Tradition of Fable; and to Reduce the Truth of Its Original Purity*. 3d ed. London: J. Walker, 1807.

Burl, Aubrey. *Prehistoric Stone Circles*. Aylesbury, UK: Shire Publications Ltd., 1983.

_____. *The Stonehenge People*. London: J.M. Dent and Sons Ltd., 1987.

Campbell, Joseph. "The Peripheries of the Indo-European World, Indian Reflections in the Castle of the Grail." In *The Celtic Consciousness*, edited by Robert O'Driscoll. New York: George Braziller, 1987.

Capra, Fritjof. *The Tao of Physics: An Exploration of the Parallels between Modern Physics and Eastern Mysticism*. New York: Fontana/Collins, 1975.

Carpenter, Edward. *The Origins of Pagan and Christians Beliefs*. London: Senate-Random House, 1996 (first published in 1920).

Carver, Robin. *The Book of Sports*. Boston: Lilly, Wait, Colman, and Holden, 1834.

Castleden, Rodney. *The Stonehenge People: An Exploration of Life in Neolithic Britain, 4700–2000 BC*. London: Routledge, 1990.

Chadwick, Henry. *The Sports and Pastimes of American Boys: A Guide and Text-Book of the Games of the Play-Ground, the Parlor, and the Field*. New York: George Rutledge and Sons, 1884.

Chadwick, Nora K. *Ancient Peoples and Places: Ancient Britain*. North Hollywood, CA: Newcastle, 1989.

Chatterjee, Gautam, and Sanjoy Chatterjee. *Sacred Hindu Symbols*. 2d. ed. New Delhi, India: Abhinav Publications, 2001.

Chetwynd, Josh. *Baseball in Europe: A Country by Country History*. Jefferson, NC: McFarland, 2008.

Churchill, Sir Winston. *A History of the English-Speaking Peoples: The Age of Revolution*. Vol. 3. New York: Bantam Books, 1957.

Cielo, Astra. *Signs, Omens and Superstitions*. London: Skeffington and Son, 1918.

Cohn, Norman. *Cosmos, Chaos and the World to Come: The Ancient Roots of Apocalyptic Faith*. 2d ed. New Haven, CT: Yale University Press, 2001.

Collingridge, Vanessa. *Boudica: The Life of Britain's Legendary Warrior Queen*. New York: Overlook Press, 2005.

Collins, Tony, John Martin, and Wray Vamplew. *Encyclopedia of Traditional British Rural Sports.* London: Routledge, 2005.

Cotterell, Arthur. *Celtic Mythology: The Myths and Legends of the Celtic World.* London: Anness, 1997.

_____. *Mythology. An Encyclopedia of Gods and Legends from Ancient Greece and Rome, the Celts and the Norselands.* London: Anness, 2000.

_____. *Norse Mythology: The Myths and Legends of the Nordic Gods.* London: Lorenz Books, 2000.

Cox, Allan E., Barbara N. Noonkester, Maxwell L. Howell, and Reet A. Howell. "Sport in Canada." In *History of Sport in Canada,* edited by Maxwell L. Howell and Reet A. Howell. Champaign, IL: Stipes, 1985.

Cox, R. Hippisley. *The Green Roads of England.* 4th ed. London: Methuen, 1934 (first Published 1914).

Cox, Simon, and Mark Foster. *An A to Z of the Occult.* Edinburgh, UK: Mainstream Publishing, 2007.

Craig, Steve. *Sports and Games of the Ancient.* Westport, CT: Greenwood, 2002.

Crooke, William. *An Introduction to the Popular Religion and Folklore of Northern India.* Northwestern Provinces and Oudh, India: Government Press, 1894.

_____. *The North-Western Provinces of India: Their History, Ethnology and Administration.* 2d ed. London: Oxford University Press, 1897.

_____. *The Popular Religion and Folk-Lore of Northern India. Vol 11.* New Delhi: Munishram Manoharalal, 1968.

Croome, Arthur C.M., ed. *Fifty Years of Sport at Oxford, Cambridge and the Great Public Schools.* Vols. 1, 2 and 3. London: W. Southwood, 1866.

Crowley, Robert. "The Scholar's Lessons." In *The Select Works of Robert Crowley,* edited by J.M. Cowper. London: N. Trubner, 1872.

Cunningham, Alexander. *The Ancient Geography of India. Vol 1., The Buddhist Period, Including the Campaigns of Alexander, and the Travels of Hwen-Thsang.* Varanasi, India: Indological Book House, 1891 (republished, 1963).

Davidson, Hilda R. Ellis. *Gods and Myths of Northern Europe.* London: Penguin, 1964.

Davies, John. *The Celts: Based upon the S4C Television Series.* London: Cassell, 2000.

_____. *Death, Burial, and Rebirth in the Religions of Antiquity.* London: Routledge, 1999.

Davis, Courtney. *Celtic Designs and Motifs.* New York: Dover, 1991.

Deane, John Bathurst. *The Worship of the Serpent Traced Throughout the World, and Its Traditions Referred to the Events in Paradise: Proving the Temptation and Fall of Man by the Instrumentality of a Serpent Tempter.* 2d ed. London: J. Hatchard and Rivington, 1830.

Dickson, Paul. *Baseball Greatest Quotations.* New York: HarperCollins, 1991.

Ditchfield, Peter Hampson. *Old English Sports.* London: Fisher Unwin, 1907.

Dobson, David. *The Original Scots Colonists of Early America Supplement, 1607–1707.* Baltimore: Genealogical Publishing House, 1998.

Dongre, Narayan Gopal. *Physics in Ancient India.* London: New Age International, 1994.

Dreifort, John E., ed. *Baseball History from Outside the Lines: A Reader.* Lincoln: University of Nebraska Press, 2001.

Drew, A.J. *A Wiccan Bible: Exploring the Mysteries of the Craft from Birth to Summerland.* Franklin Lakes, NJ: New Page Books, 2003.

Dubois, Abbe J.A. *Hindu Manners: Customs and Ceremonies.* Translated by Henry K. Beauchamp. 3d ed. London: Oxford University Press, 1906.

Dunker, Max. *History of Greece: From the Earliest Times to the End of the Persian War.* Vol. II. Translated from the German by Sarah Frances Alleyne and Evelyn Abbot. London: Iard Bentley and Son, 1886.

Dunning, Eric, Patrick Murphy, and John Williams. *The Roots of Football Hooliganism: An Historical and Sociological Study.* London: Routledge and Kegan Paul Ltd., 1988.

Durant, Will. *The Story of Civilization, Part III: Caesar and Christ; A History of Roman Civilization and of Christianity from their Beginnings to A.D. 325.* New York: Simon and Schuster, 1944.

Dyer, James. *Ancient Britain.* London: B.T. Batsford Ltd., 1990.

Edell, John, ed. *Baseball As America.* Washington, DC: National Geographic Society, 2002.

Edwardes, Michael. *Everyday Life in Early India.* New York: G.P Putnam's Sons, 1969.

Elder, Isabel Hill. *Celt, Druid, and Culdee.* 4th ed. London: The Covenant Publishing, 1962.

Elias, Robert, ed. *Baseball and the American Dream: Race, Class, Gender, and the National Pastime.* Armonk, NY: M.E. Sharpe, 2001.

Eliot, Sir Charles. *Hinduism and Buddhism: An Historical Sketch,* Vol. II. London: Edward Arnold, 1921.

Ellis, Peter Beresford. *The Celtic Dawn: A History of Pan Celticism.* London: Constable, 1999.

_____. *The Druids.* Grand Rapids, MI: William B. Eerdmans, 1994.

Fairservis, Walter A., Jr. *The Roots of Ancient India: The Archaeology of Early Indian Civilization.* New York: Macmillan, 1971.

Feachem, Richard. *Guide to Prehistoric Scotland.* London: B.T. Batsford Ltd., 1963.

Fee, Christopher R., and David Leeming. *Gods, Heroes and Kings: The Battle for Mythic Britain.* Oxford: Oxford University Press, 2001.

Fergusson, James. *Tree and Serpent Worship: Or Illustration of Mythology and Art of India in the First and Fourth Centuries of Christ from the Topes at Sanchi and Amravati.* London: W.H Allen, 1868. *Google Books.*

Feuerstein, Georg, Subhash Kak and David Frawley. *In Search of the Cradle of Civilization: New Light on Ancient India.* Wheaton, IL: Quest Books / Theosophical Publishing, 1995.

Filip, Jan. "Early History and Evolution of the Celts: The Archaeological Evidence" in *Celtic Consciousness,* edited by Robert. O'Driscoll. New York: George Braziller, 1987.

Fleming, Fergus, Sharukh Husain, C. Scott Littleton and Linda A. Malcor. *Heroes of the Dawn: Celtic Myth.* Myth and Mankind. London: Duncan Baird, 1996.

Forbes, James. *Oriental Memoirs: A Narrative of Seventeen Years of Residence in India,* Vol. 19. 2d ed. London: J.B. Nichols and Son, 1834.

Foster, Sally M. *Picts, Gaels and Scots: Early Historic Scotland.* London: B.T. Batsford / Historic Scotland, 2004.

Fox, Sir Cyril. *Life and Death in the Bronze Age: An Archaeologist's Field-Work.* London: Routledge and Kegan Paul, 1959.

Frazer, James G. *The Golden Bough: A Study in Comparative Religion,* Vols. 1 and 2. London: Macmillan, 1890.

Friedlander, Noam. *The Mammoth Book of Sports and Games of the World.* London: Robinson, 1999.

Gale, Frederick. *Echoes from Old Cricket Fields.* London: S.R. Publishers Ltd.,1972 (first published 1871).

Gannett, William Channing, Blake, James Vila, and Hosmer, Frederick (Eds.) *Unity Hymns and Chorals for the Congregation and the Home.* Chicago: Charles H. Kerr, 1889.

Gardiner, Philip. *Secret Societies: Gardiner's Forbidden Knowledge, Revelation About the Freemasons, Templars, Illuminati, Nazis, and the Serpent Cults.* Franklin Lakes, NJ: New Page Books, 2007.

Garlett, Kyle, and Patrick O'Neal. *The Worst Call Ever: The Most Infamous Calls Ever Blown by Referees, Umpires, and Other Blind Officials.* New York: HarperCollins, 2007.

Gelling, Peter, and Hilda Ellis Davidson. *The Chariots of the Sun and Other Rites and Symbols of the Northern Bronze Age.* New York: Frederick A. Praeger, 1969.

Gershman, Michael. *Diamonds: The Evolution of the Ballpark: From Elysian Fields to Camden Yards.* Boston: Houghton Mifflin Company, 1993.

Gifford, John [John Richards Green]. *The Anti-Jacobin Review and Protestant Advocate; or, Monthly Political, and Literary Sensor,* Vol. X. London: J Whittle, 1801.

Gilbert, Inga. *The Symbolism of the Pictish Stones in Scotland: A Study of Origins.* Edinburgh: Speedwell Books, 1995.

Gimbutas, Marija. *The Civilization of the Goddess.* San Francisco: Harper, 1991.

_____. *The Goddesses and Gods of Old Europe, 6500–3500 BC: Myth and Cult Images.* Rev. ed. Berkeley: University of California Press, 1982.

_____. *The Gods and Goddesses of Old Europe, 7000 to 3500 BC: Myth, Legends and Cult Images.* London: Thames and Hudson, 1974.

_____. *The Language of the Goddess.* San Francisco: Harper, 1991.

_____. "Prehistoric Religions: Old Europe." In *The Encyclopedia of Religions,* edited by Mircea Eliade. New York: Macmillan, 1987.

Glavine, Tom, with Brian Tarcy. *Baseball for Everybody: Tom Glavine's Guide to America's Game*. Worcester, MA: Chandler House Press, 1999.

Glob, P.V. *The Mound People: Danish Bronze-Age Man Preserved*. Translated from the Danish by Joan Bulman. Ithaca, NY: Cornell University Press, 1974.

Gmelch, George, ed. *Baseball Without Borders: The International Pastime*. Lincoln: University Of Nebraska Press, 2006.

Goldsmith, Oliver. "The Deserted Village." In *Annotated Poems of English Authors*, edited by E.T. Stephens and D. Morris. London: Longmans, Green, 1876.

Goldstein, Warren. *Playing for Keeps: A History of Early Baseball*. Ithaca, NY: Cornell University Press, 1989.

Gomme, Alice Bertha. *The Traditional Games of England, Scotland, and Ireland: With Tunes, Singing, Rhymes and Methods of Playing, Volume II*. London: David Nutt, 1898.

Gordon, E.O. *Prehistoric London: Its Mounds and Circles*. London: Covenant Publishing, 1946.

Gould, Steven Jay. "The Creation Myths of Cooperstown." *Journal of Natural History* 98 (November 1989): 14–24.

Grantham, W.W. *Stoolball and How to Play It*. London: Tattersall, 1941.

Gray, Herbert Louis, Arthur Berriedale Keith, and Arthur J. Carnoy. *The Mythology of All Races, Vol. VI: Indian and Iranian*. New York: Cooper Square, 1964.

Gray, Scott. *The Mind of Bill James: How a Complete Outsider Changed Baseball*. New York: Doubleday, 2006.

Gray, Thomas. *The Works of Thomas Gray: In Prose and Verse*. Vol.1. Edited by Edmund Gosse. New York: A. C. Armstrong and Son, 1885.

Greer, John Michael. *The Druidic Handbook: Ritual Magic Rooted in the Living Earth*. San Francisco: Weisler Books, 2007.

Gregor, Douglas Bartlett. *Celtic: A Comparative Study of Six Celtic Languages: Irish, Gaelic, Manx, Welsh, Cornish, Breton Seen Against the Background of Their History, Literature, and Destiny*. New York: Oleander Press, 1980.

Grimm, Jacob. *Teutonic Mythology*, Vol. III. London: George Bell and Sons, 1882.

_____. *Teutonic Mythology*, Vol. IV. New York: Dover, 1966.

Guerber, H.A. *The Myths of the Norsemen: From the Eddas and Sagas*. London: George G. Harrap, 1911.

_____. *The Norsemen: Myths and Legends Series*. London: Bracken Books, 1986.

Guhl, Ernst, and Wilhelm Koner. *The Greeks: Their Life and Customs*. London: Senate, 1994.

Guth, Delloyd J. *Late-Medieval England, 1347–1485*. Cambridge: Cambridge University Press, 1976.

Hackwood, Frederick William. *Staffordshire Customs, Superstitions and Folklore*. Lichfield, UK: Mercury Press, 1924. Republished, Yorkshire, UK: EP Publishing, 1974.

Haigh, Christopher. *The Plain Man's Pathway to Heaven: Kinds of Christianity in Post–Reformation England, 1570–1640*. Oxford: Oxford University Press, 2007.

Hall, Donald. *Fathers Playing Catch with Sons*. New York: North Point Press, 1998.

Hardy, Steven. *How Boston Played: Sport, Recreation and Community 1865-1915*. Boston: Northeastern University Press, 1982.

Harrison, Jane Ellen. *Ancient Art and Ritual*. London: Williams and Norgate, 1913.

Hartland, Edwin Sidney. *Primitive Paternity: The Myth of Supernatural Birth in Relation to the History of the Family*. London: David Nutt, 1909.

Hazlitt, Carew W. *Poetical and Dramatic Works of Thomas Randolph: New First Collected and Edited from the Early Copies and Mss. with Some Account of the Author and Occasional Notes*. London: Reeves and Turner, 1875.

Henderson, Robert W. *Ball, Bat, and Bishop: The Origins of Ball Games*. New York: Rockport Press, 1947.

Herrick, Robert. *The Poetical Works of Robert Herrick*. George Saintsbury, ed. 2 Vols. London, UK: George Bell and Sons, 1893.

Hibbert, Samuel. *A Description of the Shetland Islands: Comprising an Account of Their Scenery, Antiquities, and Superstitions*. Second Reprint. Lerwick, UK: T. and J. Manson, 1931 (originally London: Hurst, Robinson, 1822).

Holt, Richard. *Sport and the British: A Modern History*. Oxford: Clarendon Press, 1989.

Hopkins, E. Washburn. *Origin and Evolution of Religion*. New Haven, CT: Yale University Press, 1924.

Hoppel, Joe, ed. *The Sporting News Baseball: 100 Years of the Modern Era: 1901–2001.* St. Louis: The Sporting News Press, 2001.

Howell, Colin D. *Blood, Sweat, and Cheers: Sport and the Making of Modern Canada.* Toronto: University of Toronto Press, 2002.

_____. *Northern Sandlots: A Social History of Maritime Baseball.* Toronto: University of Toronto Press, 1995.

Humber, William. *A Sporting Chance: Achievements of African-Canadian Athletes.* Toronto: Natural History, 2004.

_____. *Cheering for the Home Team: The Story of Baseball in Canada.* Erin, ON: Boston Mills Press, 1983.

_____. *Diamonds of the North.* Toronto: Oxford University Press, 1995.

_____. *Let's Play Ball: Inside the Perfect Game.* Toronto: A. Lester and Orpen Dennys, 1989.

Humber, William, and John St. James, eds. *All I Thought About Was Baseball: Writings on a Canadian Pastime.* Toronto: University of Toronto Press, 1996.

Husain, Shahrukh. *Demons, Gods and Holy Men from Indian Myths and Legends.* London: Peter Lowe, 1987.

_____. *The Goddess.* London: Little, Brown, 1997.

Hutton, Ronald. *The Pagan Religions of the British Isles: Their Nature and Legacy.* Oxford: Blackwell, 1991.

_____. *The Rise and Fall of Merry England: The Ritual Year 1400–1700.* Oxford: Oxford University Press, 1994.

_____. *The Stations of the Sun: A History of the Ritual Year in Britain.* Oxford: Oxford University Press, 1996.

Jamieson, John. *An Etymological Dictionary of the Scottish Language.* Paisley, UK: Alexander Gardner, 1882.

Jayakar, Pupul. *The Earth Mother: Legends, Ritual Arts and Goddesses of India.* San Francisco: Harper and Row, 1990.

Jensen, Don. *The Timeline History of Baseball.* New York: Palgrave Macmillan, 2004.

Jiménez, Ramon L. *Caesar Against the Celts.* New York: Barnes and Noble, 2001.

Johnson, Kenneth, and Marguerite Elsbeth. *The Grail Castle: Male Myths and Mysteries in the Celtic Tradition.* St. Paul, MN: Llewellyn, 1995.

Johnston, Richard B. *The Archaeology of the Serpent Mounds Site.* Occasional Paper No. 10. Toronto: Royal Ontario Museum, 1968.

Jordan, Michael. *Dictionary of Gods and Goddesses.* 2d ed. New York: Facts on File, 2004.

Kahn, Roger. *The Boys of Summer.* New York: Harper and Row, 1972.

Katz, Victor, ed. *The Mathematics of Egypt, Mesopotamia, China, India, and Islam.* Princeton, NJ: Princeton University Press, 2007.

Kenyon, Walter Andrew. *Mounds of Sacred Earth: Burial Mounds of Ontario.* Occasional Paper No. 9. Toronto: Royal Ontario Museum, 1986.

Keri, Jonah, ed. *Baseball Between the Numbers: Why Everything You Know About the Game Is Wrong.* New York: Basic Books, 2006.

Kirsch, George B. *Baseball and Cricket: The Creation of American Team Sports, 1838–72.* Urbana: University of Illinois Press, 2007.

Kirsch, Jonathan. *Gods Against the Gods.* New York: Viking Compass, 2004.

Knickerbocker, Diedrich. [Washington Irving]. *History of New York from the Beginnings of the World to the End of the Dutch Dynasty.* London: Thomas Tegg, 1824.

Knowlson, T. Sharper. *The Origins of Popular Superstitions and Customs.* North Hollywood, CA: Newcastle, 1972.

Koppett, Leonard. *Koppett's Concise History of Major League Baseball.* Philadelphia: Temple University, 1998.

Krasskova, Galina. *Exploring the Nothern Tradition: A Guide to the Gods, Lore, Rites, and Celebrations from the Norse, German, and Anglo-Saxon Traditions.* New Page, NJ: Career Press, 2005

Krishnamurti, Jiddu. *The Awakening of Intelligence.* San Francisco: Harper and Row, 1973.

Kunz, George Frederick. *The Mystical Lore of Precious Stones.* North Hollywood, CA: Newcastle, 1986.

Kynes, Sandra. *Whispers from the Woods: The Lore and Magic of Trees.* Woodbury, MN: Llewellyn, 2006.

La Barre, Weston. *They Shall Take Up Serpents: Psychology of the Southern Snake-Handling Cult.* Minneapolis: University of Minnesota Press, 1962.

Lancashire and Cheshire Antiquarian Society. *Transactions of the Lancashire and Cheshire Antiquarian Society.* Vol. IV. Manchester, UK: A. Ireland, 1887.

Lane, C. Arthur. *Illustrated Notes on English Church History, Vol.1: From the Earliest times to the Dawn of the Reformation.* London: Society for Promoting Christian Knowledge, 1894 (first published 1886).

_____. *Illustrated Notes on English Church History, Vol. II: Its Reformation and Modern Work.* London: Society for Promoting Christian Knowledge, 1896 (first published 1886).

Lattimore, Richmond, trans. *Greek Lyrics.* 2d ed. Chicago: University of Chicago Press, 1960.

Leeming, David. *From Olympus to Camelot: The World of European Mythology.* New York: Oxford University Press, 2003.

_____. *The World of Myth: An Anthology.* Oxford: Oxford University Press, 1990.

_____, ed. *Storytelling Encyclopaedia: Historical, Cultural, and Multiethnic Approaches to Oral Traditions Around the World.* Phoenix: Oryx Press, 1997.

Leeming, David, and Jake Page. *God Myths of the Male Divine.* New York: Oxford University Press, 1996.

_____, and _____. *Goddess Myths of the Female Divine.* New York: Oxford University Press, 1994.

Leventhal, Josh, *Baseball: Yesterday and Today.* St. Paul, MN: Voyageur Press, 2006.

_____. *The Perfect Game: An All Star Anthology Celebrating the Game's Greatest Players, Teams, and Moments.* St. Paul, MN: Voyageur Press, 2005.

_____. *Take Me Out to the Ballpark: An Illustrated Tour of Baseball Parks. Past and Present.* New York: Black Dog and Leventhal, 2000.

_____. *The World Series: An Illustrated Encyclopaedia of the Fall Classic.* New York: Black Dog and Leventhal, 2001.

_____, ed. *Baseball and the Meaning of Life.* St. Paul, MN: Voyageur Press, 2005.

Levinson, David, and Karen Christensen, eds. *Encyclopedia of World Sport 1: From Ancient Times to the Present.* Santa Barbara, CA: ABC-CLIO, 1996.

Lewis, W.J. *The Language of Cricket: With Illustrative Extracts from the Literature of the Game.* Oxford: Oxford University Press, 1934.

Lorius, Cassandra. *Mandalas and Meditations for Everyday Living.* New York: CICO Books, 2008.

Lowth, Frank. J. *Everyday Problems of the Country Teacher: A Textbook and a Handbook of the Country-School Practice.* Rev. edition. New York: Macmillan Company, 1936.

Lynch, John. *The Weather.* London: Firefly Books, 2002.

Mac Cana, Proinsias. *Celtic Mythology.* Library of the World's Myths and Legends. New York: Peter Bedrick Books, 1987.

MacCulloch, J.A. *The Celtic and Scandinavian Religions.* London: Constable, 1948.

_____. *Medieval Faith and Fable.* London: George G. Harrap, 1932.

Mackenzie, A. Donald. *German Myths and Legends.* New York: Avenel Books, 1985.

Mackillop, James. *Myths and Legends of the Celts.* London: Penguin, 2005.

Macleod, Sharon Paice. *Celtic Myth and Religion: A Study of Traditional Belief, with Newly Translated Prayers, Poems and Songs.* Jefferson, NC: McFarland, 2012.

MacMullen, Ramsay. *Christianity and Paganism in the Fourth to Eight Centuries.* New Haven: Yale University Press, 1997.

Malcolmson, Robert W. *Popular Recreations in English Society 1700–1850.* Cambridge: Cambridge University Press, 1973.

Mallory, J.P. *In Search of the Indo-Europeans: Language, Archaeology, and Myth.* London: Thames and Hudson, 1989.

Mangalwadi, Vishal. *The World of Gurus: A Critical Look at the Philosophers of India's Influential Gurus and Mystics (Rev. Ed.)* Chicago: Cornerstone Press, 1987.

Mardsen, Barry, M. *The Early Barrow-Diggers.* Buckinghamshire, UK: Shire Publications, 1974.

Markale, Jean. *The Celts: Uncovering the Mythic and Historic Origins of Western Culture.* Rochester, VT: Inner Traditions, 1993.

_____. *The Great Goddess: Reverence of the Divine Feminine from the Palaeolithic to the Present.* Rochester, VT: Inner Traditions, 1997.

Marylebone Cricket Club. *The M.C.C., 1787–1937.* Reprinted from the Times M.C.C., May 25, 1937. London: Times Publishing Company, 1937.

Marshall, Julian. *The Annals of Tennis.* London: "The Field" Office, 1878.

Martin, E. Osborn. *The Gods of India: A Brief Description of Their History, Character and Worship.* London: J.M Dent and Sons, 1914.

Martin, Jay. *Live All You Can: Alexander Joy Cartwright and the Invention of Modern*

Baseball. New York: Columbia University Press, 2009.

Matthews, Caitlin. *The Elements of the Celtic Traditions*. Rockport, MA: Element, 1989.

Mayer, Robert. *Baseball and Men's Lives: The True Confessions of a Skinny-Marink*. New York: Delta, 1994.

McNeill, Marian F. "A Scottish Calendar." In *Scotland: A Description of Scotland and Scottish Life*, edited by Henry W. Meikle. Toronto: Thomas Nelson and Sons, 1947.

Mehl, Erwin. "Baseball in the Stone Age." *Western Folklore* 7, no. 2 (1948): 145–161.

_____. "Notes to Baseball in the Stone Age." *Western Folklore* 8, no. 2: 152–156, 1949.

Menninger, Karl. *Number Words and Number Symbols: A Cultural History of Numbers*. Dover Publications Inc., New York, 1969.

Menzies, Gordon, ed. *Who are the Scots?* London: British Broadcasting Corporation, 1971.

Meredith, Martin. *Born in Africa: The Quest for the Origins of Human Life*. New York: Public Affairs, 2011.

Merry, Eleanor C. *The Flaming Door: A Preliminary Study of the Mission of the Celtic Folk-Soul by Means of Legends and Myths*. Sussex, UK: New Knowledge Books, 1936 and 1962.

Metzner, Ralph. *The Well of Remembrance: Rediscovery the Earth Wisdom Myths of Northern Europe*. Boston: Shambhala, 1994.

Miekle, Henry W., ed. *Scotland: A Description of Scotland and Scottish Life*. London: Thomas Nelson and Sons, 1947.

Miller, Stephen. *The Peculiar Life of Sundays*. Cambridge, MA: Harvard University Press, 2008.

Mladen, Davidoric. *Irish-English: English-Irish Dictionary and Phrase Book*. New York: Hippocrene Books, 1991.

Monier-Williams, Monier. *Religious Thought and Life in India: An Account of the Religions of the Indian Peoples; Part 1, Vedism, Brahmanism, and Hinduism*. 2d ed. London: John Murray, 1885.

Moore, Robert, and Douglas Gillette. *King, Warrior, Magician, Lover: Rediscovering the Archetypes of the Mature Masculine*. San Francisco: Harper, 1990.

Morgan, Owen. *The Light of Britannia: The Mysteries of Ancient Druidism Unveiled; The Original Source of Phallic Worship, and the Secrets of the Court of King Arthur Revealed; The Creed of the Stone Age Restored,* *and the Holy Grael Discovered in Wales*. Cardiff: D. Owen, 1893.

Morgan, Williams. *St. Paul in Britain: Or, The Origin of British as Opposed to Papal Christianity*. London: James Parker, 1861.

Morris, Peter. *The Game on the Field*. Vol. 1 of *A Game of Inches: The Stories Behind the Innovations That Shaped Baseball*. Chicago: Ivan R. Dee, 2006.

Morrow, Don, Mary Keyes, Wayne Simpson, Frank Cosentino, and Ron Lappage. *A Concise History of Sport in Canada*. Toronto: Oxford University Press, 1989.

Morse, Michael A. *How the Celts Came to Britain: Druids, Ancient Skulls and the Birth of Archaeology*. South Gloucestershire, UK: Tempus, 2005.

Muller, Max. *A History of Ancient Sanskrit Literature: So Far as It Illustrates the Primitive Religion of The Brahmans*. 2nd ed. rev. New York: AMS Press, 1978 (first published in 1860).

Mukundcharandas, Sadhu, Das Jnaneshwar, and Swaminarayan Aksharpith. *Hindu Rites and Rituals: Sentiments and Sacraments*. Amdavad, India: Swaminarayan Aksharpith, 2001.

Mundkur, Balaji. *The Cult of the Serpent: An Interdisciplinary Survey of Its Manifestations and Origins*. Albany, NY: State University of New York Press, 1983.

Munro, William Bennett. *Crusaders of New France: A Chronicle of the Fleur-de-Lis in the Wilderness*. New Haven, CT: Yale University Press, 1921.

Nemec, David. *The Rules of Baseball: An Anecdotal Look at the Rules of Baseball and How They Came to Be*. Guilford, DE: The Lyons Press, 1994.

Newbery, John. *A Little Pretty Pocket-Book*. 1744. Facsimile of the first edition, with an introductory essay and bibliography by M.F. Thwaite. London: Oxford University Press, 1966.

O'Connell, Mark, and Raje Airey. *The Illustrated Encyclopedia of Signs and Symbols*. London: Lorenz Books, 2005.

O'Driscoll, Robert, ed. *The Celtic Consciousness*. New York: George Brazillier, 1982.

Onions, C.T, Sidney Lee, and Walter Alexander Raleigh. *Shakespeare's England: An Account of the Life and Manners of His Age*. Oxford: Clarendon Press, 1970 (first published 1916).

Otis, James. *Mary of Plymouth: A Story of the Pilgrim Settlement*. Lake Wales, FL: Lost Classics, 1997 (first published 1910).

Perinbanayagam, Robert. *Games and Sport in Everyday Life*. Boulder: Paradigm, 2006.

Peterson, Peter. *The Man Who Invented Baseball*. New York: Charles Schribner's Sons, 1969.

Philip, Jan. "Early History and Evolution of the Celts." In *The Celtic Consciousness*, edited by Robert O'Driscoll. New York: George Brazillier, 1981.

Piggott, Stuart. *Ancient Europe from the Beginnings of Agriculture to Classical Antiquity: A Survey*. Edinburgh: Edinburgh University Press, 1965.

_____. *Antiquity Depicted: Aspects of Archaeological Illustration*. London: Thames and Hudson, 1978.

_____. *The Druids*. London: Thames and Hudson, 1968.

_____. *The Earliest Wheeled Transport: From the Atlantic Coast to the Caspian Sea*. Ithaca, NY: Cornell University Press, 1983.

_____. *Prehistoric India to 1000 B.C.* London: Cassell, 1962.

_____. *The Ruins of a Landscape: Essays in Antiquarianism*. Edinburgh: Edinburgh University Press, 1976.

_____, ed. *The Prehistoric Peoples of Scotland*. London: Routledge and Kegan Paul, 1962.

Piggott, Stuart, Daniel Glyn, and Charles McBurney, eds. *France Before the Romans*. Park Ridge, NJ: Noyes Press, 1973.

Pine, L.G. *The Highland Clans: Their Origins and History*. Newton Abbot, UK: David and Charles, 1972.

Poliakoff, Michael B. *Combat Sports in the Ancient World: Competition, Violence, and Culture*. New Haven: Yale University Press, 1987.

Porteus, Alexander. *The Lore of the Forest: Myths and Legends*. London: Random House UK, 1996 (first published 1928).

Price, S.L. *Heart of the Game: Life, Death, and Mercy in Minor League America*. New York: HarperCollins Publishers, 2010.

Rader, Benjamin G. "Baseball." *Encyclopædia Britannica Online*. Accessed 24 Apr. 2013.

_____. *Baseball: A History of America's Game*. Urbana: University of Illinois Press, 2002.

Radhakrishnan, Sarvepalli, and Charles Moore, eds. *A Source Book of Indian Philosophy*. Princeton, NJ: Princeton University Press, 1957.

Raleigh, Walter A., Charles T. Onions, and Sidney Lee. *Shakespeare's England: An Account of the Life and Manners of His Age*. Oxford: Clarendon Press, 1970 (first published 1916).

Ralls-MacLeod, Karen, and Ian Robertson. *The Quest for the Celtic Key*. Edinburgh: Luath Press, 2002.

Randolph, Thomas. "An Eclogue on the Noble Assemblies Revived on Cotswold Hills by Master Robert Dover in Poetical and Dramatic Works of Thomas Randolph." Vol. 2 of *Poetical and Dramatic Works of Thomas Randolph*, edited by William Carew Hazlitt. London: Reeves and Turner, 1875.

Ranjitsinghji, K.S. *The Jubilee Book of Cricket*. London: William Blackwood and Sons, 1897.

Rankin, William. "Base Ball's Birth: Invented and Introduced by the Dutch." Mears Baseball Scrapbook, Vol. 8: *New York Clipper* Articles by Rankin, 1904–1912. Online Resource. Cleveland Public Library Digital Gallery.

Reaves, A. Joseph. *Taking in a Game: A History of Baseball in Asia*. Lincoln: University of Nebraska Press, 2002.

Reiss, Steven A. *City Games: The Evolution of American Urban Society and the Rise of Sports*. Urbana: University of Illinois Press, 1989.

Renou, Louis, ed. *Hinduism*. New York: George Braziller, 1962.

Rhys, John, and David Brynmor-Jones. *The Welsh People: Chapters on Their Origin, History, Laws, Language, Literature and Characteristics*. 4d ed. London: T. Fisher Unwin, 1906.

Rice, Stanley. *Hindu Customs and Their Origins*. New Delhi: Low Price Publications, 1937.

Richards, Eric. *Britannia's Children: Emigration from England, Scotland, Wales and Ireland since 1600*. London: Hambledon and London, 2004.

Richardson, H. D. *Holiday Sports and Pastimes for Boys*. London: William Orr, 1844.

Ritchie, Robert C. *The Duke's Province: A Study of New York Politics and Society, 1664–1691*. Chapel Hill: University of North Carolina Press, 1977.

Roberts, Peter. *The Cambrian Popular Antiquities; or, An Account of Some Traditions,*

Customs, and Superstitions of Wales with Observations as to Their Origin, &c. &c. London: E. Williams, 1815.

Ross, Alan S.C. "*Pize-Ball*" in *Proceeding of the Leeds Philosophical and Literary Society, Literary and Historical Section Vol. XIII Part II.* Leeds, England: Leeds Philosophical and Literary Society. 1986

Ross, Anne. "The Celtic Continuum." In *The Celtic Consciousness,* edited by Robert O'Driscoll. New York: George Braziller, 1987.

_____. *Everyday Life of the Pagan Celts.* New York: G.P. Putnam's Sons, 1970.

_____. *The Folklore of the Scottish Highlands.* London: B.T. Batsford, 1976.

_____. *Pagan Celtic Britain: Studies in Iconography and Tradition.* Chicago: Academy Chicago Publishers, 1996.

Ross, Anne, and Don Robins. *The Life and Death of a Druid Prince: The Story of Lindow Man, an Archaeological Sensation.* London: Summit Books, 1989.

Ross, Nancy Wilson. *Three Ways of Asian Wisdom: Hinduism, Buddhism, Zen and Their Significance for the West.* New York: Simon and Schuster, 1966.

Roud, Steve. *The Penguin Guide to the Superstitions of Britain and Ireland.* London: Penguin, 2003.

Rutherford, Ward. *Celtic Lore: The History of the Druids and Their Timeless Traditions.* San Francisco: HarperCollins Publications, 1993.

_____. *Celtic Mythology: The Nature and Influence of Celtic Myth—from Druidism to Arthurian Legend.* New York: Sterling, 1990.

Schoeps, Hans-Joachim, *The Religions of Mankind: Their Origin and Development.* Translated from the German by Richard and Clara Wilson. Garden City, NY: Doubleday, 1966.

Senzel, Howard. *Baseball and the Cold War: Being a Soliloquy on the Necessity of Baseball.* New York: Harcourt Brace Jovanovich, 1977.

Seymour, Dorothy Z., and Harold Seymour. *Baseball: The People's Game.* New York: Oxford University Press, 1990.

Sharma, S.P., and Seema Gupta. *Fairs and Festivals of India.* New Delhi: Hindology Books, 2006.

Shaw, William. *A Galic and English Dictionary: Containing All the Words in the Scotch and Irish Dialects of the Celtic, That Could Be Collected from the Voice, and the Old Books and MSS.* London: W and A Strahan, 1780.

Shorto, Russell. *The Island at the Center of the World: The Epic Story of Dutch Manhattan and the Forgotten Colony That Shaped America.* New York: Doubleday, 2004.

Simmons, Robert. *Stones of the New Consciousness: Healing, Awakening and Co-Creating with Crystals, Minerals and Gems.* East Montpelier, VT: Heaven and Earth, 2009.

Sinclair, John. *The Statistical Account of Scotland: Drawn Up from the Communications of the Ministers of the Different Parishes, Volume 19.* Edinburgh: William Creech, 1797.

Singleton, Esther. *Dutch New York.* New York: Benjamin Blom, 1968 (first published 1909).

Smith, Charles. *Games and Games Leadership.* New York: Dodd, Mead, 1932.

Smith, Sydney. *History of the Tests: A Record of all Test Cricket Matches Played Between England and Australia, 1877–1947.* Sydney: Australian Publishing, 1947.

Spalding, Albert G. *America's National Game: Historic Facts Concerning the Beginning, Evolution, Development and Popularity of Baseball.* San Francisco: Halo Books, 1991.

Spence, Lewis. *The Mysteries of Britain: Secret Rites and Traditions of Ancient Britain Restored.* London: Bracken Books, 1993.

Spence, Lewis. *Germany: Myths and Legends.* London: Bracken Books, 1985.

Squire, Charles. *Celtic Myth and Legend.* Rev. ed. Franklin Lakes, NJ: New Page Books, 2001.

Stadler, Mark. *The Psychology of Baseball: Inside the Mental Game of the Major League Player.* New York: Gotham Books, 2007.

Steele, James L. "How the National Game Developed." *Outing* 44 (June 1904): 333.

Stover, Leon T., and Bruce Kraig. *Stonehenge: The Indo-European Heritage.* Chicago: Nelson-Hall, 1978.

Stringer, Chris, and Peter Andrews. *The Complete World of Human Evolution.* Second ed. London: Thames and Hudson, 2012.

_____. *Lone Survivors: How We Came to Be the Only Humans on Earth.* New York: Times Books, 2012.

_____. *The Origins of Our Species.* New York: Allen Lane, 2012.

Strutt, Joseph. *The Sports and Pastimes of the People of England: Including the Rural and Domestic Recreations May Games, Shows, Processions, Pageants and Pompous Spectacles from the Earliest Periods to the Present Time.* Edited by William Hone. London: Chatto and Windus, 1838.

Sumner, William Graham. *Folkways: A Study of the Sociological Importance of Usages, Manners, Custom, Mores and Morals.* New York: Ginn, 1934.

Sutton, Ronald. *The Stations of the Sun: A History of the Ritual Year in Britain.* New York: Oxford University Press, 1996.

Svensson, Horvik. *The Runes: Divine the Future with this Ancient Norse Oracle.* London: Carlton Books, 1995 (reprinted 2003).

Taylor, John. *A Short Relation of a Long Journey Made Round or Ovall by Encompassing The Principalities of Wales from London.* London: n.p., 1652. Edited by James O. Halliwell and published as *A Short Relation of a Journey Through Wales by John Taylor, the Water-Poet.* London: Thomas Richards, 1859.

Thomas, Charles. *Celtic Britain.* London: Thomas and Hudson, 1986.

Thorn, John, ed. *The Armchair Book of Baseball.* New York: Collier Books, 1985.

_____. *Baseball in the Garden of Eden: The Secret History of the Game.* New York: Simon and Schuster, 2011.

Time-Life Book Editors. *Mound Builders and Cliff Dwellers.* Alexandria, VA: Time-Life Books, 1992.

Travis, James. *Early Celtic Versecraft: Origin, Development and Diffusion.* Shannon, UK: Irish University Press, 1973.

Tygiel, Jules. *Past Time: Baseball as History.* New York: Oxford University Press, 2000.

Tylor, Edward Burnett. *Primitive Culture: Religion in Primitive Culture.* Second Edition. New York: Harper Torchbooks, 1958.

Underdown, David. *Revel, Riot and Rebellion: Popular Politics and Culture in England, 1603–1660.* New York: Oxford University Press, 1985.

Valentine, Laura, ed. *The Girl's Home Companion: A Book of Pastimes in Work and Play.* New edition. London: Frederick Warne, 1891.

Van der Zee, Barbara, and Henri Van der Zee. *A Sweet and Alien Land: The Story of Dutch New York.* New York: Viking, 1978.

Vecsey, George. *Baseball: A History of America's Favorite Game.* New York: Modern Library, 2006.

Vega, Phyllis. *Celtic Astrology: How the Mystical Power of Druid Tree Signs Can Transform your Life.* Franklin Lakes, NJ: New Page Books, 2002.

Vizard, Frank, ed. *Why a Curveball Curves: The Incredible Science of Sports.* New York: Hearst Books, 2008.

Voigt, David Quentin. *From Gentleman's Sport to the Commissioner System.* Vol. 1 of *American Baseball.* State College, PA: Penn State Press, 1983.

Vyse, Stuart A. *Believing in Magic: The Psychology of Superstition.* New York: Oxford University Press, 1997.

Wallace, Joseph, ed. *The Baseball Anthology: 125 Years of Stories, Poems, Articles, Photographs, Drawings, Interviews, Cartoons, and Other Memorabilia.* New York: Harry N. Abrams, 1994.

Ward, Geoffrey C., and Ken Burns. *Baseball: An Illustrated History.* New York: Alfred A. Knoff, 1994.

Watts, Robert G., and A. Terry Bahill. *Keep Your Eye on the Ball: The Science and Folklore of Baseball.* New York: W.H. Freeman, 2000.

Westbrook, Deanne. *Ground Rules: Baseball and Myth.* Urbana: University of Illinois Press, 1996.

Westropp, Hodder M., and C. Staniland Wake. *Ancient Symbol Worship: Influence of the Phallic Idea in the Religion of Antiquity.* Escondido, CA: Book Tree, 1999 (first published 1875).

Wickham-Jones, C. R. *Scotland's First Settlers.* London: B.T. Batsford, 1994.

Wilkins, W.J. *Modern Hinduism: An Account of the Religion and Life of the Hindus in Northern India.* 2d ed. London: Curzon Press, 1887.

Wilkinson, Kathyrn, ed. *Signs and Symbols: An Illustrated Guide to Their Origins and Meanings.* New York: DK Publishing, 2008.

Williams, John ab Ithel. *Barddas: Or A Collection of Original Documents, Illustrative of the Theology, Wisdom, and Usages of the Bardo-Druidic System of the Isle of Britain.* London: D.J. Roderic, 1862.

Williams, Samuel. *The Boy's Treasury of Sports: Pastimes and Recreations.* First

American edition. Philadelphia: Lea and Blanchard, 1847.

Wills, Bret, and Gwen Aldridge. *Baseball Archaeology: Artifacts from the Great American Pastime.* San Francisco: Chronicle Books, 1993.

Willughby, Francis. *Francis Willughby's Book of Games: A Seventeenth-Century Treatise on Sports, Games, and Pastimes.* Edited by David Cram, Jeffrey L. Forgeng, and Dorothy Johnston. Aldershot, UK: Ashgate, 2003.

Wilmot, John. *A Satire Against Mankind.* In *Eighteenth Century Poetry and Prose.* 2d ed., edited by Louis I. Bredvold, Alan D. Mackillop, and Lois Whitney. New York: Ronald Press, 1956.

Wolseley, Viscountess [Frances Garnet Wolseley]. *In a College Garden.* London: John Murray, 1916.

Wood, J. G. *Athletic Sports and Recreations for Boys.* London: Routledge, Warne and Routledge, 1861.

_____. *The Boy's Modern Playmate: A Book of Sports, Games, and Pastimes.* London: Frederick Warne, 1891.

Wood, J.G., J.H. Pepper, C. Bennett, T. Miller, et al. *The Boy's Own Treasury of Sports and Pastimes.* London: George Routledge and Sons, 1866.

Zaczek, Iain. *Ireland: Land of the Celts.* London: Collins and Brown, 2000.

Index